TEACHER'S EDITION
DAYBOOK
OF CRITICAL READING AND WRITING

THE AUTHORS
* Fran Claggett
* Louann Reid
* Ruth Vinz

Great Source Education Group
A division of Houghton Mifflin Company
Wilmington, Massachusetts

THE AUTHORS

✵ **Fran Claggett**, an educational consultant, writer, and teacher at Sonoma State University, taught high school and college English for more than thirty years. Her books include *Drawing Your Own Conclusions: Graphic Strategies for Reading, Writing, and Thinking* (1992) with Joan Brown, *A Measure of Success* (1996), and *Teaching Writing: Art, Craft, and Genre* (2005) with Joan Brown, Nancy Patterson, and Louann Reid.

✵ **Louann Reid** taught junior and senior high school English for nineteen years and currently teaches courses for future English teachers at Colorado State University. She has edited *English Journal* and is the author or editor of several books and articles, including *Learning the Landscape* and *Recasting the Text* (1996) with Fran Claggett and Ruth Vinz. She is a frequent consultant and workshop presenter nationally and internationally.

✵ **Ruth Vinz**, currently a professor of English education and Morse Chair in Teacher Education at Teachers College, Columbia University, taught in secondary schools for twenty-three years. She is author of numerous books and articles that focus on teaching and learning in the English classroom. Dr. Vinz is a frequent presenter at conferences as well as a consultant and co-teacher in schools throughout the country.

The authors gratefully acknowledge the assistance of the following teachers in developing the student and teacher material for the *Daybook of Critical Reading and Writing:* Tiffany Hunt, Cammie Kim Lin, Katherine McMullen, and Lance Ozier.

DEVELOPMENT: Bonnie Brook Communications (teacher's edition)
Michael Priestley (assessment)
EDITORIAL: Sue Paro, Bev Jessen, Lisa J. Clark
DESIGN AND PRODUCTION: AARTPACK, Inc.

Printed in the United States of America

International Standard Book Number 13: 978-0-669-53484-9

International Standard Book Number 10: 0-669-53484-6

1 2 3 4 5 6 7 8 9 10 – P00 – 11 10 09 08 07 06

CONTENTS

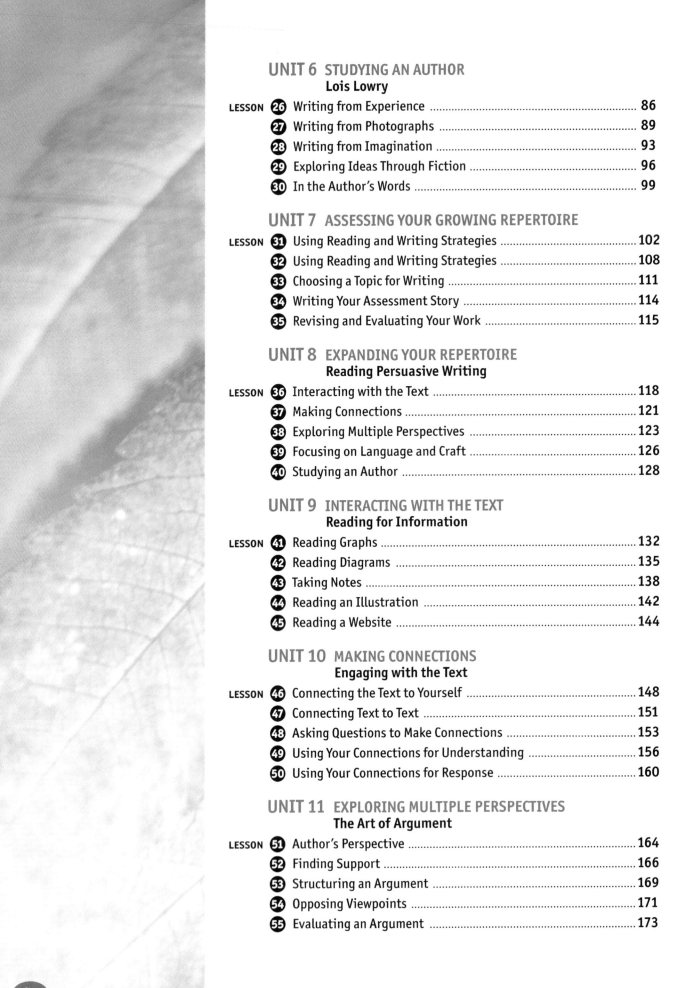

What, exactly, is a *Daybook*, and how can it help my students? Teachers often ask these questions upon their initial encounter with the *Daybook of Critical Reading and Writing*. The answers are simple and compelling:

The *Daybook*

The *Daybook* is a keepable, journal-like book that promotes daily reading and writing experiences. The integrated, interactive pages of the *Daybook* provide students with multiple opportunities to read a variety of literature and other texts, to respond to what they read, and to experiment with their own writing. The *Daybook* honors the relationship between the reader and text, conveying the message that good readers take risks, relate their reading and writing to what they know and want to know, and take ownership of the learning process.

The Literature

Many of the selections complement those commonly found in anthologies or present authors and novels known to be popular with teachers and students. The selections also support curricular content and themes for grades 6-8, reflect the diversity of our world, include a blend of traditional and contemporary authors, and present a wide variety of fiction and nonfiction. Excerpts were chosen carefully to feel "complete" and yet to inspire students to seek out and read the larger works.

The Lessons

Each *Daybook* lesson focuses on a specific strategy or strategies for critical reading and writing, providing students with the tools they need to become more proficient, confident readers and writers. The lessons include instruction on how to respond actively to many kinds of writing, as well as opportunities to practice the strategies, information about writer's craft and genre elements, and support for writing activities.

The Framework

The *Daybook* units are structured around the **Five Essential Strategies of Critical Reading and Writing:**

1. Interacting with the Text
2. Making Connections
3. Exploring Multiple Perspectives
4. Focusing on Language and Craft
5. Studying an Author

These research-based, practical strategies are introduced and summarized in the first unit, "Building Your Repertoire." Subsequent units explore each of the Five Essential Strategies in greater depth. Two assessment units also engage students in an examination of their progress as they move through the book.

HOW TO USE THE DAYBOOK

No two classrooms are alike. That's why the *Daybook* was designed to accommodate a wide range of classrooms and instructional scenarios. The *Daybook's* flexibility and versatility offer something for every teacher.

Supplement an Anthology or Core Novel List

The contemporary selections and multicultural authors provide a needed balance with the more traditional canon in older anthologies. Likewise, for teachers using a list of core novels, the *Daybook* offers a way to add daily writing and reading instruction.

Provide Direct Instruction

The lessons in the *Daybook* are ideal for helping all students develop strong literacy skills. You can use these lessons to

* teach **critical reading skills,** such as predicting, making inferences, and finding the main idea;

* teach **literary elements,** such as plot, setting, characters, and theme;

* teach **writer's craft** and literary devices, such as metaphor, imagery, and dialogue;

* teach **writing traits,** such as organization, word choice and conventions;

* prepare students for **state tests** and teach **standards and benchmarks,** such as writing for a variety of purposes and audiences.

Blend Elements

The *Daybook* allows teachers to provide truly integrated instruction by blending

* direct instruction in how to read and respond to literature critically;

* regular and explicit practice in marking up and annotating texts;

* "writing to learn" activities for each day or week;

* great selections from contemporary and multicultural literature.

WHEN TO USE THE *DAYBOOK*

Each 30-to-40 minute lesson can be used

* as the **core instruction** for a literature or language arts class;

* **before other reading or writing instruction**—to introduce a topic, genre, or author or to teach a particular skill or strategy;

* **after other reading or writing instruction**—to provide additional works by a particular author or to provide practice for students needing skill reinforcement.

Teachers who use the *Daybook* only for homework have not reported much success. The *Daybook* is designed to support interaction among teacher and students; students work collaboratively to reflect, question texts, get feedback on writing, and construct knowledge. These opportunities are lost when students use the *Daybook* in isolation.

STUDENT EDITION

Lesson title

Lesson focus

Literature excerpt

Initial response activity

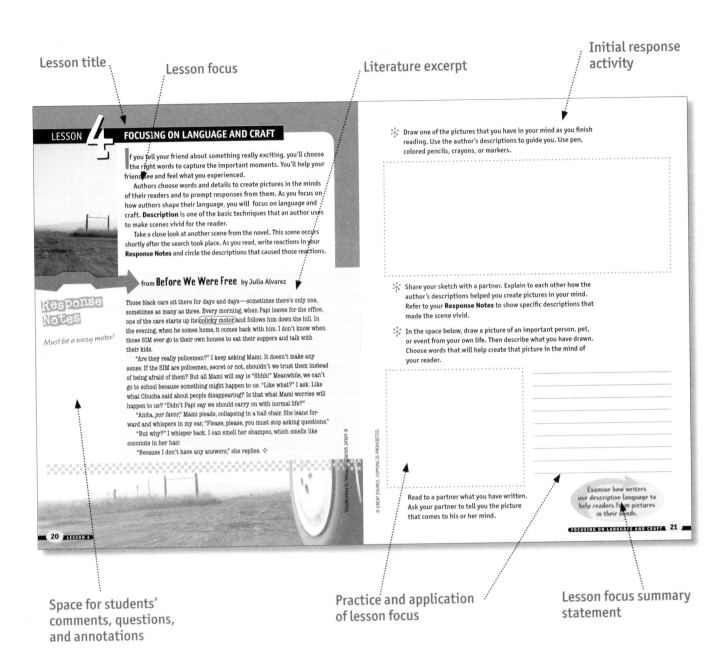

Space for students' comments, questions, and annotations

Practice and application of lesson focus

Lesson focus summary statement

TEACHER'S EDITION

Prereading activity to build background and/or activate prior knowledge

Preteaching of difficult or significant selection vocabulary

Suggestion for differentiated instruction for students who need language support

Quickly find out whether students have grasped the main focus of the lesson

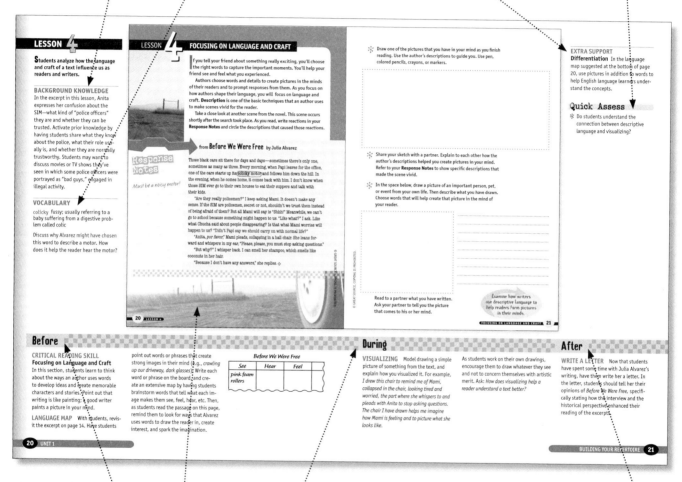

Support for introducing Critical Reading Skill and lesson focus

Support for guiding students through reading the selection and completing response activities

Extension/enrichment activities for further application of the skill or strategy

Reduced facsimiles of student pages eliminate the need for a separate book and include highlighted vocabulary

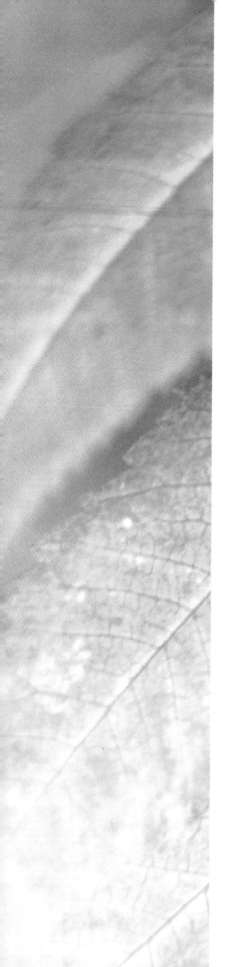

FREQUENTLY ASKED QUESTIONS

Who is the audience for the Daybook?

The *Daybook* can help all students. The length of selections and the scaffolding built into the lessons support students at all levels, while additional suggestions in the Teacher's Edition offer support for differentiated instruction, collaborative learning, and enrichment.

Are students supposed to write in the book?

Absolutely. The immediacy of responding in the *Daybook* is an integral feature of this program. Interacting with text is one of the Five Essential Strategies of Critical Reading and Writing; only by physically marking the text do students become active readers. Writing in the book provides a natural kinesthetic aid to memory and learning and allows students to refer to and reflect on their thoughts, questions, ideas, and annotations.

How do I know if the readability level is appropriate?

Helping students find materials at their individual reading levels can be a major challenge. Readability levels, which are based on text elements such as word choice, sentence length and complexity, and subject matter, provide a very rough guide. But the readability of a text also depends on the reader's interest and prior knowledge. The engaging, high-interest selections in the *Daybook,* as well as helpful background-building activities in the Teacher's Edition, provide the motivation and prior knowledge students need to access the texts. Additionally, the readability of selections throughout the *Daybook* varies so that students will gain experience reading both easier and more challenging texts.

What do you mean by "texts"?

We could call every work by a professional author *literature,* but some people associate that term only with an aesthetic or artistic approach to writing. While we do often use the term *literature* to refer specifically to "imaginative" works such as poems, short stories, and novels, we also use *literature* and *texts* as broader terms that include all written work. *Texts* also includes what students write and is therefore consistent with the *Daybook* philosophy that students are not only consumers but also creators of the written word.

May I photocopy these lessons?

No, unfortunately not. The selections, instructions, and activities are protected by copyright. To copy them infringes on the rights of the authors of the selections and the book. Writers such as Julia Alvarez, Walter Dean Myers, Laurence Yep, and Joseph Bruchac have granted permission for the use of their work in the *Daybook;* to photocopy their work violates their copyright. However, a package that includes a CD-ROM of the *Daybook* is available for purchase. Call 800-259-4490 for details.

WRITING, VOCABULARY, VISUAL LITERACY, AND ASSESSMENT

Writing in the *Daybook*

The writing activities in the *Daybook* emphasize the idea that reading is a "partnership" between author and reader.

Most of the writing activities in the *Daybook* are not intended to take students all the way through the writing process. Rather they allow students to (1) *explore* texts by questioning, analyzing, connecting with, and reacting to literature; (2) *clarify* their understanding of texts by looking at other perspectives and interpreting or reflecting on their initial impressions; and (3) *apply* what they are learning about structure, genre, and craft by modeling professional writers. The types of writing in the *Daybook* include the following:

❋ **Response Notes** Students keep track of their initial responses to literature by annotating the text as they read. In this way, students develop the habit of recording what they are thinking while they are reading.

❋ **Graphic Organizers** Students collect writing ideas in lists, charts, clusters, diagrams, and so on, while analyzing particular selections or literary elements in the process.

❋ **Short Responses** Students summarize themes and main ideas and write paragraphs of description, explanation, evaluation, interpretation, comparison, and persuasion.

❋ **Personal Narratives** Students write personal stories that connect or relate to what they have read. In some cases, the narratives tell the stories of students' prior reading experiences or how a literary selection relates to their life experiences. Other activities apply and refine students' understanding and use of narrative principles.

❋ **Creative Texts** Students write poems, character sketches, dialogues, vignettes, and descriptions as a way to apply the knowledge about language and craft they are gaining through their reading. They demonstrate and reinforce their understanding of original texts by writing imaginative reconstructions of gaps in the text—adding scenes, rewriting endings, writing from other characters' points of view, and so on.

Vocabulary in the *Daybook*

The connection between reading comprehension and word knowledge has been clear for many years. The units in the *Daybook* give students the opportunity to use words repeatedly within the context of the same theme over time, applied in different ways about different subject matter. At the beginning of most Teacher's Edition lessons, difficult or significant words from the selection are listed, along with their definitions and an activity for preteaching the words.

Visual Literacy in the *Daybook*

Visual literacy—the ability to produce and read graphics—has become an essential skill in today's media-oriented world. Teachers have long known the value of using graphic organizers, photographs, illustrations, and color-coding to present information, represent ideas metaphorically, and help students see connections.

Graphic aids are especially important for students who are just learning English or whose dominant learning mode is visual-spatial. In the *Daybook,* students read and create visuals and graphic organizers such as sequence maps, word webs, Venn diagrams, charts, and illustrations in order to

* organize ideas and information;

* visualize imagery, details, and form;

* perform close observation, personal association, and analysis;

* stimulate long-term memory by integrating both visual and verbal learning.

Several reproducible graphic organizer templates are provided at the back of the Teacher's Edition for use with the activities in the *Daybook.*

Assessment in the *Daybook*

In assessing students' work, it is important to evaluate students' growing facility with reading and writing, not just their finished products. The *Daybook* must be a safe place for students to think things through, change their minds, make mistakes, and start over. Along the way, the *Daybook* provides multiple opportunities for both teachers and students to monitor progress and identify areas of frustration or difficulty:

* **Assessment Units** Two complete units in the *Daybook,* Units 7 and 14, allow students and teachers to take stock of where students are with respect to the Five Essential Strategies of Critical Reading and Writing. Students read and respond to literature, applying all of the strategies they have learned previously, and then reflect on their achievement and identify areas for improvement. A full writing process activity at the end of each unit provides an opportunity for assessment.

* **Quick Assess** In the Teacher's Edition, suggestions are given at the end of each lesson for informal, observational assessment of students' under-standing of lesson concepts.

* **Writing Assessment Prompts** At the back of the Teacher's Edition, writing prompts tied to the texts in each unit address commonly tested modes of writing (expository, narrative, persuasive, expressive-descriptive, interpretive) and assess students' ability to interpret, reflect, evaluate, and connect to experience.

* **Reading Strategy Assessments** The assessments, found at the back of this Teacher's Edition, include a Pretest, four Reading Strategy Assessments, and a Posttest. Each assessment includes passages, based on the types of literature found in the *Daybook,* followed by a set of questions. Both multiple-choice and short answer items are included.

* **Self-Assessment** Throughout the *Daybook,* students engage in informal self-assessment as they write short reflections on what they have learned or how well they are doing.

FIVE ESSENTIAL STRATEGIES OF CRITICAL READING AND WRITING

The *Daybook* is built on a framework of Five Essential Strategies of Critical Reading and Writing.

1. Interacting with the Text

Interacting with text involves physically and mentally engaging with texts. Active readers keep their minds at work throughout reading and writing—they constantly ask questions, make inferences and predictions, and test those inferences and predictions. They write, scratch out, sketch, and rewrite. We use the metaphor of having a "conversation" with a text to describe this process.

2. Making Connections

Making connections means relating the text to oneself, to other texts, and to the rest of the world. Critical readers and writers make relevant connections—a "web of meaning"—between their reading and their experiences, knowledge, memories, and imagination.

3. Exploring Multiple Perspectives

Looking at only one side of an object gives you a limited picture of that object. But when you view it from different angles or points of view, you see the various aspects that make up a whole picture, and you may construct several versions of what the object is or resembles. Likewise, critical readers and writers explore multiple perspectives to generate a more complex understanding of a text.

4. Focusing on Language and Craft

When we take time to focus on how texts work, we analyze how the language and craft of a text—word choice, imagery, style, form, etc.—influence us as readers. This extends our own possibilities as writers. Language has not only meaning but also power, so by understanding how texts work, we gain power to create our own.

5. Studying an Author

Critical readers and writers understand that there is life behind the text and are curious about the author and his or her world. By studying authors—what influences them, where they get their ideas, and how they make decisions about language and craft—students see how they, too, can be authors of works that have personal meaning and relevance.

The Essential Strategies in Action

The essential strategies can be applied to any kind of text—fiction, nonfiction, or poetry. Through the lessons in the *Daybook,* students gradually learn which strategies to use when and why. In so doing, students become independent critical readers and writers.

ESSENTIAL STRATEGIES	STRATEGIES (PURPOSEFUL PLANS)	ACTIVITIES (ACTIONS STUDENTS TAKE)
Interacting with the Text	• underlining key phrases • writing questions/comments in the margin • noting word patterns and repetitions • circling unknown words	• Write down initial impressions. • Reread the text. • Write a summary of the text. • Generate two questions and one "certainty." Then discuss in a small group.
Making Connections	• paying attention to the story being told • connecting the story to one's own experience • speculating on the meaning or significance of incidents	• Create a character map to reveal what you have learned about a person in a story. • Make a 3-column incident chart: Incident, Significance, Related incident in your life.
Exploring Multiple Perspectives	• examining the point of view • changing the point of view • exploring various versions of an event • forming interpretations • comparing texts • asking "what if" questions	• Discuss how you might read a text differently if (1) you think the narrator is female (or male) or (2) you live in a different time or place from the narrator. • Rewrite the text from a different point of view.
Focusing on Language and Craft	• understanding figurative and sensory language • looking at the way the author uses words • modeling the style of other writers • studying various forms of literature	• Use a double-entry log to identify metaphors and the qualities implied by the comparison. • Write to model a type of text.
Studying an Author	• reading what the author says about his/her own writing • reading what others say about the author's writing • making inferences about the connections between an author's life and work • analyzing the author's style • paying attention to repeated themes and topics in the work by one author	• Read about an author's life. Make a chart to record events in the author's life, inferences about how the events affected the author, and how they are manifested in the text. • Read what a critic has said about an author's text. Write a short essay agreeing or disagreeing with the critic.

10 WAYS RESEARCH SUPPORTS THE DAYBOOK

The following research-based principles are key to effective literacy instruction and played a critical role in the development of the *Daybook*. Resources for further reading are listed for each principle.

1. Teach research-based comprehension strategies (i.e. questioning, predicting, connecting, clarifying) and comprehension monitoring strategies (i.e. checking for understanding, reflecting, self-assessing) through direct and explicit instruction. The *Daybook* provides instruction in these strategies and supports strategy development through reading, writing, and assessment activities.

   Guthrie, J. T. and Taboado, A. (2004). "Fostering the Cognitive Strategies of Reading Comprehension." In J. T. Guthrie, A. Wigfield, and K. C. Perencevich, eds. *Motivating Reading Comprehension: Concept-Oriented Reading Instruction,* pp. 87-112. Mahwah, NJ: Erlbaum.

   Melzer, J. (2002). *Adolescent Literacy Resources: Linking Research and Practice.* (ERIC Document Reproduction Service No.ED466788).

2. Integrate reading and writing strategy instruction into a wide variety of texts that build both interest and skill. The *Daybook* provides a wide range of reading and writing activities that help students build habits of mind characteristic of excellent readers.

   Allington, R. L. (2002). You can't learn much from books you can't read. *Educational Leadership, 60*(3): 16-19.

   Alvermann, D. E. (2002, Summer). Effective literacy instruction for adolescents. *Journal of Literacy Research 34(2):* 189-208. (ERIC Document Reproduction Service No. EJ672862).

3. Use modeling, scaffolding, and apprenticing to demonstrate how proficient readers and writers work strategically. The *Daybook* provides explicit step by step processing techniques to help students develop conceptual knowledge of the strategies they use.

   Gere, A. R., Fairbanks, C, & Howes, A. (1992). *Language and Reflection: An Integrated Approach to Teaching English.* Upper Saddle River, NJ: Prentice-Hall, Inc.

   Kingen, S. (2000). *Teaching Language Arts In Middle Schools: Connecting and Communicating.* Mahwah, NJ: Erlbaum.

4. Address the diverse needs of students through targeted instruction with varied reading selections and writing assignments. The *Daybook* provides a wide variety in text difficulty and genre as well as providing the appropriate background knowledge and scaffolding to support student achievement.

   Allington, R. L. (2005, 2nd edition) *What Really Matters for Struggling Readers: Designing Research-Based Programs.* Boston, MA: Allyn and Bacon.

   Kucer, S. B., (2005). *Dimensions of Literacy: A Conceptual Base for Teaching Reading and Writing in School Settings.* Mahwah, NJ: Lawrence Erlbaum.

5. Make reading and writing a daily part of literacy instruction to reinforce the common and shared processes of both sending and receiving information. The *Daybook* provides companion reading and writing activities intended to enhance reading and writing abilities.

   Booth, D. (2001). *Reading and Writing in the Middle Years.* Portland, ME: Stenhouse.

   Fitzgerald, J. (1990). *Reading and writing as "mind meeting." In T. Shanahan (Ed.), Reading and writing together: New perspectives for the classroom*, pp. 81-97. Norwood, MA: Christopher-Gordon.

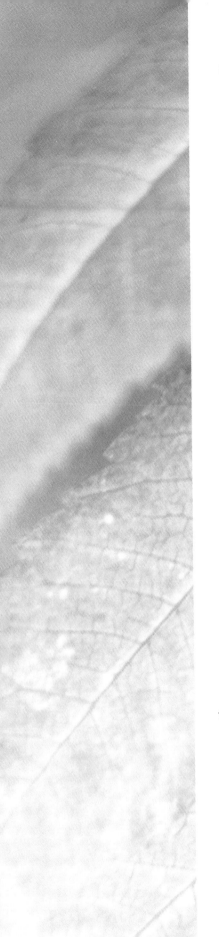

6. Incorporate visual representations and organizing devices to help students represent and organize ideas and information. The *Daybook* provides multiple and varied opportunities for students to visualize and "picture'"what they are reading, organize text graphically, and engage with visual symbols.

Bustle, L. S. (Ed.). (2003). *Image, Inquiry, and Transformative Practice: Engaging learners in creative and critical inquiry through visual representation.* New York: Peter Lang.

Bustle, L. S. (2004). "The Role of Visual Representation in the Assessment of Learning." *Journal of Adolescent & Adult Literacy.* 47(5): 416-421.

7. Complement strategy-building instruction with opportunities for students to read at their own pace and make their own decisions about what to read.The *Daybook* provides exposure to a wide range of texts and authors that are meant to entice students to read full length works that are introduced to them in excerpts.

Guthrie, J. T. and Humenick, N. M. (2004). "Motivating Students to Read: Evidence for Classroom Practices That Increase Reading Motivation and Achievement." In P. McCardle and V. Chhabra, eds., *The Voice of Evidence in Reading Research,* pp. 329-54. Baltimore, MD: Brookes.

8. Conduct multiple types of assessments and self-assessments to monitor student growth that will inform explicit instruction. The *Daybook* provides students with units for self-assessment and many opportunities for teachers to assess both students' reading and writing skills.

Cohen, J. H. and Wiener, R. B. (2003). *Literacy Portfolios: Improving Assessment, Teaching and Learning.* Upper Saddle River, NJ: Merrill/Prentice Hall.

William, D., and Black, P. (1996). "Meanings and Consequences: A Basis for Distinguishing Formative and Summative Functions of Assessment?" *British Educational Research Journal 22*(5): 537-48.

9. Determine venues for students to share expertise with one another and foster collaborative literacy projects. The *Daybook* provides opportunities for students to share their thinking and writing, and they are encouraged to do that in more depth through various extension activities suggested in the teachers' edition.

Vygotsky, L. S. (1978). *Mind in Society. The development of higher mental psychological processes.* Cambridge, MA: MIT Press.

Wood, K. D., Roser, N. L. and Martinez, M. (2001). "Collaborative Literacy: Lessons Learned from Literature." *The Reading Teacher 55*(2): 102-115.

10. Establish routines that give students ample time to read and write in the classroom, where the teacher can monitor students' progress. The *Daybook* is a resource of multiple and overlapping literacy activities that can support developing and monitoring student understanding.

Gettinger, M. (1984). "Achievement as a Function of Time Spent in Learning and Time Needed for Learning." *American Educational Research Journal 21*(3): 617-28.

Lofty. J. (1992). *Time to Write: The Influence of Time and Culture on Learning To Write.* New York: SUNY.

Contents

3

4

5

6

Focus/Skill		Selection/Author	

7

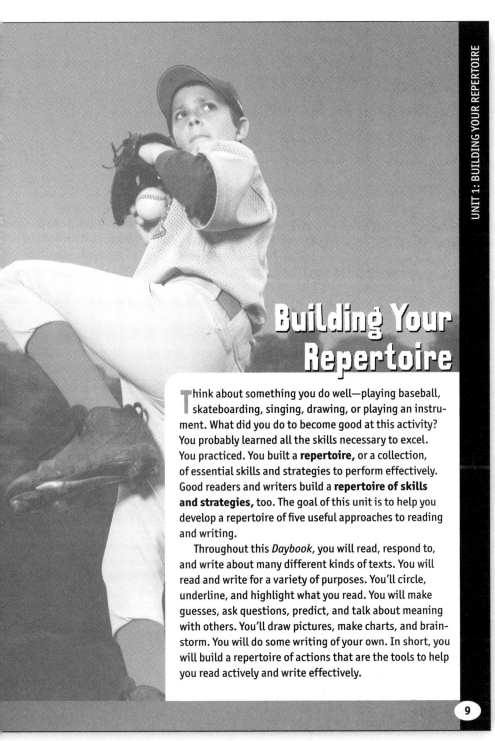

Building Your Repertoire

Think about something you do well—playing baseball, skateboarding, singing, drawing, or playing an instrument. What did you do to become good at this activity? You probably learned all the skills necessary to excel. You practiced. You built a **repertoire,** or a collection, of essential skills and strategies to perform effectively. Good readers and writers build a **repertoire of skills and strategies,** too. The goal of this unit is to help you develop a repertoire of five useful approaches to reading and writing.

Throughout this *Daybook,* you will read, respond to, and write about many different kinds of texts. You will read and write for a variety of purposes. You'll circle, underline, and highlight what you read. You will make guesses, ask questions, predict, and talk about meaning with others. You'll draw pictures, make charts, and brainstorm. You will do some writing of your own. In short, you will build a repertoire of actions that are the tools to help you read actively and write effectively.

9

UNIT 1 BUILDING YOUR REPERTOIRE

Lessons 1–5, pages 10–24

UNIT OVERVIEW
Reading excerpts from the works of award-winning author Julia Alvarez, students are introduced to five critical reading and writing strategies that will be used throughout the book.

KEY IDEA
Good readers develop a repertoire of skills and strategies to help them read and write effectively.

CRITICAL READING SKILLS
by lesson

1 Interacting with the text
2 Making connections
3 Exploring multiple perspectives
4 Focusing on language and craft
5 Studying an author

WRITING ACTIVITIES
by lesson

1 Write a note to a character or the author of *Before We Were Free*.
2 Write a paragraph about a strong connection to the text.
3 Describe an event in the story from a different point of view.
4 Draw and write about an important event, person, or pet.
5 Write an introduction to Julia Alvarez's personal story.

Literature

- *Before We Were Free* by Julia Alvarez (novel excerpts)

In this winner of the Pura Belpré Award, twelve-year-old Anita tells the story of living in the Dominican Republic in 1960, under the Trujillo dictatorship.

- "Author's Note" (*Before We Were Free* author's note excerpt)

Alvarez describes her own experiences fleeing from the Dominican Republic in 1960 and explains her reasons for writing the novel.

- *Latin American Politics and Development* by Harvey Kline and Howard Wiarda, editors (historical text excerpt)

Trujillo's 31-year period of oppression and his eventual downfall are described.

- "In her own words—A conversation with Julia Alvarez" (interview excerpt)

Alvarez describes growing up in the Dominican Republic and encourages readers to know and write about their own family histories.

ASSESSMENT To assess student learning in this unit, see pages 227.

Students will learn to mentally and physically engage with texts by asking questions and marking text.

BACKGROUND KNOWLEDGE

The opening paragraphs of *Before We Were Free* introduce the reader to the narrator, Anita, a Dominican girl attending an American school in the Dominican Republic in 1960. Help students locate the Dominican Republic on a map or globe and ask students to share what they know about the country. Explain that in 1960, the country was under the control of a dictator named Rafael Trujillo. You may wish to have students do more research on Trujillo and/or the Dominican Republic, using reliable sources and the Internet.

VOCABULARY

ridiculous silly

tic a small, repeated movement

Ask questions to check students' understanding: What is an example of something *ridiculous*? What might cause someone to have a *tic*?

Reading is like having a conversation. Instead of talking to a person, you have a conversation with the words and ideas on the page. **Interacting with the text** is like carrying on a conversation with what you are reading. When you interact, you are actively involved in your reading. Reading with your pen is one way to record how your mind works while you are reading. There is space in the **Response Notes** for you to have a conversation. As you read, react to what is going on by circling, underlining, and writing notes.

The selection below is from a novel about a young girl, Anita de la Torre, and her family. They are living in the Dominican Republic in 1960. In the **Response Notes,** you will see how one reader used her pen to interact with the text.

from **Before We Were Free** by Julia Alvarez

Response Notes

Why is there an American School in the Dominican Republic?

This doesn't seem fair

What do Davy Crockett hats look like?

Good point!

"May I have some volunteers?" Mrs. Brown is saying. We are preparing skits for Thanksgiving, two weeks away. Although the Pilgrims never came to the Dominican Republic, we are attending the American school, so we have to celebrate American holidays.

It's a hot, muggy afternoon. I feel lazy and bored. Outside the window, the palm trees are absolutely still. Not even a breeze. Some of the American students have been complaining that it doesn't feel like Thanksgiving when it's as hot as the Fourth of July.

Mrs. Brown is looking around the room. My cousin, Carla, sits in the seat in front of me, waving her arm.

Mrs. Brown calls on Carla, and then on me. Carla and I are to play the parts of two Indians welcoming the Pilgrims. Mrs. Brown always gives the not-so-good parts to those of us in class who are Dominicans.

She hands us each a headband with a feather sticking up like one rabbit ear. I feel ridiculous. "Okay, Indians, come forward and greet the Pilgrims." Mrs. Brown motions toward where Joey Farland and Charlie Price stand with their toy rifles and the Davy Crockett hats they've talked Mrs. Brown into letting them wear. Even I know the pioneers come after the Pilgrims.

"Anita"—she points at me—"I want you to say, 'Welcome to the United States!'"

Before I can mutter my line, Oscar Mancini raises his hand. "Why the Indians call it the United Estates when there was no United Estates back then, Mrs. Brown?"

The class groans. Oscar is always asking questions. "United Estates! United Estates!" somebody in the back row mimics. Lots of classmates snicker, even some Dominicans. I hate it when the American kids make fun of the way we speak English.

Before

CRITICAL READING SKILL
Interacting with the Text Ask students what they do when they have a conversation with someone. (They listen, ask questions, respond to what the other person is saying, etc.) Point out that reading is like having a conversation: you consider the ideas presented, you ask questions, and you develop a new understanding. Do a think-aloud to model interacting with the text: *I wonder why*

Mrs. Brown gives Anita the "not-so-good" parts. Is it because she's Dominican? . . . What's a Davy Crocket hat? I'll circle that and look it up later.

RESPONSE NOTES Point out the sample markings in the *Daybook,* explaining that this is how one student interacted with the text. Encourage students to mark anything they find interesting, important, or puzzling. (See *Daybook* page 225 for tips on active reading.)

READING PROCESS Explain to students that good readers keep their minds active when they read. They prepare to read by previewing the material and setting a purpose. As they read, they engage with the text and monitor their comprehension. After reading a text, successful readers take time to reflect on what they learned. (See *Daybook* page 222 for more on the Reading Process.)

✳ Circle words you don't understand, or underline phrases that catch your attention. Use the **Response Notes** to write your questions, comments, and reactions.

"That's a good question, Oscar," Mrs. Brown responds, casting a disapproving look around. She must have heard the whisper as well. "It's called poetic license. Something allowed in a story that isn't so in real life. Like a metaphor or a simile."

Just then, the classroom door opens. I catch a glimpse of our principal, and behind him, Carla's mother, Tía Laura, looking very nervous. But, then, Tía Laura always looks nervous. Papi likes to joke that if there were ever an Olympic event for worrying, the Dominican Republic would win with his sister on the team. But lately, Papi looks pretty worried himself. When I ask questions, he replies with "Children should be seen, not heard" instead of his usual "Curiosity is a sign of intelligence."

Mrs. Brown comes forward from the back of the room and stands talking to the principal for a few minutes before she follows him out into the hall, where Tía Laura is standing. The door closes.

Usually when our teacher leaves the room, Charlie Price, the class clown, acts up. He does stuff like changing the hands on the clock so that Mrs. Brown will be all confused and let us out for recess early. Yesterday, he wrote NO HOMEWORK TONIGHT in big block letters above the date on the board, THURSDAY, NOVEMBER 10, 1960. Even Mrs. Brown thought that was pretty funny.

But now the whole class waits quietly. The last time the principal came to our classroom, it was to tell Tomasito Morales that his mother was here for him. Something had happened to his father, but even Papi, who knew Señor Morales, would not say what. Tomasito hasn't come back to school since then.

Beside me, Carla is tucking her hair behind her ears, something she does when she's nervous. My brother, Mundín, has a nervous tic, too. He bites his nails whenever he does something wrong and has to sit on the punishment chair until Papi comes home.

The door opens again, and Mrs. Brown steps back in, smiling that phony smile grown-ups smile when they are keeping bad news from you. In a bright voice, Mrs. Brown asks Carla to please collect her things. "Would you help her, Anita?" she adds.

We walk back to our seats and begin packing up Carla's schoolbag. Mrs. Brown announces to the class that they'll continue with their skits later. Everyone is to take out his or her vocabulary book and start on the next chapter. The class pretends to settle down to its work, but of course, everyone is stealing glances at Carla and me.

Mrs. Brown comes over to see how we're doing. Carla packs her homework, but leaves the usual stay-at-school stuff in her desk.

ABOUT THE AUTHOR

Julia Alvarez was born in New York City on March 27, 1950. Shortly after her birth, her family moved to the Dominican Republic, where she spent the majority of her childhood. When she was ten, her family returned to New York, fleeing the Dominican Republic because of her father's involvement with an unsuccessful attempt to overthrow the Trujillo dictatorship.

In high school, Alvarez realized she wanted to pursue a career as a writer. She received her B.A. in 1971 and her M.F.A. in 1975. Since then she has written many critically acclaimed books, including *How the Garcia Girls Lost Their Accents* and *In the Time of the Butterflies*. She also writes poetry and teaches college. For more information, see her website: http://www.juliaalvarez.com/.

TEACHING TIP

Collaboration Have students work in pairs to interact further with the text. Partners can generate questions and answers together, discuss ideas and reactions, and jot down additional Response Notes.

During

SHARING RESPONSES
Invite volunteers to share some of their Response Notes with the class. Remind students that their responses are valid and unique to the reader. List the responses in columns on the board to show the different ways to interact with text, such as questioning, circling unfamiliar words, comparing, connecting to personal experiences, reacting to events in the text, etc.

After

APPLYING THE STRATEGY
Regularly provide students with newspapers, magazines, or other reading materials, and have them practice interacting with many kinds of text. Remind students to imagine they are listening and responding to the character or author as they write their questions and notes. Then have students reflect on how this strategy helps them read better. Ask questions such as the following:

✳ Does the strategy help you stay focused and interested in what you read?

✳ Does the strategy help you read through challenging parts and aid your understanding?

✳ Does the strategy help you read more critically or evaluatively?

WRITER'S CRAFT

Immediacy Point out that the excerpt students have just read is written in present tense, as if it were happening now. This convention, along with dialogue and detailed descriptions, helps the reader to closely observe the action, almost like being in the room. The author's word choice makes the scene feel "immediate." Have students use the scene as a model to write a description of a busy place. For example, they might describe the cafeteria at lunchtime or the bus ride home. Remind students to use present tense.

EXTRA SUPPORT

Differentiation Before completing the writing prompt on page 12, students who need extra support may benefit from brainstorming with a partner to form questions they want to ask the characters or the author.

Quick Assess

❋ Do students' Response Notes show a variety of interactions—questions, comments, highlights, etc.?

❋ Did students mark text that confused them or caught their attention?

❋ Do students' questions and comments demonstrate comprehension of what took place in the excerpt?

Response Notes

"Are those yours?" Mrs. Brown points at the new notebooks, the neat lineup of pens and pencils, the eraser in the shape of the Dominican Republic.

Carla nods.

"Pack it all up, dear," Mrs. Brown says quietly.

We pack Carla's schoolbag with everything that belongs to her. The whole time I'm wondering why Mrs. Brown hasn't asked me to pack my stuff, too. After all, Carla and I are in the same family.

Oscar's hand is waving and dipping like a palm tree in a cyclone. But Mrs. Brown doesn't call on him. This time, I think we're all hoping he'll get a chance to ask his question, which is probably the same question that's in everyone's head: Where is Carla going? ❖

❋ Compare your **Response Notes** with a partner's. Add additional comments as a result of your discussion.

❋ Imagine that you have the opportunity to start a conversation in writing with one of the characters of *Before We Were Free*. Whom will you choose? What questions will you ask? Write a note to one of the characters.

> When you interact with the text by jotting notes, asking questions, circling, highlighting, and stating reactions, you make it your own.

2 LESSON

Make connections between what you are reading and what you know and have experienced in your life. What you read may remind you of movies you've seen or other books you've read. You can also relate what you are reading to news of world events or places in the world you've heard about. **Making connections** helps you understand what you are reading by comparing it to something you already know.

Read another excerpt from Alvarez's *Before We Were Free*. In the **Response Notes,** record any connections you make to the characters or events in the story.

from **Before We Were Free** by Julia Alvarez

We ride home in the Garcías' Plymouth with the silver fins that remind me of the shark I saw at the beach last summer. I'm stuffed in the back with Carla and her younger sisters, Sandi and Yo, who've been taken out of their classes, too. A silent and worried-looking Tía Laura sits in front next to Papi, who is driving.

"What's happening?" I keep asking. "Is something wrong?"

"*Cotorrita,*" Papi warns playfully. That's my nickname in the family because sometimes I talk too much, like a little parrot, Mami says. But then at school, I'm the total opposite and Mrs. Brown complains that I need to speak up more.

Papi begins explaining that the Garcías have finally gotten permission to leave the country, and they'll be taking the airplane in a few hours to go to the United States of America. He's trying to sound excited, looking in the rearview mirror at us. "You'll get to see the snow!"

None of the García sisters says a word.

"And Papito and Mamita and all your cousins," Papi goes on. "Isn't that so, Laura?"

"*Sí, sí, sí,*" Tía Laura agrees. She sounds like someone letting air out of a tire.

My grandparents left for New York at the beginning of September. My other aunts and uncles were already there, having gone away with the younger cousins back in June. Who knows where Tío Toni is? Now, with the García cousins leaving, only my family will be left living at the compound.

I lean forward with my arms on the front seat. "So are we going to go, too, Papi?"

Papi shakes his head. "Somebody has to stay and mind the store." That's what he always says whenever he can't go on an outing because he has to work. Papito, my grandfather, started Construcciones de la Torre, a concrete-block business to build houses that won't blow over during hurricanes. When my grandfather retired a few years ago, Papi, being the oldest, was put in charge.

Response Notes

I was always told to speak up more in class, too.

LESSON 2

Students will learn to connect what they read to what they know.

BACKGROUND KNOWLEDGE

In the excerpts in this lesson, Anita's house is searched by the police. Explain to students that the Secret Police worked for Trujillo to find and arrest anyone suspected of acting against the government. Students may be familiar with this concept from movies they have seen or books they have read about similar situations. (Anita is named for Anne Frank.) To activate prior knowledge, invite them to imagine how they would feel if police could randomly invade and ransack the homes of citizens and threaten law-abiding families.

VOCABULARY

Plymouth an automobile that is no longer in production

gangsters criminals; outlaws

khaki sturdy, yellow-brown fabric made of cotton or wool, often used for military uniforms

guillotine an execution device with a large blade that drops down to sever a prisoner's head; here, a metaphor: the nod *chops off* any more questions

Have students share their knowledge of each word by telling what they know about each word, telling where they have seen the words, or describing an example.

Before

CRITICAL READING SKILL

Making Connections Explain that events and details in a story often remind readers of things they have heard or read about, even if they have not experienced them firsthand. Making connections means relating to what the characters have experienced and leads to a better understanding of the story. Have students recall what happened in the previous classroom scene. (Mrs. Brown asked Anita to help Carla pack her belongings. No one knew why Carla was leaving.) Have them explain when they were in a similar situation, where they didn't know why something was happening. How did it feel? What events might have led to Carla and Anita being taken out of school? Invite students to speculate based on experience, knowledge about the story setting, or other connections they made with the text.

During

RESPONSE NOTES As students read, help them make connections by asking such questions as: *How would you feel if you had been with Anita? Do the men in dark glasses remind you of others you have heard or read about? In what way? What reaction would you or your family have had?* Model making a connection: *This reminds me of the time I was called home and found out my grandpa had been taken to the hospital. Mom was* ▶▶▶

Making Connections To complete the writing prompt on page 14, have students write a short reflection on how making a personal connection to the text helped them to understand the story better.

✳ Take a moment to write about the strongest connection you've made so far.

_____

_____

_____

_____

_____

_____

_____

_____

_____

_____

_____

Response Notes

The following scene occurs the day after Anita's cousins leave for the United States. Papi and Anita's brother Mundín have already gone to work. Anita, her mother, her sister, Lucinda, and Chucha, her old nanny, are at home. As you read, continue recording connections in your **Response Notes.**

A half-dozen black Volkswagens are crawling up our driveway.

Before the cars come to a complete stop, the doors open, and a stream of men pour out all over the property. In their dark glasses, they look like gangsters in the American movies that sometimes come to town.

I run to get Mami, but she's already headed for the door. Four men stand in our entryway, all dressed in Khaki pants with small holsters at their belts and tiny revolvers that don't look real.

The head guy—or at least he does all the talking—asks Mami for Carlos García and his family. I know something is really wrong when Mami says, "Why? Aren't they home?"

But then, instead of going away, this guy asks if his men can search our house. Mami, who I'm sure will say, "Do you have a _permiso_?" steps aside like the toilet is overflowing and these are the plumbers coming to the rescue!

I trail behind Mami, "Who are they?" I ask.

Mami swings around, a terrified look on her face, and hisses, "Not now!"

After

pretending everything was OK, but I could tell it wasn't. That frightened me!

REFLECTING Have students jot down the strongest connection they made as they read. Encourage them to explain why making that connection helped them understand the passage better.

READING/WRITING CONNECTION For more practice with connections, have students choose a connection from column 2 or 3 of the chart on page 16 and write about it. Remind students to describe the connection in detail and to explain its importance.

ART CONNECTION To reinforce the concept of making connections, have students do a quick sketch that depicts the emotions in the story. Students can represent specific words and phrases with different colors or create abstract designs about the feelings created by the story.

I race to find Chucha, who's in the entryway, shaking her head at the muddy boot prints. I ask her who these strange men are.

"SIM," she whispers. She makes a creepy gesture of cutting off her head with her index finger.

"But *who* are the SIM?" I ask again. I'm feeling more and more panicked at how nobody is giving me a straight answer.

"*Policia secreta*," she explains. "They go around investigating everyone and then disappearing them."

"*Secret* police?"

Chucha gives me her long, slow, guillotine nod that cuts off any further questions.

They go from room to room, looking in every nook and cranny. When they come through the hall door to the bedroom part of the house, Mami hesitates. "Just a routine search, *doña*," the head guy says. Mami smiles wanly, trying to show she has nothing to hide.

In my room, one guy lifts the baby-doll pajamas I left lying on the floor as if a secret weapon is hidden underneath. Another yanks the covers back from my bed. I hold on tight to Mami's ice-cold hand and she tightens her hold on mine.

The men go into Lucinda's room without knocking, opening up the jalousies, lifting the bedskirt and matching skirt on her vanity, plunging their bayonets underneath. My older sister sits up in bed, startled, her pink-foam rollers askew from sleeping on them. A horrible red rash has broken out on her neck.

When the men are done searching the room, Mami gives Lucinda and me her look that means business. "I want you both in here while I accompany our visitors," she says with strained politeness. ❖

TEACHING TIP

Collaboration Have students share the connections they are making in the Response Notes, using the Think-Pair-Share technique:

1. **Think** Have individuals write down their connections in the Response Notes as they read.

2. **Pair** Have students discuss their connections with a partner and choose one to share with the rest of the class. It could be something they think others will relate to or an insight they believe others might not have reached.

3. **Share** Have pairs take turns sharing and discussing their connections with the class.

MAKING CONNECTIONS 15

Categorizing Before students complete the chart on page 16 of the *Daybook,* invite volunteers to share some of the connections they made on previous pages. Have students identify each kind, using a simple marking system—L for a connection to one's own life, T for one to other texts, or W for a connection to the world beyond. Then have students complete the chart independently.

Quick Assess

✳ Do students' Response Notes show a variety of connections, from personal to more global?

✳ In writing about their strongest connection, did students describe the connection thoroughly and explain its importance?

✳ Are students able to cite examples from the text to support their thoughts?

✳ In the table below, list the connections you made as you read. Share your lists with a partner. Add any other connections that come to mind as you discuss the lists.

Connections to you	Connections to other texts (books, movies, etc.)	Connections to world events, places, situations beyond your life

Make connections to your experiences, other texts, a neighborhood, or world events to help you better understand what you are reading.

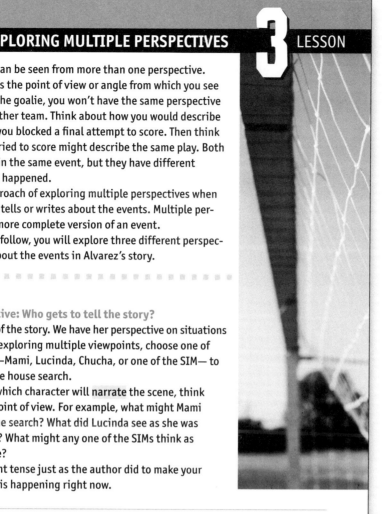

Almost anything can be seen from more than one perspective. A **perspective** is the point of view or angle from which you see a subject. If you are the goalie, you won't have the same perspective as a forward on the other team. Think about how you would describe winning the game if you blocked a final attempt to score. Then think how the player who tried to score might describe the same play. Both players participated in the same event, but they have different perspectives on what happened.

Try taking the approach of exploring multiple perspectives when you read. Notice who tells or writes about the events. Multiple perspectives give you a more complete version of an event.

On the pages that follow, you will explore three different perspectives to learn more about the events in Alvarez's story.

VANTAGE POINT **1**

Character's Perspective: Who gets to tell the story?
Anita is the narrator of the story. We have her perspective on situations and events. To begin exploring multiple viewpoints, choose one of the other characters—Mami, Lucinda, Chucha, or one of the SIM— to tell the incident of the house search.

After you choose which character will narrate the scene, think about that person's point of view. For example, what might Mami think about during the search? What did Lucinda see as she was awakened by the SIM? What might any one of the SIMs think as they search the house?

Write in the present tense just as the author did to make your retelling seem as if it is happening right now.

Students will gain a deeper understanding of an event by comparing multiple selections and perspectives.

BACKGROUND KNOWLEDGE
In this lesson, students will read excerpts from two nonfiction texts. Unlike *Before We Were Free*, the author's fictional story about a real place and time, nonfiction (informational text) presents facts and describes events without the addition of fictional elements. Activate prior knowledge by pointing out different types of nonfiction, such as articles in newspapers and periodicals, textbooks, biographies, interviews, etc., and ask students to name some they've read and enjoyed.

VOCABULARY
narrate to tell a story

native country the country in which one is born

repression the state of being silenced or kept down by force

dissent disagreement; difference of opinion

Ask how students would feel if they lived in a society that was brutally ruled by a dictator who repressed the people. Discuss ways that people express their dissenting opinions and which ways are most effective.

Before

CRITICAL READING SKILL
Exploring Multiple Perspectives Tell students: *You can think about the same text from different perspectives, or vantage points, to help you understand the text better.* Point out that the subject matter, style, theme, and other elements of a piece of writing are often determined by the perspective of the author or narrator.

Demonstrate the concept by showing students an object that looks different from different sides, such as a T-shirt with a school logo on the front or one with an acceptable slogan on the back. Ask: *If you saw only the front (or back), would you want (or not want) the shirt?* Explain to students that their "vantage point" can influence what they think or feel about something. Similarly, an author's vantage point can have an effect on the reader's understanding of the topic.

During

VANTAGE POINTS
Character's Perspective Have students role-play the house-search scene in *Before We Were Free* with a partner, taking turns playing different characters in order to experience each point of view.

Author's Perspective Model writing a response to the Author's Note: *Alvarez actually lived through some of the things she wrote about! That makes me appreciate her fictional story and characters more.* ▶▶▶

Differentiation Some students may benefit from a visual representation of the three vantage points presented in the lesson. Guide students in creating a Venn diagram to compare the vantage points of the main character and the author, and then the author and a history book editor, who would be interested in presenting accurate facts.

Read Aloud The text in Vantage Point 3 is difficult. Read it aloud or summarize it for students who need the extra support: Trujillo [troo HE oh] controlled the Dominican Republic for more than 30 years. The dictator stayed in power by mistreating people who opposed his ideas and creating a government that favored his politics. Eventually, people around the world became aware of the cruel nature of his society.

Response Notes

VANTAGE POINT 2
Author's Perspective: What is the author's story?
Sometimes an author provides interesting information about the subject or tells the purpose of what she has written.

In your **Response Notes**, write what you learn from the author that helps you understand what is going on in the story. Share with a partner what you learned from the author.

Author's Note from *Before We Were Free* by Julia Alvarez

"I won't ever forget the day in 1960 when my parents announced that we were leaving our native country of the Dominican Republic for the United States of America. I kept asking my mother why we had to go. All she would say, in a quiet, tense voice, was "Because we're lucky."

Soon after our arrival in New York City, my parents explained why we had left our homeland in such a hurry. Many of the questions in my head began to be answered.

For over thirty years, our country had been under the bloody rule of General Trujillo. The secret police (SIM) kept tabs on everybody's doings. Public gatherings were forbidden. The least breath of resistance could bring arrest, torture, and death to you as well as your family. No one dared to disobey."

VANTAGE POINT 3
Historical Perspective: What's the history behind the story?
Before We Were Free is a historical novel, meaning it draws the fictional story from real events. Read the following excerpt from a historical account of the Dominican Republic that gives information about General Trujillo. Make notes that indicate what you learn that adds to your understanding of the story.

from Latin American Politics and Development
Harvey Kline and Howard Wiarda, editors

The thirty-one year rule of Rafael Trujillo has been described as Latin America's most complete dictatorship. The Dominican Republic was controlled by one man and his extended family from 1930 to 1961, and that control was often achieved through brutal repression. The Dominican Republic during the Trujillo years became a country in which opposition politics and dissent were

After

Historical Perspective Have students discuss which might be harder, writing a historical account of something or writing a completely fictional story.

When students have finished their work on page 19 of the *Daybook,* discuss with them how the author's and the historical perspectives add to their understanding of *Before We Were Free.* Ask:

✴ How does reading Alvarez's words help you appreciate what she wrote in her novel?

✴ How does knowing details about Trujillo's dictatorship help you understand the events in *Before We Were Free?*

LISTENING/SPEAKING CONNECTION To apply the skill of exploring multiple perspectives in another context, have students choose a partner with whom they have shared an experience, such as playing on a team or doing a class project together. After partners have discussed the experience and their individual perspectives on it,

crushed and democracy was transformed into a kind of cult of personality with *el presidente* as the center of the political system.

As the world became more aware of the repressive nature of Trujilloism, the system of control that he had built gradually came tumbling down. Opposition leaders and intellectuals became more forceful in their attacks on Trujillo, the United States tired of supporting an ally who had become an embarrassment, and most important, the middle class in the country came to realize that the leader's corruption and control were harming the economy and limiting their ability to advance. ❖

❋ Ask yourself: What information did this perspective or vantage point help me notice about the events or people in the story? In the space below, summarize something important you learned from each perspective you tried out.

VANTAGE POINT 1
Character's Perspective: Who gets to tell the story?

_____

_____

_____

VANTAGE POINT 2
Author's Perspective: What is the author's story?

_____

_____

_____

VANTAGE POINT 3
Historical Perspective: What's the history behind the story?

_____

_____

_____

Examine multiple perspectives to learn more about and to evaluate what you are reading.

WRITER'S CRAFT
Word Choice Authors choose their words carefully to send a message. In the excerpt from *Latin American Politics and Development,* the editors used the word *crushed* to describe how Trujillo's government treated dissenting views. Ask: *What message does* crushed *send? How would the message be different if the editors chose to use* silenced *or* not allowed? (*Crushed* sends a very powerful, strong message. The government had absolutely no tolerance for dissent. It probably acted quickly and decisively.)

TEACHING TIP
Collaboration Before individuals begin writing, have small groups discuss what they learned from each vantage point. English learners and students needing extra support can be paired with on- or above-level students.

Quick Assess

❋ Did students use the present tense correctly on page 17? Did they show the ability to describe the same events through different eyes?

❋ Do students' Response Notes on page 18 make connections between the nonfiction selections and Alvarez's story?

❋ Did students identify at least one thing they learned from each vantage point?

have them describe the experience to the class, but with each partner presenting the other partner's point of view.

COMPARING PERSPECTIVES Have students work with other paired selections to compare authors' perspectives. For example, from a newspaper, select a news article and an editorial about the same topic. Ask students to write about how the selections are the same and how they differ. A Venn diagram will be helpful in planning the writing.

Students analyze how the language and craft of a text influence us as readers and writers.

BACKGROUND KNOWLEDGE

In the excerpt in this lesson, Anita expresses her confusion about the SIM—what kind of "police officers" they are and whether they can be trusted. Activate prior knowledge by having students share what they know about the police, what their role usually is, and whether they are normally trustworthy. Students may want to discuss movies or TV shows they've seen in which some police officers were portrayed as "bad guys," engaged in illegal activity.

VOCABULARY

colicky fussy; usually referring to a baby suffering from a digestive problem called colic

Discuss why Alvarez might have chosen this word to describe a motor. How does it help the reader hear the motor?

If you tell your friend about something really exciting, you'll choose the right words to capture the important moments. You'll help your friend see and feel what you experienced.

Authors choose words and details to create pictures in the minds of their readers and to prompt responses from them. As you focus on how authors shape their language, you will focus on language and craft. **Description** is one of the basic techniques that an author uses to make scenes vivid for the reader.

Take a close look at another scene from the novel. This scene occurs shortly after the search took place. As you read, write reactions in your **Response Notes** and circle the descriptions that caused those reactions.

Response Notes

Must be a noisy motor!

from Before We Were Free by Julia Alvarez

Those black cars sit there for days and days—sometimes there's only one, sometimes as many as three. Every morning, when Papi leaves for the office, one of the cars starts up its (colicky motor) and follows him down the hill. In the evening, when he comes home, it comes back with him. I don't know when those SIM ever go to their own houses to eat their suppers and talk with their kids.

"Are they really policemen?" I keep asking Mami. It doesn't make any sense. If the SIM are policemen, secret or not, shouldn't we trust them instead of being afraid of them? But all Mami will say is "Shhh!" Meanwhile, we can't go to school because something might happen to us. "Like what?" I ask. Like what Chucha said about people disappearing? Is that what Mami worries will happen to us? "Didn't Papi say we should carry on with normal life?"

"Anita, *por favor*," Mami pleads, collapsing in a hall chair. She leans forward and whispers in my ear, "Please, please, you must stop asking questions."

"But why?" I whisper back. I can smell her shampoo, which smells like coconuts in her hair.

"Because I don't have any answers," she replies. ❖

Before

CRITICAL READING SKILL
Focusing on Language and Craft

In this section, students learn to think about the ways an author uses words to develop ideas and create memorable characters and stories. Point out that writing is like painting; a good writer paints a picture in your mind.

LANGUAGE MAP With students, revisit the excerpt on page 14. Have students point out words or phrases that create strong images in their mind (e.g., *crawling up our driveway, dark glasses*). Write each word or phrase on the board, and create an extensive map by having students brainstorm words that tell what each image makes them see, feel, hear, etc. Then, as students read the passage on this page, remind them to look for ways that Alvarez uses words to draw the reader in, create interest, and spark the imagination.

Before We Were Free

See	Hear	Feel
pink foam rollers		

* Draw one of the pictures that you have in your mind as you finish reading. Use the author's descriptions to guide you. Use pen, colored pencils, crayons, or markers.

* Share your sketch with a partner. Explain to each other how the author's descriptions helped you create pictures in your mind. Refer to your **Response Notes** to show specific descriptions that made the scene vivid.

* In the space below, draw a picture of an important person, pet, or event from your own life. Then describe what you have drawn. Choose words that will help create that picture in the mind of your reader.

Read to a partner what you have written. Ask your partner to tell you the picture that comes to his or her mind.

Examine how writers use descriptive language to help readers form pictures in their minds.

Differentiation In the language map suggested at the bottom of page 20, use pictures in addition to words to help English language learners understand the concepts.

Quick Assess

* Do students understand the connection between descriptive language and visualizing?

During

VISUALIZING Model drawing a simple picture of something from the text, and explain how you visualized it. For example, *I drew this chair to remind me of Mami, collapsed in the chair, looking tired and worried, the part where she whispers to and pleads with Anita to stop asking questions. The chair I have drawn helps me imagine how Mami is feeling and to picture what she looks like.*

As students work on their own drawings, encourage them to draw whatever they see and not to concern themselves with artistic merit. Ask: *How does visualizing help a reader understand a text better?*

After

WRITE A LETTER Now that students have spent some time with Julia Alvarez's writing, have them write her a letter. In the letter, students should tell her their opinions of *Before We Were Free,* specifically stating how the interview and the historical perspective enhanced their reading of the excerpts.

Students go behind the story to learn where authors get ideas.

BACKGROUND KNOWLEDGE

In this lesson, students will read an interview of Julia Alvarez in which she explains how her family's experiences in the Dominican Republic and her immigration to America have influenced her writing and activism. Invite students to learn more about her experiences, beliefs, and accomplishments by researching her life story on her own website: www.juliaalvarez.com. It is a reliable source and provides a wealth of information.

VOCABULARY

underground a secret group that works to oppose a leader or government

assassinated murdered

cooperative an organized group of people or businesses that work together to produce and distribute goods or services

contradict deny; show to be false

ethnicities groups of people who have the same racial, cultural, or national background

Show students how they can determine the meaning of these words by looking at word parts and relating them to similar words. For example, *contra* means "against" and *dict* is a Latin root that means "say," as in *diction* and *dictionary*.

LESSON 5 — STUDYING AN AUTHOR

Authors often write about what they know. This doesn't mean that every book is an account of the author's life. However, many writers borrow bits and pieces from their lives. As you already know, Julia Alvarez draws heavily from her life experiences and from the time when she was a child living in the Dominican Republic. Taking the approach of studying an author offers a window into the writer's attitudes and beliefs. Knowing about the author's life might help you understand what motivates the ideas. You might see more fully what the author's attitudes are.

As you read the interview below, "In her own words—a conversation with Julia Alvarez," notice that there is a questioner [Q] and Julia Alvarez [A]. The questioner's comments are in **boldface** and the author's are not. Use your **Response Notes** to compare the information the author shares with the situation, events, and people in the novel.

Response Notes

Just like when Carla left class.

from "In her own words—a conversation with Julia Alvarez"

[Q] **We learn in your author's note that this story was inspired by your own and your family's experience in the Dominican Republic. How much of a role did your own memories and the true stories you heard play in the writing of the book?**

[A] My father was involved in the underground against the Trujillo dictatorship in the Dominican Republic. When members of his immediate "cell" were rounded up, we had to leave in a hurry for the United States. But my uncle, who was also involved in the underground, and his family remained. Some members of the group who assassinated the dictator went to my uncle's house to hide. When they were caught, my uncle was also taken away. My aunt and cousins lived under house arrest for nine months, not knowing if my uncle was dead or alive. He survived, but the members who had hidden in his house were killed by the dictator's son. These men were very close friends of my family. In fact, growing up, I called them *tíos*, uncles; their kids were my playmates. So you see, I had some connection to what actually happened. In writing the book, I conducted interviews with survivors, and I also read a lot of the history. I was particularly interested in the sons and daughters of those who had been tortured, imprisoned, or murdered—kids like my cousins and my childhood playmates. So it was a composite both of doing research and of remembering family stories.

Before

CRITICAL READING SKILL

Studying an Author Remind students that knowing about an author's background can provide valuable insight into the subject and themes of the author's writing. Reading an interview can be one way to find out about an author.

INTERVIEW Model role-playing an interview with a student. Ask the student questions, such as: *What sports do you play well? What is your favorite book, and why?* Then switch and have the student interview you. Invite other volunteers to interview each other and discuss what was learned in each case. Then ask: *How might reading an interview be different from one you watch or hear?* (You can't see the people's expressions or hear their tone of voice; some words might be changed or left out; etc.)

During

RESPONSE NOTES As students read the interview, suggest they think about and comment on Alvarez's perspective. How does it affect their understanding and attitude toward her writing?

WRITING SUPPORT Discuss the purpose of an introduction (to prepare an audience, get the audience's attention). Then brainstorm the kind of information that might be in an introduction—the

[◉] **In the book Anita's parents insist on staying in the country to fight for change. Have you continued to be committed to and involved in the future of the Dominican Republic? Do you view the writing of this book as a part of that commitment?**

[↗] Definitely. My husband and I now have an organic coffee farm [in the Dominican Republic] that is part of a cooperative of small farmers trying to save the land from erosion and pesticides. We set it up as a foundation so that the proceeds from the sale of our coffee go to fund a school on the farm. We did this when we realized that none of our neighbors could read or write: ninety-five percent illiteracy in that area! I feel so very lucky to have the opportunities we have in this country. But we can't stop there. We have a responsibility to those who are less lucky. I know I feel a special commitment to those who stayed behind in my native country, fighting for freedom and opportunities. The other way I'm still involved in my native land is by writing....

✳ Imagine that you have been asked to introduce Julia Alvarez—the writer and the person—to a group of students who will be reading *Before We Were Free*. What do you want to emphasize? What is most interesting to you? Write your introduction in the space below.

_____

_____

_____

_____

_____

_____

_____

_____

_____

_____

_____

_____

_____

_____

_____

Collaboration After students have written their introductions, partners can work together to give each other feedback. One partner can read his or her introduction while the other pretends to be the "audience" and then provides feedback.

After

person's name, what he or she is known for, one or two major achievements or interesting facts, etc. Before students write their own introductions, encourage them to make a list of what they want to include. Also remind students to think about their audience and how to get that particular audience's attention.

READING/WRITING CONNECTION To extend the author study, help students find another book by Julia Alvarez, such as *How the Garcia Girls Lost Their Accents* (written for adults), *Finding Miracles,* or *How Tia Lola Came to Stay*. Ask them to write a short review of it. The review should make connections to Alvarez's experiences and beliefs.

To reinforce the skill further, have students study other authors who base their stories on personal experiences, such as Gary Paulsen, Walter Dean Myers, Gary Soto, Linda Sue Park, or Laurence Yep. Encourage students to read autobiographies or biographies of favorite authors and share with the class how their life experiences influenced their writing.

Choosing a Topic Encourage students to tell stories they remember from their childhood or that other family members have told. If students need help thinking of a story, have them create a word web to brainstorm events, people, places, and situations in their life or community.

Writer's Craft Remind students to use present tense to make the story feel more immediate, and to use details, dialogue, and descriptive language to make the scene come alive.

Quick Assess

✻ Do students' introductions contain accurate and relevant information about Alvarez's life and work?

✻ Are the introductions interesting and appropriate for the audience?

✻ Did students choose an interesting story to tell? Does it hold the reader's attention?

✻ Did students use present tense, details, and dialogue in their story to achieve immediacy?

Response Notes

✳ Read another part of the conversation. Record your reactions in your **Response Notes.**

Can learning about others and becoming more politically aware really make a difference? Where do we start?

...I often think of that biblical phrase: "The truth shall make you free," and also that wonderful quote, "Those who cannot remember the past are condemned to repeat it." Young people as well as older people need to know the stories of their families, their communities, their countries, each other, because it's a way to be aware and experience the realities of others. In dictatorships, there is always only one story: the official story no one can contradict. All other stories are silenced. It's the knowing of each other's stories and the feeling and compassion created by knowing these stories that connect us as individuals to each other and make a humane human family out of different populations and countries and ethnicities. ❖

✳ Alvarez challenges us to know the stories of our families and communities. She encourages us to share our stories with others. Use the space below to write a story of your family or community that you want to share with others.

_____

_____

_____

_____

_____

_____

_____

> In order to understand why an author writes what he or she writes, learn what you can about the author's life and purposes for writing. This may also give you ideas for your own writing.

Interacting with the Text

What do you like to read? Fantasy? Science fiction? Mysteries? When you like what you're reading, you probably find it easy to understand.

But what happens when you have to read something new or difficult? That's when you need to become a **strategic reader.** Good readers use a repertoire of skills and strategies to help them understand what they read. Part of the repertoire is interacting with the text. When you interact with the text, you think about it and you write about it. In this unit, you will practice several strategies you can use to interact with the text.

25

UNIT 2
INTERACTING WITH THE TEXT

Lessons 6–10, pages 26–40

UNIT OVERVIEW
Students learn five essential reading strategies as they interact with two texts about people with differences.

KEY IDEA
Good readers employ certain strategies to understand and evaluate what they read.

CRITICAL READING SKILLS
by lesson

6 Predicting
7 Making inferences
8 Finding the main idea
9 Determining the author's purpose
10 Reflecting

WRITING ACTIVITIES
by lesson

6 Add to a short story.
7 Write a dialogue between two characters.
8 Describe an incident.
9 Make a web about the author's purpose.
10 Write reflective paragraphs.

Literature

- *"All Summer in a Day"* by Ray Bradbury (short story)

In this science-fiction story set on Venus in the future, children play a cruel prank on a child who is perceived to be "different."

- *"Hearing the Sweetest Songs"* by Nicolette Toussaint (personal essay)

A woman with a hearing impairment discusses how her disability affects her life and whether "disability" is an appropriate label.

ASSESSMENT To assess student learning in this unit, see pages 228 and 251.

Students will make predictions as they read to monitor their understanding of a story.

BACKGROUND KNOWLEDGE

In this lesson, students will read a science-fiction story by Ray Bradbury. Activate prior knowledge by eliciting other science-fiction books or movies that students may know. Discuss the characteristics of science fiction (e.g., often takes place in the future or in outer space; usually involves science or technology that has not yet been developed).

Point out that in 1954, when "All Summer in a Day" was published, space travel did not yet exist and no one had seen images of Venus—the setting of Bradbury's story. Bradbury imagined Venus as a rainy jungle. Now scientists know that Venus is extremely hot and dry, with almost no oxygen, a place where life could never exist.

VOCABULARY

compounded increased by combining
concussion damage from a hard blow
slackening easing up

For each word, help students think of related words that contain word parts providing clues to the word's meaning. For example: *combined, percussion, slacker*.

LESSON 6 · PREDICTING

Strategic readers interact with text by making predictions as they read to help them better understand events and characters. When you first read the title, you probably guess what the story will be about based on the words in the title and what you know about the title. That is a **prediction**. As you read further, you check to see if your prediction matches what the author wrote, or if you need to revise your prediction. Strategic readers predict and check several times while they read a story.

As you read the first part of Ray Bradbury's short story, "All Summer in a Day," use the **Response Notes** column to make notes about what you think might happen next and why. You will come back to your predictions after you finish the first part of the story.

"All Summer in a Day" by Ray Bradbury

Response Notes

"Ready?"
"Ready."
"Now?"
"Soon."
"Do the scientists really know? Will it happen today, will it?"
"Look, look; see for yourself!"
The children pressed to each other like so many roses, so many weeds, intermixed, peering out for a look at the hidden sun.
It rained.
It had been raining for seven years; thousands upon thousands of days compounded and filled from one end to the other with rain, with the drum and gush of water, with the sweet crystal fall of showers and the concussion of storms so heavy they were tidal waves come over the islands. A thousand forests had been crushed under the rain and grown up a thousand times to be crushed again. And this was the way life was forever on the planet Venus, and this was the schoolroom of the children of the rocket men and women who had come to a raining world to set up civilization and live out their lives.
"It's stopping, it's stopping!"
"Yes, yes!"
Margot stood apart from them, from these children who could never remember a time when there wasn't rain and rain and rain. They were all nine years old, and if there had been a day, seven years ago, when the sun came out for an hour and showed its face to the stunned world, they could not recall.

I think Margot knows something about the sun because she is different from the others.

Before

CRITICAL READING SKILL

Predicting Explain to students that making a prediction is more than just guessing randomly; it means using background knowledge and clues within the text to make an educated guess. Use the beginning of the story to model making a prediction: *The title reminds me of the Fourth of July. The first word, "Ready?" makes me think something exciting is*

about to happen. "It had been raining for seven years" makes me think that something strange is going on. Are there people on Venus?

RESPONSE NOTES Encourage

students to write predictions about why Margot is standing apart from the other children and how she might be different from them. Have students highlight in

the text what the author has Margot say and do in order to make and support their predictions.

Sometimes, at night, she heard them stir, in remembrance, and she knew they were dreaming and remembering gold or a yellow crayon or a coin large enough to buy the world with.

She knew that they thought they remembered a warmness, like a blushing in the face, in the body, in the arms and legs and trembling hands. But then they always awoke to the tatting drum, the endless shaking down of clear bead necklaces upon the roof, the walk, the gardens, the forests, and their dreams were gone.

All day yesterday they had read in class about the sun, about how like a lemon it was, and how hot. And they had written small stories or essays or poems about it:

I think the sun is a flower,

That blooms for just one hour.

That was Margot's poem, read in a quiet voice in the still classroom while the rain was falling outside.

"Aw, you didn't write that!" protested one of the boys.

"I did," said Margot. "I did."

"William!" said the teacher.

But that was yesterday. Now the rain was slackening, and the children were crushed in the great thick windows.

"Where's teacher?"

"She'll be back."

"She'd better hurry, we'll miss it!"

They turned on themselves, like a feverish wheel, all tumbling spokes.

Margot stood alone. She was a very frail girl who looked as if she had been lost in the rain for years and the rain had washed out the blue from her eyes and the red from her mouth and the yellow from her hair. She was an old photograph dusted from an album, whitened away, and if she spoke at all her voice would be a ghost. Now she stood, separate, staring at the rain and the loud wet world beyond the huge glass.

"What are you looking at?" said William.

Margot said nothing.

"Speak when you're spoken to." He gave her a shove. But she did not move; rather she let herself be moved only by him and nothing else.

They edged away from her, they would not look at her. She felt them go away. And this was because she would play no games with them in the echoing tunnels of the underground city. If they tagged her and ran, she stood blinking

EXTRA SUPPORT

Differentiation Some students may have trouble following dialogue without speaker tags. To help these students, read aloud the dialogue at the beginning of page 26, alternating the lines with a student or have small groups role-play the dialogue.

During

REFLECTING ON AND CONFIRMING PREDICTIONS After students have finished reading page 28, have them reflect on the predictions they have made thus far. Students can work with a partner to discuss which predictions, if any, have been confirmed and which they want to revise. Encourage students to look at any predictions that were not confirmed. Ask questions to help students determine why their predic-

tions were not confirmed. Were students confused by the dialogue or imagery? Did students read too quickly through the longer paragraphs and miss important clues? Remind students that making predictions is one way of interacting and staying engaged with the text.

After

LISTENING/SPEAKING CONNECTION To give students an opportunity to make predictions with another text, have individuals think of a suspenseful story they know and retell half of it to the class. The class can then make predictions about the ending, and the storyteller can confirm the predictions or explain how the ending was different.

TEACHING TIP

Collaboration Students may benefit from brainstorming in small groups about what might happen next in the story, using the Round Robin technique: one student suggests what happens next, the next student adds to the story, and so on.

WRITING SUPPORT

Style Before students write their story continuations on page 28, help them identify characteristics of Bradbury's writing style, such as long, descriptive sentences and short, succinct dialogue. Encourage students to mimic this style in their paragraphs.

Quick Assess

✳ Did students make predictions based on background knowledge and/or clues in the text?

✳ Do students' paragraphs continue the story in a way that shows an understanding of the setting, characters, and conflict?

✳ Does the writing reflect the style of the original author?

after them and did not follow. When the class sang songs about happiness and life and games, her lips barely moved. Only when they sang about the sun and the summer did her lips move as she watched the drenched windows.

And then, of course, the biggest crime of all was that she had come here only five years ago from Earth, and she remembered the sun and the way the sun was and the sky was when she was four, in Ohio. And they, they had been on Venus all their lives, and they had been only two years old when last the sun came out and had long since forgotten the color and heat of it and the way it really was. But Margot remembered.

"It's like a penny," she said once, eyes closed.

"No, it's not!" the children cried.

"It's like a fire," she said, "in the stove."

"You're lying; you don't remember!" cried the children.

But she remembered and stood quietly apart from all of them and watched the patterning windows. And once, a month ago, she had refused to shower in the school shower rooms, had clutched her hands to her ears and over her head, screaming the water mustn't touch her head. So after that, dimly, dimly, she sensed it; she was different and they knew her difference and kept away. ✦

✳ Put check marks next to the events in the text where your predictions were similar to the story. Using your notes, write one sentence predicting what will happen next and explain why.

_____

_____

✳ Based on your prediction, continue the story as if you were the author.

_____

_____

_____

_____

_____

_____

_____

_____

Strategic readers constantly make predictions and check them when they read.

Have you ever read all the words and still felt that something was missing? Maybe you needed to interact with the text by reading "between the lines." Writers might not tell you everything you want to know. So strategic readers **make inferences** by putting together something they have read with something they already know. Remember when Bradbury wrote that William gave Margot a shove? He was counting on you to know about a time when a boy acted the same way so you could make an inference about the kind of person William is.

Read the next part of "All Summer in a Day" to see why that matters. Notice what William says and does. Jot down notes that tell what you learn about William and what you learn about the other children.

"All Summer in a Day" by Ray Bradbury *(continued)*

Response Notes

There was talk that her father and mother were taking her back to Earth next year; it seemed vital to her that they do so, though it would mean the loss of thousands of dollars to her family. And so, the children hated her for all these reasons, of big and little consequence. They hated her pale, snow face, her waiting silence, her thinness, and her possible future.

"Get away!" The boy gave her another push. "What're you waiting for?"

Then, for the first time, she turned and looked at him. And what she was waiting for was in her eyes.

"Well, don't wait around here!" cried the boy, savagely. "You won't see nothing!" Her lips moved.

"Nothing!" he cried. "It was all a joke, wasn't it?" He turned to the other children. "Nothing's happening today. Is it?"

They all blinked at him and then, understanding, laughed and shook their heads.

"Oh, but," Margot whispered, her eyes helpless. "But this is the day, the scientists predict, they say, they know, the sun . . ."

"All a joke!" said the boy and seized her roughly. "Hey, everyone, let's put her in a closet before teacher comes!"

"No," said Margot, falling back.

They surged about her, caught her up and bore her, protesting, and then pleading, and then crying, back into a tunnel, a room, a closet, where they slammed and locked the door. They stood looking at the door and saw it tremble from her beating and throwing herself against it. They heard her muffled cries. Then, smiling, they turned and went out and back down the tunnel, just as the teacher arrived.

"Ready, children?" She glanced at her watch.

LESSON **7**

Students will make inferences about a story based on their knowledge about a topic and personal experience.

ACTIVATE PRIOR KNOWLEDGE
Help students empathize and connect with the character of Margot {MAR go} in this passage by activating prior knowledge about members of a tightly knit group rejecting an outsider. Invite students to talk about times they have witnessed bullying or teasing. Ask: *Why is bullying wrong? What did the children hold against Margot? Could Margot have changed their feelings? Could the teacher have done more to protect her?*

VOCABULARY
apparatus equipment for a specific purpose

repercussions reflection of sounds

tumultuously in a way that is full of commotion; disorderly

Have students name different kinds of *apparatus (e.g., fitness equipment)*, things that might have *repercussions* (anything with an echo), and scenes or situations that might be *tumultuous (e.g., a crowd of people all trying to grab the last sale item)*.

Before

CRITICAL READING SKILL
Making Inferences A reader makes an inference to fill in some information that the author did not state. Point out that when we make an inference, we make a connection between the text and our personal experiences, other texts, or the larger world. Model making an inference: *When I walked by the lunchroom this morning, I smelled _____ (pizza). So I inferred that we're having _____ (pizza) today. Some of you are cheering about that—I infer that you like _____ (pizza)!* Point out that inferences can be made about story characters and events, too.

RESPONSE NOTES
Do a think-aloud to model how to make an inference from the text: *At the end of the third paragraph, it says, "And what she was waiting for was in her eyes." Based on what I know about Margot, her memory of the sun, and her unhappiness on Venus, I can infer that the thing in her eyes is the sun and her strong desire to see it.* Students can underline "in her eyes" and write "desire to see the sun" in their own Response Notes.

"Yes!" said everyone.

"Are we all here?"

"Yes!"

The rain slackened still more.

They crowded to the huge door.

The rain stopped.

It was as if, in the midst of a film concerning an avalanche, a tornado, a hurricane, a volcanic eruption, something had, first, gone wrong with the sound apparatus, thus muffling and finally cutting off all noise, all of the blasts and repercussions and thunders, and then, second, ripped the film from the projector and inserted in its place a peaceful tropical slide which did not move or tremor. The world ground to a standstill.

The silence was so immense and unbelievable that you felt your ears had been stuffed or you had lost your hearing altogether. The children put their hands to their ears. They stood apart. The door slid back and the smell of the silent, waiting world came in to them.

The sun came out.

It was the color of flaming bronze and it was very large.

And the sky around it was a blazing blue tile color. And the jungle burned with sunlight as the children, released from their spell, rushed out, yelling, into the springtime.

"Now, don't go too far," called the teacher after them.

"You've only one hour, you know. You wouldn't want to get caught out!"

But they were running and turning their faces up to the sky and feeling the sun on their cheeks like a warm iron; they were taking off their jackets and letting the sun burn their arms.

"Oh, it's better than sun lamps, isn't it?"

"Much, much better!"

They stopped running and stood in the great jungle that covered Venus, that grew and never stopped growing, tumultuously, even as you watched it. It was a nest of octopuses, clustering up great arms of fleshlike weed, wavering, flowering in this brief spring. It was the color of rubber and ash, this jungle, from the many years without sun. It was the color of stones and white cheeses and ink, and it was the color of the moon.

The children lay out, laughing, on the jungle mattress, and heard it sigh and squeak under them, resilient and alive. They ran among the trees, they slipped and fell, they pushed each other, they played hide-and-seek and tag; but most of all they squinted at the sun until tears ran down their faces, they put their hands up to that yellowness and that amazing blueness and they breathed of the fresh, fresh air and listened and listened to the silence which suspended them in a blessed sea of no sound and no motion. They looked at everything and savored everything. Then, wildly, like animals escaped from their caves, they ran and ran in shouting circles. They ran for an hour and did not stop running.

Graphic Organizer: Inference Chart To help students read strategically, have them create a two-column chart on a separate piece of paper. The left column can be labeled "What the Character Said, Did, or Thought"; the right column can be labeled "My Conclusion." Have students complete the chart as they read.

During

INTERACTING WITH THE TEXT

As students read, provide prompts to remind them to make inferences: *Why do you think the children smile after they lock Margot in the closet? Outside, why does the girl cry when she sees the raindrop? At the bottom of page 31, what do the children suddenly realize? How does it make them feel?*

REFLECTING After everyone has finished reading, have students share their responses to the story. How do they feel toward Margot? What do they think of the students? Why would Ray Bradbury write such a story? Students should use their responses to the question on Daybook page 32 as a basis for their discussion.

WRITER'S CRAFT

Sentence Fluency Refer students to the discussion of Bradbury's writing style (TE page 28) and review how he mixes long, descriptive sentences with short, punchy ones. Then read aloud the paragraph at the bottom of Daybook page 30, followed by the first few sentences on page 31. Discuss how varying sentence

And then—

In the midst of their running one of the girls wailed.

Everyone stopped.

The girl, standing in the open, held out her hand.

"Oh, look, look," she said trembling.

They came slowly to look at her opened palm.

In the center of it, cupped and huge, was a single raindrop.

She began to cry, looking at it.

They glanced quickly at the sky.

"Oh. Oh."

A few cold drops fell on their noses and their cheeks and their mouths. The sun faded behind a stir of mist. A wind blew cool around them. They turned and started to walk back toward the underground house, their hands at their sides, their smiles vanishing away.

A boom of thunder startled them and like leaves before a new hurricane, they tumbled upon each other and ran. Lightning struck ten miles away, five miles away, a mile, a half mile. The sky darkened into midnight in a flash.

They stood in the doorway of the underground for a moment until it was raining hard. Then they closed the door and heard the gigantic sound of the rain falling in tons and avalanches, everywhere and forever.

"Will it be seven more years?"

"Yes. Seven."

Then one of them gave a little cry.

"Margot!"

"What?"

"She's still in the closet where we locked her."

"Margot."

EXTRA SUPPORT

Differentiation For students who need extra support reading the passage due to complex sentences and difficult vocabulary, help them identify key sensory words and phrases that describe the outdoor scene. Students can use the sensory words to create a word web or draw a picture of the scene. Read the text aloud, if it is necessary.

length—at first long and descriptive, then short and quick--moves the action along from sunny play to running from the storm. This technique creates a dramatic effect that builds tension. Discuss how it helps hold our interest and keeps the story moving. Invite students to find other examples of this technique in the passage.

WRITING SUPPORT

Dialogue Conventions To support the writing activity on *Daybook* page 32, review the rules for punctuating and formatting dialogue:

- Use quotation marks to set off a speaker's exact words from the rest of the sentence.
- Capitalize the first word of the quotation.
- Put end punctuation inside the closing quotation mark.
- Use a comma to separate the quotation from the words that introduce it or come after it. The comma goes before the quotation mark.
- Begin a new paragraph whenever the speaker changes, even if it's only one word.

Collaboration Students may enjoy working in pairs to present their dialogues to the class as short skits.

Quick Assess

❋ Did students make reasonable inferences about Margot and William in their dialogues?

❋ Are the inferences logical, based on prior knowledge, personal experience, and/or clues in the text?

❋ Did students punctuate and format their dialogues correctly?

Response Notes

They stood as if someone had driven them, like so many stakes, into the floor. They looked at each other and then looked away. They glanced out at the world that was raining now and raining and raining steadily. They could not meet each other's glances. Their faces were solemn and pale. They looked at their hands and feet, their faces down.

"Margot."

One of the girls said, "Well . . . ?"

No one moved.

"Go on," whispered the girl.

They walked slowly down the hall in the sound of cold rain.

They turned through the doorway to the room in the sound of the storm and thunder, lightning on their faces, blue and terrible. They walked over to the closet door slowly and stood by it.

Behind the closet door was only silence.

They unlocked the door, even more slowly, and let Margot out. ❖

❋ What was your initial response to what happened in the story? Did you expect it to turn out the way it did?

❋ Now return to the story. Underline any information you find about Margot and William. Make inferences about the characters, and then write a dialogue between Margot and William. What would they say to each other after Margot comes out of the closet?

> Making inferences about the characters can help you understand and remember the story.

After

READING/WRITING CONNECTION
To give students an opportunity to make additional inferences about characters, have students imagine that they are either Margot, William, or the teacher and write a journal entry about the day the sun came out.

ART CONNECTION Invite students to combine the skill of making inferences with visualizing. Provide art supplies and have students work in groups to create murals depicting the scene before, during, or after the sun was out. Then have groups show their murals to the class and explain what inferences were made in creating the art.

The **main idea** is the central focus of a piece of nonfiction. It is the most important thing the writer wants you to know. Interacting with the text by finding the main idea is key to understanding what you read.

You can usually discover the main idea by first identifying the **subject** of the writing (the person, place, or thing the author is writing about) and then figuring out what the author has to say about the subject. You can use this equation to figure out the main idea:

[subject] + [what the author says about the subject] = main idea

As you read the first part of the essay, make notes about the subject. Underline words and phrases that give you clues about the main idea.

"Hearing the Sweetest Songs" by Nicolette Toussaint

Every year when I was a child, a man brought a big, black, squeaking machine to school. When he discovered I couldn't hear all his peeps and squeaks, he would get very excited. The nurse would draw a chart with a deep canyon in it. Then I would listen to the squeaks two or three times, while the adults—who were all acting very, very nice—would watch me raise my hand. Sometimes I couldn't tell whether I heard the squeaks or just imagined them, but I liked being the center of attention.

My parents said I lost my hearing to pneumonia as a baby, but I knew I hadn't lost anything. None of my parts had dropped off. Nothing had changed: if I wanted to listen to Beethoven, I could put my head between the speakers and turn the dial up to 7. I could hear jets at the airport a block away. I could hear my mom when she was in the same room—if I wanted to. I could even hear my cat purr if I put my good ear right on top of him.

I wasn't aware of not hearing until I began to wear a hearing aid at the age of 30. It shattered my peace: shoes creaking, papers crackling, pencils tapping, phones ringing, refrigerators humming, people cracking knuckles, clearing throats and blowing noses! Cars, bikes, dogs, cats, kids all seemed to appear from nowhere and fly right at me.

I was constantly startled, unnerved, agitated—exhausted. I felt as though inquisitorial Nazis in an old World War II film were burning the side of my head with a merciless white spotlight. Under that onslaught, I had to break down and confess: I couldn't hear. Suddenly, I began to discover many things I couldn't do.

Response Notes

Students will find the central focus, or main idea, in a text to determine what the author is saying to the reader.

BACKGROUND KNOWLEDGE

In this lesson, students will read about a woman with a hearing impairment. To activate prior knowledge, ask students if they know, have read about, or have seen someone who has a hearing impairment. Point out that there are degrees of impairment, from total deafness to minor hearing loss. You might also wish to discuss or have students research famous people with hearing impairments, such as Helen Keller, Alexander Graham Bell, Beethoven, Marlee Matlin (actress), and Heather Whitestone (Miss America 1995).

VOCABULARY

inquisitorial trying to get information in a hostile, cruel, or harsh way

merciless showing no mercy or pity

onslaught overwhelming amount

vulnerable at risk of being harmed

After discussing the meaning of each word, have students imagine situations in which a person might feel *vulnerable,* experience a *merciless onslaught,* or be subjected to an *inquisitorial* person. As students use the words in sentences, write the sentences on the board.

Before

CRITICAL READING SKILL

Finding the Main Idea Point out that a main idea may be expressed directly or indirectly. Model using the equation to find the main idea of a short piece that students have already read, such as the excerpt from *Latin American Politics and Development* on Daybook page 18. Ask: *What is the subject of this piece?* (Trujillo's rule) *What does the author say about the* *subject?* (It was a brutal dictatorship.) *So, what is the main idea?* (Trujillo's rule was a brutal dictatorship.)

SETTING A PURPOSE Before students read "Hearing the Sweetest Song," have them generate one question that they have about what it's like to be hearing impaired. Students can then read the selection with that question in mind, as they look for the main idea.

During

MAIN IDEA SENTENCE As students read the selection, remind them to make notes about the subject and underline words and phrases related to the main idea. Then, after reading, invite students to share their main idea equations and the sentences they underlined. Students should tell why they believe their sentences best express the author's main idea. Point out that students will ▶▶▶

need help finding the main idea of the passage, prompt them with questions. *What is the essay mainly about? What feelings does the author express? What does the author want you to know?*

I couldn't identify sounds. One afternoon, while lying on my side watching a football game on TV, I kept hearing a noise that sounded like my cat playing with a flexible-spring doorstop. I checked, but the cat was asleep. Finally, I happened to lift my head as the noise occurred. Heard through my good ear, the metallic buzz turned out to be the referee's whistle. I couldn't tell where sounds came from. I couldn't find my phone under the blizzard of papers on my desk. The more it rang, the deeper I dug. I shoveled mounds of paper onto the floor and finally had to track it down by following the cord from the wall.

When I lived alone, I felt helpless because I couldn't hear alarm clocks, vulnerable because I couldn't hear the front door open and frightened because I wouldn't hear a burglar until it was too late.

Then one day I missed a job interview because of the phone. I had gotten off the subway twenty minutes early, eager and dressed to the nines. But the address I had written down didn't exist! I must have misheard it. I searched the street, becoming overheated, late and frantic, knowing that if I confessed that I couldn't hear on the phone, I would make my odds of getting hired even worse.

For the first time, I felt unequal, disadvantaged, and disabled. Now that I had something to compare, I knew that I had lost something; not just my hearing, but my independence and my sense of wholeness. I had always hated to be seen as inferior, so I never mentioned my lack of hearing. Unlike a wheelchair or a white cane, my disability doesn't announce itself. For most of my life, I chose to pass as abled, and I thought I did it quite well. ❖

✳ Look at your **Response Notes** and markings on the text. What seems to be the most important idea that Toussaint wants you to understand? State it in your own words using the equation on page 33.

_____ + _____ = _____
       subject   what the author   main idea
                       says about the subject

✳ Find the sentence in the essay that best expresses the author's main idea and underline it.

read the rest of the essay in the next lesson and, therefore, may need to revise their assumptions about the main idea. (Example: *"My parents said I lost my hearing to pneumonia as a baby, but I knew I hadn't lost anything."*)

WRITING SUPPORT

Brainstorming If students have difficulty thinking of a time they felt "unequal, disabled, or disadvantaged" (Daybook page 35), brainstorm as a class to generate ideas about situations in which these feelings might occur—e.g., attending a new school, being held back by a health problem or accident, being the last one chosen for a sport or activity.

✳ Now it's your turn. When have you felt "unequal, disabled, [or] disadvantaged"? Write about one incident. Explain what happened and how you felt. Before you begin, you might want to talk with a partner to help you focus on your main idea. Together, create a main idea equation for your writing

_____ + _____ = _____
        subject   what I think   main idea
                            about the subject

Use the space below to describe your incident.

_____
_____
_____
_____
_____
_____
_____
_____
_____
_____
_____
_____
_____
_____
_____
_____
_____
_____
_____
_____
_____
_____

Recognizing the main idea helps you understand what the author thinks is most important about a subject.

Quick Assess

✳ Do students' equations show that they have an understanding of the author's main idea?

✳ Did students underline a sentence in the passage that relates to the main idea?

✳ Did students adequately describe an incident in which they felt unequal, disabled, or disadvantaged?

✳ Did students' writing have a clear subject and main idea?

After

READING/WRITING CONNECTION

To further explore the author's main idea and extend it to another context, have students imagine they are Nicolette Toussaint writing a letter to someone, such as the employer whose job interview she missed. The letter should explain her condition and how she works around it. Students can use what they know so far about Toussaint and the main idea of "Hearing the Sweetest Songs" to craft the letter.

LESSON **9** DETERMINING THE AUTHOR'S PURPOSE

Students will determine an author's purpose in writing a text to understand the author's ideas.

ABOUT THE AUTHOR

A Colorado native, Nicolette Toussaint has written articles for *Education Week* and *Newsweek* and has worked for many years in advertising, media, and public relations for nonprofit groups. She has won awards for her work in education and women's issues and is listed in *Who's Who of American Women.*

VOCABULARY

eccentric strange; odd

disabled impaired; not able to function properly

transcendent extraordinary; going beyond the usual limits

Point out that all three words are adjectives. Brainstorm nouns that each word might modify and have students show their understanding of the adjective-noun pairs by using them in sentences.

DETERMINING THE AUTHOR'S PURPOSE

Strategic readers look for the **author's purpose** to better understand the author's ideas. Authors write for a variety of reasons, including the following: to entertain, to inform or teach, to persuade or argue, and to express personal thoughts and feelings. Sometimes an author will combine purposes in a piece of writing, such as informing you about a situation and persuading you to do something about it. You can determine an author's purpose or purposes by paying attention to what he or she emphasizes in the writing.

Finish reading the essay "Hearing the Sweetest Songs" to get a sense of what the author wants you to understand. In the **Response Notes,** write your impressions—what puzzles you, what you relate to, and what you like.

Response Notes

"Hearing the Sweetest Songs" by Nicolette Toussaint *(continued)*

But after I got the hearing aid, a business friend said, "You know, Nicolette, you think you get away with not hearing, but you don't. Sometimes in meetings you answer the wrong question. People don't know you can't hear, so they think you're daydreaming, eccentric, stupid—or just plain rude. It would be better to just tell them."

I wondered about that then, and I still do. If I tell, I risk being seen as unable rather than disabled. Sometimes, when I say I can't hear, the waiter will turn to my companion and say, "What does she want?" as though I have lost my power of speech.

If I tell, people may see only my disability. Once someone is labeled "deaf," "crippled," "mute" or "aged," that's too often all they are. I'm a writer, a painter, a slapdash housekeeper, a gardener who grows wondrous roses; my hearing is just part of the whole. It's a tender part, and you should handle it with care. But like most people with a disability, I don't mind if you ask about it.

In fact, you should ask, because it's an important part of me, something my friends see as part of my character. My friend Anne always rests a hand on my elbow in parking lots, since several times, drivers who assume that I hear them have nearly run me over. When I hold my head at a certain angle, my husband, Mason, will say "It's a plane" or "It's a siren." And my mother loves to laugh about the things I thought I heard: last week I was told that "the Minotaurs in the garden are getting out of hand." I imagined capering bullmen and I was disappointed to learn that all we had in the garden were overgrown "baby tears."

Before

CRITICAL READING SKILL
Determining Author's Purpose
Point out that an author's purpose(s) may be expressed directly or indirectly. Strategic readers pay attention to what the author emphasizes in the writing to better understand his or her reasons, or motivation, for writing. Have students think of a story, article, or other text the class has recently read, and discuss the author's purpose. Was it to entertain? To educate? To persuade? Was there more than one purpose?

SETTING A PURPOSE Have students refer to the main idea equations they wrote on page 34. Point out that the main idea can be a clue to the author's purpose(s). As students read, remind them to keep in mind the main idea of the passage and to ask themselves: *What does Toussaint want me to understand? What does this have to do with her purpose for writing?*

Not hearing can be funny, or frustrating. And once in a while, it can be the cause of something truly transcendent. One morning at the shore I was listening to the ocean when Mason said, "Hear the bird?" What bird? I listened hard until I heard a faint, unbirdlike, croaking sound. If he hadn't mentioned it, I would never have noticed it. As I listened, slowly I began to hear—or perhaps imagine—a distant song. Did I really hear it? Or just hear in my heart what he shared with me? I don't care. Songs imagined are as sweet as songs heard, and songs shared are sweeter still.

That sharing is what I want for all of us. We're all just temporarily abled, and every one of us, if we live long enough, will become disabled in some way. Those of us who have gotten there first can tell you how to cope with phones and alarm clocks. About ways of holding a book, opening a door and leaning on a crutch all at the same time. And what it's like to give up in despair on Thursday, then begin all over again on Friday, because there's no other choice—and because the roses are beginning to bud in the garden.

These are conversations we all should have, and it's not that hard to begin. Just let me see your lips when you speak. Stay in the same room. Don't shout. And ask what you want to know. ❖

✳ Discuss this selection with a partner or small group and compare your impressions. What do you think Toussaint wants you to understand?

Collaboration In paragraph 2, Toussaint makes a distinction between *disabled* and *unable.* Use the Jigsaw technique to have students discuss how the words are different and why the distinction is important.

1. Divide students into groups and have them hold their discussions.
2. Regroup students so that each new group has at least one member from each former group.
3. Have students share their earlier conclusions with the new group, putting the "puzzle" together.

WRITER'S CRAFT

Present a Balanced Argument

Point out that in giving her position on having a disability, Toussaint presents two sides of the issue. She gives reasons both for and against keeping her disability a secret. This makes her writing more balanced and her opinion more persuasive.

Give students a simple argument, such as "The school year should be shorter (or longer)." Have students write a paragraph in which they take a position and give at least one reason in support of the argument and one against it. Students can read their paragraphs aloud and discuss how presenting both sides of the argument helped them write a more persuasive paragraph.

During   After

INTERACTING WITH THE TEXT

After students have finished reading the passage, ask: *What does "We're all just temporarily abled" mean?* ("Abled" is the opposite of "disabled"; most people lose some abilities as they grow older.) Then ask: *Why does the author make this point? What does she want us to understand?* Partners or small groups can use this as a starting point for their discussions in which they compare impressions before completing the writing prompt.

APPLYING THE STRATEGY

For more practice determining an author's purpose, have students review the story "All Summer in a Day" on Daybook pages 26–32. Have small groups work together to determine Bradbury's purpose(s) for writing (e.g., to entertain, to persuade children to accept others' differences, to show how thoughtless acts can have real, unintended, or lasting, consequences). Then have groups present their conclusions to the class.

Differentiation Before completing the web, students who need extra support may benefit from looking through the passage and making a list of details. Students can then cross out unimportant details and circle details that are related to the author's purpose.

Quick Assess

❉ Did students correctly identify the author's purpose(s) in their web? (Toussaint's purposes could include informing readers about what it's like to have a disability and persuading readers not to judge others with disabilities.)

❉ Do students' webs show a connection between the author's purpose(s) and the details the author uses? Do only relevant details appear on the webs?

❉ What do you think Toussaint's purpose is? In the center of the web, write your answer. Write the details that she emphasizes to support her purpose in the other ovals.

Toussaint's purpose

Authors select and emphasize details that support their purposes for writing.

38 LESSON 9

W hen you take time to think about what you read, you are **reflecting**. This strategy can be used with any type of writing. It is especially useful when you are reading something new or difficult to understand. One way to interact with the text through reflection is to connect your experiences to those in the writing.

Look again at the two selections in this unit. They both dealt with differences. In "All Summer in a Day" (page 26), Margot felt separated from the other children. In "Hearing the Sweetest Songs" (page 33), Nicolette discussed how having a hearing impairment made her different. Choose one of the selections. Write a paragraph to answer each of the following questions.

✳ What relevant connections can you make between the experiences in the selection and your experience?

REFLECTING 39

Students will use the strategy of reflecting to understand new or difficult material and to connect their experiences to the writing.

BACKGROUND KNOWLEDGE
To help students apply the concept of "reflecting" to their own lives, have them think of a memorable experience or special occasion—e.g., a celebration, or the first time they used a skill successfully. Then invite students to share their memories with the class and to say what was significant about the experience. Point out that when you *remember,* you look back. But when you *reflect,* you do more—you ask yourself questions about an experience and think about what you learned from it.

Before

CRITICAL READING SKILL
Reflecting Point out that reading critically involves reflecting—not just thinking back on what you have read but considering it in light of personal experience, other texts, and conversations about the text that you have had.

During

GRAPHIC ORGANIZER
Venn Diagram With students, create a Venn diagram to compare Margot to the other children in "All Summer and a Day." Ask: *How is Margot different?* (She hasn't been on Venus as long, she remembers the sun, she misses Earth, etc.) Then ask: *What do Margot and the others have in common?* (They all want to see the sun.) Repeat the process for Nicolette Toussaint

to show ways in which she is both the same as and different from other people.

CONNECTING TO THE TEXT Help students make relevant connections to the selections by inviting them to reflect on ways in which they themselves feel the same as or different from other people. The following questions can be used to start a discussion about connections. *Can differences be "abling"? Do you* ▶▶▶

Collaboration After students have completed the writing prompt, have them use the following technique to share their responses:

1. Partners read each other's paragraphs and discuss them together to make sure each understands the other's response.

2. Students present their partners' responses to the class in their own words (paraphrase).

Quick Assess

✢ In answering the question on page 39, do students show the ability to make relevant connections?

✢ In answering the question on page 40, do students show that they have learned something about being a strategic reader?

✳ What do you learn by making connections?

Reflecting on what you read by making connections to your experience helps you understand new or difficult material.

40 LESSON 10

After

have anything in common with Margot? With Nicolette? What would you want to say to either of them?

READING/SCIENCE CONNECTION
To give students practice reflecting on a different kind of text, have students find an article about one of the following topics on the Internet or in a magazine, textbook, or other source

✳ a rain forest

✳ the effects of the sun on plants, people, or animals

✳ how the ear works

✳ advances in technology for people with hearing loss

Remind students that, as they read informational text, they can make connections to their reading and their own experiences to help them understand new information. Afterwards, have students reflect on what they learned about their topics and share their reflections with the class.

Making Connections

Your life is like a story because it has the same basic elements that are developed in most stories: people, places, and events. Think how the basic elements of a story are present in one of your strongest memories. Who were the people involved? Where were you? What events created joy, conflict, or suspense? What lessons did you learn? A good author will skillfully blend these basic elements to create a story. A good reader understands the elements and appreciates how they work together.

In this unit, you'll learn about five of the basic elements of a story:

- setting
- story line and plot
- character
- theme
- point of view

You'll also discover how authors use and combine these elements to create stories.

41

Lessons 11–15, pages 42-56

UNIT OVERVIEW

In this unit, students will see how master writers like Madeleine L'Engle, Natalie Babbitt, Judith Ortiz Cofer, and Roald Dahl use the key elements of great storytelling to create unforgettable stories.

KEY IDEA

Good writers develop elements of a story to entertain, inform, intrigue, and move the reader. Readers connect to one or more story elements.

CRITICAL READING SKILLS
by lesson

11 Visualize setting

12 Understand characters

13 Understand point of view

14 Connect story line and plot

15 Connect plot and theme

WRITING ACTIVITIES
by lesson

11 Write about setting.

12 Create a character map.

13 Write about an experience.

14 Fill in a Plot Diagram.

15 Analyze the important parts of a story using a Theme Organizer.

Literature

- **The Search for Delicious** by Natalie Babbitt (novel excerpt)

Babbitt opens her book with a clear, engaging description of time and place.

- **A Wrinkle in Time** by Madeline L'Engle (novel excerpt)

L'Engle creates a vivid picture of the warm, fragrant, and blooming setting.

- **Danny the Champion of the World** by Roald Dahl (novel excerpts)

Dahl develops the unforgettable character of Danny's father, while revealing much about the narrator, Danny, and his point of view.

- **"Abuela Invents the Zero"** by Judith Ortiz Cofer (short story)

Cofer engages the reader's interest by beginning with the climax of the story, inviting the reader to read on to find out

how the characters reached this defining moment.

- **"There's No Sweet Revenge"** by Ruth Vinz (short story)

This story is used to illustrate how the connections among events are crucial to the plot.

ASSESSMENT To assess student learning in this unit, see pages 229 and 254.

Students will learn about story elements to understand how an author uses setting to develop a story.

BUILD BACKGROUND

Remind students that the setting of a story shows *where* and *when* the story takes place. Good writers use their craft to paint a picture of the setting, building on the connection between the place in the story and places we all may know or have visited. Even in fantasy writing, the author will use descriptive words and comparisons that allow us to make the connection between what we know and what is being described. Invite volunteers to describe settings in stories and novels they have read to discuss the connections they made and how the author helped them make those connections.

VOCABULARY

woldwellers fictional creatures that live alone in forest trees

glint a sparkle; a flash of light

ineffable impossible to describe

Discuss the words and their meanings, inviting students to think of examples of something off which light might glint (*a diamond*) and something ineffable (*a feeling of complete happiness*).

Setting is the time and place of a story, when and where the action occurs. Think about a favorite memory. Could it have taken place anywhere else but where it did?

In some stories, the setting is one of the most important elements. It's hard to imagine Peter Pan without Neverland or Batman without Gotham City. In other stories you might not focus on the setting, although it's there if you look for it.

Read this short passage from Natalie Babbitt's novel *The Search for Delicious*. Circle any words or phrases that relate to the setting. Use your **Response Notes** to describe when and where the story takes place.

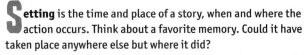

Response Notes

Sounds like the country.

from **The Search for Delicious** by Natalie Babbitt

There was a time once when the earth was still very young, a time some call the oldest days. This was long before there were any people about to dig parts of it up and cut parts of it off. People came along much later, building their towns and castles (which nearly always fell down after a while) and plaguing each other with quarrels and supper parties. The creatures who lived on the earth in that early time stayed each in his own place and kept it beautiful. There were dwarfs in the mountains, woldwellers in the forest, mermaids in the lakes, and, of course, winds in the air.

Next, read the following passage from Madeleine L'Engle's novel *A Wrinkle in Time*. Circle any words or phrases that relate to *setting*. Use your **Response Notes** to describe when and where you think the story takes place.

from **A Wrinkle in Time** by Madeleine L'Engle

"But where am I?" Meg asked breathlessly, relieved to hear that her voice was now coming out of her in more or less a normal way.

She looked around rather wildly. They were standing in a sunlit field, and that air about them was moving with the delicious fragrance that comes only on the rarest of spring days when the sun's touch is gentle and the apple blossoms are just beginning to unfold. She pushed her glasses up on her nose to reassure herself that what she was seeing was real.

Before

CRITICAL READING SKILL

Visualize Setting Ask students to picture a setting. It can be a real setting or an imagined one. Have them close their eyes and think of the time of day, month, year, or season; the historical period—past, present, or future; and the physical characteristics of the place, including objects, weather, and other descriptive elements. Students can then open their eyes and describe the settings they imagined, orally or in writing.

Explain that writers use their memories and imaginations to create settings that serve as landscapes in which their stories take place.

RESPONSE NOTES Remind students to look for words and phrases suggesting the time of the action, such as "when the earth was very young" and "on the rarest of spring days," as well as descriptions of the place (mountains, lakes, forests; sunlit field, apple blossoms). Have students highlight descriptions in the text by circling them and, perhaps, making brief notes in the Response Notes.

They had left the silver glint of a biting autumn evening; and now around them everything was golden with light. The grasses of the field were a tender new green, and scattered about were tiny, multicolored flowers. Meg turned slowly to face a mountain reaching so high into the sky that its peak was lost in a crown of puffy white clouds. From the trees at the base of the mountain came a sudden singing of birds. There was an air of such ineffable peace and joy all around her that her heart's wild thumping slowed. ❖

* With a partner, discuss when and where these stories take place. Write the type of story each setting might introduce.

* You have been hired to illustrate the cover for either Babbitt's or L'Engle's novel. Imagine what scene you would draw to show the setting. Choose the novel that is most interesting to you. Use colored pencils, markers, crayons, or pastels to create the cover in the space below.

The time and place of the setting can influence a story.

ABOUT THE AUTHORS

Madeline L'Engle was born in New York City, where her family regularly entertained all sorts of artists. When Madeline was twelve, she moved to Europe to attend a Swiss boarding school. L'Engle became fascinated by quantum physics and wrote *A Wrinkle in Time,* which won the 1963 Newbery Medal. This was particularly satisfying to L'Engle since the book had received many rejections before it was published.

Natalie Babbitt grew up in Ohio. As a child, she enjoyed reading fairy tales and myths, as well as drawing. Babbitt has written and/or illustrated many books. She wrote her first two books, *Dick Foote and the Shark* and *Phoebe's Revolt,* in verse. *The Search for Delicious* is a long story, which has its roots in the fairy tales and myths she read as a child.

Quick Assess

Can students

* identify words and phrases that help the reader picture the setting for a story?

* describe when and where a story takes place?

* make the connections between the setting and places they know or have visited?

* identify key elements of the setting that indicate the type of story?

During

RESPONSE NOTES Have students compare the two writers' methods of creating a setting. Help students see that Babbitt's writing sounds like other myths and fairy tales, setting up the expectation that this story will also be a fantasy. L'Engle applies another technique, using sensory language to help her readers feel as if they are right there. Encourage students to think about what type of story the author is fashioning as they create their book covers.

After

SETTING MAP Talk about how a movie director will use a "story board" to map out each scene of a movie. That way the director knows where each shoot will need to take place and can plan ahead. Help students make the connection between plotting out each scene of a movie and plotting out each scene of a story.

A visual Setting Map is a story board that is drawn to show the setting for each scene. A verbal Setting Map is a written or oral description of the setting of each scene in the story. Ask students to make a visual or verbal Setting Map for one of their favorite stories. Invite students to share their Setting Maps with the class.

Students will learn about story elements to understand how an author develops memorable characters.

BACKGROUND KNOWLEDGE

Help students' connect with the idea of characterization by asking them to think of a memorable story or movie character they've encountered. Have them think about how the author or screenwriter helped make that character unforgettable. Prompt them to pay attention to things like how the character spoke or dressed and what the character did or said. Tell them that as they read the selection in this lesson, they should focus on how the author makes the characters come alive for the reader.

VOCABULARY

stern strict; severe

serials stories presented in installments, or in a series

unconscious not aware

Have students circle each vocabulary word as it appears in the selection and underline clues to the meaning of each word. (*Stern* is compared with *serious* and contrasted to *wildly funny; serials* is followed by the phrase *went on for many nights running; unconscious* is preceded by *still and distant*. Ask volunteers to share the clues they found for each word.

Characters are the people, animals, and even imaginary creatures that "live" through the events in a story. Some characters are memorable because of how the author describes them—how they look, act, or talk. Some authors make their characters interesting by giving details about what the characters think and feel. The way an author develops the character is called **characterization**. The better you know a character, the more you will be able to understand the character and the story.

Read the following excerpt from the novel *Danny the Champion of the World*. According to the narrator, Danny, what makes his father special? As you read, list details in your **Response Notes** that characterize, or describe, his father.

Response Notes

from **Danny the Champion of the World** by Roald Dahl

You might think, if you don't know him well, that he was a stern and serious man. He wasn't. He was actually a wildly funny person. What made him appear so serious was the fact that he never smiled with his mouth. He did it all with his eyes. He had brilliant blue eyes and when he thought of something funny, his eyes would flash and, if you looked carefully, you could actually see a tiny little golden spark dancing in the middle of each eye. But the mouth never moved.

I was glad my father was an eye-smiler. It meant he never gave me a fake smile because it's impossible to make your eyes twinkle if you aren't feeling twinkly yourself. A mouth-smile is different. You can fake a mouth-smile any time you want, simply by moving your lips. I've also learned that a real mouth-smile always has an eye-smile to go with it. So watch out, I say, when someone smiles at you with his mouth but his eyes stay the same. It's sure to be a phony.

My father was not what you would call an educated man. I doubt he had read twenty books in his life. But he was a marvelous storyteller. He used to make up a bedtime story for me every single night, and the best ones were turned into serials and went on for many nights running.

One of them, which must have gone on for at least fifty nights, was about an enormous fellow called "The Big Friendly Giant," or "The BFG" for short. The BFG was three times as tall as an ordinary man and his hands were as big as wheelbarrows. He lived in a vast underground cavern not far from our filling station and he only came out into the open when it was dark. Inside the cavern he had a powder factory where he made more than one hundred different kinds of magic powder.

Before

CRITICAL READING SKILL

Understand Characters As students read these passages, have them focus on how the author makes a character memorable. Help them recognize that understanding characters and their traits will help them follow the plot developments and themes in the story.

RESPONSE NOTES Encourage students to make note of the descriptive words and phrases Danny uses to describe his father, as well as some of the clues to the father's character that come through his actions. Encourage students to circle or underline descriptions in the text and to list reactions in the Response Notes.

During

RESPONDING Check with students as they are reading to see if they are able to find details that characterize Danny's father. Prompt them to think about (1) Danny's description of his father; (2) why Danny believes his father is "a marvelous storyteller"; (3) the father's purpose in telling the tall tale; (4) how students respond to Danny's father. As students write words they think best describe Danny's father, encourage them to think

"The Big Friendly Giant makes his magic powders out of the dreams that children dream when they are asleep," he said.

"How?" I asked. "Tell me how, dad."

"Dreams, my love, are very mysterious things. They float around in the night air like little clouds, searching for sleeping people."

"Can you see them?" I asked.

"Nobody can see them."

"Then how does The Big Friendly Giant catch them?"

"Ah," my father said, "that is the interesting part. A dream, you see, as it goes drifting through the night air, makes a tiny little buzzing-humming sound, a sound so soft and low it is impossible for ordinary people to hear it. But The BFG can hear it easily. His sense of hearing is absolutely fantastic."

I loved the intent look on my father's face when he was telling a story. His face was pale and still and distant, unconscious of everything around him.

"The BFG," he said, "can hear the tread of a ladybug's footsteps as she walks across a leaf. He can hear the whisperings of ants as they scurry around in the soil talking to one another. He can hear the sudden shrill cry of pain a tree gives out when a woodman cuts into it with an ax. Ah yes, my darling, there is a whole world of sound around us that we cannot hear because our ears are simply not sensitive enough."

"What happens when he catches the dreams?" I asked.

"He imprisons them in glass bottles and screws the tops down tight," my father said. "He has thousands of these bottles in his cave."

"Does he catch bad dreams as well as good ones?"

"Yes," my father said. "He catches both. But he only uses the good ones in his powders."

"What does he do with the bad ones?"

"He explodes them."

It is impossible to tell you how much I loved my father. When he was sitting close to me on my bunk I would reach out and slide my hand into his, and then he would fold his long fingers around my fist, holding it tight. ❖

❋ List three words or phrases that best describe Danny's father.

_____

_____

_____

_____

CHARACTERS 45

ABOUT THE AUTHOR

Roald Dahl was born in Wales, of Norwegian parents. While attending schools in Wales and England, Dahl was shocked to find that teachers and older students were allowed to terrorize the younger ones. These experiences later inspired him to write stories in which children fight against cruel adults and authorities. *Danny the Champion of the World* carries this theme as well, but in Danny's father, Dahl has created a devoted, lovable, and memorable adult character.

EXTRA SUPPORT

Differentiation If students need extra support finding details about Danny's father's character, model with a think-aloud: *Danny says his father is a funny man. What are some of the details he gives? He says his father's eyes "flash" when he thinks of something funny. Danny's father also makes up funny stories and calls the Big Friendly Giant "the BFG."*

about how Danny's description makes the father a memorable character for the reader.

REFLECTING After students have completed their lists, ask them to think about the importance of other people in their lives. How do their encounters and relationships with others influence their own beliefs and actions? Help students make the connection to why characters can be such a central part of a story.

GRAPHIC ORGANIZER Have students work with partners or in small groups to discuss the characterization of Danny's father and then use their observations to complete a Character Map (page 46). Invite students to share their maps and discuss what is similar and different about them.

Collaboration Have students meet in small groups to discuss the three words they've come up with to describe Danny's father. Tell students to give each other reasons for why they chose the words they did. Make sure they use evidence from the story for their choices. After students have discussed their choices, have a representative from each group report on what they discovered about Danny's father through their discussion.

Quick Assess

Can students

✻ identify details the author provides to create a characterization?

✻ evaluate a character based on those details?

✻ map a character using evidence from the text?

✻ recognize the connection between characterization, plot, and theme in a story?

A Character Map is a way to organize information about characters. Create a Character Map for Danny's father. Record what you have learned about Danny's father in the space provided. The prompts on the map show the types of information to include.

CHARACTER MAP

How Danny feels about him

What he says

How I feel about him

Draw Danny's father here.

What he looks like

His actions

Notice details about characters to learn what they are like and why they behave the way they do.

After

READING/WRITING CONNECTION Using Dahl's story as a model, have students write character sketches about people whose lives have influenced others. Students can compile, illustrate, and design a *Book of Champions* and display it in the classroom.

AUTHOR STUDY Roald Dahl is famous for his wacky, memorable characters. Ask students to help you set up a "Who's Who" display of Dahl's books, with character maps clipped to the book jackets. Invite students to compare and contrast characters from Dahl's stories and share their analyses with the class.

Your perspective, or **point of view**, is how you see an event. If someone else were to tell part of your life story, think how different the perspective would be. How might a close friend tell the story of a moment that was embarrassing to you? What would be different about how you told the story and how your friend told the story?

In order to understand a story's point of view, you must first determine who the narrator is and what the narrator knows. Notice whether the narrator is a character in the story or someone outside the story who describes what takes place.

Read another excerpt from *Danny the Champion of the World*. The narrator is Danny, who is a character in the story. The way Danny tells the story will give you clues to his character. Use your **Response Notes** to jot down things you learn about Danny from his description of his father and the events of the day. What type of person do you think Danny is?

Response Notes

from **Danny the Champion of the World** by Roald Dahl

And so life went on. The world I lived in consisted only of the filling station, the workshop, the caravan, the school, and of course the woods and meadows and streams in the countryside around. But I was never bored. It was impossible to be bored in my father's company. He was too sparky a man for that. Plots and plans and new ideas came flying off him like sparks from a grindstone.

"There's a good wind today," he said one Saturday morning. "Just right for flying a kite. Let's make a kite, Danny."

So we made a kite. He showed me how to splice four thin sticks together in the shape of a star, with two more sticks across the middle to brace it. Then we cut up an old blue shirt of his and stretched that material across the framework of the kite. We added a long tail made of thread, with little leftover pieces of the shirt tied at intervals along it. We found a ball of string in the workshop, and he showed me how to attach the string to the framework so that the kite would be properly balanced in flight.

Together we walked to the top of the hill behind the filling station to release the kite. I found it hard to believe that this object, made only from a few sticks and a piece of old shirt, would actually fly. I held the string while my father held the kite, and the moment he let it go, it caught the wind and soared upward like a huge blue bird.

"Let out some more, Danny!" he cried. "Go on! As much as you like!"

Higher and higher soared the kite. Soon it was just a small blue dot dancing in the sky miles above my head, and it was thrilling to stand there

---

Students will learn about story elements to understand how point of view affects the telling of a story.

BACKGROUND KNOWLEDGE
Review with students what they already know about Danny and his father from the previous passage. You may wish to share more information, included in the book but not in the excerpts, about Danny's childhood: Danny's mother died when Danny was a baby. Danny's father owned a *filling station,* and they lived in an old *caravan* behind the station.

VOCABULARY
filling station gas station

caravan a trailer; a large truck with furniture in it that can be used as a home

grindstone a large stone that is used to sharpen or polish knives and tools

intervals spaces between each point

Ask students to locate and circle the three vocabulary words in the first paragraph. Define the words for students and have them make a quick sketch of each in the margin. As students read the passage on their own, they can use their sketches as visual cues.

Before

CRITICAL READING SKILL
Understand Point of View Remind students that Danny is both the narrator and a central character in the story. He tells the story from the first-person point of view. Have students highlight the pronouns *I, me, my,* and *we* on the first page. Then have students replace them with third-person pronouns as they read the same passage. Invite them to reflect on how a different narrator's point of view would affect the story.

RESPONSE NOTES Remind students to listen to the author's "voice" to see what it reveals about the narrator. Students should notice what the narrator says and how he says it.

During

As students read, encourage them to think about the mental picture they had of Danny and his father before reading this second excerpt. Suggest that they revise that picture as the story unfolds.

WRITING SUPPORT
Using Notes As students write their paragraphs on page 48, encourage them to refer to the Response Notes ▶▶▶

EXTRA SUPPORT

Differentiation Some students may need extra support as they work on their drafts. Help them brainstorm experiences they could write about by suggesting they make a list before they begin writing and then narrowing their topic to the one that they think is the best choice. Once they've selected the experience they want to describe, help them think about what they want to say about it. Prompt them with questions, such as *How did you feel at first? What words or actions could you use to show the reader how you felt? How did you feel while [it] was happening? What details can you use to describe the experience?*

Quick Assess

❊ Can students recognize voice in a piece of writing?

❊ Did students use first person in their narrative?

---

holding on to something that was so far away and so very much alive. This faraway thing was tugging and struggling on the end of line like a big fish.

"Let's walk it back to the caravan," my father said.

So we walked down the hill again with me holding the string and the kite still pulling fiercely on the other end. When we came to the caravan we were careful not to get the string tangled in the apple tree and we brought it all the way around to the front steps.

"Tie it to the steps," my father said.

"Will it still stay up?" I asked.

"It will if the wind doesn't drop," he said.

The wind didn't drop. And I will tell you something amazing. That kite stayed up there all through the night, and at breakfast time next morning the small blue dot was still dancing and swooping in the sky. After breakfast I hauled it down and hung it carefully against a wall in the workshop for another day. ❖

❊ Write what you learned about Danny by the way he narrates the story of the kite-flying incident.

_____

_____

_____

❊ Like Danny, you have stories to tell. Think of an experience that was important to you. Write a quick draft that describes the experience. Remember, the way you tell the story reveals the type of person you are.

_____

_____

_____

_____

_____

_____

_____

_____

_____

> Determine who is telling the story. Look for clues about what type of person the narrator is.

After

they took as they were reading. What does Danny's account of the kite-flying incident tell us about *him?* How can students frame their experiences to help us learn about *them?*

PERSONAL NARRATIVE Discuss with students the concept of *voice,* the personality and feelings of the writer as they are revealed in the writer's work. A personal narrative usually has a strong voice, since it is written in the first person and relates a personal experience.

After students write their quick draft, ask them to read their work to a partner. Partners should describe what was

revealed about the narrator through the details in the story.

ALTERING THE POINT OF VIEW
Have students select another story or book that has a clear point of view. Encourage them to rewrite a scene from that selection from the point of view of one of the other characters. For example, what would a scene from *Before We Were Free* (Unit 1) be like if it were told from the point of view of Mrs. Brown, the teacher?

"There's No Sweet Revenge" by Ruth Vinz

The **story line** is the sequence of events in the order they are told in a story. A story line is a timeline. You can list everything that happened in the order it appears in the story. Take a look at the events on the story line below.

Band practice was cancelled.	A boy broke his arm.	The band took 3rd place.	A rainstorm created a sink-hole in a field.
#1	#2	#3	#4

Just listing the events in the order in which they appear in the story doesn't tell a story. Something is missing. One way to examine what's missing is to see how the events are presented in the story. As you read the short story "There's No Sweet Revenge," circle each of the events listed above when you come across it. In your **Response Notes,** explain what you think each event contributes to the story.

"There's No Sweet Revenge" by Ruth Vinz

Band practice is cancelled and we all jump up and down like there is no tomorrow. My first thought is that Jerry and I have time to go for ice cream before heading home. No one expects us for at least an hour. If I go home my mom will nag me about my homework. We all head off at full steam, running to our lockers. We've been practicing for months. We want to keep our title as Jefferson Middle School #1 Best Band in the State. But no practice is a higher priority. At least, for now.

As we get to our lockers, we hear the new kid in the trumpet section yelling his head off. He annoys me anyway because he thinks he's the best trumpet player we've got. I'm thinking about him for about one second before I hear the sound of voices. "Who? Who? What happened?" It's Mr. Zino, our principal, sounding as excited as ever. He chirps when he talks. We yell, "hey, hurry up" to our friends and take off running before Zino can stop us. We rule the afternoon.

It isn't until the next day we learn what happened. Our band teacher stands in the doorway, looking like he swallowed a pickle. The whole band is chirping like Zino, passing around information. Seems that the new kid broke his arm. Can't play trumpet for at least six weeks. That means I lead the section. I'm having little grinning fits about that. Until I think about the competition in three days.

As it turns out, we don't take last place but not the top one either. We place 3rd and everybody is quiet. The new kid stands on the sidelines jumping up and down like a grasshopper and annoying me all over again. That red cast on his

Response Notes

Students will use a timeline to examine a story line and use a plot diagram to show relationships between events in a story.

BACKGROUND KNOWLEDGE

Both passages in this lesson show how a narrator views a particular character and what happens to change the narrator's mind. In "There's No Sweet Revenge" the narrator expresses disdain for the new kid in the trumpet section. In "Abuela Invents the Zero," the narrator feels embarrassed in the company of her grandmother. Invite students to talk about ways in which they may jump to conclusions about relatives or friends and what they might learn by trying to see things from the other person's point of view.

VOCABULARY

revenge punishment of somebody in return for harm done

full steam without any hesitation

rule the afternoon to have complete control over

sinkhole a sunken area where waste collects

Before

CRITICAL READING
Connect Story Line and Plot

Explain to students that the story line is the sequence of events that happens in the story, while the plot is how the author connects those events. Ask students, "What makes for an interesting or exciting story?" Elicit that the best plots are the ones that strike a balance between conflict, tension, and action. These elements can hold a reader's attention through an entire story so that he or she wants to find out how it's going to end. Sometimes the events of a story are presented in time sequence, but other times, authors choose to present the events in a different sequence.

RESPONSE NOTES After students have noted the events that take place in "There's No Sweet Revenge," have them think about how these events connect to each other and to the characters, forming the plot of the story.

Collaboration Have partners map the events of the story. Have them compare the events they circled and explained in their Response Notes and agree on which event fits each label on the diagram. Once they have reached consensus, they can both label their Plot Diagrams.

arm pokes into Melanie Brooks as he pitches a fit about our losing first place. He looks up. And then for no reason that I can recall, I stretch back in my mind to imagine the moment he fell in that sinkhole, the one that opened up when the heavy rains came. And, I'm almost glad he did. And, I'm almost glad we didn't take first with him as section leader. And I'm almost, well, feeling the sting in my eyes that brings tears. But instead, I look straight at him and flash a big smile, teeth and all. "Next time," I yell. "come on over to my house if you want. We're having a celebration party." And I march off just like that. ❖

A story line is the sequence of events as they occur in the story. The **plot** emphasizes how events and characters are connected.

✳ Think about what each of the four events on the story line contributes to the plot of the story. Discuss with a partner how each part forms a connection to other parts of the story.

A *plot* can be divided into five parts: *exposition, rising action, climax, falling action,* and *resolution.*

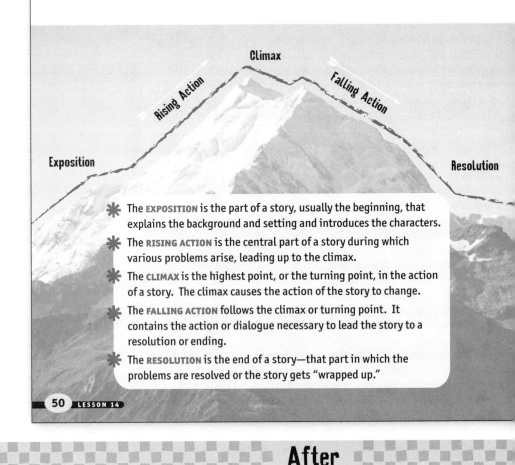

* The EXPOSITION is the part of a story, usually the beginning, that explains the background and setting and introduces the characters.

* The RISING ACTION is the central part of a story during which various problems arise, leading up to the climax.

* The CLIMAX is the highest point, or the turning point, in the action of a story. The climax causes the action of the story to change.

* The FALLING ACTION follows the climax or turning point. It contains the action or dialogue necessary to lead the story to a resolution or ending.

* The RESOLUTION is the end of a story—that part in which the problems are resolved or the story gets "wrapped up."

50 LESSON 14

During

WRITER'S CRAFT

A Strong Beginning Cofer begins this story with a powerful opening paragraph. If students are puzzled about why "this angry little old woman" is saying, "You made me feel like a zero, like a nothing," encourage them to read further to see what caused the outburst. Point out that good writers grab the reader's attention right away to make them want to read

more. Explain that in this instance, Cofer works outside of time order, starting with the climax of the story and then revealing the events that led up to it.

After

Have students create a Plot Diagram for another story they've read recently. Remind them to plot only the major events in the story that move the plot forward. Invite them to share their diagrams, with you or with the class, and discuss whether they think the author's story line and plot are as effective as Cofer's, providing reasons for why or why not (for example, *"This is like Cofer's story because*

Now that you have an idea about how a plot works, read the first part of the story "Abuela Invents the Zero," by Judith Ortiz Cofer. In your **Response Notes,** keep track of the major events that may be important in the story's plot.

"Abuela Invents the Zero" by Judith Ortiz Cofer

"You made me feel like a zero, like a nothing," she says in Spanish, *un cero, nada.* She is trembling, an angry little old woman lost in a heavy winter coat that belongs to my mother. And I end up being sent to my room, like I was a child, to think about my grandmother's idea of math.

It all began with Abuela coming up from the Island for a visit—her first time in the United States. My mother and father paid her way here so that she wouldn't die without seeing snow, though if you asked me, and nobody has, the dirty slush in this city is not worth the price of a ticket. But I guess she deserves some kind of award for having had ten kids and survived to tell about it. My mother is the youngest of the bunch. Right up to the time when we're supposed to pick up that old lady at the airport, my mother is telling me stories about how hard times were for *la familia* on *la isla,* and how *la abuela* worked night and day to support them after their father died of a heart attack. I'd die of a heart attack too if I had a troop like that to support. Anyway, I had seen her only three or four times in my entire life, whenever we would go for somebody's funeral. I was born here and I have lived in this building all my life. But when Mami says, "Connie, please be nice to Abuela. She doesn't have too many years left. Do you promise me, Constancia?"—when she uses my full name, I know she means business. So I say, "Sure." Why wouldn't I be nice? I'm not a monster, after all.

So we go to Kennedy to get la abuela and she is the last to come out of the airplane, on the arm of the cabin attendant, all wrapped up in a black shawl. He hands her over to my parents like she was a package sent airmail. It is January, two feet of snow on the ground, and she's wearing a shawl over a thin black dress. That's just the start.

Once home, she refuses to let my mother buy her a coat because it's a waste of money for the two weeks she'll be in *el Polo Norte,* as she calls New Jersey, the North Pole. So since she's only four feet eleven inches tall, she walks around in my mother's big black coat looking ridiculous. I try to walk far behind them in public so that no one will think we're together. I plan to stay very busy the whole time she's with us so that I won't be asked to take her anywhere, but my plan is ruined when my mother comes down with the flu and Abuela absolutely has to attend Sunday mass or her soul will be eternally damned. She's more Catholic than the Pope. My father decides that he should stay home with my mother and that I should escort la abuela to church. He tells me this on Saturday night as I'm getting ready to go out to the mall with my friends.

STORY LINE AND PLOT 51

ABOUT THE AUTHOR
Born in Hormigueros, Puerto Rico, Judith Ortiz Cofer was part of a military family. As she was growing up, her father's position in the U.S. Navy prompted many moves back and forth between Puerto Rico and the mainland United States. She compares her bicultural upbringing to feeling like a "perpetual student."

TEACHING TIP

Collaboration   Invite Spanish-speaking students to work with class-mates to pronounce the Spanish words.

EXTRA SUPPORT

On the board or on chart paper, arrange the vocabulary terms and their English definitions into columns with the heads *Spanish* and *English*. Then invite students to compare and contrast the words in each pair. Challenge students to think of similar words in English that relate to the Spanish word.

la familia [lah fah MEE lee ah] family
la isla [lah EES lah] island
la abuela [lah ah BWAY lah] the grandmother
el Polo Norte [el POH loh NOR tay] the North Pole

the author really surprises you by show-ing you the climax of the story in the first sentence" or "This isn't as good as Cofer's because there are so many events, it's hard to follow."

Using a Graphic Organizer: Plot Diagram Using a graphic organizer like the Plot Diagram helps students to stop and reflect on the part of a story they've read and to organize those reflections. Students can also use a Plot Diagram to analyze what they've read once they have finished a story. Remind students that the events they're filling in now are part of the exposition and rising action and that they'll continue to fill out the diagram as they read the next passage.

Quick Assess

Can students

* identify the main events in a story passage?

* connect the five essential parts of a plot to events in a story?

* identify events that lead up to a story's climax?

* state the difference between the story line and the plot?

"No way," I say.

I go for the car keys on the kitchen table: he usually leaves them there for me on Friday and Saturday nights. He beats me to them.

"No way," he says pocketing them and grinning at me.

Needless to say, we come to a compromise very quickly. I do have a responsibility to Sandra and Anita, who don't drive yet. There is a Harley-Davidson fashion show at Brookline Square that we *cannot* miss.

"The mass in Spanish is at ten sharp tomorrow morning, *entiendes?*" My father is dangling the car keys in front of my nose and pulling them back when I try to reach for them. He's really enjoying himself. ❖

✳ Fill in as much of the Plot Diagram as you can. You won't have everything filled in yet, nor will the order of events be clear until you've read the entire story.

Climax

Falling Action

Rising Action

Exposition

Resolution

Plot Summary

Look at the relationships and connections between events in the story to determine the plot.

A story's **theme** is its central idea. The theme is the statement or message from the author. Often you can connect a story's plot and theme to your own life. Ask yourself: What does this author want me to think or understand from the story? Sometimes the author will make the theme obvious by stating the idea directly. Other times you'll need to make inferences, or reasonable guesses, about the theme from what the author says and the way the plot is constructed.

Continue reading "Abuela Invents the Zero" by Judith Ortiz Cofer. Use your **Response Notes** to note major events and to tie these to the lessons Cofer seems to be emphasizing.

"Abuela Invents the Zero" by Judith Ortiz Cofer
(continued)

Response Notes

"I understand. Ten o'clock. I'm out of here." I pry his fingers off the key ring. He knows that I'm late, so he makes it just a little difficult. Then he laughs. I run out of our apartment before he changes his mind. I have no idea what I'm getting myself into.

Sunday morning I have to walk two blocks on dirty snow to retrieve the car. I warm it up for Abuela as instructed by my parents, and drive it to the front of our building. My father walks her by the hand in baby steps on the slippery snow. The sight of her little head with a bun on top of it sticking out of that huge coat make me want to run back into my room and get under the covers. I just hope that nobody I know sees us together. I'm dreaming, of course. The mass is packed with people from our block. It's a holy day of obligation and everyone I ever met is there.

I have to help her climb the steps, and she stops to take a deep breath after each one, then I lead her down the aisle so that everybody can see me with my bizarre grandmother. If I were a good Catholic, I'm sure I'd get some purgatory time taken off for my sacrifice. She is walking as slow as Captain Cousteau exploring the bottom of the sea, looking around, taking her sweet time. Finally she chooses a pew, but she wants to sit in the *other* end. It's like she had a spot picked out for some unknown reason, and although it's the most inconvenient seat in the house, that's where she has to sit. So we squeeze by all the people already sitting there, saying, "Excuse me, please, *con permiso*, pardon me," getting annoyed looks the whole way. By the time we settle in, I'm drenched in sweat. I keep my head down like I'm praying so as not to see or be seen. She is praying loud, in Spanish, and singing hymns at the top of her creaky voice.

I ignore her when she gets up with a hundred other people to go take communion. I'm actually praying hard now—that this will all be over soon.

Students will determine the theme, or central idea, of a story and relate the author's message to their lives.

BACKGROUND KNOWLEDGE
Remind students that Judith Ortiz Cofer was born in Puerto Rico but moved to New Jersey as a child. Help students understand that her story is as much about wrestling the demands of two cultures as it is about wrestling the demands of childhood and adulthood.

Invite volunteers to relate experiences they may have had of trying to "live in two worlds," whether those worlds are two different cultures or situations that make them feel pulled between two conflicting forces, such as sports and school requirements.

VOCABULARY

pew a long bench of seats in a church

drenched soaking wet

periscope an instrument with lenses and mirrors that helps one see things that are not in the direct line of sight

After introducing the vocabulary words, invite students to share what they know about any of the words. Challenge them to predict how the words will be used in the story. After students have read the selection, compare their predictions with the story.

Before

CRITICAL READING
Connect Plot and Theme Help students understand that the theme is the message the author wants to convey to the reader. The primary theme of a story is usually a lesson learned through the experience of one or more of the story's characters.

RESPONSE NOTES As students read the second passage from this story, remind them to continue to note the major events in the story. As they do, invite them to think about how those events and the interactions between the characters tie to the theme, or message, of Cofer's story. Remind students to jot notes (which can be brief and in incomplete sentences) in the margin.

During

WRITE A SUMMARY
Before they add the rest of the events to the Plot Diagram (page 52), ask students to write a brief plot summary of "Abuela Invents the Zero." Have them collaborate with a partner and check to see if they have included all the main events that tie to the plot and theme of the story.

WRITER'S CRAFT

Voice Cofer is masterful in her ability to capture the "voice" of an adolescent whose life is not quite the way she would like it to be. You may want to read part of the selection aloud or invite a student to do so. Ask students to listen for the voice of the narrator as the story is read. After reading, discuss which words help to make the narrator—a teenage girl—sound convincing. Also point out examples in which the narrator moves back and forth between English and Spanish and discuss how this technique authenticates the story.

TEACHING TIP

Responding Encourage students to think of the events in the story as clues to how the narrator's grandmother became so hurt and angry. Have them make note of each event in the story that they think is important to the plot.

But the next time I look up, I see a black coat dragging around and around the church, stopping here and there so a little gray head can peek out like a periscope on a submarine. There are giggles in the church, and even the priest has frozen in the middle of a blessing, his hands above his head like he is about to lead the congregation in a set of jumping jacks.

I realize to my horror that my grandmother is lost. She can't find her way back to the pew. I am so embarrassed that even though the woman next to me is shooting daggers at me with her eyes, I just can't move to go get her. I put my hands over my face like I'm praying, but it's really to hide my burning cheeks. I would like for her to disappear. I just know that on Monday my friends, and my enemies, in the barrio will have a lot of senile-grandmother jokes to tell in front of me. I am frozen to my seat. So the same woman who wants me dead on the spot does it for me. She makes a big deal out of getting up and hurrying to get Abuela.

The rest of the mass is a blur. All I know is that my grandmother kneels the whole time with *her* hands over her face. She doesn't speak to me on the way home, and she doesn't let me help her walk, even though she almost falls a couple of times.

When we get to the apartment, my parents are at the kitchen table, where my mother is trying to eat some soup. They can see right away that something is wrong. Then Abuela points her finger at me like a judge passing a sentence on a criminal. She says in Spanish, "You made me feel like a zero, like a nothing." Then she goes to her room.

I try to explain what happened. "I don't understand why she's so upset. She just got lost and wandered around for a while," I tell them. But it sounds lame, even to my own ears. My mother gives me a look that makes me cringe and goes in to Abuela's room to get her version of the story. She comes out with tears in her eyes.

"Your grandmother says to tell you that of all the hurtful things you can do to a person, the worst is to make them feel as if they are worth nothing."

I can feel myself shrinking right there in front of her. But I can't bring myself to tell my mother that I think I understand how I made Abuela feel. I might be sent into the old lady's room to apologize, and it's not easy to admit you've been a jerk—at least, not right away with everybody watching. So I just sit there not saying anything.

My mother looks at me for a long time, like she feels sorry for me. Then she says, "You should know, Constancia, that if it wasn't for this old woman whose existence you don't seem to value, you and I would not be here."

That's when *I'm* sent to *my* room to consider a number I hadn't thought much about—until today. ❖

After

USING A GRAPHIC ORGANIZER

Theme Organizer The Theme Organizer (page 55) provides students with a structured way of organizing their thoughts about the author's message, or theme of the story. Filling out the organizer also requires students to provide evidence to back up their analyses.

Ask students to write about a short story or novel they've read or a movie they've seen that explores the theme of growing up. What were the story's specific themes? Did they find that the themes related to their own life experiences? What questions came to mind, and what did they learn through the themes?

Invite students to make a Theme Organizer for that story, book, or movie. Then have them write a short essay on why it affected them and what they learned. Encourage students to share their essays with the class.

✳ First, add events from this part of the story to the Plot Diagram on page 52. Share your thinking with a partner. Discuss how you think the events are related. Then write a summary of the plot.

✳ In the Theme Organizer, organize your thinking about the important messages from the story.

THEME ORGANIZER

1. Important Quotes	What I Think About This

2. What Characters Do and Say

Meaning to the Story

3. Big Ideas

4. Lessons Learned

Differentiation If students are having difficulty connecting quotes from the story and a character's actions with a theme, model using a think-aloud: *In the story, Abuela says about her granddaughter, "You made me feel like a zero, like a nothing." It's clear that Abuela's feelings are really hurt. I think one of the messages of the story is how much we can hurt people who love us when we don't treat them with respect. I think that's one of the story's themes.*

Identifying the Main Theme

Remind students to use their Theme Organizers to help them as they write about a theme of the story (page 56). Answers may vary: *It's wrong to think only of yourself; becoming more mature is remembering to think of how other people feel; it's important to respect your elders,* and so on. Students should provide evidence from the story to support their analyses.

Connecting to Personal Experiences

The last activity of the lesson (page 56) asks students to connect the theme that they wrote about to their own lives. As a prewriting activity, have them consider what the granddaughter learned from the experiences with her grandmother.

Quick Assess

Can students

✳ identify a theme?

✳ convey clearly how the theme relates to their lives?

✳ Write a paragraph describing what you see as one of the themes of the story. Use your Theme Organizer to provide evidence or use quotes to support your opinions.

✳ Connect this theme to your own life. Describe an experience or situation you've had that relates to the story's theme. What did you learn from your experience?

If you can connect the theme from the story to your own experiences, then you will understand the story better.

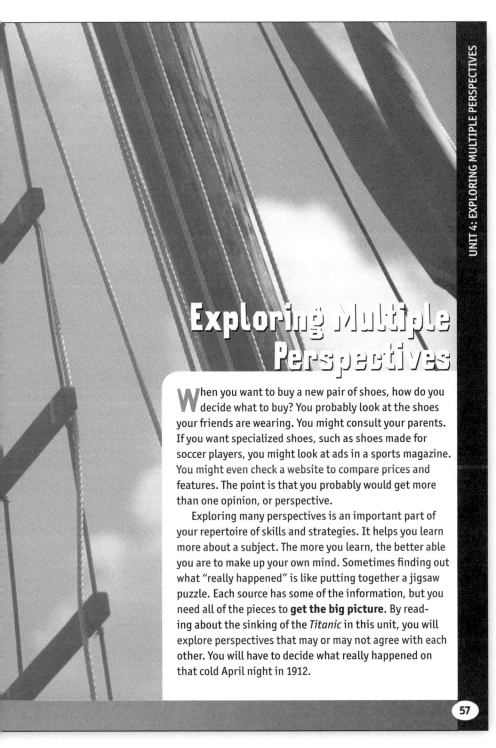

Exploring Multiple Perspectives

When you want to buy a new pair of shoes, how do you decide what to buy? You probably look at the shoes your friends are wearing. You might consult your parents. If you want specialized shoes, such as shoes made for soccer players, you might look at ads in a sports magazine. You might even check a website to compare prices and features. The point is that you probably would get more than one opinion, or perspective.

Exploring many perspectives is an important part of your repertoire of skills and strategies. It helps you learn more about a subject. The more you learn, the better able you are to make up your own mind. Sometimes finding out what "really happened" is like putting together a jigsaw puzzle. Each source has some of the information, but you need all of the pieces to **get the big picture**. By reading about the sinking of the *Titanic* in this unit, you will explore perspectives that may or may not agree with each other. You will have to decide what really happened on that cold April night in 1912.

57

Lessons 16-20, pages 58-70

UNIT OVERVIEW
By studying a famous event, students will learn ways to find and evaluate different perspectives, important strategies they can then apply to other topics.

KEY IDEA
Multiple perspectives help a reader understand an event or topic more fully.

CRITICAL READING SKILLS
by lesson

16 Establishing the sequence of events

17 Determining cause and effect

18 Considering the author's credibility

19 Evaluating eyewitness accounts

20 Comparing different versions of an event

WRITING ACTIVITIES
by lesson

16 Chart a sequence of events

17 Write an "official" report on the causes of a disaster

18 Write a paragraph evaluating an author's credibility

19 Draft the beginning of a survivor's "eyewitness account" of the sinking of a ship

20 Write an analysis of an eyewitness account of a current event

---

Literature

- *The Titanic* by Richard Wormser (nonfiction book excerpt)

Documentary filmmaker and writer Richard Wormser describes the collision with the iceberg and the reactions of passengers and crew.

- **"John Thayer: Becoming a Man Aboard the *Titanic*"** from *We Were There, Too! Young People in U.S. History* by Phillip Hoose (biographical nonfiction)

Author Phillip Hoose profiles a 17-year-old survivor, using excerpts from Thayer's self-published report of the disaster.

- **"I Survived the *Titanic*"** from *National Geographic World:* June 1996 by Jennifer Kilpatrick (biographical nonfiction)

Ruth Becker was 12 years old when she and her family boarded the ship in Southampton.

ASSESSMENT To assess student learning in this unit, see pages 230 and 257.

Students will follow the sequence of events in personal narratives to compare accounts of a historical event.

BACKGROUND KNOWLEDGE

Use these facts to expand on what students already know about the *Titanic*.

❋ The *Titanic* was as long as four city blocks.

❋ It set sail for New York from Southampton, England, on April 10, 1912.

❋ On the night of April 14, 1912, the *Titanic* hit an iceberg and sank in a little over two hours.

❋ There weren't enough lifeboats, so many people dove into the icy water or went down with the ship.

❋ Out of 2,223 people on board, only 706 survived. Approximately 320 bodies were recovered, many of which were buried in Halifax, Nova Scotia.

VOCABULARY

crow's nest a small lookout platform that is near the top of a ship's mast

binoculars a device made up of two small telescopes to make distant things look closer

Ask students to predict how these terms might be important in a selection about the *Titanic*.

The first step in exploring multiple perspectives is to figure out what happened. You need to know the order, or **sequence**, of events. When you know the sequence of events, you can compare what people say about the event to what you know about it. For example, soon after a disaster occurs, the facts are not always clear. You should know that if you read about a disaster right away, you should question whether the facts are correct. As you can see on the front page of Baltimore's *The Evening Sun*, the first reports about the *Titanic* were not accurate.

THE EVENING SUN
ALL TITANIC PASSENGERS ARE SAFE; TRANSFERRED IN LIFEBOATS AT SEA
PARISIAN AND CARPATHIA TAKE HUMAN CARGO

As you read the following excerpt, pay attention to the sequence of events. Circle words and phrases that show when events happened.

Response Notes

from **The Titanic** by Richard Wormser

The night was bitter cold. Stars shone like diamonds in the dark sky, but there was no moon. The water was calm, and smooth as glass. High in the crow's nest, two young sailors, Frederick Fleet and Herbert Lee, were watching for icebergs. These men were the "eyes of the ship"—part of the team of lookouts. From their perch above the *Titanic*'s deck, they could gaze far out into the open sea and spot any danger before it seriously threatened the ship. Radar and other electronic scanning devices had not yet been invented, so watching closely was the only way to spot objects in the water. But these lookouts didn't even have a pair of binoculars.

By 11:30 P.M., most passengers were in bed. Fleet and Lee were glad their shift would be over in another 20 minutes. They were numb with cold and their eyes hurt from the strain of trying to see in the dark. Then at 11:39 P.M., Fleet suddenly spied an object which at first seemed small but rapidly increased in

Before

CRITICAL READING SKILL

Sequence Understanding the order in which events happen is important when reading informational text and can help readers determine the facts. In the case of the *Titanic,* the series of events that led to the rapid sinking of the ship help us understand what actually happened.

RESPONSE NOTES Remind students to look for and circle all words that signal sequence, such as *then, next,* and *later,* as well as other terms, such as *night* and *by 11:30 P.M.* Tell them these words and phrases will help them fill in the sequence chart on page 59. (See *Daybook* page 225 for tips on active reading.)

During

After students finish reading the first selection by Wormser, discuss how they might decide on the most important events. It is possible to include more than four in the chart, depending on what students consider key events. Ask them to defend their choices. (Suggested answers: Fleet notifies the officers, officers give the order to change course, the ship begins to swerve, the ship scrapes the iceberg)

size. Within seconds he realized that the *Titanic* was headed straight for an iceberg. He snatched up the telephone and rang the bridge, the officer's control center. As soon as the officer answered, Fleet cried out:

"Iceberg dead ahead!"

The great ship was about to meet her fate.

It only took 37 seconds for the *Titanic* to begin its swing away from the 100-foot-high, 500-foot-deep iceberg in its path. To lookouts Fleet and Lee, that was way too long. It seemed certain that the *Titanic* would crash head-on into the mountain of ice. William Murdoch, the first officer in charge, had already given orders to change the ship's course. A ship as large as the *Titanic*, however, needed time to reposition. Fifteen seconds more and the *Titanic* would have escaped. But time was the one thing the *Titanic* didn't have.

The *Titanic* was about to crash into the iceberg when it suddenly began to swerve out of the iceberg's path. To the officers on the bridge, it seemed that their last-minute attempts to change course had worked. The ship appeared to have only lightly scraped the iceberg. But many passengers and crew below were aware that something much more serious had happened. ❖

❊ What is the sequence of events that Wormser describes? Use the diagram below to show what happened first, what happened next, and so on.

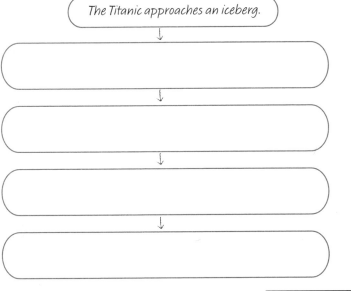

Once you establish the sequence of events, you have a foundation to use in exploring different perspectives.

Richard Wormser has produced more than 100 film and video programs and has won more than 20 awards for his films. He has also written many nonfiction books for young people on a wide variety of topics. Students will learn more about Richard Wormser in Lesson 18: Considering the Author's Credibility

EXTRA SUPPORT

Using a Graphic Organizer: Sequence Chart Remind students to focus on the main events and to use terms they circled in the passage to help them list the events in the correct order.

Differentiation If students need help understanding sequence, relate the concept to an everyday process, such as tying your shoes or brushing your teeth. Have a volunteer describe the steps involved in that process, using time-order words such as *first, next, then,* and *finally.*

Quick Assess

❊ Did students select key events?

❊ Are they listed in the correct order according to the article?

After

MAKE A SEQUENCE CHART

Invite students to locate information on another disaster, for example the 1906 San Francisco earthquake, the volcanic eruption of Mt. St. Helens in 1980, the tsunami in Indonesia in 2004, or Hurricane Katrina in 2005. Ask them to diagram the sequence of events leading up to the disaster.

Students will examine cause and effect in eyewitness accounts of a historical event and write an account of their own.

BACKGROUND KNOWLEDGE

Refer to a diagram or model of a ship to help students locate the accommodations for first-, second-, and third-class passengers. Understanding the structure of the ship and where the people were located will help students visualize as they read. (See http://www.historyonthenet.com/Titanic/largecutaway.htm for a good cutaway diagram of the ship.)

VOCABULARY

lounge a place for people to relax

jolt a sudden bump

tremor a trembling, shaking movement; a small earthquake

compartment a separate space

bulkhead a wall that separates a section of a ship

Discuss *lounge, compartment,* and *bulkhead* regarding where they might be located on a ship. Then talk about the meanings of *jolt* and *tremor.* Have students predict how those words will be used and then check their predictions.

Before judging other people's perspectives on an event, you need to understand the event thoroughly. Besides knowing the sequence of events, you need to know the possible **causes and effects**. This means trying to figure out how one event, the cause, brings on related events, the effects. Determining the causes of a disaster, like the sinking of the "unsinkable" *Titanic,* is not easy. Immediately after hitting the iceberg, some passengers and crewmembers knew that something was wrong. But no one knew how devastating the effects would be.

As you read, underline or highlight possible causes of the disaster.

Response Notes

from **The Titanic** by Richard Wormser

Four crew members relaxing in a first-class lounge heard a grinding noise from deep inside the ship. It sounded, one said, as if "a propeller had fallen off." Many first-class passengers felt a shock. To Marguerite Frolicher, a young Swiss woman, it seemed, "as if the ship were landing." Lady Duff Gordon, a dress designer married to a British nobleman, commented that it was as if "someone had run a giant finger along the side of the ship."

On the ship's lower decks, the noise was even louder. Some people in second class were awakened by the jolt. Major Arthur Godfrey Peuchen, a Canadian, thought "a heavy wave" had struck the ship. Mrs. Walter Stephenson, who had lived through the 1906 San Francisco earthquake, thought the shock felt like an earthquake tremor.

Deep within the ship, the men tending the boilers that powered the *Titanic* knew exactly what had happened. In one of the boiler rooms, a tremendous rumbling, scraping sound was heard, followed by a terrifying roar as tons of sea water came crashing into the ship. The whole left side of the ship seemed to collapse suddenly. The men barely escaped with their lives.

In the third-class area, Carl Bohme, a Finnish immigrant, got out of bed to see what was going on and found himself up to his ankles in water. In the mailroom, the water was already covering the knees of the postal workers, who were frantically trying to keep the mail from getting wet.

Most passengers still didn't realize how serious things were. Some third-class passengers had discovered that their deck was covered with ice that had fallen from the iceberg. Some began to have a snowball fight. Soon passengers from every class were picking up pieces of ice. Some even used the ice to cool their drinks. Whatever the problem, they seemed confident that it would soon be solved.

60 LESSON 17

Before

CRITICAL READING SKILL

Cause and Effect Understanding the cause-effect relationships of events helps the reader understand what is happening. As students read, have them pay attention to what seems to cause different events to take place on the *Titanic.* In this selection, Wormser focuses on how different reactions of the crew and passengers led

to confusion on board and how lack of time and not realizing the seriousness of the situation led to the great loss of life.

RESPONSE NOTES Point out that some details in a text might seem unimportant at first but may turn out to be important in the long run. For example, the fact that the postal workers were trying to keep the mail from getting wet

may have delayed their leaving their work area to escape to safety. The snowball fight seems foolish in retrospect, but the passengers' perspective was based on incomplete information.

A few passengers, however, were well aware that something was terribly wrong. Lawrence Beasley, a schoolteacher traveling in second class, had started back to his cabin when he noticed that somehow his feet weren't falling in the right place. The stairs were level, but he felt slightly off balance. It was as if the steps were suddenly tilting forward toward the *bow*, the front part of the ship. In fact, they were.

Below the decks was Thomas Andrews, the chief engineer who had supervised the design of the *Titanic*. He was on board to see how the ship would perform on her maiden voyage and whether any adjustments needed to be made. No one knew the *Titanic* better than Andrews. No man, not even Captain Smith, commanded more respect from the crew. Now the ship's officers were anxiously waiting for him to tell them what was happening.

Andrews studied the reports of the damage and then gave Captain Smith the bad news: The rock-hard base of the iceberg had scraped the *Titanic*'s hull below the waterline, gashing some holes in her side and loosening the steel plates that held her together. Water was rushing into the front of the ship. Andrews explained there were 16 water-tight compartments on the ship from bow to stern, the back end of the ship. The ship could float if the first four were filled. But if the fifth compartment, or bulkhead, was filled, the bow would begin to sink so low that water would spill over that bulkhead into the sixth compartment. Because the *Titanic*'s bulkheads were not high enough to prevent this from happening, the spillover would continue from compartment to compartment until the whole ship filled with water and sank.

The *Titanic* was doomed.

"How long have we got?" the captain asked.

"About two hours," Andrews replied.

Smith and Andrews both knew that there were 2,207 passengers and crew on board, but room for only about 1,178 people in the lifeboats. Unless a rescue ship arrived within two hours, more than 1,000 people would drown. There was no time to waste.

Using Details Wormser paints a very clear picture of the confusion aboard the *Titanic* after the ship hits the iceberg. By recounting the different reactions to the jolt, the loud noise, and the rushing water, Wormser takes the reader inside the events of the story. Ask students to find examples of details that help them picture what is happening, such as the reactions of people in the different sections of the ship, the scene in the boiler room, the snowball fight, the delivery to the Captain of the bad news from the chief engineer, and so on.

EXTRA SUPPORT

Differentiation Part of the authenticity of Wormser's report lies in the amount of detail he includes. However, these details might make the passage difficult for less confident readers. If students get confused as they read, help them locate the different people and places mentioned, using a layout or model of the ship. *(See Background Knowledge on page 60.)*

During

USING THINK-ALOUD

So much is happening in this selection that it's often hard to distinguish between cause and effect. Many of the effects of events in this selection then become the cause of another effect. To help students understand how to identify the causes, model by using a think-aloud: *In the third paragraph, it says that the sea water came crashing into the boiler room. The iceberg* **caused** *a leak, and tons of water was coming into the ship. If the ship's crew can't stop it, this will* **cause** *the ship to sink.*

RESPONSE NOTES While some connections between cause and effect may be obvious, encourage students to draw inferences as they read. For example, apparently unimportant events (such as when passengers used the ice for a snowball fight) may have caused a critical delay in passengers getting to the lifeboats.

USING A GRAPHIC ORGANIZER

Causes Chart Have students use their Response Notes to fill in the causes on the diagram. Remind students to keep in mind the big picture of what happened: *The ship hit an iceberg, which tore a hole in the side. The ship's bow took on water and began to sink. At first the crew and passengers didn't know the severity of the problem, which led to a lot of confusion.*

▶ ▶ ▶

✻ On the diagram below, list some of the causes of the *Titanic* disaster.

1.

2.

3.

4.

After

Students can include causes from the first passage (pages 58-59). If students find it easier to write the causes *and* the effects on the diagram, allow them to do so, but ask them to underline the causes and draw an arrow from the causes to their effects.

APPLY CAUSE-EFFECT Have students write an official report about something that happened to them or in their community. They can write it from their own perspective or from a different one. In their reports, they should focus on the causes and effects that led up to the final outcome. If students have trouble thinking of a topic, suggest that they write about helping someone in an emergency, facing a crisis at school, or dealing with a crisis the community faced, such as a flood or a fire.

✳ Imagine that you are one of the surviving crew members. You have been asked to explain the cause of the disaster. Use your diagram and the Sequence Chart you made in Lesson 16 (page 59) to write your official report.

Official Report

Prepared By: ....

> Recognizing cause-and-effect relationships helps you connect events and ideas.

Purpose and Audience Explain to students that before you write, it's important to think about *why* you are writing (your purpose) and *to whom* you are writing (your audience). Model a way to begin the official report using a think-aloud: *As a surviving crew member of the Titanic, I have very strong emotions about the events. However, I am writing an official report, which means I need to stick to the facts and keep my tone as objective as possible. I want people to learn from what happened so that it never happens again. They should understand the horror of the experience, so I will include those details, but I also want to give a clear account of what happened and why.*

Remind students to use the Sequence Chart from Lesson 16, as well as the Causes Chart they just filled out, to complete the report.

Quick Assess

✳ Do students understand that a cause can lead to an effect, which, in turn, can lead to another effect?

✳ Does the writing assignment show that students comprehended the article?

LESSON 18

Students will use guidelines to determine the reliability of a source and the author's perspective.

BACKGROUND KNOWLEDGE

If you haven't already, you may want to share the information on Richard Wormser found in **About the Author** on page 59. Students will learn more about Wormser on page 65. To complete the Background Check on this page, students will rely on inferences they've made from the reading and the information you've shared from **About the Author**.

VOCABULARY

social related to issues that are important to society

dispossessed deprived of possessions or a place to live

Preview the words and their meanings with students to make sure they understand the words as they are used in this lesson. Also make sure students understand how *social* is used in this lesson to mean larger issues that affect everyone.

LESSON 18 — CONSIDERING THE AUTHOR'S CREDIBILITY

How do you know what to believe if you get many perspectives on a subject? Do you know which sources are believable? You cannot believe everything you hear, see, or read. You have to make some judgments. Fortunately, there are guidelines that will help you ask good questions. In this lesson, you will learn what questions to ask when your source is the author.

The selections you read in Lessons 16 and 17 were by Richard Wormser, author of the book *The Titanic*. Unless you have researched him, you may not know whether he is **credible**, or believable. Look at those selections again to complete the Background Check. Briefly note the reason for your answer in the space below each item. Answer as best you can for now, given the information you have.

BACKGROUND CHECK ON AN AUTHOR

☐ What is Richard Wormser's purpose for writing about the *Titanic*?

_____

_____

☐ Why did he tell about people on each level of the ship—passengers in first class, second class, and third class, and crew members in first class and in the boiler room?

_____

_____

☐ Where do you think Richard Wormser got his information?

_____

_____

☐ What is Richard Wormser's background?

_____

_____

✳ Evaluate your conclusions with a partner. If you want to make changes to your answers, make them now.

Before

CRITICAL READING SKILL

Author's Credibility Help students understand that although we are surrounded by information from many media sources, not all the information we read or hear is accurate. Good readers evaluate the source of their information.

Help students evaluate a source with the following examples: (1) In which ways would an autobiography of a president differ from a biography written by a political opponent? (2) How might an article on skateboarding be different if it were written not by an enthusiast, but by someone who had never ridden a skateboard? Would the article be as credible? Invite students to think of other examples where credibility can affect the reliability of information, such as advertising firms writing their own product endorsements or politicians writing editorials.

Help students understand that because there can be multiple perspectives on any subject, as critical readers, they need to be aware of an author's background and purpose in order to evaluate that author's credibility on a given subject.

✴ The next step is to find out more about the author to check your conclusions. The quotations below will give you additional data and perhaps another perspective. Richard Wormser wrote an essay for the reference source *Something About the Author Autobiography Series* (1998). He is also listed in *Contemporary Authors Online* (2004). Read the quotations to make **inferences**, or reasonable guesses, about the author's perspective. Write notes about the information in the spaces around the quotations.

"Richard Wormser is a filmmaker-turned-writer who has published several works of nonfiction for young adult readers on such varied topics as teens at risk, Vietnam, hoboes, railways, American Islam, and even a biography of Allan Pinkerton, the first private investigator in the United States. Wormser's writings generally have a social slant...." (CA)

"In the 1970s and 1980s he continued to make documentary films. By the 1990s, though, he 'found it increasingly difficult to produce his social and political documentaries, and turned to writing instead.'" (CA)

"His first book was so well received that he decided to continue writing for young adults. He wrote, 'Perhaps through my books I can reach an audience that is not yet indifferent to the plight of America's dispossessed—those for whom society seems to have no place.'" (SAAS)

✴ Return to the Background Check on page 64 and revise your answers as necessary.

Collaboration Working together is important in this lesson because students will need someone to help them generate and test ideas. Just as the lesson proceeds by supplying additional perspectives on Richard Wormser, so students will benefit from peer perspectives.

Depending on the needs of students in your class, you may want to pair students using one of these methods:

✴ pair a more-proficient student with a less-proficient one

✴ have students turn to the person on their right or left

✴ encourage students to select their own partners

During

Review with students what they have read about the *Titanic* so far. Ask them to look back over their Response Notes and other writing they did for the lessons as they complete the Background Check. Stress that they are making inferences, or reasonable guesses, based on what they have read. Let them know that opinions and evaluations are bound to vary among classmates since perspectives will differ.

Once all students have completed the Background Check on an Author, have them talk with a partner and make any changes they want after listening to that perspective. It is important for students to learn that keeping their minds open to multiple perspectives (in this case theirs and that of their partner) can change their conclusions.

READING BAR GRAPHS The bar graph of survivors and victims (page 66) connects with the information Wormser provides in Lesson 17 and helps answer the question of why he tells so much about people in each class of the ship. Assist students in interpreting the information presented in the graph and connecting it with what they've read in the passages from Wormser's *The Titanic*. ▶▶▶

✻ Do students' paragraphs provide more than one reason to support the writer's position? (For example, students could say that Wormser seems credible because publishers have found his work worthy enough to publish in books.)

✻ Do students use details from the excerpts in Lessons 16–18?

Good authors do a lot of research to establish the details of their story. There is evidence in the selections that Richard Wormser relied on research, too. One piece of information that was not widely reported right after the disaster was the great differences in who died and who survived. There were lifeboats for only about half the passengers. Look at the chart. Who had the best chances of surviving? How might this relate to the author's purpose for writing *The Titanic*? Note your conclusions below the chart.

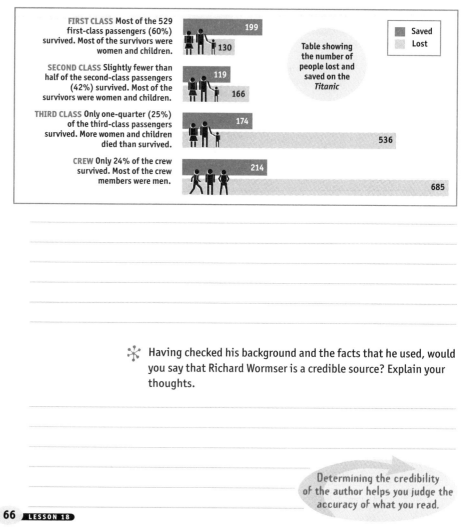

FIRST CLASS Most of the 529 first-class passengers (60%) survived. Most of the survivors were women and children. — 199 / 130

SECOND CLASS Slightly fewer than half of the second-class passengers (42%) survived. Most of the survivors were women and children. — 119 / 166

THIRD CLASS Only one-quarter (25%) of the third-class passengers survived. More women and children died than survived. — 174 / 536

CREW Only 24% of the crew survived. Most of the crew members were men. — 214 / 685

Table showing the number of people lost and saved on the *Titanic*

Saved
Lost

✻ Having checked his background and the facts that he used, would you say that Richard Wormser is a credible source? Explain your thoughts.

Determining the credibility of the author helps you judge the accuracy of what you read.

After

Students will get additional opportunities to work with diagrams, maps, and graphs in Unit 9.

WRITING SUPPORT
Providing Support for an Opinion
Remind students to use their Background Check to find examples and details to support their opinions. Explain that effective argument involves presenting an opinion with examples that support it.

VIEWING CONNECTION
Ask students to compare Wormser's account of the *Titanic* disaster to a documentary, movie, or television version of the same event. Have them discuss which version seems more credible and why.

RESEARCH CONNECTION
Encourage students to research an author they are reading to help them evaluate the author's credibility. Students can conduct searches on the Internet or in reference materials. Many public and school libraries have copies of *Contemporary Authors* and *Something About the Author,* which are good sources of biographical information and bibliographies of authors' works. Whichever source students use, they must evaluate the validity of each and cite each properly.

People at the scene of an event provide important perspectives. But, as readers, we need to remember that they know only what they see and hear. Usually, eyewitnesses do not have the whole picture. As you read this account from a survivor of the *Titanic* disaster, think about what must have been going through his head at the time.

John Thayer, Jr., was 17 when he took a trip to Europe with his parents during spring break. It was his last year in high school, and his father had mapped out John's future in banking. John and his parents were returning to New York on the *Titanic,* traveling first-class. Author Phillip Hoose wrote John's story based on Thayer's 1940 self-published book, *The Sinking of the S. S. Titanic.*

"John Thayer: Becoming a Man Aboard the *Titanic*"
from *We Were There, Too! Young People in U.S. History* by Phillip Hoose

John thought the *Titanic* was astounding. It was really a floating city, four blocks long. You could work out in the gymnasium, take steam baths, or lounge around the pool. There were shops everywhere; even the barber shop sold flags from around the world. As a first-class passenger, John could go anywhere and talk to anyone he wanted to, even the ship's owner.

On the evening of Sunday, April 14, after a dinner conversation with a judge's son named Milton Long, John stepped out onto the deck for some fresh air. He later wrote: "there was no moon and I have never seen the stars shine brighter—they sparkled like cut diamonds . . . It was the kind of night that made one glad to be alive." Yawning, he went down to his stateroom, said good night to his parents, and slipped on his pajamas. He was about to climb into bed when he felt the ship sway very slightly. He wrote, "If I had had a brimful glass of water in my hand not a drop would have been spilled."

The engines stopped and then started up again, and he heard voices outside his door. He put on his overcoat and went to the deck to see what was happening. There were chunks of ice scattered about. A crew member told him they had struck an iceberg. The deck seemed to be tilting a little to the right. A few minutes later John passed the ship's designer, Thomas Andrews, in a corridor. Shaken, Andrews told John he didn't think the ship could float for more than an hour. John's heart began to race. He got dressed, woke his parents, and rushed back to the deck with them to put on life vests and wait for a lifeboat. Milton Long appeared and asked if he could join them.

There was room in the lifeboats for only about half the passengers and crew, so choices had to be made. "Women and children first," people were yelling. John didn't even ask whether he qualified. He could see that much

Response Notes

Students will evaluate an eyewitness account in order to form a whole picture of a historical event.

BACKGROUND KNOWLEDGE
Remind students that there were just over 700 survivors from the *Titanic*. The survivors' accounts provide a perspective for what happened. Help students understand that there are many perspectives on historical events and that part of what helps us discern what actually happened is *primary source material,* written and oral accounts provided by eyewitnesses (people who were actually there). Invite students to think of other eyewitness accounts they may have read, such as *The Diary of Anne Frank*. Discuss the importance of primary sources.

VOCABULARY
lounge relax, hang out

deafening so loud as to cause hearing loss

arcing moving in a curved path

surging moving forward powerfully

Point out that *lounge* was used as a noun in Lesson 18, referring to a place on the ship, and here is used as a verb. *Deafening* can mean literally "loud enough to cause hearing loss," but it also means extremely loud. Talk with students about using context to understand unfamiliar words.

Before

CRITICAL READING SKILL
Evaluating Eyewitness Accounts
Help students to think about eyewitness accounts by calling on their knowledge of detective shows and stories. How do detectives find out what has happened? How do they get all sides of a story? Help students make the connection between getting multiple perspectives and evaluating those accounts.

RESPONSE NOTES As students read, have them think about what would be going through John's head as he discovers that the ship is going to sink. Encourage them to jot down what his thoughts might have been.

During

Ask students to think about what is *not* told in this story. How would the story change if it were told by someone else—possibly a passenger in another class of the ship? Discuss some ideas with students to help them draft an eyewitness account from another perspective.

* Do students' drafts use first-person point of view consistently?

* Do students include details not found in John Thayer's account, yet seem credible?

Response Notes

younger boys than he were being kept from the boats. John knew that on this, maybe the last night of his life, he was considered a man.

At 12:45 A.M. John hugged his mother good-bye, watched her step into a lifeboat, and hurried to the deck on the other side of the boat with his father and Milton. The roar of the steam was deafening. Sailors sent rockets arcing high into the sky to try to attract passing ships. The ship's orchestra was still playing in the background. People were screaming. A surging crowd separated John and Milton from John's father.

* What do you think John was thinking while all this was going on? Jot down a few thoughts that might go through someone's head at this point.

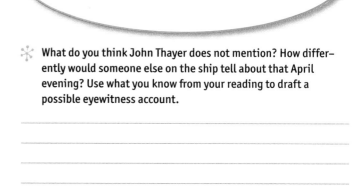

* What do you think John Thayer does not mention? How differently would someone else on the ship tell about that April evening? Use what you know from your reading to draft a possible eyewitness account.

_____

_____

_____

_____

_____

_____

The author's perspective on a subject determines what information is presented.

68 LESSON 19

After

WRITING SUPPORT

Using First-Person Point of View

Point out that John Thayer's own account, *The Sinking of the S.S. Titanic*, is told in the first person. The narrator, John, uses *I* and *me* because he's telling the story from his own point of view. This retelling of John's story by Phillip Hoose is told in the third person, using *he, she,* and *they,* except when quoting John's actual words and thoughts. Explain that a first-person account reflects only what the narrator knows and sees. Remind students that they should write their accounts using *I* and *me* to reflect the first-person point of view.

READING/WRITING CONNECTION Have students find other eyewitness accounts of important events. Good sources are newspaper and magazine articles, as well as autobiographies of historical figures. Ask students to write an analysis of what makes the eyewitness account interesting and to consider the value of a contribution from a primary source.

There can be many versions of a story. The viewpoints of people involved in the event will vary, depending on who they are and how they were involved. People studying the event might look at it from the vantage point of their own special interests, such as science or history. Some authors might want to make a point about social injustice or other concerns that they have.

Critical reading requires that you understand and evaluate information. As you read the rest of John Thayer's story, underline or highlight places where you can tell what he's *thinking*. Make notes about what he might be *feeling*.

"John Thayer: Becoming a Man Aboard the *Titanic*"
from *We Were There, Too! Young People in U.S. History* by Phillip Hoose

As one side of the ship continued to list, John and Milton climbed to the upper deck and looked down onto the scene. They had few choices, and none of them was good. They thought about trying to fight their way aboard one of the last two lifeboats, but it looked like those boats would be crushed under the ship anyway. John wanted to slide down a rope, leap into the water, and swim for a lifeboat, but Milton convinced him to wait to jump until the water was close to the deck. The two climbed onto the deck railing as the water drew nearer. "So many thoughts passed so quickly through my mind! I thought of all the good times I had had, and of all the future pleasures I would never enjoy; of my Father and Mother; of my Sisters and Brother . . . It seemed so unnecessary, but we still had a chance, if only we could keep away from the crowd and the suction of the sinking ship."

When the water reached them, John and Milton shook hands and wished each other luck. Milton jumped first, and then John sat on the rail, placed his feet outward, gulped as much air as he could, and leaped. He and the *Titanic* went down at about the same time. "The shock of the water took the breath out of my lungs. Down and down I went, spinning in all directions." John stayed under for at least a minute and then struggled to the surface, popping up just in time to see the great ship split in two. Then the suction dragged him under again. Swimming with all his might, he broke the surface with his hand and grabbed onto an object. It was an overturned lifeboat. Soon twenty-seven other passengers were clinging to it as well.

They hung on in the freezing sea for five hours, singing hymns and trying to keep talking, until they were rescued by sailors from the ocean liner *Carpathia*. John was able to climb the rope ladder by himself. At the top of the ladder, the first face he saw was that of his mother. Hours later, they realized John's father had not survived. ❖

Students will compare and contrast eyewitness accounts in order to see multiple perspectives of a historical event.

BACKGROUND KNOWLEDGE
Share this knowledge about the subject of the second selection: Passenger Ruth Becker, her mother, brother, and sister were headed back to the United States from India, where they had been missionaries. Her father planned to join the family later. "After their rescue Ruth and her family traveled safely to Michigan. They were joined by Ruth's father a year later. Ruth went to college, married, raised a family, and taught school. She lived to age 90," according to Jennifer Kilpatrick, who wrote the *National Geographic* story students will read.

VOCABULARY
steward assistant to passengers on a ship

distress confused anxiety

frantically in a hurried and disorganized manner

somber sadly serious

bow the front part of a ship

stern the back part of a ship

To help students understand *bow* and *stern,* refer to a model or cutaway of the ship (see page 60 for suggestions).

Before

CRITICAL READING SKILL
Comparing Different Versions As students have already learned, different points of view provide different accounts of the same events. Critical readers compare different versions and think about where the accounts differ. This helps them evaluate the source.

As students read, they may notice differences in the facts presented. For example,

John Thayer says that the ship had about an hour before sinking after hitting the iceberg. Richard Wormser reports that Andrews said the ship had two hours. Encourage students to think about why there might be these discrepancies.

RESPONSE NOTES Tell students to look for words and phrases that indicate Thayer's personal feelings and thoughts, such as "They thought about trying to

fight their way aboard," and "So many thoughts passed through my mind. . . ." Have them highlight those words and phrases and make notes about what they think John was feeling.

WRITING SUPPORT

Tone Remind students that while the account is from John Thayer's or Ruth Becker's point of view, the tone of the account should be that of an official report. Refer students to the official report they wrote on page 63.

Quick Assess

✴ Do students' reports use one perspective consistently?

✴ Do the reports include only the information that Ruth or John could know?

✴ Is the tone appropriate for an official report (formal, factual)?

Ruth Becker was only 12 when she boarded the *Titanic*, along with her mother, brother, and sister. As you read, note how this account compares to John Thayer's.

Response Notes

"I Survived the *Titanic*" by Jennifer Kilpatrick

"My mother had just gone to bed when she was awakened by the engines stopping," described Ruth. Their steward told Mrs. Becker to get on deck. "We had to climb five flights of stairs to a room full of women," Ruth recalled. "They were all weeping—in all states of dress and undress. Everyone was frightened—no one knew what would happen to them. But I was never scared. I was only excited. I never for one minute thought we would die." . . .

On deck, the crew fired distress rockets. Mrs. Becker sent Ruth back to their cabin for blankets. Ruth returned to find officers loading women and children in a nearby lifeboat. "One officer grabbed my sister, another carried my brother into the lifeboat and yelled, 'All full!' My mother screamed. They let mother on, but they left me behind.

"My mother yelled at me to take the next lifeboat, and before I knew it, an officer picked me up and dumped me into a boat." . . .

Officers frantically loaded the remaining lifeboats. Passengers prayed. The band played somber hymns. The lights went out as the ship split apart. People screamed and jumped overboard. First the bow went down quietly—then the stern sank. ✧

Ruth was later reunited with her entire family.

✴ Imagine that either Ruth or John had to write an official report about the sinking of the *Titanic* and the rescue of passengers. Draft the beginning of the report. Remember to include only what she or he would know. Capture only the perspective that you would get from one or the other of these two survivors.

_____

_____

_____

_____

_____

_____

_____

> Comparing versions of an event helps you piece together the whole picture.

During

You may want to read aloud the passages to emphasize the drama of the narratives. As students read the last part of John Thayer's story, they should think about his thoughts and feelings. After reading, students can discuss their impressions and reactions before going on to the next account.

Discuss with students the differences between Ruth's story and John's and possible reasons for the differences. Then ask students to take on the perspective of either Ruth or John to draft the beginning of an official report about the sinking and rescue.

After

READING/WRITING CONNECTION

Have students interview eyewitnesses to get their account of an event at school, such as a performance, an election, a celebration, or even an emergency drill. After they've recorded at least two versions of the event, have students write an analysis comparing the different accounts.

Focusing on Language and Craft

The beauty of poetry lies in how poets shape and use language to create feelings and images. Often, poetry is able to convey more images with fewer words than prose. That's because poets use certain techniques that help them craft ideas into an effective piece of writing.

In this unit, you're going to read a number of poems about different sports. You will also look at the **figurative language** in the poems. You will learn to recognize and use techniques such as the following:

- metaphor
- word choice
- simile
- sensory language
- imagery

71

Literature

ASSESSMENT To assess student learning in this unit, see page 231.

Students will analyze the use of metaphor to understand how comparisons contribute to a poem's meaning.

BACKGROUND KNOWLEDGE

Invite students to share what they know about karate or other types of martial arts. Point out that karate is a particular kind of martial art, or style of self-defense, from the island of Okinawa, near Japan. It also incorporates elements of Chinese martial arts. Have students who are studying karate or any other martial art describe some of its features and, if possible, demonstrate simple movements or forms.

VOCABULARY

crane a long-legged, long-necked bird that wades in marshes and wetlands and soars over open areas

lofty high; soaring

Show students a picture of a crane and discuss how someone doing karate might resemble a crane in flight.

LESSON 21 METAPHOR

Many students are now studying martial arts, such as *tae kwon do, aikido,* and *karate*. Perhaps you are, too. Read this poem by Jane Yolen. Notice that she repeats some words and phrases. Mark those sections. Write what you think about the poem in the **Response Notes**.

Karate Kid by Jane Yolen

Response Notes

Repeating "I am" makes the poet sound powerful

I am wind,
I am wall,
I am wave,
I rise, I fall.
I am crane
In lofty flight,
Training that
I need not fight.

I am tiger,
I am tree,
I am flower,
I am knee,
I am elbow,
I am hands
Taught to do
The heart's commands.

Not to bully,
Not to fight
Dragon left
And leopard right.
Wind and wave,
Tree and flower,
Chop.
    Kick.
        Peace.
           Power. ❖

Before

CRITICAL READING SKILL

Understanding Metaphor Have students listen as you read the poem aloud. Tell them that as they listen, they should picture the things the speaker compares. Explain that these comparisons are carefully crafted to give the poem a sense of rhythm and balance, similar to the movements of karate. Be sure to model intonation, enunciation, and pacing as you read slowly, emphasizing the repeated phrase "I am."

During

PERFORMING THE POEM Go over the instructions on page 73 with students. Then organize the class into groups to practice and perform the poem. After each group has performed, discuss what the performances had in common as well as how they were different. Point out that poems can be "open to interpretation"— different readers may see and respond to different things in the same poem.

PERFORMING THE POEM

Your teacher will organize the class into small groups to read and act out the poem. Each group will organize its own performance.

✳ Here are the instructions for each group:

- Read the poem aloud together, as a group.
- Mark up the poem, underlining any words you don't quite understand.
- Discuss any parts or words you don't understand.
- Talk about words for which you may understand one meaning, but you don't understand how it is used in the poem or story, "Dragon left and leopard right," for example.
- Decide who the speakers and actors will be.
- Decide what actions your group will use to dramatize the poem. Some may speak their lines or strike poses while other students read the lines. They may read lines individually, in pairs, or as a whole group.
- Practice!

✳ Perform the poem for the class. Be attentive while other groups are performing. After the performances, discuss the choices that each group made. Emphasize the effective choices made by each group.

UNDERSTANDING METAPHOR

You may already know the word **metaphor.** Here are a few examples of metaphors that do not come from this poem:

- "I am hawk."
- "Paul Bunyan was a mountain."
- "The moon is a coin."

✳ Work with a partner. Describe how

- a person might be thought of as a hawk
- Paul Bunyan might be considered a mountain
- the moon and a coin are alike

ABOUT THE POET

Jane Yolen is an award-winning author and poet who has written more than 250 books for both children and adults. She is most well known for her fantasy and science fiction stories. Her picture book *Owl Moon* won a Caldecott medal in 1988.

Yolen was born in 1939 in New York City and spent most of her childhood there and in Connecticut. She wrote her first book of poems while attending Smith College, where she won several awards for poetry and journalism and wrote the lyrics to her senior class musical. She published her first children's book at the age of 22. For more information, see http://www.janeyolen.com.

METAPHOR   Before reading the metaphors on page 73, review the comparisons in "Karate Kid." Explain that the statements aren't literal. The speaker isn't really the wind, a wall, or a wave. The metaphors are images that help the reader understand what the poet is saying. Review the characteristics of a hawk (a large predatory bird with keen eyesight and sharp talons) and, if necessary, explain who Paul Bunyan is (a giant lumberjack featured in several tall tales). Then have students work in pairs to discuss the meaning of each metaphorical statement. Afterward, have partners share their responses with the class.

WRITING SUPPORT

Analyzing the Statement Before students write their paragraphs about the poem (page 74), discuss the statement by breaking it down into smaller chunks.

Underline the phrase *tranquility in the midst of conflict or danger* and discuss the definition of *tranquility* (peace, calmness). Then underline the phrases *control our bodies, minds, and emotions; avoid conflict; defend ourselves;* and *protect others* and discuss how the phrases relate to the poem.

TEACHING TIP

Collaboration   For the second writing prompt, have students use the Think-Pair-Share technique:

1. **Think** Have students think about a metaphor from "Karate Kid."

2. **Pair** Have students discuss the metaphor with a partner and write notes about what it makes them see or think.

3. **Share** Have students share their written responses with the class.

Quick Assess

In the performance

✳ Did readers speak clearly and slowly, maintaining eye contact? Did they read their lines dramatically?

✳ Did actors' movements depict the images in the poem?

In the writing

✳ Did students define *metaphor* accurately?

✳ Did students identify a metaphor in "Karate Kid"? Did they explain what it made them think or see?

✳ Did students demonstrate an understanding of how the poem connects to the statement? Did they use words from the poem to show how it supports the statement?

✳ From your discussion, write what the word *metaphor* probably means. Robert Frost said it meant talking about one thing in terms of another, for example, saying the moon is (like) a coin. Notice that the word *like* does not appear in the examples of metaphor on page 73.

✳ What do the three words "I am tiger" make you think or see in your mind? Look for other metaphors in "Karate Kid." Choose one and tell how it helps you think about ideas beyond the words.

Here is a statement of what some people who practice karate believe: "We seek tranquility in the midst of conflict or danger and strive to control our bodies, minds, and emotions to be able to avoid conflict when possible, defend ourselves when necessary, and protect others when able."

✳ Write a paragraph about how you think the poem "Karate Kid" supports that statement. When you write, try to use some of the words in the poem.

A metaphor can help the reader access ideas beyond the literal meaning of the words.

After

READING/WRITING CONNECTION   Give each student an index card. On one side, have students write three metaphors to describe themselves, using the sentence starter "I am a/an/the ___." Instruct students to save their metaphors for possible use in poems they will write later in the unit.

Y ou have already learned something about metaphor. Now you
will read a poem that makes very definite comparisons by using a
particular kind of **metaphor** called a **simile.**

Read the poem "Skiing" by Bobbi Katz. Put check marks next to
lines that help you see images in your mind.

Skiing by Bobbi Katz

Skiing is like being
part of a mountain.
On the early morning run
before the crowds begin,
my skis make
        little blizzards
as they plough
        through untouched powder
to leave fresh tracks
        in the blue-white snow.
My body bends and turns
        to catch each
bend and turn
        the mountain takes;
and I am the mountain
and the mountain is me. ❖

Response
Notes

✳ Do a quickdraw of the poem in the space below. Underline the
   parts of the poem you included in your drawing.

Students will study figures of
speech and learn the difference
between metaphor and simile.

BACKGROUND KNOWLEDGE
Ask students if they have ever skied
or have seen skiing on TV. Invite
those who have skied to describe the
experience. Was it fun? Scary? Cold?
Have students who haven't skied tell
whether they'd like to try it, and why
or why not.

ABOUT THE POET
As a young child, Bobbi Katz started
writing poetry by listening to jazz
songs on the radio and making up
lyrics to them. Since then, in addition
to writing children's books, she has
worked as a fashion editor, a social
worker, a radio talk-show host, a
teacher, and a house cleaner. For
more information, see:
http://www.bobbikatz.com/bio.htm.

Before

During

CRITICAL THINKING SKILL
Understanding Simile Review the definition of *metaphor*. Then remind students
that *similes* use the words *like* or *as* to
show how two things are *similar.* Copy the
metaphors from *Daybook* page 73 onto
the board, and then change each one into
a simile—e.g., *I am like a hawk. Paul Bunyan was as big as a mountain. The moon is
as shiny and bright as a coin.* Then invite
students to suggest additional similes to
write on the board.

SIMILE Read "Skiing" aloud, telling
students to pay particular attention to
the beginning and ending lines of the
poem. Ask students to find a simile.
(Skiing is like being part of a mountain.)
Then ask students to find a metaphor.
*(I am the mountain and the mountain is
me.)* Then have partners work together to
complete the prompts.

PERFORMING THE POEM
Reread the poem, modeling proper volume, speed, and phrasing. Use gestures
and voice to show how the flow of the
poem mimics the movements of skiing.
Then go over the guidelines on page 76
and have groups practice and perform
the poem.

Differentiation Invite students who need extra support to use the metaphors in "Karate Kid" to practice writing similes—e.g., *I am like a tiger. I am as fast as the wind.*

WRITER'S CRAFT

Print Conventions Point out the indented lines of the poem and ask: *Why do you think the poet set the text this way?* (To make it zig-zag back and forth, like the tracks of a skier.) Explain that poets often set the text of a poem in a special way to achieve a certain effect.

Quick Assess

✳ Do students understand the difference between the simile at the beginning and the metaphor at the end?

✳ Do students' similes use the words *like* or *as* to describe a skier?

Look at the underlined parts of the poem to identify any metaphors that you drew. Remember that a metaphor shows characteristics of one thing by using words associated with something else.

✳ Explain the differences between the lines "Skiing is like being part of a mountain" at the beginning of the poem and "I am the mountain and the mountain is me" at the end of the poem. Discuss your answers with a partner.

_____

_____

_____

✳ You probably recognized the last lines as metaphors. You may see the first line as a metaphor, too, which it is. A metaphor that uses the word *like* in the comparison is a special kind of metaphor called a **simile.** Think of your experiences skiing or watching skiing on television. What similes can you think of to describe a skier?

_____

_____

_____

PERFORMING A POEM

Reread "Skiing." Get into the same group you were in when you performed "Karate Kid" in Lesson 21. Review the guidelines that tell you how to perform a poem. (See page 73.)

✳ For this advanced performance, add four more items to the list:

■ Show confidence when you're in front of the class.

■ Wait for the audience's attention before you begin.

■ Stay near each other when reading or acting.

■ After the applause, take a bow.

Practice your performance of "Skiing," then dramatize it for the class. After all the groups have performed, talk about how your second performance was either better than or not as good as your first.

> The power of poetry comes from how well the poet uses figurative language, such as similes and metaphors.

After

READING/WRITING CONNECTION

Have students write a short poem about their favorite sport or activity, using at least one simile and one metaphor. Provide an example:

> *Playing soccer is like*
> *dancing on the grass.*
> *I am a shooting star,*
> *streaking across the field.*

Suggest that students place line breaks and indents in ways that give their poems rhythm and shape. Then have students illustrate their poems and display them in the library or other common area.

Wen you read, do you see pictures of what you're reading about? This is a strategy that good readers use. It is called **visualizing.** We learn about things by making pictures in our minds. We call these pictures **images.** The use of it in poetry is called **imagery.**

Read "The Swimmer" by Constance Levy. Notice the images you make as you read. Put check marks next to lines that help you "see" the swimmer and the setting of the poem.

Response Notes

The Swimmer by Constance Levy

The sun
underwater
makes chains of gold
that rearrange
as I reach through.
I feel at home
within this world
of sunlit water, cool and blue.
I sip the air;
I stroke;
I kick;
big bubbles bloom as I breathe out.
Although I have no tail or fin
I'm closer than I've ever been
to what fish feel
and think about. ❖

✳ Reread the lines that you marked. In the **Response Notes** column, draw pictures of the images that these lines of poetry help you see. When you finish, choose two or three of the images you drew. Explain how the poet's language helps you *see* the swimmer.

Students will analyze a poem to understand how a writer creates vivid word pictures and how a reader connects with those images.

BACKGROUND KNOWLEDGE
Ask students if they like to swim, and ask volunteers to explain why or why not. Invite students who have been in both a pool and a natural body of water to compare the experiences. Which do they enjoy more? Why? How is the water different?

ABOUT THE POET
Constance Levy has written several critically acclaimed poetry books and has been published in *Cricket* and *Spider* magazines. Her book *Splash! Poems of the Watery World* won the Lee Bennett Hopkins award in 2003. In 2004, she was inducted into the Writers Hall of Fame of America.

Before

CRITICAL READING SKILL
Visualizing Imagery Revisit the poem "Skiing" on page 75. Read the line *my skis make little blizzards*. Ask: *What do the words make you see?* Invite a volunteer to draw a picture on the board. Explain that these words are an example of imagery—language that helps you visualize, or create an image in your mind. Then have students close their eyes as you read "The Swimmer" aloud. Tell students to listen for specific words that create images and to try to visualize what is being described.

During

VISUALIZING SWIMMERS
Have students discuss the images they drew and wrote about on page 77. Then, to help students come up with other images to describe a swimmer, ask: *Have you ever seen a swimming race on TV? Have you ever watched children playing in a pool?*

Collaboration Students can work in small groups to write their poems, using the Round Robin technique. Have students sit in a circle. The first student chooses one of his or her swimming images to start the poem. Have the next student add another image, and so on.

WRITER'S CRAFT

Rhyme Point out that many poems contain rhymes. Sometimes the rhymes are obvious; sometimes they're not. Ask students if they noticed the rhymes in "The Swimmer." Then read the poem aloud, stressing the rhyming words *(through/blue; out/about; fin/been)*. Have students underline the rhyming words as they listen.

Quick Assess

✳ Did students write strong images of swimmers?

✳ Do students' poems use imagery to help a reader visualize swimming?

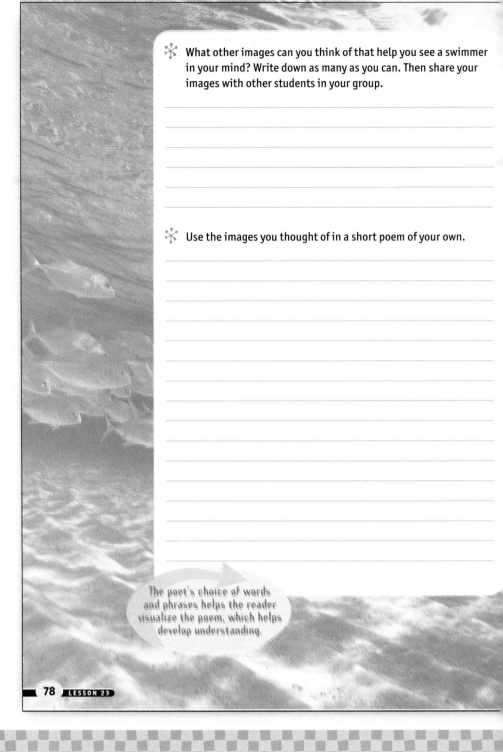

✳ What other images can you think of that help you see a swimmer in your mind? Write down as many as you can. Then share your images with other students in your group.

✳ Use the images you thought of in a short poem of your own.

The poet's choice of words and phrases helps the reader visualize the poem, which helps develop understanding.

After

ART CONNECTION   Have students use one of the poems in this unit or another poem with strong imagery to create a painting or drawing. Students can then share their artwork with the class and explain how it illustrates the images in the poem.

LISTENING/SPEAKING CONNECTION   Have students choose another poem by Constance Levy or a poet of their choice to read to a partner. Partners can then discuss the imagery in the poem and what they visualized as they listened to the words.

Choosing just the right words for a poem is an important part of a poet's work. You've seen how poets use words in metaphors and similes. Sometimes **word choice** is very important, such as in the poem by Robert Francis about a base stealer during a game of baseball.

As you read the poem, notice the words that the poet uses to tell how the base stealer moves. Underline them.

Response Notes

The Base Stealer by Robert Francis

Poised between going on and back, pulled
Both ways taut like a tightrope-walker,
Fingertips pointing the opposites,
Now bouncing tiptoe like a dropped ball
Or a kid skipping rope, come on, come on,
Running a scattering of steps sidewise,
How he teeters, skitters, tingles, teases,
Taunts them, hovers like an ecstatic bird,
He's only flirting, crowd him, crowd him,
Delicate, delicate, delicate, delicate—now! ❖

✳ Look at the words you underlined. Write about these words. Which part of speech are most of the words? How do they show a base stealer at work? Do they speed up the poem or slow it down?

_____

_____

_____

_____

_____

_____

_____

_____

_____

_____

_____

Students will look closely at how a poet uses specific nouns and vivid verbs and examine the role of word choice in conveying precise images and meaning.

BACKGROUND KNOWLEDGE
Ask students who are familiar with baseball to explain base stealing—i.e., how it's done and when a player might try to do it.

ABOUT THE POET
Robert Francis (1901-1987) was an American poet and novelist whose style has been compared to Robert Frost and Emily Dickinson. He won the Poetry Society of America's 1939 Shelley Memorial Award.

VOCABULARY
poised balanced in readiness, waiting

taunts teases; insults

ecstatic extremely happy; joyful

flirting behaving in a tempting way

Ask students for examples of when someone might appear poised (in an interview), give a taunt (when feeling threatened), feel ecstatic (after acing a test), and flirt (when trying to gain someone's attention).

Before

CRITICAL READING SKILL
Word Choice Tell students: *In a poem, every word counts. A strategic reader notices the words that a poet uses because each word carries a great deal of meaning.* Remind students that as they read "The Base Stealer," they should think about each word and ask themselves: *Why did the poet choose this particular word?*

During

MARKING THE TEXT Remind students that they should read with their pens or pencils in hand. In this case, they should circle the verbs that show action.

VIVID VERBS After students have read "The Base Stealer," point out that it contains a lot of specific, or *vivid*, verbs. Write the line *How he teeters, skitters,* *tingles, teases* on the board. Then change it to "How he stops, walks, stands, pauses." Ask: *Which gives you a clearer picture?* Help students brainstorm more vivid verbs. Make a list of students' favorite sports on the board and invite students to call out specific verbs associated with each sport.

WRITER'S CRAFT

Poetic License Ask: *What's grammatically incorrect about the long sentence in "The Base Stealer"?* (It's a run-on sentence; it doesn't have a clear subject and verb; it isn't punctuated correctly.) Ask: *Why do you think Robert Francis took poetic license with sentence mechanics in this poem?* (So the sentence would mirror the action in the poem.) To show how the sentence "moves" like the base stealer, you might read the poem aloud as a volunteer dramatizes the action.

EXTRA SUPPORT

Differentiation Before writing their poems, students who need extra support may benefit from working with you or a partner to create a word web of vivid verbs associated with the topic they chose. Encourage students to express their ideas orally before they write.

Quick Assess

* ✳ Do students' poems contain vivid verbs and other carefully chosen words?

* ✳ Did students convey an image?

✳ You probably have noticed that the poet used a lot of verbs, or action words, in the poem. Below are some of the verbs from "The Base Stealer." Make notes about as many of them as you can, either drawing the actions or describing them in other words:

teeters

tingles

taunts

teases

skitters

hovers

Did you notice that this poem is all one sentence? It is not a conventional or traditional sentence, but it works like one sentence. When a poet bends the rules a bit, it is called **poetic license.**

✳ Try writing a poem about an athlete setting a record. Use verbs that are vivid and specific. You may wish to use a thesaurus to help you find dramatic word choices. If you want, try to write the poem in one sentence, as Robert Francis has done.

> Poets use vivid and specific verbs to help readers see and feel the action of a poem.

After

APPLYING THE SKILL To practice analyzing word choice, have students read another poem about baseball, such as the classic "Casey at the Bat" by Ernest Lawrence Thayer. Students can work with a partner or in small groups to discuss the poet's choice of words and to identify vivid verbs.

LISTENING/SPEAKING CONNECTION Have students read aloud the poems they wrote, as their classmates listen carefully for vivid verbs. Challenge the audience to list as many of the verbs they heard as possible.

In "Foul Shot," poet Edwin A. Hoey used many verbs, as Robert Francis did in "The Base Stealer." Hoey also used language that appeals to your senses, which is **sensory language.**

As you read the poem, mark where the poem uses sensory language. Underline those words and phrases.

Response Notes

Foul Shot by Edwin A. Hoey

With two 60's stuck on the scoreboard
And two seconds hanging on the clock,
The solemn boy in the center of eyes,
Squeezed by silence,
Seeks out the line with his feet,
Soothes his hands along his uniform,
Gently drums the ball against the floor
Then measures the waiting net,
Raises the ball on his right hand,
Balances it with his left,
Calms it with fingertips,
Breathes,
Crouches,
Waits,
And then through a stretching of stillness,
Nudges it upward.

The ball
Slides up and out,
Lands,
Leans,
Wobbles,
Wavers,
Hesitates,
Exasperates,
Plays it coy
Until every face begs with unsounding screams—.

And then
    And then
        And then,
Right before ROAR-UP,
Dives down and through. ❖

Students will use figures of speech, imagery, and precise language to write an original poem based on a model sports poem.

BACKGROUND KNOWLEDGE

Ask students who are familiar with the game of basketball to describe the rules and to help you explain a foul shot. (In a basketball game, physical contact between players on opposing teams during play is against the rules. When there is contact, the player who was touched is said to have been "fouled" by the other player. When a player has been fouled, he or she gets to take a "free throw"; the player stands at the foul line and gets one or two chances, depending on the type of foul, to shoot a basket.)

Before

CRITICAL READING SKILL
Sensory Language Draw a chart on the board with the following headings: *Sights, Sounds, Smells, Tastes, and Feelings.* Title the chart "At the Game." Then ask students to think about a time they watched or played in an exciting basketball game (or other sport). Have students list words to describe what they saw, heard, smelled, etc. (school colors, flashing scoreboard, loud buzzer, screaming crowd, buttery popcorn, hard bleacher seats). Write the words in the chart and point out that these are examples of sensory language. Say: *Paying attention to sensory language when you read helps you "experience" a poem.*

LISTENING TO THE POEM Read the poem aloud. Have students close their eyes and imagine they are in the stands. Afterward, ask them to jot down what they saw, heard, and felt as they listened to the poem.

Edwin Hoey is best known as the former editor of *READ, Weekly Reader's* middle school classroom magazine. During the 36 years that he wrote for, edited, and managed the magazine, Hoey introduced many young readers to the works of such young-adult fiction authors as Robert Cormier, Lois Lowry, Walter Dean Myers, Jerry Spinelli, and Katherine Paterson. Every year, the National Council of Teachers of English (NCTE) gives an award in his name, honoring an outstanding middle school English teacher.

TEACHING TIP

Collaboration Have students use the Interview technique to share their responses to the writing prompt:

1. Partners read their responses to each other and explain why they chose the verbs they did.

2. Students present their partners' responses to the class and explain why their partner chose the verbs.

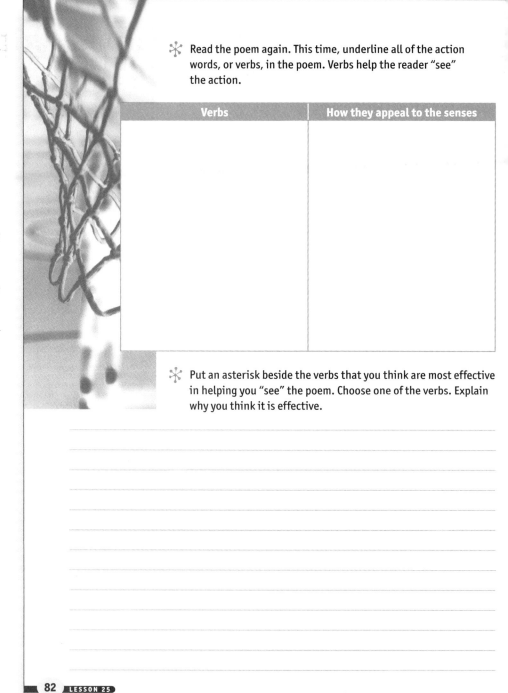

✳ Read the poem again. This time, underline all of the action words, or verbs, in the poem. Verbs help the reader "see" the action.

Verbs	How they appeal to the senses

✳ Put an asterisk beside the verbs that you think are most effective in helping you "see" the poem. Choose one of the verbs. Explain why you think it is effective.

During

SENSORY VERBS Have students tell which words they underlined on page 81 and which sense(s) the words appeal to—for example, *solemn boy* (sight); *gently drums* (sound); *soothes his hands along his uniform* (touch). Point out that sensory language often includes strong verbs. Ask: *How does the verb "soothes" appeal to the senses?* (It helps you "feel" the soothing softness of the uniform.) Then have students complete the chart and the writing prompt.

After

LISTENING/SPEAKING CONNECTION Hold a "Sports Poetry Slam" and invite another class to be the audience. Have your students perform their poems and, after each performance, provide an opportunity for the audience to ask questions and to say what they liked about the poem.

WRITE A POEM

✳ Working alone or with a group, list as many names of sports as you can. Use a large sheet of paper, leaving a lot of space between names of sports. Consider including sports other than the usual team sports, like cross-country, skating, dancing, or cheerleading. For each sport listed, create a web of words associated with that sport. Remember to use verbs and images. Use a different color for each sport.

From the big list, choose one sport with which you have experience to serve as the subject of a sports poem you will write. Copy the web for your sport in this space.

EXTRA SUPPORT

Differentiation Students who need extra support creating their word web can start with words from "Foul Shot" or the other poems in this unit. Then help students brainstorm their own words about a sport by giving them prompts such as: *What does the court/field/room look like? What sounds do you hear? How does your body feel? What comparisons can you make to other experiences or places?*

✳ Expand the word web with your own experiences in that sport. Use a second color for these words and phrases. Here you can be specific, making notes about "a time when I . . ."

WRITING POETRY 83

FURTHER READING For additional opportunities to analyze the language and craft of poetry, students may enjoy reading more sports poems from the following books:

Opening Days: Sports Poems, selected by Lee Bennett Hopkins. Harcourt Brace and Company, 1996.

Motion: American Sports Poems, edited by Noah Blaustein. University of Iowa Press, 2001.

This Sporting Life: Poems about Sports and Games, edited by Emilie Buchwald & Ruth Roston. Milkweed Editions, 1998.

WRITING SUPPORT

Language and Craft Review the guidelines for writing a poem.

❋ Point out that the beginning of a poem, like a story, should draw the reader in; the middle should elaborate, build suspense, or develop an idea through details; the ending should leave the reader feeling satisfied—it should make a point or offer a conclusion to the action.

❋ Remind students to choose words that create images for the reader to visualize, and encourage students to use sensory language that helps the reader experience what is being described.

❋ Review the definitions of *metaphor* and *simile*.

Quick Assess

❋ Do students' poems have a clear beginning, middle, and end?

❋ Did students use colorful adjectives, vivid verbs, important details, and strong imagery?

❋ Did students include metaphors and similes?

❋ (optional) Do students' poems have rhythm? Did students effectively use rhyme, line breaks, indents, or other conventions?

Sensory language is a technique that poets use to make their poems effective and memorable.

❋ Next, follow the guidelines listed below for writing your sports poem. Consider writing your draft on a separate sheet of paper and then copying the final poem into your *Daybook*.

■ Create a beginning, a middle, and an end for your poem.

■ Use colorful adjectives and vivid verbs.

■ Include important details and create interesting images.

■ Use at least a couple of similes or metaphors. You might also consider using rhyme, rhythm, and line design.

Studying an Author

It was simply what I always wanted to do, from childhood: what I did best, loved best. I have never wanted to do anything but write. To shape, to create and compose, to shed light, to perceive and pass on. —Lois Lowry

Where do writers get their ideas? Most writers will tell you that it's a good idea to "write what you know," that the subjects for writing come from life experiences. In many of Lois Lowry's novels, you get glimpses of people in Lowry's family, flashes of places where she has lived, and memories of events she has experienced. But Lowry also charts new worlds that grow out of her imagination.

In this unit, you'll take a close look at Lois Lowry's writing, which includes more than twenty novels, two of them Newbery Medal winners. You'll think about where she gets ideas, as well as the types of issues she explores in her stories. By studying an accomplished author, you will learn how to communicate your thoughts as stories. Your stories will reflect who you are and what you know and imagine.

UNIT 6 STUDYING AN AUTHOR

Lessons 26-30, pages 86-100

UNIT OVERVIEW

In this author study of Lois Lowry, students examine where the author gets her ideas and how authors' experiences influence their writing.

KEY IDEA

Writers draw on their experiences in life. Knowing an author and his or her experiences helps a reader explore the author's themes and appreciate the author's craft.

CRITICAL READING SKILLS

by lesson

26 Studying an author

27 Reading an excerpt inspired by photographs

28 Reading an excerpt that uses imagination

29 Exploring ideas through fiction

30 Understanding the author's experience through the author's words

WRITING ACTIVITIES

by lesson

26 Write about a significant personal experience.

27 Write a story about a photograph.

28 Write about a future world.

29 Compare *The Giver* and *Gathering Blue.*

30 Write a book blurb for an author.

Literature

- ***A Summer to Die*** by Lois Lowry (novel excerpt)

This story of how Meg copes with her sister Molly's terminal cancer is based in part on the author's own experiences.

- ***The Silent Boy*** by Lois Lowry (novel excerpt)

Inspired by photographs, this novel is set in the early 1900s and is told from the perspective of four-year-old Katy.

- ***The Giver*** by Lois Lowry (novel excerpt)

Jonas struggles in a community of sameness when he is assigned the prestigious job of the Receiver of Memory and learns that long ago, people had choices they no longer have.

- ***Gathering Blue*** by Lois Lowry (novel excerpt)

This companion novel to *The Giver* presents a society that has regressed to a way of life filled with indifference and savagery.

- ***"The Remembered Gate and the Unopened Door,"*** Sutherland Lecture, Chicago Public Library, April, 2001, Lois Lowry

This speech provides insights into Lowry's view of herself as a writer.

ASSESSMENT See page 232 for a writing prompt based on this unit.

Students will examine how personal experiences influence an author's message and will make connections to their own personal experiences in their writing.

BACKGROUND KNOWLEDGE

Tell students that *A Summer to Die* has its roots in Lowry's own experience of losing her older sister, Helen, to cancer when both were young girls. Activate students' prior knowledge by reading the opening quote about childhood on *Daybook* page 86. Then ask students to think about an important conversation they have had. Without asking them for details of their conversations, ask volunteers if they think they could write about them. Discuss possible pros and cons of sharing your challenges in the form of a novel that others would read. While students may be reluctant to share the specifics of their own conversations, they should be able to relate to the issue in general terms.

VOCABULARY

solitary alone

After discussing the meaning of *solitary,* ask students to talk about how the author might use that word in a story about someone who is dying. After they've read the story, have them talk about the statement, "Dying is a very solitary thing."

So often we remember childhood as a continuous bright street of cheerful pleasure, the bright street where we roller-skated over a geography of sidewalks memorized by our feet. The softball games at sunset, the smell of fresh-baked oatmeal cookies, the soft voices of mothers, the stern-but-just wisdom of fathers, and endless summer days – the nights flickering with fireflies – and the clean sheets at bedtime. We forget the dark paths that all children must travel as well.
—from Lois Lowry's speech, *Bright Streets and Dark Paths,* Brown University, March 2001

Life experiences shape our thoughts about the world. Lowry draws on her experiences and the relationships within her family for her stories. In her first novel, *A Summer to Die*, Lowry centers the story on the death of a sister. Thirteen-year-old Meg realizes that her older sister Molly is dying of cancer. Lowry had a similar experience when her sister Helen died of cancer.

In the following excerpt, Meg and her father have a conversation about what is happening to Molly. As you read the dialogue, underline passages that you think are powerful. Reflect on their meaning in your **Response Notes.**

from **A Summer to Die** by Lois Lowry

Dad drove me to Portland, and on the way he tried to tell me what it would be like at the hospital. "You have to keep reminding yourself," he said, "that it's still Molly. That's the hard thing, for me. Every time I go in her room, it takes me by surprise, seeing all that machinery. It seems to separate you from her. You have to look past it, and see that it's still Molly. Do you understand?"

I shook my head. "No," I said.

Dad sighed. "Well, I'm not sure I do either. But listen, Meg—when you think of Molly, how do you think of her?"

I was quiet for a minute, thinking. "I guess mostly I think of how she used to laugh. And then I think of how, even after she got sick, she used to run out in the field on sunny mornings, looking for new flowers. I used to watch her, sometimes, from the window."

"That's what I mean. That's the way I think of Molly, too. But when you get to the hospital, you'll see that everything is different for Molly now. It will make you feel strange, because you're outside of it; you're not part of it.

Response Notes

Before

CRITICAL READING SKILL

Studying an Author As students read this selection, they will focus on powerful passages and reflect on what makes them so. Ask students to note as they read whether this selection sounds like a real conversation and why.

RESPONSE NOTES
Remind students to underline the parts of the selection that move them. Have them write down their reflections on why they think these parts are so powerful. (See *Daybook* page 225 for tips on active reading.)

LISTENING TO THE LANGUAGE

This is a particularly good selection to read slowly, allowing the quietness of the scene and the power of the words to sink in. Help students see that because the scene sounds natural it draws you in, making you believe that Lowry knows how such an experience really feels. After you have read, have students reread silently, "listening" to the power of Lowry's language.

"She'll be very sleepy. That's because of the drugs they're giving her, so that she'll feel comfortable. And she can't talk to you, because there's a tube in her throat to help her breathe.

"She'll look like a stranger to you, at first. And it'll be scary. But she can hear you, Meg. Talk to her. And you'll realize that underneath all that stuff, the tubes and needles and medicines, our Molly is still there. You have to remember that. It makes it easier.

"And, Meg?" He was driving very carefully, following the white line in the center of the curving road.

"What?"

"One more thing. Remember, too, that Molly's not in any pain, and she's not scared. It's only you and I and Mom, now, who are hurting and frightened.

"This is a hard thing to explain, Meg, but Molly is handling this thing very well by herself. She needs us, for our love, but she doesn't need us for anything else now." He swallowed hard and said, "Dying is a very solitary thing. The only thing we can do is be there when she wants us there." ❖

✳ Describe what strikes you as the most powerful moment in the exchange between Meg and her Dad. Explain what you learned in that moment about the experience Meg, Molly, and their mom and dad were going through.

_____

_____

_____

✳ Explain how the moment you described makes you feel.

_____

_____

_____

✳ What details in the passage convey the message that Meg's father is trying to express?

_____

_____

_____

ABOUT THE AUTHOR

Lois Lowry has written more than 20 novels, including two Newbery Medal winners, *Number the Stars* and *The Giver*. Lowry moved around often as a child because her father was in the military. Her varied experiences and interests have resulted in books that deal with a wide variety of topics and settings. Many of her themes, however, are consistent: the importance of connecting to others, the need for all of us to find a place where we belong, and the importance of memory as something that comes from the past but affects how we live our lives in the present. To find out more about Lois Lowry, visit her website at www.loislowry.com.

EXTRA SUPPORT

Rereading Have the students read the selection at least twice and compare what they notice in the first and second readings. Relate this to the experience of listening to an unfamiliar song. Ask students: *When you hear a new song, do you understand its meaning the first time you hear it, or do you need to hear it several times for the meaning to sink in?* Help them understand that reading can be like listening to a song: a reader may need to read something more than once to understand what the author is saying.

Differentiation Some students will benefit from hearing this passage read aloud the first time they encounter it.

During

IDENTIFYING POWERFUL LANGUAGE
Model how to select powerful words or passages and how to extrapolate meaning from them using a think-aloud: *When the father says, "That's the hard thing for me," it shows me that he is having a hard time dealing with seeing his daughter in the hospital. It's also powerful when he says he's surprised every time he sees "all that machinery."*

After students have finished reading, give them several minutes to write or talk about what they have underlined and why. Encourage them to talk about their opinions on whether or not this scene is effective, giving reasons for their opinions.

Choosing a Topic After students have jotted down some conversations and their importance, help them figure out about which one they want to write. Have them ask themselves these questions: *Is this conversation something I want to share with others? Is there enough to say about it? Do I remember the important details? Is the message, or what I learned from it, something that other people could relate to?*

Punctuating Dialogue Remind students how to correctly place punctuation marks in dialogue. (See Writing Support on page 31.)

Quick Assess

✳ Did students underline examples of powerful language in the selection?

✳ Did students include reasons in their Response Notes for why they thought the words and phrases were powerful?

✳ Did students write an effective dialogue?

✳ Like Lowry, you can write about experiences that were powerful moments and ones that helped you learn more about life and relationships. In the Memory Catalog below, list three important conversations in your life. They don't need to be sad or serious.

MEMORY CATALOG

Important conversations	Notes on what is important in each and why

✳ Write a scene that portrays one of the conversations in your Memory Catalog. Remember, when you write dialogue, you use quotation marks to show your reader that someone is speaking.

_____

_____

_____

_____

_____

_____

_____

_____

_____

_____

_____

_____

Writers draw on personal experiences and relationships to bring to life powerful moments.

After

WRITING VIGNETTES Have students use their Memory Catalogs for additional writing assignments. They can create "vignettes," or short scenes, of different events in their lives to create their own memoir project. Remind students of the importance of choosing language carefully to evoke the tone, mood, and feeling of incidents. Each vignette could explore a specific aspect of a writer's craft, such as using visual imagery, figurative language, or dialogue. Students can add to their memoir project over the year, adding photos or illustrations and even revising earlier vignettes, as they gain insight into the significance of what they learned from their important conversations.

Few things give me more pleasure than looking at photographs. To glimpse other lives, caught and captured in moments that live on long after the circumstances of the moment have passed, makes me shiver with imagination. —Lois Lowry from "Acknowledgments" in The Silent Boy

Lois Lowry compares the craft of a writer to a photographer's eye: both must learn to capture details, knowing which things to focus on and which to blur. One of Lowry's novels, *The Silent Boy*, was inspired by a collection of photographs. These photographs—taken of family and others and found in an antique shop—inspired her characters and the events of the novel. A photo introduces the events of each chapter. In the following scene, the narrator, Katy, sees a photograph that reminds her of a summer day when she was four.

As you read the excerpt from *The Silent Boy*, try to imagine the setting. Think about what pictures come to your mind as you read. Underline words and phrases that help you see, hear, touch, taste, and smell the scene. Make notes about the connections you make to your life.

from **The Silent Boy** by Lois Lowry

I peered at the photograph of two solemn little girls, side by side, wearing hats, and gradually I remembered that day at the lake. It was summer. It came to me in fragments, in little details.

Jessie had black shoes, and mine were white.

The air smelled like pine trees.

A cloud was shaped like my stuffed bear. Then its ears softened and smeared, and it was just a cloud, really, not a bear at all (I knew it all along); then, quickly, the cloud itself was gone and the sky was only blue.

And there were fireworks! We were visiting at the Woods' cottage there. Cottage sounded like a fairy tale: a woodcutter's cottage. Hansel and Gretel and their cottage.

But the Woods' cottage was not a fairy-tale storybook one. It was just a house. They invited my family to come to their cottage for the holiday called Fourthofjuly, which I didn't understand, and for fireworks.

I remembered the scent, the sky, the heat, the wide-brimmed straw hats we wore to protect our faces from the sun, and the white shoes and black. The shoes and stockings and dresses—even the hats—were removed, at some point, because my memory told of Jessie and me, wearing only our bloomers,

Response Notes

Students will read a descriptive story based on a photograph to learn how sensory details help create a picture for the reader.

BACKGROUND KNOWLEDGE

Explain that the story is told from the viewpoint of a four-year-old girl. Preview some of the things that Lowry includes in this selection that help you see this through a child's eyes: the reference to *Hansel and Gretel and their cottage, Fourthofjuly, Our mothers rubbed us dry...,* and to the envy Katy feels about the pail "with the bright painted picture printed on its metal side." As they read the selection, have students think about how well Lowry captures the world from a child's view.

VOCABULARY

bloomers loose-fitting women's underwear

fretted worried

reeds tall swamp grasses

scamper to run quickly and playfully

squatting crouching

scolding yelling at; criticizing

Have students think of synonyms for the vocabulary words (for example, *run* for *scamper*). When they find the words in the selection, have them substitute their words. Discuss which word is more effective.

Before

CRITICAL READING SKILL
Reading Writing Inspired by Photographs Help students get an understanding of how and why writers might use photographs as inspiration. Bring in a collection of old photographs, and give students time to browse through them, encouraging each student to select one that is interesting. Ask students to imagine using this photograph as a

prompt for a story. What type of story might the photograph inspire? Ask students to share their chosen photos with a partner and discuss their story ideas. Then have them read the introduction on page 89 and the excerpt from *Silent Boy*.

RESPONSE NOTES Remind students to underline words and phrases in this selection that use sensory language to evoke setting. Students also should note any parts of the story that connect to something they've experienced themselves.

Chunking the Reading The excerpt is long but not difficult. If students struggle to keep focused on their reading, you might want to break up the excerpt into two or three parts and stop to draw a plot line, pointing out the rising tension. You might also stop at intervals to discuss what pictures come to mind as students read. Have students imagine photographs that would capture some of the main events of the story. (Suggested stopping points: before the last paragraph on page 89, before *stealthily* on page 90, and before *It was silent* on page 91.)

Differentiation Use a Five Senses Chart to help students identify sensory language. Have students make a chart with these headings: *Hear, See, Taste, Touch, Smell.* Then have students go back through the selection from *The Silent Boy,* and have them write words and phrases under the appropriate heading. Then review what students have charted and talk about how such charts can help readers picture what's happening in a story.

wading at the edge of the lake. We chased tiny silvery fish—minnows! Someone told us they were called minnows, and we said that to each other, laughing: "Minnows! Minnows!"

After a while we were shivering, even though the day was hot. My fingertips were puckered, pale lavender. Our mothers rubbed us dry with rough towels. Jessie fretted because there were pine needles stuck to her damp feet. We played in the sand at the edge of the lake.

The parents sat on the porch, talking, while Jessie and I amused ourselves, still half-naked in the sunshine, digging with bent tin shovels in the damp sand. Jessie had a pail and I didn't. I pretended that I didn't care about her pail, though secretly I wished it were mine, with the bright painted picture printed on its metal side: pink-faced children building castles, green-blue water, foamed with white, curling behind them.

Stealthily I followed a beige toad that hopped heavily away into the grasses edging the small beach. Soon I could no longer see the toad (I had begun to think of him as "my" toad) but when I waited, silent, I saw the grass move and knew that he had hopped again. I waited, watched. I followed where the grass moved. It was taller than my head, now, and I was surrounded by it and was briefly frightened, feeling that I had become invisible and not-there with the high reeds around me. But the world continued close by. I could hear the grownups talking on the porch, still.

"Where's Katy?" I heard my mother ask, suddenly.

"Jessie where did Katy go?" Mrs. Wood called in an unconcerned voice.

"I don't know." Jessie's voice was not that far away from me.

"She was right there. I saw her just a minute ago." That was my father's voice.

"It's amazing, how quickly they scamper off, isn't it?" Mrs. Wood again. She was using a cheerful voice, but I could tell that now she was worried, and I was made pleased and proud by the worry.

"Katy!" My mother was calling now. "Katy!"

I should call back, I knew. But I liked the feeling of being concealed there, squatting in the moist earth, with the high grass golden above me, being an

During

WRITER'S CRAFT

Word Choice Refer to earlier discussions of the ways Lowry uses precise language and words that relate to the five senses to create a picture for the reader. Remind students that Lowry was inspired by photographs to create this story, and that the narrator's memory is triggered by a photograph. Ask students these questions: *How does the use of vivid words draw the reader into the setting? What pictures linger in your mind after you've read this excerpt? How are the language and details similar and different from those Lowry used in the excerpt from* A Summer to Die?

observer, but hidden. The breeze blew the grass and it closed above my head, creating a small, secret place where I fit. I had already forgotten my toad in the new excitement of being lost to the grownups. So I held still.

"You go that way, Caroline," my father said. "Check over there behind the woodpile and by the shed. I'll look in this direction."

"She wouldn't have gone into the house, would she? She would have had to pass us, to go into the house. We would have seen her. Katy!"

"Jessie, are you sure you don't know where she went?" Mr. Wood sounded angry, as if he were scolding his little girl.

Jessie began to cry. It pleased me somehow, that she was crying. She deserved to cry, because she owned a tin pail with bright paintings on its side.

"Katy! Katy!" My mother's voice was quite far from me now.

"Let's think." Jessie's mother said this. "*Hush*, Jessie." (Jessie was still crying loudly.) "She wouldn't have gone far because she was barefoot. It's stony out there beyond the house. It would hurt her feet."

"Kaaaaty!" It was like a song in my mother's voice, when she called it that way. "Henry," she called to my father, "she isn't over this way."

"Everyone be absolutely quiet for a moment," Mr. Wood commanded. "She might be calling and we wouldn't hear her."

It was silent except for Jessie, who was now howling. In my mind, I scolded Jessie for not obeying her father. "Shhhh," Mrs. Wood said to her angrily, and finally Jessie was quiet.

Now, into that important silence, was when I should have called out. "Surprise!" I should have shouted. "Here I am!"

But I didn't. I waited. There was a bug near my toe, and I watched it waddle across the slick surface of wet earth. I put my hand near it and hoped that it would mount my finger and walk on me. But carefully it found a path around my hand. I began thinking very hard about the bug, and I forgot my family and their worry. I crouched there, and then lay down, slowly curling into the warm mud that was as soft and private as a bed. The sun was hot on my head and back, coming down through the curtain of grass that surrounded me, and things became dreamlike. ❖

⚹ A storyboard helps you keep track of different scenes in passages that you are reading. Use the frames on the next page to sketch three "snapshots" from the scene you just read. Under each sketch write a quote from the text that shows where the idea came from. When you finish, share your sketches and quotes with a partner.

Using a Graphic Organizer: Storyboard Model for students how to make selections for a storyboard, using the opening scene from *The Silent Boy* excerpt: *The first real scene in the story takes place at the lake, with Katy and Jessie chasing minnows and then digging in the sand, while the parents sit on the porch. In the first storyboard frame, I'll draw a picture of the kids digging and the parents on the porch, because that image is clear in my mind. It's also important to what happens in the story.* Give students time to sketch the scenes and encourage them to use a variety of colors to add details. Then invite them to share their storyboards with a partner or with the whole class and to discuss why these scenes are so clear to them.

Reflecting Ask students to reflect on how visualizing a story is helpful to understanding the events. Have them compare experiences of reading a text with pictures and reading a text without them. Can they give examples of how an illustrator's version of a story did or did not coincide with their own?

Storyboard for Scenes

1	2	3

Word Choice Students are asked to imagine what story the picture on page 92 tells. Before they start to write, have them ask themselves these questions: *Who are the people in the photo? What is happening? When and where was the photograph taken? Can I tell who took the picture?* These questions give students a chance to brainstorm words and phrases that focus on creating a visual picture of what they're going to write. Remind students to use sensory language and precise words as they write. You may wish to have students continue their stories on a separate sheet of paper after they have finished their opening paragraphs.

Quick Assess

✳ Did students highlight words and phrases that provide sensory details?

✳ Did they make notes about connections to their lives?

✳ Were students able to sketch vivid scenes based on the selection?

✳ Did students apply the use of visual imagery in their own writing?

✳ Lowry worked from a photograph to imagine the scene you read. Now, it's your turn. Use this scene in the photograph to tell a story. Remember to use visual and sensory details in the way that Lowry used them in her scene.

> Writers use the world around them to get ideas for stories in which they explore people, situations, and issues.

After

WRITE A PERSONAL NARRATIVE

Ask students to bring photographs from home or to locate some in another source that remind them of a personal experience. Have them write a personal narrative based on one or more of those pictures. If students have been working on the memoir project mentioned on page 88, they may want to include the narrative and the photos in that collection.

WRITE A SHORT STORY

Students can write a story based on a postcard, poster, or illustration. Encourage students to use their imaginations to come up with a story based on what they see. (Students can use the Plot Diagram on page 270 to plan their story.) Display the short stories for other students to read during their reading time. Have students respond to the writer on Comment Cards (note cards).

The Giver *begins with a boy on a bicycle, riding through the clean and safe streets of his community to the dwelling where he lives with his happy, cheerful, busy family. It concludes with the same boy riding a bicycle at night—hiding by day—for many miles, through terrible danger. He saves himself—quite literally saves himself; warms and nourishes himself and finds courage—by recalling the stories from the past that have been told to him by an old man.*—from Lois Lowry's speech, *Bright Streets and Dark Paths,* Brown University, March 2001

What kind of world could Lowry be imagining that would have the boy's life change so dramatically? *The Giver* is set in the future. Lowry creates a world of *sameness* where the climate is controlled and the inhabitants' lives are monitored. Each family has two parents, a daughter, and a son, but they are not biologically related; they are developed through careful observation and placement.

As you read the following excerpt, use your **Response Notes** to ask questions about the type of world in which the characters live. List issues that you think Lowry examines in her imagined world.

from **The Giver** by Lois Lowry

Response Notes

"I heard about a guy who was absolutely certain he was going to be assigned Engineer," Asher muttered as they ate, "and instead they gave him Sanitation Laborer. He went out the next day, jumped into the river, swam across, and joined the next community he came to. Nobody ever saw him again."

Jonas laughed. "Somebody made that story up, Ash," he said. "My father said he heard that story when *he* was a Twelve."

But Asher wasn't reassured. He was eyeing the river where it was visible behind the Auditorium. "I can't even swim very well," he said. "My swimming instructor said that I don't have the right boyishness or something."

"Buoyancy," Jonas corrected him.

"Whatever. I don't have it. I sink."

"Anyway," Jonas pointed out, "have you ever once known of anyone—I mean really known for sure, Asher, not just heard a story about it—who joined another community?"

"No," Asher admitted reluctantly. "But you can. It says so in the rules. If you don't fit in, you can apply for Elsewhere and be released. My mother says that once, about ten years ago, someone applied and was gone the next day." Then he chuckled. "She told me that because I was driving her crazy. She threatened to apply for Elsewhere."

Students will read a story about an imagined world and draw conclusions about the society from the text.

BACKGROUND KNOWLEDGE

Share this information about *The Giver*: Jonas, the main character, lives in a community where every aspect of life is controlled. At twelve, children are assigned their lifetime job. In this selection, Jonas is still happy with his world as he waits to find out what his lifetime job will be.

VOCABULARY

Engineer someone who designs or plans things

Sanitation Laborer someone who cleans up garbage

buoyancy ability to float

reluctantly not eagerly

meticulously carefully

weighty serious and important

disposition usual temperament

scrupulously thoroughly

Ask students to brainstorm the qualities an *Engineer* or a *Sanitation Laborer* needs. After reading the selection, ask students how Lowry uses the rest of the words to paint a picture of Jonas's world.

Before

CRITICAL READING SKILL
Reading Writing That Uses Imagination In this selection, students see how an author uses her imagination to create a world. Ask students if they ever imagined the world differently from the way it is. Solicit examples. Ask what inspired them to imagine a different world. Was it a song or movie, a worry or situation beyond their control, or was

it just a flight of fancy? Talk about the genre of science fiction and how it usually depicts a vision of a future world.

RESPONSE NOTES Tell students to write down questions they have about the world Lowry is describing. Have them underline any clues Lowry provides about that world. Tell students that they will be filling in a Drawing Conclusions chart on page 95 after they read the selection, so they should also mark any places in the story that give clues to the issues Lowry is exploring.

WRITING SUPPORT

Empathizing with Characters

Encourage students to picture themselves as one of the characters in the story as they think about their reactions (take on the perspective of the character). What would they feel like if they were one of the characters in the story? Would they be anxious like Asher, or would they trust in the system like Jonas? Why? Have students provide examples from the selection about what the rules for this society seem to be. Then have them discuss what they think of those rules.

"She was joking."

"I know. But it was true, what she said, that someone did that once. She said that it was really true. Here today and gone tomorrow. Never seen again. Not even a Ceremony of Release."

Jonas shrugged. It didn't worry him. How could someone not fit in? The community was so meticulously ordered, the choices so carefully made.

Even the Matching of Spouses was given such weighty consideration that sometimes an adult who applied to receive a spouse waited months or even *years* before a Match was approved and announced. All of the factors—disposition, energy level, intelligence, and interests—had to correspond and to interact perfectly. Jonas's mother, for example, had higher intelligence than his father; but his father had a calmer disposition. They balanced each other. Their Match, which like all Matches had been monitored by the Committee of Elders for three years before they could apply for children, had always been a successful one.

Like the Matching of Spouses and the Naming and Placement of new children, the Assignments were scrupulously thought through by the Committee of Elders.

He was certain that his Assignment, whatever it was to be, and Asher's too, would be the right one for them. He only wished that the midday break would conclude, that the audience would reenter the Auditorium, and the suspense would end.

As if in answer to his unspoken wish, the signal came and the crowd began to move toward the doors. ❖

❋ Write a paragraph describing your reactions and feelings about the type of society in which Asher and Jonas are living. What type of society is this? What do the rules seem to be?

_____

_____

_____

_____

_____

_____

_____

During

ASKING QUESTIONS TO CLARIFY

This is a short enough excerpt for most students to read independently, but many of the ideas and situations are unfamiliar to them. After students have finished reading, ask clarifying questions, such as: *Who are the two main characters?* (two boys: Jonas and Asher) *What are they waiting to find out?* (what their lifetime jobs will be) *How do they feel about it?*

(Asher is scared and nervous, but Jonas seems calm and unworried.) *What kind of world do these characters live in?* (a world where all decisions are made for everyone by the Committee of Elders) Then have them write their paragraph about how they feel about that type of society.

USING A GRAPHIC ORGANIZER

Drawing Conclusions Chart Remind students that *drawing conclusions* means "using what you know to form an opinion about something." Have students review their Response Notes and then fill in the Drawing Conclusions chart (page 95) with quotations from the story and the conclusions they drew from those quotations.

✳ What issues in society does Lowry seem to be exploring through this imagined world? Use the following chart to help you look back at the text and draw conclusions from information in the text.

DRAWING CONCLUSIONS

Quotes from the text	What I conclude

✳ If you could design a future world, what would it be like? Take a minute to brainstorm the characteristics of your society, using the Future-World Chart to prompt your thinking.

FUTURE-WORLD CHART

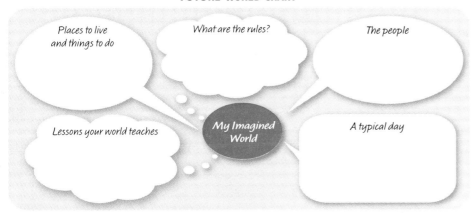

Places to live and things to do

What are the rules?

The people

Lessons your world teaches

My Imagined World

A typical day

✳ Now that you have some ideas of what this world will be like, write a short scene that describes one incident that occurs in this world.

Authors use their imaginations to depict their hopes, dreams, fears, and criticisms of the world in which we live.

Collaboration You may want students to work in pairs or in small groups to brainstorm the Future-World Chart. One student can act as a recorder and write down the rules and other details of the group's future world. The recorder should post the final Future-World Chart where everyone in the group can see it. Then have students work independently to write a scene from the world they have created.

EXTRA SUPPORT
Differentiation Help students understand that the issues that concern society are big questions with which all people struggle: *how to have freedom and still have rules that provide order in society; how children can learn to make their own decisions without having so much freedom that they put their lives in danger; how governments can make rules that are good for everyone.* Lowry uses her imagination to explore these issues.

Quick Assess

✳ Were students able to draw conclusions about key issues, using examples from the selection?

✳ Did students work to design a future world? Were they able to create an effective scene that reflects that world?

After

CONNECTING TO OTHER AUTHORS' WORKS Have students find other books that present a fantasy world. The world can be in the future, such as another science fiction story, or in the past, such as a fairy tale. *The Chronicles of Narnia* by C.S. Lewis, and the Harry Potter books by J. K. Rowling are other popular choices. Ask students to write a list of rules for the society presented in one story. Then meet as a group to share the different sets of rules and discuss what sorts of worlds these authors have created. Ask students if they would want to live in any of them, and why or why not. You may want to have students vote on which of the worlds would be the best/ worst place to live.

LESSON 29 EXPLORING IDEAS THROUGH FICTION

Students will read a story about an imagined world and use a Venn diagram to compare two stories.

BACKGROUND KNOWLEDGE

Explain to students that *Gathering Blue,* also set in the future, is a companion novel to *The Giver;* Lowry wrote it after *The Giver* was published in order to present a different view of the future. Unlike the community in *The Giver,* which sacrifices individual need for the good of society, this community is based on selfishness and savagery— where one's own needs are placed above even the most basic needs of others.

VOCABULARY

cadence rhythmic sound of speech

bickering spiteful quarreling

taunting mocking; teasing

wary cautious; worried

refuse (REF yōōs) garbage

fowls domesticated birds that are used for food, such as chickens

devoured eaten up

forage to search for food

Use the Word Splash blackline master on page 272 to familiarize students with the vocabulary.

There is always a period of time, after I have written a book, before it is published, when I begin to worry that my brain has simply run out and become empty, the way a cookie jar does, and all the good stuff is gone; only a stiff raisin and some stale crumbs left. I worry then that I will never be able to write the next one. —from Lois Lowry's speech, How Everything Turns Away, University of Richmond, March 2005.

Lowry doesn't seem to come up short on ideas, although she worries that she will. Not long after *The Giver* was published, she completed a companion novel, *Gathering Blue.* In it, Lowry explores a different *"what if"* proposition than she did in *The Giver. What if* a society hasn't moved forward technologically as in *The Giver* where everything is controlled and engineered? *What if* the society has become primitive and savage? *What if,* instead of controlling everything, even memory, organized society has collapsed?

As you read the following excerpt from *Gathering Blue,* underline words or phrases that demonstrate the decline of this society compared to the society in *The Giver.*

Response Notes

from **Gathering Blue** by Lois Lowry

With the boy still beside her, Kira paused at the well and filled her container with water. Everywhere she heard arguing. The cadence of bickering was a constant sound in the village: the harsh remarks of men vying for power; the shrill bragging and taunting of women envious of one another and irritable with the tykes who whined and whimpered at their feet and were frequently kicked out of the way.

She cupped her hand over her eyes and squinted against the afternoon sun to find the gap where her own cott had been. She took a deep breath. It would be a long walk to gather saplings and a hard chore to dig the mud by the riverbank. The corner timbers would be heavy to lift and hard to drag. "I have to start building," she told Matt, who still held a bundle of twigs in his scratched, dirty arms. "Do you want to help? It could be fun if there were two of us.

"I can't pay you, but I'll tell you some new stories," she added.

The boy shook his head. "I be whipped iffen I don't finish the fire twiggies." He turned away. After a hesitation, he turned back to Kira and said in a low voice, "I heared them talking. They don't want you should stay. They be planning to turn you out, now your mum be dead. They be putting you in the Field for the beasts. They talk about having draggers take you."

Before

CRITICAL READING SKILL
Exploring Ideas Through Fiction

When writers create fiction, they often start with the thought "What if...?" In this lesson, students are asked to consider three "What if...?" questions about the futuristic society that Lowry created in *The Giver.* Before students read this excerpt, ask them to predict what this other world might be like. As a class, make a list of adjectives to describe the community in *The Giver* as completely as they can from reading the excerpt in Lesson 28. In a second column, list adjectives that mean the opposite. Then ask students to read the excerpt from *Gathering Blue* and make note of how Lowry uses her "What if...?" propositions to create this brutal world.

RESPONSE NOTES Tell students to underline words and phrases as they read that will help them compare the worlds of *Gathering Blue* and *The Giver* in the exercise on page 98. For example, the last sentence of the first paragraph indicates a general loss of order, which is the opposite of the highly regulated society in *The Giver.*

Kira felt her stomach tighten with fear. But she tried to keep her voice calm. She needed information from Matt and it would make him wary to know she was frightened. "Who's 'they'?" she asked in an annoyed, superior tone.

"Them women," he replied. "I heard them talking at the well. I be picking up wood chippies from the refuse, and them didn't even notice me listening. But they want your space. They want where your cott was. They aim to build a pen there, to keep the tykes and the fowls enclosed so they don't be having to chase them all the time."

Kira stared at him. It was terrifying, almost unbelievable, the casualness of their cruelty. In order to pen their disobedient toddlers and chickens, the women would turn her out of the village to be devoured by the beasts that waited in the woods to forage the Field. ❖

❉ Write a paragraph describing your reactions and feelings about the type of society in which Kira and Matt are living. What type of society is this? What do the rules seem to be?

_____

_____

_____

_____

_____

_____

_____

_____

❉ Be the author and write the next scene in *Gathering Blue*.

_____

_____

_____

_____

_____

_____

_____

_____

_____

_____

_____

During

LOOKING FOR EXAMPLES IN THE TEXT As students read, have them think about what types of things show that this world has regressed, or become less civilized, than the world of Jonas. Prompt them to look for things like how the characters talk, what they say about their society, how the people in that world treat each other, and the plans for Kira. Model looking for examples, using a think-aloud: *In the beginning of the passage, Kira hears arguing everywhere. She says that's a constant sound in the village. It doesn't sound like a very nice place to live. They even kick crying children. It doesn't sound like a very civilized place.*

USING A GRAPHIC ORGANIZER
Venn Diagram Have students use their Response Notes from this lesson and Lesson 28 to review their notes about the two worlds Lois Lowry has created. The bulleted list on page 98 will help them focus on details to include in their diagrams. Instruct students to use the overlapping area in the middle to list adjectives describing what the two societies have in common and to use the outer parts of the circles to list adjectives that describe what is different in each society.

WRITING SUPPORT

Comparing and Contrasting

The writing assignment offers plenty about which students can write. Offer students the option of focusing on one part or the other. If they choose the compare/contrast paragaph, the Venn diagram provides an organization for students to use. Students should write a topic sentence that describes their main point (the societies are similar/different), sentences based on notes in the diagram that support their topic sentence, and a concluding sentence that wraps up their discussion. If students choose the second part of the assignment, the topic sentence should state their opinion, followed by examples from the text that support that opinion.

Quick Assess

* Were students able to identify words and phrases that represent the regression of society in *Gathering Blue?*

* Did students describe their feelings and reactions to the selection?

* Were students able to compare and contrast the two worlds presented by Lowry, using a Venn diagram?

* Do students understand how *The Giver* and *Gathering Blue* can be considered companion novels?

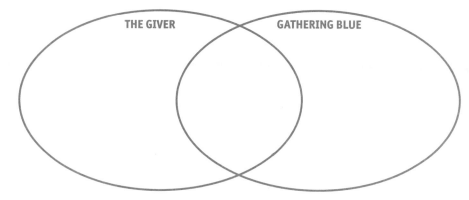

✳ Now that you have read excerpts from *The Giver* and *Gathering Blue*, list the characteristics of each society.
- Compare characters' concerns and fears.
- Compare what life is like.
- Compare the relationships within families.

✳ Write a paragraph that compares and contrasts the two worlds that Lowry imagines. What aspect of these two cultures is most disturbing to you? Tell why.

> Writers use their writing to explore *what if* certain things happened in the world.

After

READING/WRITING CONNECTION

Give students an opportunity to expand one of their scenes into a story. Have them ask "What if...?" questions as they write their stories. Encourage them to list the key issues they are exploring so they can refer to them as they write. Once students have written their stories, set aside time for authors to read them aloud

REFLECTING
Ask the students to consider how Lowry's stories require them to compare her imagined worlds with the real world. Ask them to think about how we all benefit from reading fiction that makes us answer the question "What if...?" Ask them what they've learned about the real world by reading about these imagined worlds.

"*I practiced in my spiral-bound notebooks: making sentences, rearranging them to say the same thing in a different ordering of words, then saying it again in new words so that I could compare the sound, and the way the words looked on the page.*" —from Lois Lowry's speech *The Remembered Gate and the Unopened Door*, Chicago Public Library, May 4, 2001.

Writing was what Lois Lowry always wanted to do. She began to write in elementary school. In the excerpt below, Lowry tells the story of her first typewriter and its importance to her work as a writer.

In your **Response Notes,** note what Lowry reveals about the importance of writing and her purposes for writing.

from "**The Remembered Gate and the Unopened Door**"
The Sutherland Lecture, May 4, 2001

On my thirteenth birthday, my father gave me a typewriter. Today, of course, half the 13-year-olds you know have their own computers. But this was in 1950. And in 1950 this was an astounding gift: a Smith-Corona portable typewriter with smooth dark green keys; and my name was engraved on the case, just below the handle.

Why did he give it to me? I don't know. It may have been simply that he was sick of my sneaking into his office and using <u>his</u> typewriter; maybe he was nervous about the damage I might inflict as I endlessly, noisily taught myself how to type.

But I like to think that he gave it to me because he recognized who I was, and what my dreams were, for the future. And I am <u>immeasurably</u> grateful that he never—never once—leaned over my shoulder, to see what I was doing with my gift.

I used that typewriter through high school and college. It went into a closet, along with my dreams of being a writer, and stayed there, unused, through an early marriage and the arrival of four children. But it came out of storage and was dusted off when I went to graduate school and began to write, in my thirties. I used the old Smith-Corona to write my first book for kids, *A Summer to Die*. I was thirty-nine.

My father was over seventy by then: retired, living in Florida. He sent me a gift to celebrate the publication of that first book, in which he appeared, as Meg's father. It was an electric typewriter.

Response Notes

Students will read an excerpt from an interview with an author to reflect on the writer's craft and identify the techniques that will inform and influence their writing.

BACKGROUND KNOWLEDGE
Explain that some authors like to talk about the actual experience of writing—where their inspirations come from and how they go about getting their ideas down on paper. Invite students to share any experiences they have had with hearing an author speak about writing or anything they've read on the subject. Invite students to consider how reading the author's comments about her craft and her passion for writing might influence their attitudes toward her work.

VOCABULARY

immeasurably impossible to measure

protracted extended; taking place over a long time

vestibule a waiting area or room

Discuss the words and their definitions. Then ask whether the vocabulary words make Lowry's writing more interesting. Have students give reasons for their opinions (such as "*immeasurably grateful* seems to capture the feelings she has about her father's gift better than *very grateful* would").

Before

CRITICAL READING SKILL
Connecting the Author's Life to Her Work In this lesson, students will synthesize the information they have gathered about Lois Lowry from these lessons to get a fuller picture of her background and a greater understanding of her writing. Review with students what they have learned about Lowry so far. Have students create a double-entry journal (a page with two columns) where

they can record on one side what Lowry has said about her writing or demonstrated through her writing. On the other side, students can record what qualities they believe Lowry possesses as a writer.

RESPONSE NOTES
Have students mark places in the text that show how important writing is to Lois Lowry (for example, she loved to write so much as a child that she would sneak into her

father's office to use his typewriter), as well as those that reveal why she writes (she talks about her desire to write for children). Tell students that they will be using these notes to help them write a book blurb about Lois Lowry after they've finished reading.

WRITING SUPPORT

Describing Words If students are not sure where to begin with writing the book blurb, have them start by making a word web. In the center, they should write "Lois Lowry's Writing." In the outer circles, they should write words and phrases that describe the best aspects of Lowry's writing, such as *exciting, vivid, makes me think, easy to read, can't put her books down,* and so on. Remind students to use the double-entry journals they created to help them think of words and phrases to use. Then have students use those descriptions to create a book blurb that would make someone pick up a book by Lowry and read it.

Quick Assess

❉ Were the students able to identify statements in Lowry's speech that demonstrate her passion for writing?

❉ Could they synthesize the information presented about Lowry in this unit into a short bio about Lowry?

❉ Did students make connections between Lowry's life and her writing?

I began—after a protracted education, after interruptions, (sometimes happy ones like the births of babies), and after a few false starts, as a writer for adults. . . . But it was not until I went back and timidly pulled at unopened doors in my past that I realized I should be speaking to children.

I am not certain how I knew I must do that. But it was as if, as a writer, I was still in a passageway, or a vestibule, and had not reached the place I needed to go. ❖

❉ You've been chosen to write about the author for the cover of Lois Lowry's new book. In your critical acclaim, use what you have learned—about Lowry as a person and as a writer—to describe the author and her writing.

❉ What can you use as a lesson from Lowry in your future writing? What have you learned about yourself as a writer through the writing you have done in this unit? Think about the ways in which you work, what you like to write about, and what sources you draw on for ideas.

> Writers use many different sources of information and inspiration to express the purposes and subjects of their writing.

During

CONNECTING TO STUDENTS' OWN EXPERIENCES   As students read Lowry's account of what writing means to her, they should think about how this is reflected in the works of hers they have read. Encourage them to think about how they feel about writing. Ask them to reflect on these questions: *Does reading about Lowry's experience as a writer make me want to write more? Why or why not?* This will help students answer the questions in the second writing exercise on page 100.

After

READING/WRITING CONNECTION
Writing a Letter Ask students to make a list of questions they would like to ask Lois Lowry about her writing experiences. Then have students write a letter to Lowry (see www.loislowry.com for contact information). Review with them the five parts of a letter (the heading, the salutation, the body, the closing, and the signature) and make sure they edit their final copy before sending it to the author.

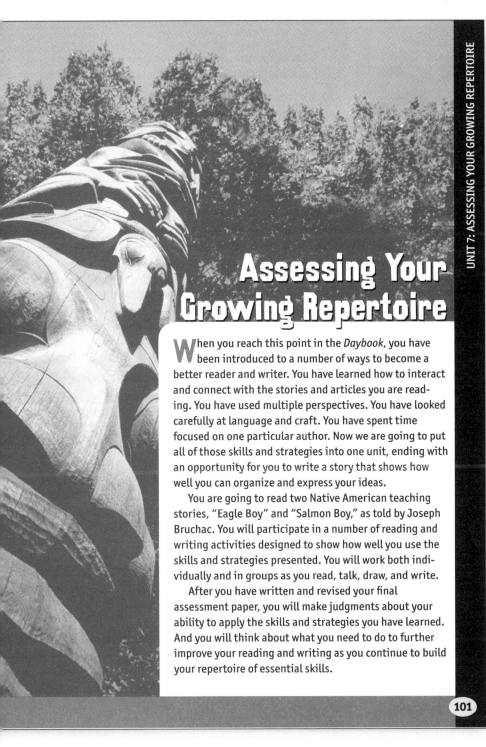

Assessing Your Growing Repertoire

When you reach this point in the *Daybook*, you have been introduced to a number of ways to become a better reader and writer. You have learned how to interact and connect with the stories and articles you are reading. You have used multiple perspectives. You have looked carefully at language and craft. You have spent time focused on one particular author. Now we are going to put all of those skills and strategies into one unit, ending with an opportunity for you to write a story that shows how well you can organize and express your ideas.

You are going to read two Native American teaching stories, "Eagle Boy" and "Salmon Boy," as told by Joseph Bruchac. You will participate in a number of reading and writing activities designed to show how well you use the skills and strategies presented. You will work both individually and in groups as you read, talk, draw, and write.

After you have written and revised your final assessment paper, you will make judgments about your ability to apply the skills and strategies you have learned. And you will think about what you need to do to further improve your reading and writing as you continue to build your repertoire of essential skills.

101

UNIT 7
ASSESSING YOUR GROWING REPERTOIRE

Lessons 31-35, pages 102-116

UNIT OVERVIEW
In this unit, students will use the reading and writing strategies and skills they have studied so far to write a story that will help them (and you) assess whether or not they have mastered the material.

KEY IDEA
This assessment unit provides students with a chance to apply the reading strategies and what they've learned about writing to read new selections and write a story.

CRITICAL READING SKILLS
by lesson

31, 32 Using reading and writing strategies

33 Comparing stories

34 Writing a story

35 Revising and evaluating your work

WRITING ACTIVITIES
by lesson

31 Write a personal response to a story

32 Write about a story's main idea and message

33 Planning a piece of writing

34 Write a story with a message

35 Write a reflection

Literature

- *"Eagle Boy"* from *Native American Teaching Stories* by Joseph Bruchac (Native American folktale)

In this story, a young boy learns a lesson about listening and learning from a wise eagle.

- *"Salmon Boy"* from *Native American Teaching Stories* by Joseph Bruchac (Native American folktale)

In this story, a young boy learns an important lesson about respecting life in all forms.

Students will try out different strategies to make personal connections to a Native American story that is translated from the oral tradition.

BACKGROUND KNOWLEDGE

Talk about how folktales are stories through which different cultures teach their children important lessons about life. Native American teaching stories are folktales that focus on the relationships between human beings and animals. In most stories, the human beings have much to learn from their animal teachers. Invite students to talk about other folktales they've read that use animals as a way of conveying a message, such as Aesop's fables or folktales from Africa.

VOCABULARY

game wild animals, fish, and birds hunted for food

sorrow sadness

troubled worried; bothered

Point out that early societies on every continent hunted wild game for food. Then talk about the words *sorrow* and *troubled*. Ask students what expectations those words set up: *Do you think this will be a happy story, or will there be a problem that needs to be solved?* Then have students read the story to see how these words are used.

In the previous units, you practiced using reading strategies such as making connections to the text and examining the author's perspective. Each lesson focused on one strategy or idea. A successful reader, however, knows which strategy to choose and often uses more than one per selection.

BEFORE YOU READ

You should know that this story is one that Native American parents, aunts, and uncles use to teach their values to their children. Most native people of North America think of animals as beings equal to humans. Stories of animals becoming people and people becoming animals are common. They believe that animals have their own families and traditions and that human beings can learn how to live in harmony with the earth by understanding the animal world.

DURING YOUR READING

Use the Response Notes column to record your ideas and feelings as you read "Eagle Boy." Remember, you can make predictions, write questions, notice what surprises you, and make connections to what you already know.

Response Notes

"Eagle Boy" by Joseph Bruchac

Long ago, a boy was out walking one day when he found a young eagle had fallen from its nest. He picked that eagle up and brought it home and began to care for it. He made a place for it to stay, and each day he went out and hunted for rabbits and other small game to feed it. His mother asked him why he no longer came to work in the fields and help his family. "I must hunt for this eagle," the boy said. So it went on for a long time and the eagle grew large and strong as the boy hunted and fed it. Now it was large enough to fly away if it wished, but it stayed with the boy who had cared for it so well. The boy's brothers criticized him for not doing his part to care for the corn fields and the melon fields, but Eagle Boy did not hear them. He cared only for his bird. Even the boy's father, who was an important man in the village, began to criticize him for not helping. But still the boy did not listen. So it was that the boy's brothers and his older male relatives came together and decided that they must kill the eagle. They decided they would do so when they returned from the fields on the following day.

When Eagle Boy came to his bird's cage, he saw that the bird sat there with its head down. He placed a rabbit he had just caught in the cage, but the eagle did not touch it.

Before

CRITICAL READING SKILL

Using Reading and Writing Strategies Review with students the key reading strategies they have studied in the *Daybook:* interacting with the text, making connections, exploring multiple perspectives, focusing on language and craft, and studying an author. Tell them that they will apply some of these strategies as they read "Eagle Boy," a story shared for generations among Native

Americans. Encourage students to think about the story from the different perspectives of the characters and to make connections between the lesson Eagle Boy learns and similar lessons they have learned in their lives.

At the end of the lesson, students will work in groups of three to five to talk about what they have read. You may want to assign students to groups before

they read. Allow members of each group to support one another if they have questions or difficulty understanding something as they read.

RESPONSE NOTES Review the paragraph under During Your Reading on page 102 and talk with students about the kinds of comments they might write in their Response Notes. You may want to model a think-aloud: *The title of this story*

"What is wrong, my eagle?" said the boy.

Then the eagle spoke, even though it had never spoken before. "My friend, I cannot eat because I am filled with sorrow," said the eagle.

"Why are you troubled?" said the boy.

"It is because of you," said the eagle. "You have not done your work in the fields. Instead, you have spent all of your time caring for me. Now your brothers and your older male relatives have decided to kill me so that you will again return to your duties in the village. I have stayed here all of this time because I love you. But now I must leave. When the sun rises tomorrow, I will fly away and never come back."

"My eagle," said the boy, "I do not wish to stay here without you. You must take me with you."

"My friend, I cannot take you with me," said the eagle. "You would not be able to find your way through the sky. You would not be able to eat raw food."

"My eagle," said the boy, "I cannot live here without you." So he begged the eagle and at last the great bird agreed.

"If you are certain, then you may come with me. But you must do as I say. Come to me at dawn, after the people have gone down to their fields. Bring food to eat on our long journey across the sky. Put the food in pouches that you can sling over your shoulders. You must also bring two strings of bells and tie them to my feet."

That night the boy filled pouches with blue corn wafer bread and dried meat and fruits. He made up two strings of bells, tying them with strong rawhide. The next morning, after the people had gone down to the fields, he went to the eagle's cage and opened it. The eagle spread its wings wide.

"Now," he said to Eagle Boy, "'tie the bells to my feet and then climb onto my back and hold onto the base of my wings."

Joseph Bruchac is well known for his retellings of Native American traditional stories. He has authored more than 70 books for adults and children and edited many anthologies of poetry and fiction. Bruchac draws on what he has learned from his Abenaki [ah buh NAHK ee] community in his storytelling, and he and members of his family work on many projects devoted to preserving Abenaki culture. Joseph Bruchac lives in New York's Adirondack foothills. For more information, go to www.josephbruchac.com.

WRITER'S CRAFT
Anthropomorphic Characters
Many folktales rely on animal characters with human traits to impart important life lessons. Good writers and storytellers are careful when they employ this technique to preserve some of the nature of the animal while giving it human behaviors, such as speech. Help students appreciate how this story manages to do that by discussing what they know about eagles (they are often seen soaring; they are large, powerful, predatory birds; they build their nests at great heights). Then list what the eagle does in the story that a real eagle can't do (talk, fly with a boy on its back). Brainstorm why a storyteller might create a humanlike animal to teach a lesson.

During

is "Eagle Boy." From what I know about folktales, I think it's going to be about a boy who becomes an eagle. I'm going to write that prediction in my Response Notes and then read to find out if my prediction is correct.

Tell students that they will refer back to their Response Notes later to discuss what they have read and what they thought about it.

READ ALOUD AND MODEL USING READING STRATEGIES Folktales lend themselves to oral reading, so you might want to read the story aloud before students read it on their own. As you read, pause to model the strategies for interacting with the text, such as predicting, making inferences, connecting, and reflecting. For example, use a think-aloud to model making inferences: *The eagle says he loves the boy. The boy begs the*

eagle to take him away, saying, "I cannot live here without you." I can tell that the boy loves the eagle, too.

After you have finished the read aloud, ask students to reread the story, using the Response Notes to record their understanding of what they've read.

Differentiation Some students may need support visualizing the fantasy setting of the middle part of the story. Go over the details about Sky Land with students and have them underline the parts of the story that describe the setting, such as "Turquoise Mountain," "[e]verything was smooth and white," and "[t]hey looked like people."

Help students understand that Eagle Boy lives with the eagles for a long time, but once he is able to fly, he becomes eager to explore. It is his curiosity that leads him to break the rule of "Never fly to the South Land."

Before students read the rest of the passage on page 105, have them guess why Eagle Boy isn't supposed to fly to the South Land and have them predict what will happen to him there. Then have students read on to find out if their predictions are correct.

Response Notes

Eagle Boy climbed on and the eagle began to fly. It rose higher and higher in slow circles above the town and above the field. The bells on the eagle's feet jingled and the eagle sang and the boy sang with it:

Huli-i-i, hu-li-i-i

Pa shish lakwa-a-a-a . . .

So they sang and the people in the fields below heard them singing, and they heard the sounds of the bells Eagle Boy had tied to the eagle's feet. They all looked up.

"They are leaving," the people said. "They are leaving." Eagle Boy's parents called up to him to return, but he could not hear them. The eagle and the boy rose higher and higher in the sky until they were only a tiny speck and then they were gone from the sight of the village people.

The eagle and the boy flew higher and higher until they came to an opening in the clouds. They passed through and came out into the Sky Land. They landed there on Turquoise Mountain where the Eagle People lived. Eagle Boy looked around the sky world. Everything was smooth and white and clean as clouds.

"Here is my home," the eagle said. He took the boy into the city in the sky, and there were eagles all around them. They looked like people, for they took off their wings and their clothing of feathers when they were in their homes.

The Eagle People made a coat of eagle feathers for the boy and taught him to wear it and to fly. It took him a long time to learn, but soon he was able to circle above the land just like the Eagle People and he was an eagle himself.

"You may fly anywhere," the old eagles told him, "anywhere except to the south. Never fly to the South Land."

All went well for Eagle Boy in his new life. One day, though, as he flew alone, he wondered what it was that was so terrible about the south. His curiosity grew, and he flew further and further toward the south. Lower and lower he flew and now he saw a beautiful city below with people dancing around red fires.

▶ **104** LESSON 31

After

REFLECTING   Remind students that Native American teaching stories were told to children to help explain lessons they needed to know about life. Ask students to consider why an adult would tell a child the story of Eagle Boy: *What lesson(s) do you think that adult would want the child to learn?* Have students write their thoughts about this on page 107.

COMPARING TEXTS   Have students read another folktale that conveys a message important to young people, such as one of the Anansi tales from Africa or one of Aesop's fables. Ask students to present an oral or written report to compare the pair of stories and their messages. Encourage students to delve into how the stories are told, how effective they are in

conveying the message (or lesson), and why the message is an important one for young people.

"There is nothing to fear here," he said, and flew lower still. Closer and closer he came, drawn by the red fires, until he landed The people greeted him and drew him into the circle. He danced with them all night and then, when he grew tired, they gave him a place to sleep. When he woke next morning and looked around, he saw that the fires were gone. The houses no longer seemed bright and beautiful. All around him there was dust, and in the dust there were bones. He looked for his cloak of eagle feathers, wanting to fly away from this city of the dead, but it was nowhere to be found. Then the bones rose up and came together. There were people made of bones all around him! He rose and began to run, and the people made of bones chased him. Just as they were about to catch him, he saw a badger.

"Grandson," the badger said, "1 will save you." Then the badger carried the boy down into his hole and the bone people could not follow. "You have been foolish," the badger said. "You did not listen to the warnings the eagles gave you. Now that you have been to this land in the south, they will not allow you to live with them anymore."

Then the badger showed Eagle Boy the way back to the city of the eagles. It was a long journey and when the boy reached the eagle city, he stood outside the high white walls. The eagles would not let him enter.

"You have been to the South Land," they said. "'You can no longer live with us."

At last the eagle the boy had raised took pity on him. He brought the boy an old and ragged feather cloak.

"With this cloak you may reach the home of your own people," he said. "But you can never return to our place in the sky."

So the boy took the cloak of tattered feathers. His flight back down to his people was a hard one and he almost fell many times. When he landed on the earth in his village, the eagles flew down and carried off his feathered cloak. From then on, Eagle Boy lived among his people. Though he lifted his eyes and watched whenever eagles soared overhead, he shared in the work in the fields, and his people were glad to have him among them. ❖

AFTER YOU READ

Look at your **Response Notes.** Write a few lines about what this story made you think about and how this story made you feel.

Writing a Personal Response

Remind students to look back at their Response Notes for predictions, inferences, and connections to their own lives. Remind them also to look for any words or phrases they may have marked in the selection itself. Have them consider the story's ending and what it makes them think about in their own lives. Then have students write about this connection at the bottom of page 105.

Collaboration If you assigned student groups before reading, have them meet to discuss "Eagle Boy." If not, assign groups of three to five students to complete the activity on page 106.

Remind students to take turns speaking and to listen to the person talking. Assign the questions at the top of page 106. A recorder should write down the responses. Once the groups have finished discussing the story and come to consensus on the recorder's notes, have groups fill in the chart on page 106.

Each group can select a reporter to share with the rest of the class a summary of the group's discussion.

✳ Get together with your group and talk about the story "Eagle Boy." Below are three questions that might help you as you think and talk about the story. After you have talked with your group, write the group's ideas and your ideas that address these questions.

1 What did you find hard to understand about the story?
2 Why did Eagle Boy go to the South Land?
3 What did Eagle Boy learn from his experience?

What the Group Thought	What I Think Now
1 What the group found hard to understand	1 What I find hard to understand
2 Why the group thought Eagle Boy went to South Land	2 Why I think Eagle Boy went to South Land
3 What the group thought Eagle Boy learned	3 What I think Eagle Boy learned

✳ What did you learn by discussing the three questions with your group? What ideas did you contribute to the group? Did any of you change your minds or understand the story better as the result of what other members said? Write a few sentences that tell what was important about your group discussion.

What do you think children who were told this story were supposed to learn?

Effective readers sometimes use more than one strategy when they read a piece of writing.

USING READING AND WRITING STRATEGIES **107**

Students will decide on the most important part of a Native American story.

BACKGROUND KNOWLEDGE

To help students understand the action of the salmon in this story, share this information: A Pacific salmon spends part of its life in salt water and part in fresh water. Pacific salmon hatch in fresh water, but they migrate to the ocean while still young. When Pacific salmon are fully grown, they leave the Pacific Ocean to reach the place they were born and where they will spawn, or lay and fertilize eggs. After spawning, they die. If the salmon do not spawn, the species will become extinct.

Point out to students that "Salmon Boy" is a story that comes from the Haida [HI duh] people, Native Americans who live in the Pacific Northwest. The Haida have always been expert fishermen, and salmon are central to their culture. Thus, it is essential to the Haida that the salmon be respected.

VOCABULARY

gratitude thankfulness, appreciation

Talk with students about the word *gratitude*. Ask them to think of things for which they are grateful. Then ask how this word might be important in the story.

BEFORE YOU READ

You should know that the story about Eagle Boy is told by the Zuni people who live in the southwestern part of the United States. The next story you will read is from the Haida nation, which is in the Pacific Northwest. The Haida people depend on salmon for their livelihoods. It is very important to the Haida people that everyone in the community respects the salmon.

DURING YOUR READING

Use the **Response Notes** to record your ideas and feelings as you read. You can make predictions, sketch what you visualize, or write connections that you make.

Response Notes

"Salmon Boy" by Joseph Bruchac

Long ago, among the Haida people, there was a boy who showed no respect for the salmon. Though the salmon meant life for the people, he was not respectful of the one his people called Swimmer. His parents told him to show gratitude and behave properly, but he did not listen. When fishing he would step on the bodies of the salmon that were caught and after eating he carelessly threw the bones of the fish into the bushes. Others warned him that the spirits of the salmon were not pleased by such behavior, but he did not listen.

One day, his mother served him a meal of salmon. He looked at it with disgust. "This is moldy," he said, though the meat was good. He threw it upon the ground. Then he went down to the river to swim with the other children. However, as he was swimming, a current caught him and pulled him away from the others. It swept him into the deepest water and he could not swim strongly enough to escape from it. He sank into the river and drowned.

There, deep in the river, the Salmon People took him with them. They were returning back to the ocean without their bodies. They had left their bodies behind for the humans and the animal people to use as food. The boy went with them, for he now belonged to the salmon.

When they reached their home in the ocean, they looked just like human beings. Their village there in the ocean looked much like his own home and he could hear the sound of children playing in the stream which flowed behind the village. Now the Salmon People began to teach him. He was hungry and they told him to go to the stream and catch one of their children, who were salmon swimming in the stream. However, he was told, he must be respectful and after eating return all of the bones and everything he did not intend to eat to the water. Then, he was told, their child would be able to come back to

Before

CRITICAL READING SKILL
Using More Reading Strategies
Remind students of the reading strategies they have studied: interacting with the text, making connections, exploring multiple perspectives, focusing on language and craft, and studying an author. Ask volunteers to review the strategies, reminding students of what they've learned about applying some of these strategies to their reading. Tell them they will be applying these strategies as they read "Salmon Boy," by Joseph Bruchac.

As in Lesson 31, students will work in small groups to talk about what they have read. You may want to assign students to new groups, or you may prefer to have them work in the same groups.

RESPONSE NOTES Remind students to record their thoughts and feelings as they read the story. Encourage them to make predictions, sketch what they're picturing, and make notes about points in the story that connect to their own lives. Point out to students that they will be referring to these notes later on in the lesson.

life. But if the bones were not returned to the water, that salmon child could not come back.

He did as he was told, but one day after he had eaten, when it came time for the children to come up to the village from the stream he heard one of them crying. He went to see what was wrong. The child was limping because one of its feet was gone. Then the boy realized he had not thrown all of the fins back into the stream. He quickly found the one fin he had missed, threw it in and the child was healed.

After he had spent the winter with the Salmon People, it again was spring and time for them to return to the rivers. The boy swam with them, for he belonged to the Salmon People now. When they swam past his village, his own mother caught him in her net. When she pulled him from the water, even though he was in the shape of a salmon, she saw the copper necklace he was wearing. It was the same necklace she had given her son. She carried Salmon Boy carefully back home. She spoke to him and held him and gradually he began to shed his salmon skin. First his head emerged. Then, after eight days, he shed all of the skin and was a human again.

Salmon Boy taught the people all of the things he had learned. He was a healer now and helped them when they were sick.

"I cannot stay with you long," he said, "you must remember what I teach you."

He remained with the people until the time came when the old salmon who had gone upstream and not been caught by the humans or the animal people came drifting back down toward the sea. As Salmon Boy stood by the water, he saw a huge old salmon floating down toward him. It was so worn by its journey that he could see through its sides. He recognized it as his own soul and he thrust his spear into it. As soon as he did so, he died.

Then the people of the village did as he had told them to do. They placed his body into the river. It circled four times and then sank, going back to his home in the ocean, back to the Salmon People. ❖

※ What are your first thoughts and feelings after reading "Salmon Boy"? Review your **Response Notes** for ideas about what to write. Write what this story made you think or wonder about and how it made you feel.

_____

_____

_____

_____

Show, Don't Tell Explain that good writers reveal characters through the characters' actions and dialogue, rather than telling the reader how a character feels. In "Salmon Boy," Bruchac helps us understand the change that takes place in the boy as he grows to respect the salmon. Ask students to find examples in the beginning of the story where the writer shows the boy's lack of respect for the salmon (_he steps on their bodies and throws the bones into the bushes; he rejects good salmon meat, saying "This is moldy," and throws it on the ground_). Then have them find examples from later in the story that show how he's changed (_when he sees the limping, crying salmon child, he finds the missing fin and disposes of it properly_).

During

MODEL USING READING STRATEGIES

As with "Eagle Boy," you may want to read this story aloud and model using the strategies. For example, use a think-aloud to model making connections: _When the boy's mother serves him salmon, and he says, "This is moldy," it reminds me of when I was a child and acted rude to my mother who had prepared a meal that I didn't appreciate._ After you have modeled using one or two of the strategies, ask students to reread the story using the Response Notes to record their own understanding of what they've read.

REFLECTING As students think about "Salmon Boy," have them focus on what stood out in their minds and what lesson they feel the story is teaching. There are many vivid images in this story, and as students choose the one to draw and write about, encourage them to think about what makes it such a strong image and why they think it's important to the story. ▶▶▶

✳ Pick out a part of the story that you thought was important. In the space below, draw what you think this part looked like.

✳ On the lines below, write why you chose this part of the story.

_____

_____

_____

AFTER READING

✳ Get together with your group and talk about the story "Salmon Boy." The questions below might help as you think and talk about it. Record your thoughts about each question on the lines.

1 What was hard to understand about this story? _____

_____

_____

2 What did Salmon Boy learn from the salmon? _____

_____

_____

3 Why do you think Salmon Boy thrust his spear into the old

salmon at the end of the story? _____

_____

_____

> Many teaching stories deal with the survival of the tribe.

After

After students have discussed the story in their groups, invite a reporter from each group to share the keys points of the discussion with the class.

EVALUATING THE STRATEGIES
Ask students to think about the reading strategies they used to read the folktales. Which ones were the most useful? Which ones didn't they use? Have them read another folktale and apply the strategies. Encourage them to list the strategies they try and to keep track of which ones worked best for the folktales. Then have

them report back on what they found. Remind them that when they write stories, good readers will use the same strategies when reading them.

Remember that the Native peoples used these stories because they believed animals had important lessons to teach human beings. What qualities or values do the eagle and the salmon represent for the Native American people in these stories?

The EAGLE represents _____

The SALMON represents _____

✳ Native American parents, aunts and uncles told these stories to help teach children about values and behavior important to their people. In the chart below, write what you think each story was trying to teach.

What Parents Were Trying to Teach in "Eagle Boy"	What Parents Were Trying to Teach in "Salmon Boy"

CHOOSING AN ADVENTURE

If you could have one of these two adventures, which would you prefer? Would you rather be Eagle Boy and learn how it is to live among the eagles in Sky Land? Or would you rather learn how to live in a village in the ocean?

✳ I would rather have the adventures of

_____

✳ Here are my reasons for choosing this adventure:

_____

_____

_____

_____

Students will compare and contrast the message or lesson in two Native American tales and develop ideas for writing a similar story for assessment.

BACKGROUND KNOWLEDGE

Discuss the words *qualities* and *values*. Invite students to share what they know about the words' meanings. Help them understand that all cultures are different, but there are certain *qualities,* or characteristics, that each culture thinks are important. From these qualities come the culture's *values,* the qualities that are essential to the survival of the culture.

Use an example to help students understand. For instance, most cultures believe that the wisdom that comes from learning about the past is necessary to ensure survival—both of the individual and of the culture. Cultures that regard the quality of *wisdom* highly would encourage young people to learn from their elders, the oldest and wisest members of their society.

Before

CRITICAL READING SKILL
Comparing and Contrasting Stories

Review with students the comparing and contrasting they've done in earlier units: of different perspectives in Unit 1 and Unit 4 and of author's techniques in Unit 3. Point out that when they compare things, they think about how they are alike, but when they contrast things, they think about how they are different. In this lesson, students will be comparing and contrasting "Eagle Boy" and "Salmon Boy" and then making a judgment about which of the two adventures they'd rather experience.

WRITTEN RESPONSES While there are no Response Notes in this lesson, there are many places where the students are asked to stop and write in response to a question or a prompt. Tell the students to read the text carefully and to think about what they want to say before they write. Encourage students to seek help if they don't understand what they are supposed to do at any point.

Collaboration You may wish to have students work in the same groups, or you may wish to assign them to new groups. Have one student in each group read the discussion prompts found in the second and third paragraphs on page 112 to keep the discussion focused. After the groups have finished their discussions, invite a reporter from each group to share what his or her group learned.

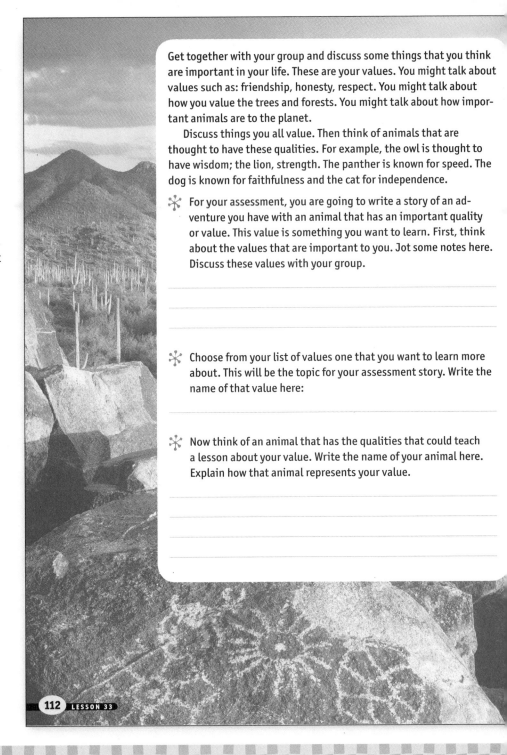

Get together with your group and discuss some things that you think are important in your life. These are your values. You might talk about values such as: friendship, honesty, respect. You might talk about how you value the trees and forests. You might talk about how important animals are to the planet.

Discuss things you all value. Then think of animals that are thought to have these qualities. For example, the owl is thought to have wisdom; the lion, strength. The panther is known for speed. The dog is known for faithfulness and the cat for independence.

✳ For your assessment, you are going to write a story of an adventure you have with an animal that has an important quality or value. This value is something you want to learn. First, think about the values that are important to you. Jot some notes here. Discuss these values with your group.

_____

_____

✳ Choose from your list of values one that you want to learn more about. This will be the topic for your assessment story. Write the name of that value here:

_____

✳ Now think of an animal that has the qualities that could teach a lesson about your value. Write the name of your animal here. Explain how that animal represents your value.

_____

_____

_____

112 LESSON 33

During

SYMBOLIC CHARACTERS Have students talk about what the eagle and salmon represent in the stories. Responses will vary. *(Possible answers: the eagle stands for wisdom, love, the law; the salmon stands for life, learning, respect)* Encourage students to use examples from the stories to support their opinions.

Have students fill out the boxes about what the Native American children were

supposed to learn from the stories and then choose which of the two adventures they would rather experience.

Ask students to explain the reasons for their choices. Then have them meet with their groups.

Finally have students start planning their assessment story. Guide them to choose an animal and a lesson to be learned.

Students can work with a partner or with the group to brainstorm and explore the topic they will write about in the next lesson.

WRITING SUPPORT

Exploring a Topic Ask students to think about the main topics of the two stories they have just read, as well as how the animal characters helped teach the lesson. Have them answer the questions on

Here are some ideas to talk and think about as you prepare to write. Share your ideas with your partner or group. Be sure everyone has a chance to share.

- What value do you want to learn? What animal did you choose to teach it to you?
- What kind of adventure would teach you the lesson you have to learn?
- How does it feel when you change into that animal?
- What happens to you when you are changed into this animal?
  - * Where do you go?
  - * What do you do?
  - * How do you learn your lesson?
  - * How do you feel when you are changed back?

Make notes here:

_____

_____

_____

_____

_____

_____

✻ In the box below, draw a picture of your animal teaching you an important lesson.

```



```

Thinking about values helps readers focus on key issues.

✻ Were students able to compare and contrast "Eagle Boy" and "Salmon Boy"?

✻ Did they indicate which adventure they'd rather have and give reasons for their choice?

✻ Did students choose a value they want to explore in their assessment story?

✻ Did students choose an animal to teach that value?

✻ Have students completed the planning exercises in this lesson in preparation for writing their assessment stories?

After

page 113 and discuss their answers with a partner or a small group. Students should make notes during their discussions as they get ideas about how their stories will unfold. Once students have ideas about their animal characters, invite them to draw them. Encourage students to use details in their drawings. They may wish to add words to their drawings to describe the characters' strengths.

COMPARING TEXTS Have students compare two other folktales. Have them use a comparison chart to identify the main characters in each story, the characters' qualities, the events of each story, and the values that are being taught. Students can share their findings with a partner, or you may want to make a display of the comparison charts to encourage the class to read some of the stories.

Students will write and share a story for assessment that is based on two Native American tales that present a message or teach a lesson.

TEACHING TIP

Collaboration As students work in small groups to give feedback on each other's papers, remind them to use the list of characteristics of an outstanding story as their criteria for evaluating the work. Remind them of the procedures for a small group review:

✳ Take turns reading their stories aloud to the group.

✳ Tell what they like about each story after it is read.

✳ Give helpful suggestions for how the writer might improve the story, using the criteria on this page.

You are now ready to write your story for the assessment. Your main character has already been transformed into an animal. On a separate sheet of paper, write about an adventure that the main character has with the teacher animal. The character must learn the lesson taught by the animal. (Remember that the teacher and the learner are now the same type of animal.)

SHARING THE FIRST DRAFT WITH YOUR PARTNER OR GROUP
Meet with your partner or group to share the first draft of your story. Before you read each other's papers, consider these criteria for a successful story.

An outstanding story will

✳ identify the value that the main character is going to learn.

✳ explain how the main character meets the animal that is to teach the lesson.

✳ explain how it feels for the main character to transform into an animal.

✳ describe the adventure, telling
- where the main character goes
- what the main character does
- how the main character learns his or her lesson
- how the main character feels when he or she is changed back

✳ use an interesting selection of words.

✳ use a variety of sentence types: simple, compound, complex.

✳ use correct punctuation, capitalization, and spelling.

Read your story aloud to a partner or a small group. Listen carefully to each story. At the end of each story, tell what you liked about it. Use the list in the box above to help give constructive feedback.

As your group talks about your story, make notes so that when you revise it, you will remember what they suggested.

Setting criteria for writing helps in drafting and revising.

Before

CRITICAL WRITING SKILL
Writing a Story You might want to review the elements of a story covered in Unit 3. Students will need to establish a setting for the story, introduce the main character, and create a situation in which she or he shows the need to learn an important lesson.

During

WRITING THE FIRST DRAFT
As students begin working on their stories, remind them to use the planning notes they made in Lesson 33. Refer them to the list of characteristics of an outstanding story found on page 114. Tell students that the important part of creating a first draft is getting their ideas down on paper. They will have time to revise and correct their story later.

After

APPLYING THE FEEDBACK
Make sure students take notes as they get feedback from you and from their classmates. Have them review the feedback and decide what they want to focus on as they revise their work. Then have students turn to Lesson 35 to complete their stories.

REVISING AND EVALUATING YOUR WORK 35 LESSON

Reread the list of criteria for an outstanding paper on page 114. Using your notes, review your draft carefully to decide how you can improve it.

Now make a clean copy of the final draft of your story. Remember to give it a title that hints at the story.

A FINAL REFLECTION

As you worked through this book, you have had many opportunities to learn and practice skills and strategies to become a better reader and writer. You have developed and practiced five essential strategies for critical reading and writing:

- Interacting with the text
- Making connections
- Exploring multiple perspectives
- Focusing on language and craft
- Studying an author

You have read a lot of stories, poems, and essays, using such skills and strategies as predicting, questioning, summarizing, visualizing, and reflecting.

In the reflection on page 116, consider how much you have improved as a reader and writer through your work with this first half of the Daybook. Think about the elements and skills that you still need to practice to become a more effective and confident reader and writer.

Students will evaluate their goals and reflect on their progress toward becoming stronger readers and writers.

Before

CRITICAL WRITING SKILL
Revising and Evaluating Your Work
Remind students that the stories they are writing will be used as a writing assessment, an opportunity to show what they have learned.

First have students look at the notes they made regarding the feedback they've received on their stories. Other members of their group may have made some sug-gestions that they do not want to follow. Be sure students know that they have the final say. Have students reread their story to decide what changes they're going to make and how to go about making them.

During

REVISING AND CREATING THE FINAL DRAFT
Once students have decided on the final content of their stories, have them create their final versions. Remind them to focus on sentence fluency (the way the words flow from one another) as well as the conventions of writing (grammar, mechanics, usage, and spelling). ▶▶▶

✳ Write a paragraph reflecting on how you have improved and what you can do to become an even stronger reader and writer.

> Reflecting on progress provides guidelines for improvement.

After

Have each student make a clean copy of his or her story, reflecting on the last changes made while doing so. Then have the students read their stories again to make sure they have corrected all errors. You may want to allow students to read each other's stories for errors. Once students have made their corrections, remind them to give their stories titles.

SETTING GOALS   Have students set specific goals for improving their reading and writing skills. Encourage them to be specific in their goals and to write them down in their writing folder or notebook. Prompt them to think about these questions: *Which reading strategies are hard for me? Which ones would I like to learn more about? What parts of my writing could use*

improvement? How will I go about improving those writing skills?

Periodically, encourage students to submit regular progress reports on their progress toward those goals.

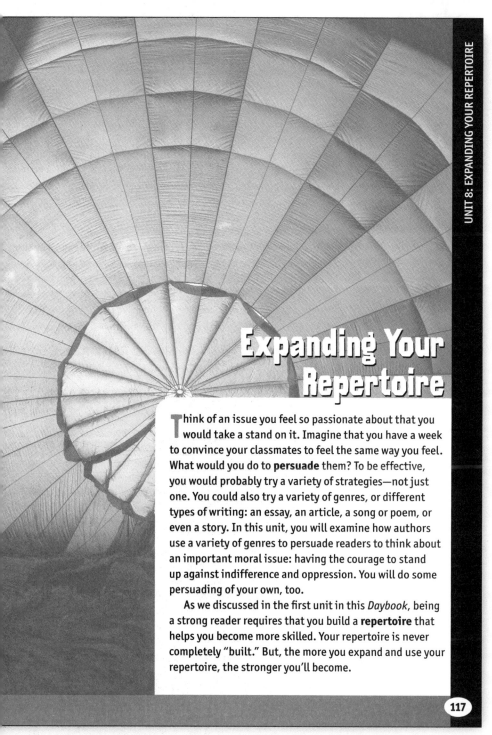

UNIT 8
EXPANDING YOUR REPERTOIRE

Lessons 36–40, pages 118–130

UNIT OVERVIEW
Students build on the basic strategies they have learned as they read about people who stand up against indifference and oppression.

KEY IDEA
Good readers recognize persuasive writing and consider both the author's perspective and their own in order to make informed decisions.

CRITICAL READING SKILLS
by lesson

36 Interacting with the text

37 Making connections

38 Exploring multiple perspectives

39 Focusing on language and craft

40 Studying an author

WRITING ACTIVITIES
by lesson

36 Interact with text by having a written "conversation."

37 Record and compare personal connections to a fictional story.

38 Write how perspective influences personal response.

39 Compare persuasive language and writing styles.

40 Write persuasively.

Expanding Your Repertoire

Think of an issue you feel so passionate about that you would take a stand on it. Imagine that you have a week to convince your classmates to feel the same way you feel. What would you do to **persuade** them? To be effective, you would probably try a variety of strategies—not just one. You could also try a variety of genres, or different types of writing: an essay, an article, a song or poem, or even a story. In this unit, you will examine how authors use a variety of genres to persuade readers to think about an important moral issue: having the courage to stand up against indifference and oppression. You will do some persuading of your own, too.

As we discussed in the first unit in this *Daybook*, being a strong reader requires that you build a **repertoire** that helps you become more skilled. Your repertoire is never completely "built." But, the more you expand and use your repertoire, the stronger you'll become.

117

Literature

- **"The Perils of Indifference"** by Elie Wiesel (speech excerpt)

A speech made at the White House by this author and activist warns against inaction in a world of oppression and suffering.

- **"To You"** by Langston Hughes (poem)

This simple poem bears a hopeful message about our world and our dreams.

- *Farewell to Manzanar* by Jeanne Wakatsuki Houston and James D. Houston (memoir excerpt)

Wakatsuki Houston poignantly reflects on an incident that occurred at age 11, when she'd just been released from a Japanese-American internment camp.

- *The Gold Cadillac* by Mildred D. Taylor (novel excerpt)

In the 1950s, adults speak of dangers in the segregated South, and a young African American girl is amazed at the bravery of those around her.

- *Interview with Mildred D. Taylor*

The award-winning author discusses how oral history, storytelling, and strong family roots inspired her to share her world with others.

ASSESSMENT See page 233 for a writing prompt based on this unit.

36

Summarize the author's message, interact with two types of text, and determine the author's purpose and perspective.

BACKGROUND KNOWLEDGE

Students will read part of a speech by author and activist Elie Wiesel. Gauge prior knowledge of the Holocaust by asking questions such as: *When did the Holocaust happen? Who was involved?* Help students understand that this happened in Europe during World War II (1939–1945) and that Nazis imprisoned and killed millions of people, most of them Jews.

VOCABULARY

peril danger

elicit to bring forth

denounce to publicly speak out against

aggressor a person or country that attacks another

political prisoner a person who has been put in jail for his or her political views

plight a bad or difficult situation

unfettered not restrained

Help students apply each word to the context of a war with which they are familiar, such as the Revolutionary War. Ask: *In this war, who were the aggressors? Who denounced King George III?*

When you engage with text, you don't simply see the words on the page. You **interact** with them. That means you react, remember, wonder about, ask questions, and get ideas. Also, you allow space for the text to "talk back to you," as if you're having a conversation with the text. To do this, you need to listen to what the text has to say. It's important to stop reading sometimes. Give yourself time to think and "listen." Reread sentences or sections if that will help you "converse" with the text. In this lesson, you'll practice not only carrying on your side of the "conversation," but also working hard to "listen" to what the text says to you.

The first excerpt is from a **speech** given at the White House by the author and Nobel Peace Prize winner, Elie Wiesel. One of his most famous books, *Night*, is about his experience surviving in a concentration camp during the Holocaust. In your **Response Notes**, jot down thoughts, questions, or reactions that help you consider what Wiesel **persuades** listeners to think about. Remember, it's okay to pause to think and "listen" as you have a conversation with the text.

Response Notes

from "The Perils of Indifference" by Elie Wiesel

In a way, to be indifferent to that suffering is what makes the human being inhuman. Indifference, after all, is more dangerous than anger and hatred. Anger can at times be creative. One writes a great poem, a great symphony. One does something special for the sake of humanity because one is angry at the injustice that one witnesses. But indifference is never creative. Even hatred at times may elicit a response. You fight it. You denounce it. You disarm it.

Indifference elicits no response. Indifference is not a response. Indifference is not a beginning; it is an end. And, therefore, indifference is always the friend of the enemy, for it benefits the aggressor—never his victim, whose pain is magnified when he or she feels forgotten. The political prisoner in his cell, the hungry children, the homeless refugees—not to respond to their plight, not to relieve their solitude by offering them a spark of hope is to exile them from human memory. And in denying their humanity, we betray our own.

Indifference, then, is not only a sin, it is a punishment. ❖

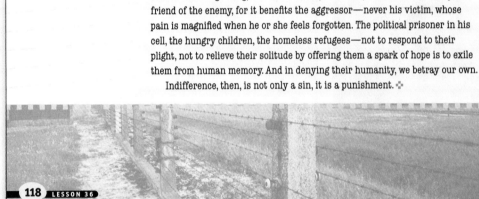

Before

CRITICAL READING SKILL

Interacting with the Text Ask: *When you listen to someone and you don't understand what he or she is saying, what do you do?* (ask questions, ask the speaker to repeat the part you didn't understand) Then help students understand that they can use the same approach when reading. Say: *When you read, try to "listen" to the author's message. Stop to think, ask questions, make comments, or reread the text.*

Then read the first few sentences of the selection and model an interaction. For example, ask: *What does "makes the human being inhuman" mean?* Or ask What does the author mean when he says, *"When I'm suffering, I hate being ignored"? Let's see if these comments can help me understand what Elie Wiesel means about the effect of indifference on others.*

KEY CONCEPT Discuss indifference, or not caring. Ask: *How does someone who feels indifferent react to suffering in the world? What do you think causes indifference? Give examples from other texts or history to support your claim.* (If a person is indifferent to something, he or she is not interested in it and, therefore, not likely to do anything about it.)

✳ In every sentence, Wiesel makes us think. Summarize what you think he is **persuading** us to think about. Is he also asking us to do something?

_____

_____

_____

_____

_____

_____

✳ Choose one sentence from the excerpt that you responded to in your notes—one you don't agree with or understand or one that just makes you think. Record the sentence in the chart below, then have a "conversation" with it. If it would help to reread parts of the speech, to look up something in the dictionary, or to ask another reader a question, do that.

THE SENTENCE	YOUR "CONVERSATION" WITH THE SENTENCE What do you have to say about it? What does it have to say back to you?

ABOUT THE AUTHOR
Elie Wiesel (born in 1928) lost his father, mother, and sister during the Holocaust. After surviving the Auschwitz concentration camp, he became a journalist, professor, and author of more than 40 books. His most famous work was _Night_, an account of his survival. A Nobel Laureate, Wiesel delivered this speech before a group of distinguished guests at the White House on April 12, 1999.

WRITING SUPPORT
Summarizing Help students distill Wiesel's speech by asking: _What is his most important message?_ Remind students to use their own words to summarize the speaker's ideas.

TEACHING TIP
Collaboration Another option to complete the charts on pages 119 and 120 is to have students complete the left side of the chart and then pair up to complete the "conversation" together.

During

RESPONSE NOTES   Review ways to interact with text: circling, underlining, writing questions, etc. As they read, prompt students to continually revisit their notes. For example, ask: _Now that you've read more, has the author answered your question?_ (For tips on marking text, see _Daybook_ page 225.)

INTERACTING WITH THE TEXT
To help students complete the chart on page 119, have a volunteer propose a sentence from the text and write it on the board. For example: _"Indifference is not a beginning; it is an end."_

✳ Solicit a reaction to the sentence from students, such as: _To what is indifference an end?_

✳ Brainstorm what the author might say in response.

✳ List the responses under the sentence, and have students choose one response to complete their chart.

ABOUT THE AUTHOR

Langston Hughes started writing poetry in the eighth grade. Throughout his life, he wrote poems, novels, short stories, and musicals. His large body of work centered on themes relating to the lives of African Americans and feelings of racial pride.

Quick Assess

✳ Do students write in the Response Notes for each text?

✳ Are students able to have a conversation with a text?

Persuasive writing can also take the form of a poem. Read the poem below. In your **Response Notes** jot down questions and reactions as you think about what Hughes is **persuading** you to consider.

Response Notes

"To You" by Langston Hughes

To sit and dream, to sit and read,
To sit and learn about the world
Outside our world of here and now—
    Our problem world—
To dream of vast horizons of the soul
Through dreams made whole,
Unfettered, free—help me!
All you who are dreamers too,
    Help me to make
Our world anew.
I reach out my dreams to you. ✧

✳ Explain what Hughes is persuading us to think about or do.

_____

_____

_____

✳ Choose two or three lines from the poem. Record the lines in the Double-entry Journal below, then have a "conversation" with them.

LINES FROM POEM	YOUR "CONVERSATION" WITH THESE LINES What do you have to say about them? What do these lines have to say back to you?

Interact with the text by making notes, "listening" to what the text says to you, and pausing to think what you have to say back to the text.

After

APPLYING THE STRATEGY

For further application of text interaction, have students use self-stick notes to record their "conversations" with assigned reading from another class. Students can share their notes in small groups. Invite each group to share one question that was answered by "listening" to the text.

LISTENING/SPEAKING EXTENSION

Assign partners a short poem to read and with which to interact. Then have each pair present a "live" interaction for the class. One student plays the Speaker and reads the poem. Another student plays the Listener, stopping the reading whenever he or she has a question or comment.

As you already know, there are many ways to **make connections** as you read. You can connect the text to you, to other texts, and to other things you know about. It 's important to connect *back* to the text, using your connection to better understand and respond to what you read. One way of connecting is to think about the author's intentions. In this lesson, you will work to make connections and use them to understand what the author is saying to you, the reader.

Just as speeches and poems can persuade, *memoirs*—stories about peoples' lives—can be persuasive too. These stories illustrate issues that the author wants the reader to think about. *Farewell to Manzanar* was written by Jeanne Wakatsuki Houston, a Japanese American woman who was sent to live in internment camps during World War II.

In the excerpt below, Jeanne's family has just left the camps to return to "normal" American life. As you read about her return to school, consider what her story **persuades** you to think about. In your **Response Notes** record connections you make that persuade you to "listen" to her words.

from **Farewell to Manzanar** by Jeanne Wakatsuki Houston and James D. Houston

Response Notes

When the sixth-grade teacher ushered me in, the other kids inspected me, but not unlike I myself would study a new arrival. She was a warm, benevolent woman who tried to make this first day as easy as possible. She gave me the morning to get the feel of the room. That afternoon, during a reading lesson, she finally asked me if I'd care to try a page out loud. I had not yet opened my mouth, except to smile. When I stood up, everyone turned to watch. Any kid entering a new class wants, first of all, to be liked. This was uppermost in my mind. I smiled wider, then began to read. I made no mistakes. When I finished, a pretty blond girl in front of me said, quite innocently, "Gee, I didn't know you could speak English."

She was genuinely amazed. I was stunned. How could this have even been in doubt?

It isn't difficult, now, to explain her reaction. But at age eleven, I couldn't believe anyone could think such a thing, say such a thing about me, or regard me in that way. I smiled and sat down, suddenly aware of what being of Japanese ancestry was going to be like. I wouldn't be faced with physical attack, or with overt shows of hatred. Rather, I would be seen as someone foreign, or as someone other than American, or perhaps not be seen at all.

Students will read a poignant memoir, make personal connections to the text, and explore the author's ideas about making false assumptions.

BACKGROUND KNOWLEDGE

To familiarize students with the context of this memoir, ask them to share any prior knowledge of the internment of Japanese Americans during World War II. Explain that shortly after the Japanese attacked Pearl Harbor, the U.S. government ordered more than 110,000 people of Japanese ancestry to move to internment camps. Even though most of these people were U.S. citizens, they were forced to live in isolated camps across the American West.

VOCABULARY

benevolent showing kindness or generosity

guileless not deceitful

illumination understanding; awareness

Oriental Asian; from the region that includes Asia south of the Himalaya Mountains. NOTE: *Asian* is now strongly preferred.

On a world map, point out the Asian continent, the country of Japan, and regions within the U.S. where Japanese Americans were interned.

Before

CRITICAL READING SKILL

Making Connections Review what happens when you make a personal connection to a story: you relate something you've seen, heard, or experienced to something in the text. Then explain that this reading centers on an incident where someone makes an assumption, or thinks something is true about a group of people. Prepare readers to examine how a classmate's false assumption makes the author feel like an outsider.

Prompt students to think about this as they read the excerpt. Ask: *Does this remind you of something that has happened to you or someone you know? What do you think the author wants to say about making this kind of assumption?*

TEACHING TIP

Sensitivity If students seem hesitant to share personal experiences, ask if anyone has witnessed a similar situation portrayed in a movie, play, or book.

Jeanne Wakatsuki Houston lived in the Manzanar internment camp during her teen years. She relates her memories in the critically-acclaimed *Farewell to Manzanar*. On writing the memoir as an adult, Houston says, "I began to make connections I had previously been afraid to see."

EXTRA SUPPORT

Differentiation If students are having difficulty completing the prompt at the bottom of page 122, ask what they would want the girl to think about or do next. Then discuss whether or not the author would agree.

Quick Assess

✷ Did students make connections to the excerpt?

✷ Do students understand what the authors want them to think about (the effects of prejudice and misunderstanding)?

During the years in camp I had never really understood why we were there, nor had I questioned it much. I knew no one in my family had committed a crime. If I needed explanations at all, I conjured up vague notions about a *war* between America and Japan. But now I'd reached an age where certain childhood mysteries begin to make sense. This girl's guileless remark came as an illumination, an instant knowledge that brought with it the first buds of true shame.

From that day on, part of me yearned to be invisible. In a way, nothing would have been nicer than for no one to see me. Although I couldn't have defined it at the time, I felt that if attention were drawn to me, people would see what this girl had first responded to. They wouldn't see me, they would see the slant-eyed face, the Oriental. This is what accounts, in part, for the entire evacuation. You cannot deport 110,000 people unless you have stopped seeing individuals. ✧

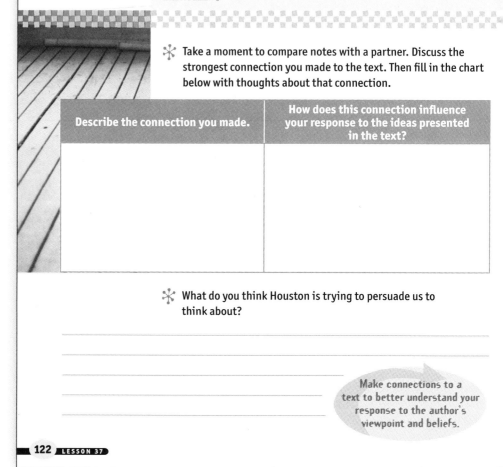

✷ Take a moment to compare notes with a partner. Discuss the strongest connection you made to the text. Then fill in the chart below with thoughts about that connection.

Describe the connection you made.	How does this connection influence your response to the ideas presented in the text?

✷ What do you think Houston is trying to persuade us to think about?

> Make connections to a text to better understand your response to the author's viewpoint and beliefs.

122 **LESSON 37**

During

WRITING SUPPORT Use a think-aloud to model how to complete the chart. For example: *My connection to the text was that I was 16 when I got my first job at a store. Because I was so young, some people thought that I wouldn't do a good job. So, how does this connection influence my response? I feel like the author understands what has happened to me, so I'm more willing to listen to what she has to say.*

Then discuss the importance of the connection. Ask: *If I didn't have that personal connection, would I respond to the text the same way?*

After

APPLYING THE STRATEGY Invite students to brainstorm a list of other stories. Ask them to think about the personal connections they've made to the places, people, or events in the stories. Then have students create their own chart to record elements from the stories and their personal connection to each element.

In Unit 1, you took the approach of *Exploring Multiple Perspectives* when you read. You looked at a character's perspective, the author's perspective, and a historical perspective. Another way to explore multiple viewpoints is to examine different readers' responses. Readers respond differently to texts depending on their life experiences, beliefs, and connections. In this lesson, you'll examine how your own perspective influences your responses. And you'll examine how other readers' perspectives influence their responses.

In addition to nonfiction writing that **persuades** readers to think about an issue, fiction often does the same thing. The excerpt below, taken from *The Gold Cadillac* by Mildred D. Taylor, is told from the perspective of the narrator, a young girl nicknamed 'lois. As you read, consider what the author may be trying to **persuade** readers to think about. In your **Response Notes,** pay special attention to how your perspective influences your understanding and response to the story. Think about who you are and what connections you make to the text because of that perspective.

from The Gold Cadillac by Mildred D. Taylor

Response Notes

Though my mother didn't like the Cadillac, everybody else in the neighborhood certainly did. That meant quite a few folks too, since we lived on a very busy block. On one corner was a grocery store, a cleaner's, and a gas station. Across the street was a beauty shop and a fish market, and down the street was a bar, another grocery store, the Dixie Theater, the café, and a drugstore. There were always people strolling to or from one of these places and because our house was right in the middle of the block just about everybody had to pass our house and the gold Cadillac. Sometimes people took in the Cadillac as they walked, their heads turning for a longer look as they passed. Then there were people who just outright stopped and took a good look before continuing on their way. I was proud to say that car belonged to my family. I felt mighty important as people called to me as I ran down the street. "'Ey, 'lois! How's that Cadillac, girl? Riding fine?" I told my mother how much everybody liked that car. She was not impressed and made no comment.

Since just about everybody on the block knew everybody else, most folks knew that my mother wouldn't ride in the Cadillac. Because of that, my father took a lot of good-natured kidding from the men. My mother got kidded too as the women said if she didn't ride in that car, maybe some other woman would.

LESSON 38

Students will read a story based on the author's own experiences and reflect on how personal perspectives influence the reader's response.

BACKGROUND KNOWLEDGE

Point out that the story is set in the 1950s, when Mississippi was still a segregated state. Point out that during the same time period, Ohio was an integrated state in which, for the most part, African Americans enjoyed the same rights as white Americans.

Up until this time, many southern states had laws that segregated, or kept apart, African Americans from white Americans. For example, African Americans were required to sit or stand in the backs of public buses, were denied service in most restaurants and shops, were prevented from buying homes or property in white neighborhoods, and were barred from attending schools with white children.

VOCABULARY

Negro a person of African descent. NOTE: *African American* is now strongly preferred.

lynch to murder by hanging

heedful carefully paying attention

Check for understanding by asking questions such as: In what state(s) were people heedful of segregation?

Before

EXPLORING MULTIPLE PERSPECTIVES Briefly review what makes up a reader's perspective: experiences, beliefs, and connections to the text. Explain that, as no two readers have the same experiences or beliefs, each reader's perspective is unique.

EXPRESSING PERSONAL PERSPECTIVES Before reading, invite students to write a journal entry expressing their own perspective. Assure students that it will not be judged, graded, or made public.

Have students freely write about each of these questions:

✳ What do you think of segregation or laws that separate certain groups of people?

✳ Have you felt discrimination—someone treating you unfairly because of who you are?

✳ What would you do if someone you cared about wanted to do something dangerous in order to take a stand against discrimination?

ABOUT THE AUTHOR

Mildred D. Taylor was born in Mississippi and raised in Ohio. Like the narrator in *The Gold Cadillac,* Taylor would often visit family in the rural South. Family and setting have served as rich inspiration for Taylor, as many of her novels parallel her own family history. Her most famous novel, *Roll of Thunder, Hear My Cry,* earned the Newbery Medal in 1977.

EXTRA SUPPORT

Differentiation For students who may have difficulty grasping the subtlety of this excerpt, consider reading it aloud, using your tone of voice to emphasize clues to the characters' fear.

TEACHING TIP

Collaboration Encourage students to circle any words with which they are unfamiliar. Students can also underline context clues. When students are finished reading, make a list of words that students circled. Then have students form groups to

✳ choose a word from the list;

✳ infer its meaning from context;

✳ look up the word in a dictionary to confirm that the meaning is correct;

✳ share the meaning with the class.

Response Notes

And everybody laughed about it and began to bet on who would give in first, my mother or my father. But then my father said he was going to drive the car south into Mississippi to visit my grandparents and everybody stopped laughing.

My uncles stopped.

So did my aunts.

Everybody.

"Look here, Wilbert," said one of my uncles, "it's too dangerous. It's like putting a loaded gun to your head."

"I paid good money for that car," said my father. "That gives me a right to drive it where I please. Even down to Mississippi."

My uncles argued with him and tried to talk him out of driving the car south. So did my aunts and so did the neighbors, Mr. LeRoy, Mr. Courtland, and Mr. Pondexter. They said it was a dangerous thing, a mighty dangerous thing, for a black man to drive an expensive car into the rural South.

"Not much those folks hate more'n to see a northern Negro coming down there in a fine car," said Mr. Pondexter. "They see those Ohio license plates, they'll figure you coming down uppity, trying to lord your fine car over them!"

I listened, but I didn't understand. I didn't understand why they didn't want my father to drive that car south. It was his.

"Listen to Pondexter, Wilbert!" cried another uncle. "We might've fought a war to free people overseas, but we're not free here! Man, those white folks down south'll lynch you soon's look at you. You know that!"

Wilma and I looked at each other. Neither one of us knew what *lynch* meant, but the word sent a shiver through us. We held each other's hand.

My father was silent, then he said: "All my life I've had to be heedful of what white folks thought. Well, I'm tired of that. I worked hard for everything I got. Got it honest, too. Now I got that Cadillac because I liked it and because it meant something to me that somebody like me from Mississippi could go and buy it. It's my car, I paid for it, and I'm driving it south."

My mother, who had said nothing through all this, now stood. "Then the girls and I'll be going too," she said.

"No!" said my father.

My mother only looked at him and went off to the kitchen.

My father shook his head. It seemed he didn't want us to go. My uncles looked at each other, then at my father. "You set on doing this, we'll all go," they said. "That way we can watch out for each other." My father took a moment and nodded. Then my aunts got up and went off to their kitchens too. ✦

124 LESSON 38

During

RESPONSE NOTES As students read, help them remain aware of their own perspectives by posing questions. For example: *Though the narrator is frightened by the adults' anxiety, mostly she is puzzled by it. What do the adults know that she doesn't? Does this scene remind you of any situation you've seen or experienced?*

AUTHOR'S PERSPECTIVE Point out how the author uses dialogue to give important information about the characters. For example, one of 'lois's uncles says, *"We might've fought a war to free people overseas, but we're not free here!"* Ask students what they can infer about the uncles. (Possible answers: They are veterans of World War II.) Then pose the question: *Why does the author include this information? How does she want you to look upon these men?* (She wants you to understand the injustice of inequality.)

✳ Through the use of a story, what do you think Taylor is persuading readers to think about? What makes you think so?

_____

_____

_____

_____

✳ How does your perspective influence your response to the story? Do you feel fear for 'lois's family when they make the trip South? Tell why or why not. What new perspectives do you have on indifference or oppression from reading Taylor's story?

_____

_____

_____

_____

✳ Compare what you've written with another classmate's responses. What differences did you notice? What similarities? Fill in the chart below to show how your different perspectives influenced your reading responses.

How your perspective influenced your reading response	How _____'s perspective influenced her/his reading response

Your life experiences, beliefs, and connections to the text shape your perspective on an issue.

WRITING SUPPPORT

Reflecting Use a think-aloud to model how to complete the second prompt. For example: _I've seen racial discrimination, but I've never feared traveling to visit family (or friends) in another state. Now I see how racism and oppression affect people's everyday lives._ Or: _I've never dealt with racism, so it's hard to relate to what 'lois is feeling. But now I understand how people might feel a need to take a stand for equality despite the risks._

After students complete the prompt, have a few volunteers share their responses. Then have students form groups of three to complete the comparison chart.

TEACHING TIP

Sharing Responses Assure students that because each person has a unique perspective, there is no one correct way to interpret a text.

Quick Assess

✳ Do students understand the connection between an author's life and her or his writing?

✳ Can students state a purpose for Taylor's story? (Taylor uses the story as a way to persuade readers to think about racial injustice.)

After

READING/HISTORY CONNECTION

Have students increase their historical perspective of the story by researching the South of the 1950s.

✳ Set up a class K-W-L chart. In the first column, list what students know about this period.

✳ For the middle column, ask what details students want to know.

✳ Have small groups pick an entry from the middle column and turn it into a research question. Each group can research and present its findings, summarizing them in the third column.

✳ Briefly revisit the story and solicit new reflections based on what students learned.

READING/WRITING CONNECTION

To help students process the story's sensitive subject matter:

✳ Assign additional journal entries for students to explore their feelings or new perspectives.

✳ Encourage students to write a letter to a character in the story, telling how they feel or giving advice.

Students will examine persuasive elements (language and craft) in a selection and model the same elements in an original speech.

BACKGROUND KNOWLEDGE

Briefly review the purposes of the previous three selections.

✳ In "The Perils of Indifference," Elie Wiesel aimed to convince readers that indifference is dangerous to humanity. In "To You," Langston Hughes asked others to share his dream for a new world.

✳ In *Farewell to Manzanar,* Jeanne Wakatsuki Houston wrote persuasively about how making unfounded assumptions hurts all people.

✳ In *The Gold Cadillac,* Mildred D. Taylor showed readers how scary it can be to stand up against oppression.

Then invite students to share their experiences of persuading others. Perhaps they have asked a parent or teacher for something. Ask students: *What kinds of words and tone of voice do you use when you want to persuade? Do you speak like you normally would to a friend, or do you use more formal language and a serious tone? Why?* Help students understand that the goal of persuasion is either to make others take action or to change their minds about something.

Think about a time when you tried very hard to **persuade** someone about something. Chances are, you chose your language carefully. When authors write persuasively, they make careful language choices. They want to draw out from their readers the most powerful responses possible. And, as you've seen, they can choose to write in a variety of genres, such as speeches, poems, memoirs, or fictional stories.

In this unit, you've seen several examples of authors using various genres and different topics to take a stand against oppression and indifference. Now let's look at the language they chose to support their opinions. Use the chart below to analyze and compare how two different authors did this. Choose to compare Wiesel's speech with either Langston Hughes's poem or with Houston's memoir. Write the name of the piece at the top of the blank column on the right. You may need to skim the selections again and use your **Response Notes** to complete the chart.

Language and Craft	Elie Wiesel's speech, "The Perils of Indifference"	
Describe the *vocabulary* used. Does the author use "big" words or common words or both? Does the author use powerful words to get ideas across? Give examples. What is the effect of the vocabulary used?		
What is the *tone* the author uses (for example, serious, sad, sarcastic, funny)? Describe and give examples.		
Where and when did the author use *repetition* (repeating words or phrases)? What effect did it have on you?		
Did the selection convince you that it is important to stand up against oppression? Why or why not?		

Before

CRITICAL READING SKILL

Focusing on Language and Craft

Explain that good readers recognize persuasive language. Then direct students to complete the chart. Read through each question and, as necessary, model finding examples from the selections. For example: Elie Wiesel uses the words *aggressor, political prisoner,* and *homeless refugees.* Ask students what effect these words have

on the reader. (Possible responses: *These are strong words, which makes me realize the seriousness of Wiesel's message.* Or: *Big words are OK, but it's harder for me to understand his message.*)

TEACHING TIP

Distinguishing Tone If students are having difficulty detecting the tone of each piece, ask them to pair up and read the pieces aloud to each other. Ask: *As you listen, picture the writer saying the words. Does he or she appear to be smiling, serious, amused, or angry?*

✳ Which selection elicited the strongest reaction in you as a reader? Explain why, using specific details from the chart on the previous page to describe how the author's language and style prompted your response.

_____
_____
_____
_____
_____
_____
_____

✳ Explain what aspect of indifference or oppression the author persuaded you to think about. Describe how the author reinforced or changed your mind on the issue.

_____
_____
_____
_____
_____
_____
_____
_____
_____
_____
_____
_____
_____

Determine how language and style contribute to an author's ability to persuade you to consider his or her opinions and viewpoints.

WRITING SUPPORT

Brainstorming For the second prompt on page 127, help students brainstorm different aspects of indifference and oppression that they have read about in the unit. For example: the damage indifference can cause (from Wiesel), the pain of the oppressed (from Houston), and the personal courage needed to take a stand (from Taylor).

Quick Assess

✳ Do students' charts have at least one example of vocabulary from each selection?

✳ Have students' responses shown an understanding of persuasive language and tone?

✳ Do students give candid answers as to whether or not each selection persuaded them? Responses should include reasons why or why not.

During

SHARING RESPONSES
After students have completed their charts, compose a chart together as a class. Invite students to share their responses.

TEACHING TIP
Acknowledging Contributions
Write down students' names next to their additions to the class chart. This acknowledges each contributor and helps build confidence.

After

READING/ART CONNECTION
Have students find or create visual images (sketches, photos, or art) to accompany the most powerful or persuasive words and phrases from their charts. Students can then craft a collage for the classroom wall. View the collage with students and discuss the images, emphasizing the ways the crafted language leaves images in the reader's mind.

READING/WRITING CONNECTION
Have students create a short, persuasive piece of their choice—a speech, a poem, a personal account, or a short story—modeling their writing after one of the unit selections. Have students use their Response Notes and chart entries to include vocabulary from the selection. Remind them to model the writer's tone.

Students will learn that an authors' experiences and perspectives influence their writing.

BACKGROUND KNOWLEDGE

In this lesson, students will read an interview with Mildred D. Taylor in which she explains how her childhood and family relations influenced her writing. Students should share prior knowledge about Taylor's life from previous lessons. Remind students that Taylor's family had experienced segregation in Mississippi. Ask: *If you had lived there in that time, what would you want to write about? What would you want people to know about your everyday life?*

VOCABULARY

pathos something that makes people feel sympathy or sorrow

foibles small weaknesses or mistakes

Black student movement a group of African American college students who fought for equal rights during the 1960s

To check for understanding, ask questions about each word. For example: *What might the* Black student movement *have fought against?* (segregation) *What is a common* foible *of some people you know?* (gossiping) *What's an example of* pathos *that you've read about in this unit?* (spending part of one's childhood in an internment camp)

Writers often write about what they know. Knowing about an author's life can help you understand the author's opinions and viewpoints. Of course, this doesn't mean that every book is an autobiography, or an author's account of his or her life. But writers borrow tidbits from their own lives or the lives of people they know to persuade others of their viewpoints.

As you read the following interview, pay special attention to the connections between Taylor's life and her viewpoints about oppression that are evident in *The Gold Cadillac*. You can reread the excerpt in Lesson 38. In your **Response Notes**, record the insights you have about the source of Taylor's ideas about indifference and oppression. Why do you think she became a writer?

Response Notes

from a interview with **Mildred D. Taylor**

"From as far back as I can remember my father taught me a different history from the one I learned in school. By the fireside in our Ohio home and in Mississippi, where I was born and where my father's family had lived since the days of slavery, I had heard about our past. It was not an organized history beginning in a certain year, but one told through stories about great-grandparents and aunts and uncles and others that stretched back through the years of slavery and beyond. It was a history of ordinary people. Some brave, some not so brave, but basically people who had done nothing more spectacular than survive in a society designed for their destruction. Some of the stories my father had learned from his parents and grandparents as they had learned from theirs; others he told first-hand, having been involved in the incidents himself. There was often humor in his stories, sometimes pathos, and frequently tragedy; but always the people were graced with a simple dignity that elevated them from the ordinary to the heroic.

"Those colorful vignettes stirred the romantic in me. I was fascinated by the stories, not only because of what they said or because they were about my family, but because of the manner in which my father told them. I began to imagine myself as storyteller, making people laugh at their own human foibles or nod their heads with pride about some stunning feat of heroism. But I was a shy and quiet child, so I turned to creating stories for myself instead, carving elaborate daydreams in my mind.

"I do not know how old I was when the daydreams became more than that, and I decided to write them down, but by the time I entered high school, I was confident that I would one day be a writer. I still wonder at myself for feeling

---

Before

CRITICAL READING SKILL

Studying an Author Explain that, while not every story includes autobiographical details, authors frequently draw from their own experiences to create stories. Then give reasons why studying an author can help your understanding of a text. For example: *When you know about an author's life, you can make connections between the author and the text. When you*

know why they want to write, you can make a better guess about their purpose and what they want you to get out of the story.

RESPONSE NOTES As students read, encourage them to underline biographical information that Taylor uses in *The Gold Cadillac.* Model finding an example: *In the first paragraph, the second sentence starts, "by the fireside in our Ohio home and in Mississippi... ." 'lois's family also lived in these states. This is something Taylor used from her own life.*

so confident since I had never particularly liked to write, nor was I exceptionally good at it. But once I had made up my mind to write, I had no doubts about doing it. It was just something that would one day be. I had always been taught that I could achieve anything I set my mind to. Still a number of years were to lapse before this setting of my mind actually resulted in the publication of any of my stories.

"In those intervening years spent studying, traveling, and living in Africa, and working with the Black student movement, I would find myself turning again and again to the stories I had heard in my childhood." ❖

Collaboration After reading the interview, have students share the connections between Taylor's life and fiction. Use the Think-Pair-Share technique:

1. **Think** Have individuals write down the connections in the Response Notes as they read.
2. **Pair** Have students discuss the connections they found with a partner and choose one to share with the rest of the class.
3. **Share** Have pairs take turns sharing and discussing their connections with the class.

❄ Now that you've read Mildred Taylor's words, you have additional information about her viewpoints. Based on your perspective, experiences, and what you have read, what would you say to persuade students to stand up against oppression? Write a draft of the speech you would give. Be as creative as you'd like, and draw on what Taylor says in the interview and in the excerpt from *The Gold Cadillac* that you read.

Speech About Standing Up Against Oppression

During

AUTHOR'S PERSPECTIVE To prepare for the writing prompt, discuss the following questions:

❄ What do you think might be the purpose(s) of Mildred D. Taylor's writing?

❄ What effect do you think her writing has on readers?

❄ What do her stories persuade readers to consider?

WRITING SUPPORT

Writing to Persuade Review some tips for writing a persuasive speech:

❄ Decide on one or two main points, or reasons, that support your opinion.

❄ Each reason should then have details to support it. Students can find examples from their own experiences, events in *The Gold Cadillac,* and details from the interview with Mildred Taylor.

❄ Remind students that, as covered in the previous lesson, good writers use special language to craft their persuasive writing.

❄ Provide paper for students who need extra room for writing.

WRITING SUPPORT

Choosing a Topic Before completing the first prompt, students may benefit from brainstorming possible topics. Solicit topics that affect students, such as: dress codes, testing, school funding for sports, and school safety issues. Or, ask open-ended questions such as: *What needs to change in your school, your community, or the world? What seems unfair? What do you wish people would do to bring about change?*

Gathering Details Model filling out the graphic organizer with a simple topic, explaining the parts of the diagram. Say:

✳ *An example is something that shows what is wrong with the situation.*

✳ *The details describe the example.*

✳ *An issue to consider is an opposing viewpoint, or a point that someone might make to contradict your position, such as, "Your solution won't work because no one agrees with you." What would you say in response?*

Quick Assess

✳ Do students use examples from the texts to support their point of view?

✳ Do you have the power to persuade someone? First decide what you want to convince someone else to consider from one of the pieces you've read. Choose the issue and write a few sentences describing why it is important to you.

_____

_____

_____

✳ Brainstorm a list of details and examples that will help you persuade someone to agree with you.

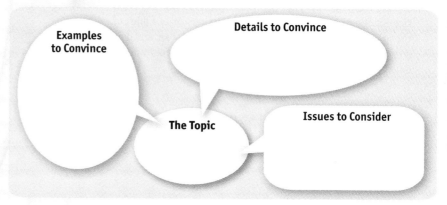

✳ Write a paragraph that is as persuasive as you can make it. Convince your readers to think about your point of view on the issue.

_____

_____

_____

_____

_____

Determine what an author wants to persuade you to believe and how convincingly he or she presents the issues and point of view.

After

LISTENING/SPEAKING CONNECTION Have students turn their speeches or persuasive paragraphs into oral presentations.

✳ Encourage students to practice good oral presentation skills, such as speaking clearly, pacing the speech, and looking at the audience.

✳ Students can practice and refine their speeches in pairs.

✳ After each speech, briefly analyze its persuasive qualities and discuss whether it addresses opposing viewpoints.

ORAL HISTORY PROJECT As Mildred D. Taylor uses oral history for her stories, students can complete oral history projects of their own.

✳ Have students choose an older family member or friend to interview. Students should then write questions about this

person's life and times. For example: *Who lived in your community when you were growing up? What are the most memorable moments of your life?*

✳ Students should take notes and use them to write a short essay about the person.

✳ Have each student give a finished copy of the essay to the interviewee.

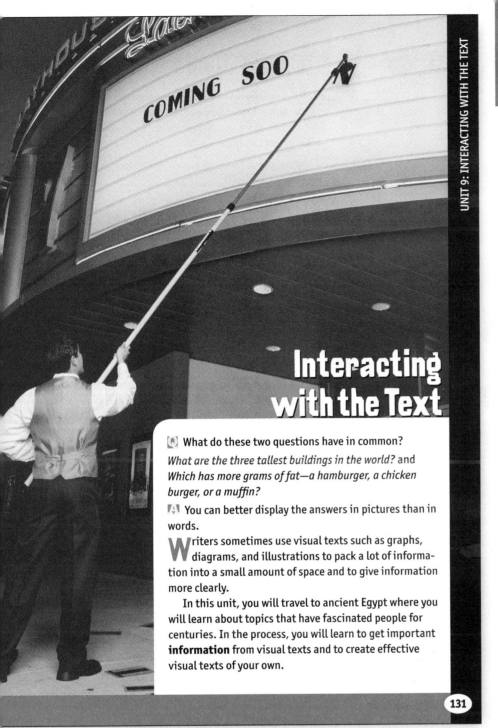

Interacting with the Text

What do these two questions have in common?

What are the three tallest buildings in the world? and *Which has more grams of fat—a hamburger, a chicken burger, or a muffin?*

A You can better display the answers in pictures than in words.

Writers sometimes use visual texts such as graphs, diagrams, and illustrations to pack a lot of information into a small amount of space and to give information more clearly.

In this unit, you will travel to ancient Egypt where you will learn about topics that have fascinated people for centuries. In the process, you will learn to get important **information** from visual texts and to create effective visual texts of your own.

(131)

UNIT OVERVIEW

In reading informational text about ancient Egypt and the practice of mummification, students will learn how to use visual texts such as graphs, diagrams, illustrations, maps, graphic organizers, and websites.

KEY IDEA

Nonfiction (informational) writing often includes visual texts to present and enhance information.

CRITICAL READING SKILLS
by lesson

41 Reading a graph
42 Reading a diagram
43 Using graphic organizers to visualize information
44 Reading an illustration
45 Reading a website

WRITING ACTIVITIES
by lesson

41 Create a pictograph.
42 Write a summary statement.
43 Complete a sequence map; complete a comparison chart; write a paragraph for a report.
44 Write about an illustration.
45 Create and explain a visual text.

Literature

- **"Famous Pyramids"** by Anne Steel (reference book excerpt)

In this excerpt from *Egyptian Pyramids,* Steel describes different types of pyramids.

- **"The Pyramid Builders"** by Anne Steel (reference book excerpt)

Steel describes how the pyramids were built in this excerpt from *Egyptian Pyramids.*

- *The Ancient Egyptians* by Elsa Marston (reference book excerpt)

Marston gives an overview of the origin and process of mummification.

- **"Accidental Mummies"** (online article excerpt)

Readers learn about bodies that were mummified by the forces of nature.

- *Cat Mummies* by Kelly Trumble (reference book excerpt)

The text and accompanying illustration give information about how Egyptians mummified cats.

- **"The Kittens of Egypt"** by James M. Deem (online article)

From the website Mummy Tombs, the article discusses the history of cat mummification.

ASSESSMENT To assess student learning in this unit, see pages 234 and 251.

LESSON 41 READING GRAPHS

Students will read a pictograph and create a K-W-L Chart and a pictograph based on informational text.

BACKGROUND KNOWLEDGE

Have students locate Egypt on a globe or a map of the world. Ask students what they already know about ancient Egyptian culture (e.g. the Sphinx, the pyramids, King Tut). Explain to students that in this lesson they will learn more about the pyramids. Show photos of pyramids and point out that these giant structures were built as burial monuments to Egyptian kings. Check websites, such as www.national-geographic.com/pyramids, for photos.

VOCABULARY

burial chamber a room that serves as a tomb

pharaoh a king of ancient Egypt

Have students discuss what might be placed in a burial chamber (a coffin, personal possessions of the dead person, etc.). Then help students think of other words that are used for *king* in different cultures (emperor, ruler, monarch, czar, etc.).

When they want to compare different amounts to each other, writers often use graphs. You can use a bar graph to show the amount of fat in different foods, for example. You would set up a **bar graph** like this:

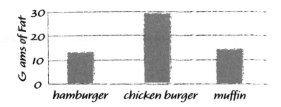

A pictograph is another kind of graph that uses symbols or pictures rather than bars. As you read the first paragraph of the excerpt below, try to **visualize** the height of the Great Pyramid. In the **Response Notes**, sketch symbols or pictures you could use in a **pictograph**.

Response Notes

"Famous Pyramids" from *Egyptian Pyramids* by Anne Steel

The earliest Egyptian graves were very simple and could easily be broken into and robbed. To prevent this, the Egyptians began to build tombs called mastabas. These were rectangular buildings placed over a burial chamber. Pharaohs had mastabas built with many rooms inside to protect the burial chamber from thieves, but the graves were still robbed.

The first pyramid was built for Pharaoh Zoser at Sakkara. There were six huge steps built on top of the tomb to make it safer from robbers. The Pharaoh's spirit was believed to have climbed the steps of the pyramid to the stars. Later pyramids were built without steps, like the famous group at Giza. The largest of these is the Great Pyramid, built for Pharaoh Khufu. Each side is 450 feet (144 m) high and measures 756 feet (230 m) at the base. It would have taken at least twenty years to build. ✧

✳ Does the Great Pyramid seem very tall to you? What evidence is there in the text?

Before

CRITICAL READING SKILL

Reading a Graph Help students name different types of graphs—e.g., line graphs, bar graphs, pie graphs—and show what they look like. Then point out that we read graphs not only to see and compare data but to make inferences or draw conclusions about the data.

INTERACTING WITH THE TEXT

Have students study the bar graph. Then ask questions such as: *Which food has the most grams of fat? Which has the least? How can you tell?* Model drawing a conclusion about the information, e.g.: *People who want less fat in their diet should avoid eating chicken burgers.*

During

FEATURES OF A GRAPH
Point out that bar graphs have two *axes:* a vertical *axis,* or line, going up the left side, and a horizontal *axis,* or line, going across the bottom. Units of measurement (such as grams of fat) are shown along one axis, and the things being compared (such as types of food) are shown along the other. But in a pictograph, units of measurement

Now there are other buildings taller than the Great Pyramid. But for 4,000 years, it was the tallest structure in the world. Anne Steel gave its current size of 450 feet, but when it was built, it was 31 feet (9.5 m) taller. The creator of the pictograph that follows claims that the pyramid is 449.5 feet high and rounds that number down for the graphic. Read the pictograph and answer the questions that follow.

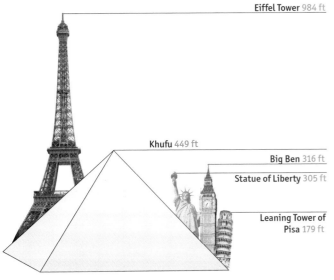

Eiffel Tower 984 ft

Khufu 449 ft

Big Ben 316 ft

Statue of Liberty 305 ft

Leaning Tower of Pisa 179 ft

✳ What is the one building taller than the Great Pyramid?

_____

✳ How much taller is it?

_____

✳ Which is taller—the Statue of Liberty or the Leaning Tower of Pisa?

_____

✳ Is it easier or harder to read the graph instead of the words? Explain.

_____

_____

Differentiation Before reading the selection, have students create a K-W-L chart. In the first column (K), have students write what they already know about Egyptian pyramids. Then, for the middle column (W), have students work with a partner to generate questions about what they want to learn. Students can fill in the third column (L) as they read this selection and the one in the next lesson. As students encounter answers to their questions in the text, they can write the answers in the chart.

are shown through pictures or symbols, rather than being marked off along an axis. Ask: *What is being compared in this pictograph?* (heights of structures) *What is the unit of measurement?* (meters/feet)

Collaboration Have students share their pictographs with the class, using the following interview technique:

1. Students present their pictographs to a partner and "quiz" their partner about the data shown to make sure he or she is reading and interpreting it correctly.

2. Partners present each other's pictographs to the class and quiz the class about what the pictographs show.

Quick Assess

✻ Do students' pictographs use symbols accurately to reflect units of measurement?

✻ Do the pictographs compare data?

✻ Create your own pictograph to display information. You can use information familiar to you, such as the height of people in your family. You can do some research on tall buildings to find other comparisons to the Great Pyramid. Or you can look for information on a topic you are studying in science or social studies.

Pictographs and bar graphs are useful when a writer wants to show or compare different amounts.

After

MATH CONNECTION Divide students into groups to gather data about your school, such as the number of male and female students in each class, the amount and types of food served in the cafeteria each week, the number of doors, stairs, and windows in the building, etc. Then have groups create bar graphs or pictographs to present their data. What inferences can be made from the graphs? Combine the graphs into an illustrative brochure to share with visitors and new students.

A **diagram** is another kind of visual text. Diagrams may show the parts of something, or they may show how something works. If you have background knowledge about the topic, the diagram might give you more information than if you don't have some background. In this lesson, you will learn about building the pyramids before you look at the parts of the pyramid.

When you read in Lesson 41 that the Great Pyramid took at least twenty years to build, did you wonder why? One reason is that pyramids were very complex structures, with a lot of rooms and passageways. As you read the next section from *Egyptian Pyramids*, circle words and phrases that show how difficult it was to build the pyramids.

Response Notes

"The Pyramid Builders" from *Egyptian Pyramids* by Anne Steel

Many thousands of people were needed to build a pyramid. Some of them, such as the architect and planners, were highly skilled. Their plans had to be accepted by the pharaoh before any work could begin. Quarry men were needed to get the stone out of the ground, and masons worked to shape the rough stone. Painters decorated the walls inside the tomb, and sculptors made statues and carvings.

The heavy work of moving the stones was done by people with no special building skills. Some of them were farmers who had to leave their land for some time each year when the Nile flooded. Others may have been prisoners, or people paying labor tax to the pharaoh. As there was no money in Ancient Egypt, the workers were paid with food, wine, clothes, and other goods. ❖

Review the words or phrases you circled. Make a note of two important facts that you learned from this excerpt.

_____

_____

_____

_____

_____

_____

_____

_____

READING DIAGRAMS **135**

Students will read informational text and study a diagram about the pyramids of ancient Egypt and then write a summary.

BACKGROUND KNOWLEDGE
In this lesson, students will read informational text about how the pyramids were built. Ask students if they have ever seen a building under construction. What kind of equipment and materials were being used? Who was working there and what work were they doing? How quickly was the building completed? Point out that the ancient Egyptians built the pyramids without the benefit of modern equipment, materials, and electricity, and yet these structures are still standing after thousands of years. Invite students to speculate how this could be. (engineering design, materials, climate, etc.)

VOCABULARY
architect a person who designs buildings or other large structures

quarry a large area from which stone is dug, blasted, or cut out

mason a stoneworker; a craftsman who works with stones or bricks

Discuss what it might be like to work as an architect, a mason, or a quarry worker. Have students tell which job they would like most/least and why.

Before

CRITICAL READING SKILL
Reading a Diagram Ask students if they have ever used a diagram to figure out how something worked or was put together. What made the diagram helpful? What could have made it more helpful? Bring in books or other materials containing diagrams (such as *The Way Things Work* by David Macaulay, craft or hobby magazines, instruction manuals). Have students identify common features of diagrams: labels, leader lines, specialized language, etc. Then have students work in small groups to look through the materials and choose two diagrams that they find interesting or informative. Discuss advantages and disadvantages of using a diagram or a written description.

Writing a Summary Statement

Before they write the summary statement, have students tell in their own words the main idea of "Pyramid Builders." Use a graphic organizer to capture the main idea and supporting details. Sketch the outline of a hand with palm facing the reader. Write the main idea in the palm of the hand. Write supporting details in each finger. You may prefer to write a summary statement together as a class, for example: *The ancient pyramids were built not only by highly skilled architects, engineers, and artisans, but also by thousands of laborers, including farmers and prisoners.*

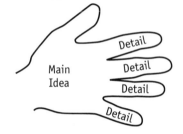

EXTRA SUPPORT

Differentiation Remind students to continue adding to their K-W-L charts as they read the selections on page 135 and 137. Referring to the chart will also help students write and revise their summary statements.

✻ Use the notes you made in Lesson 41 and the two facts you just wrote to write a summary of the excerpts from *Egyptian Pyramids*. Restate the main idea in your own words. Include some of the most important facts you have learned to give details about the main idea.

During

CONNECTING DIAGRAMS TO TEXT

Point out that knowing how to read a diagram is important. Not only does a diagram illustrate or further explain details in a main text, it may also provide additional information. After students have matched the parts of the diagram on page 137 to the text, ask: *What else does the diagram show? Does it teach you anything that you couldn't tell from just reading the text?* (It shows the actual layout, i.e. the location of specific chambers and passageways; it shows the scale, or size relationship.) Point out that successful readers integrate information from both visual and print sources for a full understanding of the author's message.

RELATING TO THE MAIN IDEA

Have students share their responses to the question at the bottom of page 137. Then discuss how the diagram is related to the main idea or supports the reader's understanding of it. (By helping the reader visualize the inside of a pyramid, it shows the work that went into designing and building the pyramids.)

✳ Diagrams often go with printed text. Look at the diagram of the pyramid below. As you read the excerpt that goes with it, use colored markers to match the parts of the diagram to the sentences that describe those parts.

The pharoah's burial chamber

Ante-chamber

The grand gallery

False burial chamber

The corridor blocked by huge stone slabs

The entrance to the pyramid

Inside, the pyramid was a maze of passages and rooms. The main aim of the builders was to hide the burial chambers so that thieves could not steal its treasures. The entrance was usually on the north side of the pyramid and it was always well hidden. Inside, the passages might lead to false burial chambers or dead ends. In the Great Pyramid there was a false chamber underground. The real chamber was blocked off with huge stone slabs. But this was not enough to keep robbers from stealing everything except the stone tomb. ✥

✳ Did the diagram help you visualize? Did the diagram help you understand pyramids better? Why or why not?

Diagrams can help a reader see the parts of something or understand how things work.

After

SOCIAL STUDIES CONNECTION

For further practice working with diagrams, have students work in small groups to research and draw diagrams of the pyramids built by the Incas, Mayans, or Aztecs. Then have each group present its diagram to the class and discuss how these pyramids are different from the Egyptian pyramids.

To encourage students to collaborate, assign specific roles within each small group, such as researcher, illustrator, note-taker, and presenter, to match tasks to students' strengths or needs.

Students will learn ways to take notes from informational text.

BACKGROUND KNOWLEDGE

Activate prior knowledge by having students tell what they know or believe about mummies. Discuss any misconceptions students may have, based on how mummies are portrayed in movies or on TV. Point out that in ancient Egypt and other cultures, mummifying the dead was a practice tied to a religious belief in the "afterlife," a place where a person goes after death. Egyptians thought a person's body needed to be preserved so his or her spirit, or *ka,* could live on forever.

VOCABULARY

forensic referring to the use of science or technology to find facts or evidence

radiocarbon dating a way to determine the approximate age of an ancient object by measuring the amount of carbon-14 it contains

dehydrating causing a lack of moisture

peat partially decomposed vegetation found in bogs

After discussing the definitions of the words, have students brainstorm professions or scientific fields in which these words are used (e.g. medicine, chemistry, crime solving, archaeology, anthropology).

If you've ever had to write a research report, you probably read about your topic in several different places, such as reference books, magazine articles, and the Internet. But how did you keep track of all that information? One way to organize your information is by **taking notes** as you read. Some people use a combination of words and pictures to take notes; some just use words. Here are a few tips about note-taking:

- Notes do not need to be in complete sentences. You can jot down words or phrases.
- There is no one right way to take notes. Some people make formal outlines or lists, while other people use webs or other graphic organizers. Pick a style that works for you.
- Don't take notes about everything that you read. Write only the most important ideas.
- Organize your notes with headings, titles, or whatever system works for you.
- Use numbers, symbols, and/or abbreviations to help you take notes more quickly.

Imagine that you are an archaeologist, studying one of the most fascinating topics in ancient Egypt—mummies. As you read the excerpt, jot down comments and questions in the **Response Notes.** Remember that you can use words, pictures, or symbols for your notes.

Response Notes

from **The Ancient Egyptians** by Elsa Marston

Why did the ancient Egyptians mummify their dead? The procedure was an essential part of their belief in the afterlife. For a person to enjoy eternal life, his or her body had to be preserved.

The Egyptians probably got the idea by observing that desert sands would sometimes dry and preserve a body naturally. Then they learned how to mummify artificially. Though at first only the royal and rich had the privilege of being preserved, later almost everyone but the very poor expected to be mummified. There were different grades of mummification, from the quick, cheap job to the full seventy days' treatment for kings.

The first step in mummification was to take out most of the internal organs and preserve them. The heart was left in the body to be weighed by the gods; the brain, though, was discarded because it was not thought to be of

Before

CRITICAL READING SKILL
Visualizing the Information Prompt students to recall times they have created word webs or story maps in writing, used tables or charts in math or science, or employed other graphic organizers. Ask students how a visual presentation of information can be useful. Tell students: *You can also use graphic organizers to take*

notes while you read informational text, to help you understand and remember the information better.

TAKING NOTES Before students fill in the sequence map and chart on pages 139 and 141, demonstrate how to paraphrase specific details from the text. Read aloud the last paragraph in *The Ancient Egyptians,* pausing to list details given

in the text, e.g. Egyptians kept the heart in the body for the gods; they discarded the brain; the body was soaked in salt for days. Point out that when details are listed in sequence, organizers are helpful for review.

any value. After being immersed for many days in a special kind of salt called natron, the body was treated with special ointments and finally wrapped carefully in long strips of linen. The mummification business was always a thriving one, and it lasted well into Roman times. ✧

✳ Using a graphic organizer can help you keep track of information. Review the notes you made. Then use this sequence map to list the steps involved in mummification.

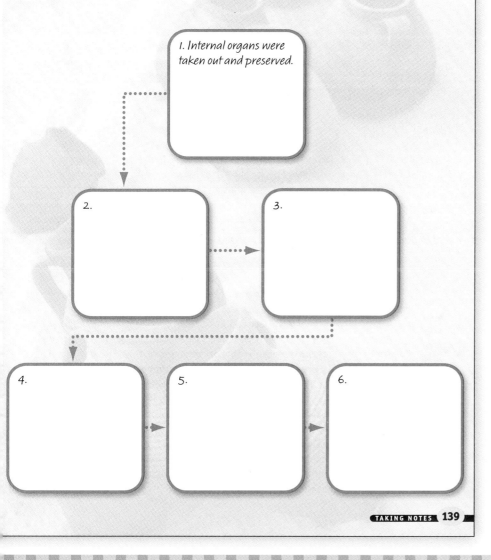

1. Internal organs were taken out and preserved.

2.

3.

4.

5.

6.

SEQUENCE MAP The information for the sequence map is in the last paragraph. Answers should be similar to the following: (2) leave the heart in the body, (3) throw away the brain, (4) immerse other organs in natron, (5) treat body with special ointments, and (6) wrap body in linen strips.

Graphic Organizer: Timeline Point out that a timeline is another way to visualize information. Invite students who can benefit from an extra challenge to create a timeline showing when each "accidental mummy" was discovered, as well as when he or she is thought to have died. Students can then present their timelines to the class.

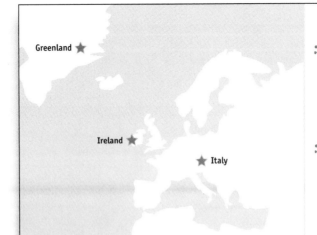

Greenland ★

Ireland ★

★ Italy

⁂ Although Egypt is the best-known location of mummies, they have also been found in other parts of the world. Look at the map and think about how those mummies might have been made.

⁂ Talk with a partner about the map. Looking at it, and using what you know about geography, discuss whether you think all mummies were made the same way. Read "Accidental Mummies" to find out.

Response Notes

"Accidental Mummies" from *Nova* Online

Some of the most spectacular mummies were created accidentally. In 1991, German climbers found a body frozen on top of a glacier near the Austrian-Italian border. Initially, the police and forensic experts who arrived on the scene didn't realize how old the body was—even though he was wearing a grass cape, carrying a bow and arrows and had shoes stuffed with grass for warmth. Later, radiocarbon dating determined that the "Iceman" died sometime between 3350 and 3300 B.C.—making him the oldest well-preserved mummy in the world.

In 1972, hunters found some of the best naturally-preserved human bodies at a remarkable abandoned settlement called Qilakitsoq, in Greenland. The "Greenland Mummies," who died about 500 years ago, consisted of a six-month old baby, a four-year-old boy, and six women of various ages. Protected by a rock that overhung a shallow cave, the bodies were naturally mummified by the sub-zero temperatures and dry, dehydrating winds. Accompanying the eight bodies were seventy-eight items of clothing, most made out of sealskin.

Over the years, peat cutters working the bogs of northwest Europe have uncovered hundreds of mummies. The spongy top layer of a peat bog tends to seal off oxygen from the layers below. A bog's naturally acidic environment also helps to create mummies and gives them a distinctively brown, leathery and life-like appearance. The oldest "bog mummies" are from the Iron Age (between 400 B.C. and 400 A.D.) and were Celtic or Germanic contemporaries of the Romans. Strangely, many of the mummies found in the European bogs show evidence of violent deaths. With slit throats and broken skulls, these individuals may have been victims of ritual sacrifice, not unlike the mummies of the high Andes. ❖

■ **140** LESSON 43

During

READING A MAP To help students think about how mummies might have been made in each place identified on the map, discuss the climate and geography of each location. Ask: *Is the climate cold and snowy? Hot and dry? What might have happened to a body that was exposed to the elements in this area?* Then, as students read "Accidental Mummies," they can confirm or correct their predictions

and take notes to record what they learn about the locations where mummies have been found.

USING A CHART Before students complete the chart on page 141, discuss the notes that are provided. Work with students to find the places in the selection that correspond to the notes. Point out that, like regular class notes, the notes in a chart or other graphic

organizer can be key words and phrases, questions, short answers, and notes to the reader. Then have students work in pairs or alone to fill in the rest of the chart. (*Egypt*—for the afterlife, everyone; *Greenland*—cold temperatures and dry winds, 500 years ago, 6 women and 2 children; *Northwest Europe*—bogs, more than 1600 years ago, result of the weather)

✳ Use a chart when you need to sort information into categories. Imagine that you are going to write a report on different ways that people have been mummified. Look over the information in this lesson. Make notes in the boxes below.

	Egypt	Greenland	Northwest Europe
What was used to dry or preserve the bodies?	First sand, then salt		
When were people mummified?	"ancient"— check the years		
Why were people mummified?		Accident?	
Who was mummified?			Maybe human sacrifices

✳ Using the information from the chart, write one paragraph that could be a part of your report on mummies. You can use one of the questions in the chart as your first sentence or you can write a different one.

_____

_____

_____

_____

_____

_____

Taking notes helps readers and writers organize information and communicate important ideas.

WRITING SUPPORT
Paragraph Development To help students focus their writing, you might suggest one of two approaches:

1. Students can select a question from the first column and write the answer for all three locations.

2. Students can focus on one location and answer all of the questions for it.

Quick Assess

✳ Are students' charts complete?

✳ Is all of the information in the chart taken from the readings?

✳ Do students' paragraphs have a clear focus?

✳ Do the paragraphs include relevant details from the chart and the readings?

After

SOCIAL STUDIES/ART CONNECTION

For more practice visualizing information, have students do additional research on mummies to expand their charts. (For example, they might add a column on Chinese or South American mummies.) Students can then turn the charts into posters, adding illustrations, photos, and maps to accompany the notes in each column. Display the posters on a wall titled "Mummies Around the World" in the library or another common area.

LESSON 44

Students will study an illustration and compare their observations with the information they find in the text.

BACKGROUND KNOWLEDGE

In this lesson, students will read about the Egyptian practice of mummifying cats. Explain that cats were considered sacred in ancient Egypt, where they were first domesticated as house pets. They were highly valued for protecting houses against rats and mice, and they were even used for hunting birds and fish. Cats were worshipped and treated like gods, and Egyptians believed that when cats died, they, like humans, needed their bodies preserved for the afterlife.

VOCABULARY

papier-mâché (PAY per muh SHAY) a material made from paper mixed with glue or paste that can be shaped when wet and becomes hard when dry

Invite students who have worked with papier-mâché to explain the process and to describe how it looks, feels, and smells.

READING AN ILLUSTRATION

You have probably heard that "a picture is worth a thousand words." Authors of informational texts know this. They often use photos and illustrations to emphasize key points or to make an important point. When the subject is unfamiliar, an illustration can help you better understand what you are reading. In fact, a good way to preview what you are going to read is to look at the illustrations.

Did you know that the ancient Egyptians mummified animals as well as humans? In this lesson, you will read about one type of animal mummy—cats. The following picture comes from the book *Cat Mummies*. Look at it for several minutes. Write your questions or reactions in the **Response Notes.**

✳ Talk with one or two other students about your observations. Write two questions that you still have.

_____

_____

_____

_____

Before

CRITICAL READING SKILL

Reading an Illustration Show students pictures from informational texts such as magazines, textbooks, nonfiction picture books, or newspapers. Discuss the images and encourage students to share their reactions. Ask: *What is the purpose of this photo? What did you learn from this illustration? What questions do you have about it?* Point out that pictures in text can serve different purposes—to clarify something in the text, to provide additional information, to draw a conclusion from the text, or to create a feeling or mood.

During

INTERACTING WITH THE TEXT

Tell students that, as they read the passage, they should note information that is in the text but isn't included in the picture. (Heads were covered with masks; ears were made of palm leaf midribs.)

Then, after reading, have students share what they learned from the text and what questions they still have.

Laszlo Kubinyi drew the illustration on page 14 to accompany a description of how cats were mummified. Read the description.

from **Cat Mummies** by Kelly Trumble

Sometimes a cat was mummified in an elaborate way. The body was wrapped in strips of linen that had been dyed in two colors. The linen strips were woven together to form beautiful patterns. The head was covered with a mask made of a material similar to papier-mâché. Pieces of linen were sewn on the mask to look like eyes. Ears were made from the midribs of palm leaves, set in a natural position.

Other cats were mummified in a simple way. They were rolled up only in a piece of plain linen. But the rolling was done with the care and respect that a sacred animal deserved. ✣

✳ Did this passage answer more of your questions? If so, go back and write the answers by your questions. Circle any questions you still have.

✳ Illustrations often set a tone for the information. When you see the picture, you get a certain feeling about the subject. Look again at the illustration of the cat mummies. What feeling does it give you? What mood does it suggest? Common words for mood are *scary, exciting, tense, calm, funny,* and so on. Write one or two words here that you think fit the picture and tell why.

_____

_____

✳ Do you think that the illustration better fits the *information* in the excerpt by Kelly Trumble or the *mood*? Explain.

_____
_____
_____
_____
_____
_____
_____
_____

Illustrations emphasize information in a text or add new information. They can also set the mood or tone of informational text.

Collaboration For the Listening/ Speaking Connection below, have students present their pictures to each other, using the Inside-Outside Circle technique:

1. Have students form two circles, one within the other, with students facing each other.

2. Have each student present his or her pictures to the facing student.

3. Have circles rotate in opposite directions, forming new pairings, and repeat step 2.

Quick Assess

✳ Do students' responses show an understanding of mood?

✳ Did students state an opinion and give clear reasons for it in their responses?

After

MOOD Review the definition of *mood* (the feeling or emotion inspired in the observer) and point out that an art piece's style, medium (materials used), and subject matter all contribute to the mood it creates. Then have students complete the prompts on the page. Afterward, have students share their responses. Compile a list on the board of all the words students wrote to describe the mood.

LISTENING/SPEAKING CONNECTION Have students look through a variety of informational texts to find two pictures, one that provides or clarifies information and one that creates a mood (or does both). Have students present their pictures to the class and explain what purpose(s) the pictures serve.

Students will read a sample website to understand how pictures relate to a topic and create their own visual to coordinate with informational text in the unit.

BACKGROUND KNOWLEDGE

Most students will have had prior experience using the Internet for an assignment or project. Invite students to talk about times they used the Internet for research. What subjects were they researching? What websites did they use? How did students find the sites and what information was included?

VOCABULARY

Egyptologist person who studies artifacts of ancient Egypt

communal shared by many people

gruesome horrifying, disgusting; repulsive

pulverize to pound, grind, or crush into small pieces

Have students use the Word Splash blackline master on page 272.

Websites can be good sources of factual information if you know how to read them. Perhaps you still have unanswered questions about mummies or ancient Egyptians. Perhaps you just want to learn more about them. Or maybe you have a big report coming up, and you have decided to write about some aspect of ancient Egypt. You need to know more.

A website consists of pages and links. The links allow you to explore a subject in greater detail. You can preview the website by looking at the links, pictures, and icons. You want to know whether it has the information you need. Let's say you do have questions about animal mummies. Look at the web page to see if it would be helpful.

When you click on the link "Egyptian Mummies" you find another link to "Egyptian Animal Mummies." Read the article and see if it answers any of your questions.

Websites have lots of information, but you have to be sure the information is accurate. Ask yourself questions such as these to **evaluate a website:** Is the source of the site legitimate and well known? Are the people who contribute to the page knowelgeable? What is the purpose of the website? When was the site last updated? Can the information be verified by another source? The answers to these questions should tell you whether you can trust a website.

Before

CRITICAL READING SKILL

Reading to Answer Questions Have students think about questions they still have about mummies. Ask: *What are some ways to find answers to your questions?* (Search the Internet, read books or magazines, talk to an expert.) Explain that when you read to answer questions, you start by looking at sources and deciding if they will have the information you need.

USING THE INTERNET Ask students how they would use the Internet to find answers to their questions. What key words would they use to search? (*ancient Egypt, mummies,* etc.) For what kinds of websites should they look? (university sites, museum sites, archaeological societies, etc.) Discuss how to tell if a website is a credible source. Was it created by experts? Can the information

be verified in at least two other places? When was it last updated? Where do the links take you? Familiarize students with your school's policy on Internet use and demonstrate on a computer how to search for and evaluate websites.

"The Kittens of Egypt" by James M. Deem

Mummies come in all shapes and sizes–and species. The ancient Egyptians mummified reptiles and animals such as dogs, apes, bulls, rams, and even an occasional hippopotamus. However, one of the most common animal mummies in Egypt was the cat. To determine how, when, and why cats were mummified, Egyptologists have had to piece together many clues. It appears, for example, that by 1350 B.C., cats were occasionally buried with their owners, according to author Jaromir Malek.

But by 900 B.C., a striking change had taken place in the Egyptians' religious beliefs. Many animals were now thought to be the embodiment of certain gods and goddesses; cats were believed to represent the goddess Bastet. Consequently, they were raised in and around temples devoted to Bastet. When they died, they were mummified and buried in huge cemeteries, often in large communal graves.

An even more important change took place over the centuries. From about 332 B.C. to 30 B.C., animals began to be raised for the specific purpose of being turned into mummies. The mummies were sold to people on their way to worship a god and left at the temple as offerings. Scientists have uncovered a gruesome fact: many cats died quite premature and unnatural deaths. Two- to four-month-old kittens seemed to have been sacrificed in huge numbers, perhaps, as Malek supposes, because they fit into the mummy container better. So many cat mummies were made that researchers can only guess that there were millions of them. In fact, one company bought 38,000 pounds of cat mummies in the late 1800s to pulverize and sell as fertilizer in England; this shipment alone probably contained 180,000 mummified cats. ✧

✳ What three things did you learn from this article? What questions does it answer? What new questions do you have? Talk with one or two other students to get your questions answered. Write two or three important points from your discussion.

Differentiation Students who need extra support for reading expository text may benefit from creating a graphic organizer such as a timeline or sequence map (see page 139) to show the events described in the article.

During

REVIEWING THE WEBSITE

Discuss the website shown on page 144. Ask: *What can you tell about this website— what information might be found here? Does the site look reliable and easy to use? Where might the links take you?*

RESPONSE NOTES

Before students read the online article, have them jot down at least two questions they have about animal mummification. Then remind students to use their Response Notes to mark text where the questions are answered and to note any additional questions that occur as they read.

Collaboration Students can work with partners to go through the unit and look for texts that could be illustrated. You might pair visual learners with students who have strong verbal skills and have them work together to design their visual texts. Have each pair share their work with the class.

WRITING SUPPORT

Understanding the Prompt Ask questions to help students think about how to answer the writing prompt: *Why is the visual that you chose the best way to present the information? Does it organize the information in a sequence? Sort it into categories? Does it help the reader understand how something looks or works? Does it create a mood or send a message?*

Quick Assess

✳ Do students' visuals clarify the text, provide additional information, or serve another appropriate purpose?

✳ Did students write a clear explanation of how and why they developed that specific visual text?

✳ Apply what you know about using visual texts. Select one written text from this unit. Design a visual that will go with that text and provide information at a glance. Of course, if the piece already has a visual text, such as a diagram or a pictograph, give it a different treatment, such as an illustration or a graphic organizer.

Selection Title: _____

✳ Explain why you chose to use the visual text that you did.

_____
_____
_____
_____
_____
_____
_____
_____
_____
_____
_____
_____

Understanding how to read websites is important for finding useful information.

After

LISTENING/SPEAKING CONNECTION With the class, make a list of questions students still have about one of the topics covered in this unit or other aspects of Egyptian culture. Then divide the class into small groups and have each group choose a topic to research. Each group should work together to find answers to their questions and develop an oral presentation about the topic. Build in time for students to search the Internet, books, and magazines to find answers and to create visuals for their presentation. Remind students that information available in books and on the Internet is copyrighted, which means that they must put the information in their own words to avoid plagiarism. Then have each group make their presentation to the class or to another class.

Making Connections

Imagine this: A dance group visits your school to do a performance of merengue, a type of dance that began in the Dominican Republic. Two weeks later, you attend your uncle's wedding. At the reception, you make a connection—you hear music that sounds like the music from the merengue performance at your school. You say to your cousin, "That reminds me of the merengue performance at school. Let me tell you about it."

When you read, you connect what you are thinking or remembering to the text you are reading. Connections like this can also give you ideas for writing. In this unit, you will work at connecting what you read to your life, to movies, to books, or to others' stories, events, or situations. Notice how **making connections** can influence your reading.

147

Literature

- *The Egypt Game* by Zilpha Keatley Snyder (novel excerpt)

This is a novel about friendship and imagination, with a sprinkling of history and mystery. Melanie and April, both eleven years old, become enthralled with Egyptian history, which leads to their involvement in a contemporary mystery.

- *Project Mulberry* by Linda Sue Park (novel excerpt)

Korean American narrator Julia Park and her new friend Patrick develop a science project based on a traditional Korean practice, raising silkworms. At the same time, Julia struggles with her bicultural identity.

ASSESSMENT To assess student learning in this unit, see pages 235 and 254.

Students will learn to make connections from the text to their own lives.

BACKGROUND KNOWLEDGE

To help students make connections between a text and their own experience, share examples of strong personal connections you have made to various books, movies, TV shows, songs, or poems. Explain your connection to the text, for example: *I really related to the conversation between Meg and her father in the passage from "A Summer to Die." The car is where my father and I would have our most serious conversations. Those talks meant a lot to me when I was growing up.*

Ask students to share examples of times they made personal connections to texts.

VOCABULARY

associate be with; play with

stole a long scarf worn around the shoulders

haughtiness snobbishness; pride

Say: *Visualize a person of great haughtiness. Explain why you would or would no wish to associate with him or her.*

Response Notes

As we discussed in previous units, it is important to **make connections** between what you are reading and what you know and have experienced. For example, something you read might make you remember a similar experience or feeling you've had. These kinds of connections can help you relate to the story, even if the characters seem very different from you. "To relate" means that you understand or feel involved or concerned about the situation or the characters.

Sometimes the connections come easily. Other times it can be difficult to make them. Take time to think about and find connections even when they don't come easily. The more connections you make, the more personal meaning you will find in what you read.

The following excerpt is from Zilpha Keatley Snyder's novel, *The Egypt Game*. It is about friendship and imagination, and has a sprinkling of history and mystery. In the **Response Notes,** make notes about connections you make to your life experiences.

from **The Egypt Game** by Zilpha Keatley Snyder

On that same day in August, just a few minutes before twelve, Melanie Ross arrived at the door of Mrs. Hall's apartment on the third floor. Melanie was eleven years old and she had lived in the Casa Rosada since she was only seven. During that time she'd welcomed a lot of new people to the apartment house. Apartment dwellers, particularly near a university, are apt to come and go. Melanie always looked forward to meeting new tenants, and today was going to be especially interesting. Today, Melanie had been sent up to get Mrs. Hall's granddaughter to come down and have lunch with the Rosses. Melanie didn't know much about the new girl except that her name was April and that she had come from Hollywood to live with Mrs. Hall, who was her grandmother.

It would be neat if she turned out to be a real friend. There hadn't been any girls the right age in the Casa Rosada lately. To have a handy friend again, for spur-of-the-moment visiting, would be great. However, she had overheard something that didn't sound too promising. Just the other day she'd heard Mrs. Hall telling Mom that April was a strange little thing because she'd been brought up all over everywhere and never had much of a chance to **associate** with other children. You wouldn't know what to expect of someone like that. But then, you never knew what to expect of any new kid, not really. So Melanie knocked hopefully at the door of apartment 312.

Before

CRITICAL READING SKILL
Connecting the Text to Yourself

Explain to students that proficient readers are able to make connections between stories they read and their own lives, even when the story or characters seem very different from them. Making these connections helps add a new dimension as the reader relates to story events, feels empathy for the characters, and visualizes the setting and the action.

RESPONSE NOTES Tell students to write the connections they're making as they read. Tell them to prompt themselves with these questions: *How would I feel in the character's place? What parts of the story remind me of something I've experienced?* Remind students that they do not need to write complete sentences, but they must write enough so that they remember later what their notes mean.

Meeting people had always been easy for Melanie. Most people she liked right away, and they usually seemed to feel the same way about her. But when the door to 312 opened that morning, for just a moment she was almost speechless. Surprise can do that to a person, and at first glance April really was a surprise. Her hair was stacked up in a pile that seemed to be more pins than hair, and the whole thing teetered forward over her thin pale face. She was wearing a big, yellowish-white fur thing around her shoulders, and carrying a plastic purse almost as big as a suitcase. But most of all it was the eyelashes. They were black and bushy looking, and the ones on her left eye were higher up and sloped in a different direction. Melanie's mouth opened and closed a few times before anything came out.

 What connections can you make to the story? If you have difficulty, pause and think about what you read. In what ways do the characters or the feelings or the situation seem familiar to you?

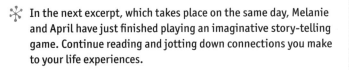 In the next excerpt, which takes place on the same day, Melanie and April have just finished playing an imaginative story-telling game. Continue reading and jotting down connections you make to your life experiences.

As they walked to the door Melanie asked, "Do you want to play some more tomorrow?"

April was adjusting her fur stole around her shoulders for the trip upstairs. "Oh, I guess so," she said with a sudden return to haughtiness.

But Melanie was beginning to understand about April's frozen spells, and how to thaw her out. You just had to let her know she couldn't make you stop liking her that easily. "None of my friends know how to play imagining games the way you do," Melanie said. "Some of them can do it a little bit but they mostly don't have any very good ideas. And a lot of them only like ball games or other things that are already made up. But I like imagining games better than anything."

April was being very busy trying to get her stole to stay on because the clasp was a little bit broken. All at once she pulled it off, wadded it all up and tucked it under her arm. She looked right straight at Melanie and said, "You know what? I never did call them that before, but imagining games are just

ABOUT THE AUTHOR
Zilpha Keatley Snyder was born on May 11, 1927, in Lemoore, California. Having grown up before the age of television, she read books for entertainment. At the age of eight, she decided she wanted to become a writer.

As an adult, Snyder has enjoyed much success as a writer of children's books. Three of her novels—*The Egypt Game, The Headless Cupid,* and *The Witches of Worm*—have achieved "runner up" status for the Newbery Medal. Snyder says that she has based much of her writing on people she knows and her own experiences. For more information, visit the Zilpha Keatley Snyder homepage: www.zksnyder.com.

During

REREADING   Students who find it difficult to read and note their connections at the same time should read the excerpt twice. First, have them follow along as you model reading the passage for connections, pausing two or three times to note connections to your experiences. Then have students reread silently, writing their own connections.

Organization Before students write their story, have them plan how to organize it. Point out two options: They can tell their stories in chronological order, or they can start with the main event and go back to tell what led up to it. If students are writing about meeting someone for the first time, have them consider whether they will describe that person based on their first impression or based on reflection. Have students use a graphic organizer, such as a sequence chart or a web, to help them plan their writing. Then tell them to use the organizer to guide them as they write.

Quick Assess

❋ Did students record several connections in their Response Notes?

❋ Were they able to explain the connections in a way that makes sense to someone else?

❋ Did they write a coherent narrative about one of those connections?

about all I ever play because most of the time I never have anybody to play with."

She started off up the hall. Then she turned around and walked backward, waving her fur stole around her head like a lasso. "You've got lots of good ideas, too," she yelled. ❖

❋ Share and compare your **Response Notes** with a partner's. Have your partner help you choose your strongest connection. In your conversation, explain the connection by telling the story you were reminded of while reading this one. That's how many ideas for stories are formed—by reflecting on life stories and connections. Below, write the story behind the connection, as if you were telling it to a friend.

_____

_____

_____

_____

_____

_____

_____

_____

_____

_____

_____

_____

_____

_____

> Connecting life experiences to the text helps readers relate to and become involved in what they are reading. These connections also offer ideas for writing.

After

READING/WRITING CONNECTION

Have students write a report on a favorite story of theirs, one with which they really connected. Instead of focusing on what happened in the story, have students focus on their response to the story: why that story means a lot to them and what made them connect with it. Encourage them to use examples from the story to make their point.

Variation Students can write about a favorite movie or song, explaining their strongest connection and why the piece is important to them.

In earlier units of the Daybook, you made connections to another text, such as a book or short story, a movie, a piece of artwork, a poem, or a song. Somehow the texts are related, but your mind begins to wonder how and why. You ask yourself, "How are they the same? How are they different? How does one text help me understand the other?" Often, you make the connections in the back of your mind without really noticing.

In this lesson, you're going to practice noticing what connections you make while you read. Read the following excerpt, also from Zilpha Keatley Snyder's novel *The Egypt Game*. Note that Caroline is April's grandmother and Marshall is Melanie's little brother. In the **Response Notes**, record connections you make to other texts.

from The Egypt Game by Zilpha Keatley Snyder

Response Notes

All through the month of August, Melanie and April were together almost every day. They played the paper-families game and other games, both in the Rosses' apartment and in Caroline's. They took Marshall for walks and to the park while Mrs. Ross was gone to her class, and almost every day they went to the library. It was in the library in August that the seeds were planted that grew into the Egypt Game in September in Professor's deserted yard.

It all started when April found a new book about Egypt, an especially interesting one about the life of a young pharaoh. She passed it on to Melanie, and with it a lot of her interest in all sorts of ancient stuff. Melanie was soon as fascinated by the valley of the Nile as April had been. Before long, with the help of a sympathetic librarian, they had found and read just about everything the library had to offer on Egypt—both fact and fiction.

They read about Egypt in the library during the day, and at home in the evening, and in bed late at night when they were supposed to be asleep. Then in the mornings while they helped each other with their chores they discussed the things they had found out. In a very short time they had accumulated all sorts of fascinating facts about tombs and temples, pharaohs and pyramids, mummies and monoliths, and dozens of other exotic topics. They decided that the Egyptians couldn't have been more interesting if they had done it on purpose. Everything, from their love of beauty and mystery, to their fascinating habit of getting married when they were only eleven years old, made good stuff to talk about. By the end of the month, April and Melanie were beginning work on their own alphabet of hieroglyphics for writing secret messages, and at the library they were beginning to be called the Egypt Girls.

LESSON 47

Students will read a story and use a chart to find their strongest connections to the story and relate their connections to another text.

BACKGROUND KNOWLEDGE

Extend your discussions about Egypt from the previous unit by explaining that Egypt is an African country with a long and interesting history of civilization. Have students locate Egypt on a map. Invite students to share what they already know about ancient Egyptian civilization and the things about it that interest them the most. If you have time, gather books from the library or visit informational sites online so that students can read more about the three pyramids of Giza, the pharaohs, mummies, temples, and the tomb of the boy king, Tutankhamen.

VOCABULARY

pharaoh a king of ancient Egypt

Nile the longest river in the world, flowing about 6,677 km (4,150 mi) through eastern Africa

monoliths large blocks of stone

hieroglyphics an ancient system of writing that includes pictures and symbols

Use the Word Splash blackline master on page 272.

Before

CRITICAL READING SKILL

Connecting Text to Text In addition to making personal connections, a proficient reader makes meaning by finding connections between the text he or she is reading and other texts, such as books, movies, TV shows, songs, poems, and so on. These connections deepen understanding, support visualization, and help the reader fill in gaps and answer questions.

RESPONSE NOTES As students read, have them ask themselves these questions: *In what way does this remind me of something I've read or watched? How are the characters like other characters I've read about? How is the setting or plot similar to something I've read or seen before?* As they make connections, they should write them in their Response Notes. Let students know they'll use these notes later in the lesson.

During

PROVIDING INDIVIDUAL SUPPORT

As students are reading independently, circulate around the room, conferring quietly with them. You might have a deskside conference with a student who needs to find more connections, perhaps prompting her or him or rereading the text together. You could also confer with a student who makes connections easily, engaging her or him in a discussion about both texts.

**Using a Graphic Organizer:
Connections Chart** Filling in the
Connections Chart will help students
organize the information they've gathered in their Response Notes. It will
help them understand the connections
with other texts, as well as why they
made them. Discussing their connections with a partner will help solidify
the meanings of those connections
for them.

Quick Assess

✳ Did students record several connections in their Response Notes and
discuss them with a partner?

✳ Were they able to explain why they
made each connection?

✳ Did students choose their strongest
connection and describe it effectively?

But in between all the good times, both April and Melanie were spending
some bad moments worrying about the beginning of school. April was worried because she knew from experience—lots of it—that it isn't easy to face
a new class in a new school. She didn't admit it, not even to Melanie, but she
was having nightmares about the first day of school. There were classroom
nightmares, and schoolyard nightmares and principal's office nightmares. ✧

✳ Using the connections you made, fill in the following
Connections Chart.

This part of *The Egypt Game* . . .	reminded me of this other text . . .	because . . .

✳ Compare your Connections Chart with a partner's and discuss the
types of connections you each made.

✳ Now describe the strongest connection you made. Was the other
text a song, picture, movie, or another book? What was the subject
of the connection? How did the connection make you feel? Explain.

Comparing
texts helps you
make your
reading more
meaningful.

After

SOCIAL STUDIES CONNECTION

Have students work in small groups on
a mini research project about a specific
aspect of ancient Egypt. Have each group
create a multimedia report or a skit with
props. The report can take the form of a
slide show or video, and include labeled
drawings, hieroglyphics, graphics, or
maps. Once the groups have finished their
projects, set aside time for each group to
share their presentation with classmates.

ASKING QUESTIONS TO MAKE CONNECTIONS — 48 LESSON

As they read, good readers make connections to things they know. Sometimes readers come across situations about which they know little or nothing. What happens then? One way to connect to unfamiliar experiences and places is to ask questions such as these: Why would a person act that way? What would life be like if I lived in this place with these rules? What would I do if I were in that position? Take time to think about and ask questions that help you connect to the issues, the people, and the events in what you read.

In the following excerpt, April, Melanie, and Marshall have been playing "The Egypt Game" that they created. In the **Response Notes,** make connections by asking questions about what is unfamiliar to you or what makes you curious.

Response Notes

from The Egypt Game by Zilpha Keatley Snyder

...Nobody ever planned [the Egypt Game] ahead, at least, not very far. Ideas began and grew and afterwards it was hard to remember just how. That was one of the mysterious and fascinating things about it.

On that particular day, the game about Marshamosis, the boy pharaoh, and Set, the god of evil, didn't get very far. They'd no more than gotten started when April and Melanie decided they just had to have some more equipment before they could play it well. So they postponed the game and went instead to scout around in the alley for boards and boxes to use in making things like thrones and altars. They found just what they needed behind the doughnut shop and the furniture store in the next block, and brought them back to Egypt. And it was on the same trip that they had the good luck to rescue an old metal mixing bowl from a garbage pail. April said it would be just the thing for a firepit for building sacred fires.

When they had everything as far as the hole in the fence, they ran into a problem. The bowl and boards went through all right, but the boxes were just too big. The only solution was to throw them over the top of the fence. It wasn't easy, and in landing they made quite a bit of noise.

It wasn't long afterwards that the curtain on the small window at the back of the Professor's store was pushed very carefully to one side. But April and Melanie were so busy building and planning that they didn't notice at all. Only someone with very sharp eyes would have been able to see the figure that stood silently behind the very dirty window in the darkened room.

...That was about where they were in the Game, when something happened that almost put an end to the Egypt Game; and not to the Egypt Game alone,

---

LESSON 48

Students will read a story and use Response Notes to ask questions about the story in order to monitor understanding and make connections.

ACTIVATE PRIOR KNOWLEDGE

Invite volunteers to talk about games they have invented with friends or family members that required a good deal of imagination. Encourage students to share the focus, setting, characters, and rules of their childhood games. Remind students that in this exercise, they are making a connection between the game played by the two girls in the story and their own "imagining games."

VOCABULARY

dungeon an ancient prison often found in a castle basement

languishing losing strength; withering away

pillar architectural column

bonds something, like rope, that is used to restrain

Talk about the words and their definitions. Ask students what sort of setting the words make them picture. Encourage them to draw on previous encounters with any of the words. Have students then read the selection to see if their images were similar to what's being described in the story.

Before

CRITICAL READING SKILL
Asking Questions to Make Connections Tell students that good readers often ask themselves questions as they're reading to monitor their understanding and to interact with the text. Review the questions in the introduction at the top of page 153. Make sure students understand that it's OK if they don't "get" something that they're read-

ing right away. Asking questions is a way of figuring out what isn't clear.

RESPONSE NOTES Direct students to write in their Response Notes any questions they have. After they finish reading, they can go back to those questions and answer them if they can.

During

ASKING QUESTIONS WHILE
READING Students can read the passage independently, or you may want to read it aloud, emphasizing the building suspense. Model asking questions while reading, using a think-aloud: *Who's looking through the window in the Professor's store? Is it someone dangerous to the girls? I'm going to read more to see if I can find out who it is.*

WRITER'S CRAFT

Building Suspense Good writers build suspense so that the reader is eager to discover what happens next. In this selection from *The Egypt Game*, Snyder indicates that something very important, something very frightening, has happened, but she doesn't let us know right away what it is. She builds the suspense by dropping clues, such as the worry in Mrs. Ross's voice, the fear the children feel, and the indication in the first sentence at the top of page 154 that whatever it is, it will have a huge impact on the children in the story. By building suspense, Snyder is drawing in her readers and making sure they'll constantly ask questions, make predictions, and then read on to find out what happens.

Response Notes

but to all the outdoor games in the whole neighborhood. On that particular afternoon, the girls had built a dungeon out of cardboard boxes in the corner of the storage yard. Elizabeth and Marshall were languishing in the dungeon, tied hand and foot, victims of the priests of Set. April and Melanie were creeping cautiously from pillar to pillar in the Temple of Evil, on their way to the rescue. Melanie was crouching behind an imaginary pillar, when suddenly she straightened up and stood listening. In the dungeon Elizabeth heard it too, and quickly untied her bonds. April ran to help Marshall with his. They were really only kite string and knotted easily. From somewhere not too far away, perhaps the main alley behind the Casa Rosada, Mrs. Ross's voice was calling, "Melanie! Marshall! Melanie!" There was something about the tone of her voice that made Melanie's eyes widen with fear.

"Something's wrong," she said.

"It's too early," April nodded. "She never gets home this early."

They scrambled through the hole in the fence and, dragging Marshall to hurry him up, they dashed for the main alley behind the Casa Rosada. From there they could safely answer without giving the location of Egypt away.

Mrs. Ross met them near the back door of the apartment house. Even though they all clamored to know what was the matter, she only shook her head and said, "There's been some trouble in the neighborhood. April, you and Elizabeth come up to our apartment until your folks get home."

Of course they were all terribly curious, but Mrs. Ross wouldn't say any more. "We'll wait to discuss it until we have the facts," she said. "What I know right now amounts only to rumors. There may not be any truth in the story at all."

It occurred to all of them, though, that the rumors had been frightening enough to make Mrs. Ross cancel her after-school remedial reading class— which she almost never did—and come home early. And Melanie noticed a strangeness in her voice and that her hand shook as she put milk and cookies on the table. It had to be something serious. ❖

154 LESSON 48

✳ Compare your **Response Notes** with a partner's. Discuss the questions you asked. Add any new questions that arise from your conversation.

After

As students share their Response Notes with a partner, have them try to find answers to their questions. They should highlight the parts of the text that provide the answers.

READING/WRITING CONNECTION
Have students write the next chapter of the story to answer the question "What happens next?" If students know the story, tell them to write something different from what they know will happen next. Because the excerpt here ends with the characters (and readers) curious about the problem in the neighborhood,

this stopping point presents an opportunity for students to engage with the story and use their imaginations.

✳ Choose one of the questions and try to answer it. Describe how your question and possible answer help you make sense of the story.

_____

_____

_____

_____

_____

_____

_____

_____

✳ REFLECT: Take a moment to think about the three kinds of connections you've made in this unit: connecting text to yourself; connecting text to other texts; and connecting text to big questions. For you, which type seems to come most easily with *The Egypt Game* excerpts? Why do you think so? Write about it below.

_____

_____

_____

_____

_____

_____

_____

_____

_____

_____

Asking questions will help you make connections to texts that are about unfamiliar situations and places.

ASKING QUESTIONS TO MAKE CONNECTIONS **155**

Differentiation Some students may need help with their reflection on the different types of connections they've learned about in this unit. Review the types of connections: connecting text with your own experience, connecting this text with something else you've read or seen, and making connections by asking questions. Ask: *Which type of connection helped you the most in understanding and enjoying the selections from* The Egypt Game? Ask students which connection worked best, and help them to express why. Then have them reflect on the three strategies for making connections to a story.

Quick Assess

✳ Do students ask questions while they read?

✳ Are they able to make connections to what they read?

Students will learn that making personal connections helps them understand what they are reading.

BACKGROUND KNOWLEDGE

Ask students if they know what *kimchee* is. If students are unfamiliar with it, explain that kimchee is a kind of pickled cabbage that is a staple of Korean cuisine. It is a hot and spicy dish, with a distinctive, pungent odor. Invite students to share special or traditional dishes that are popular in their homes and tell whether or not they like them.

VOCABULARY

unreasonable unwilling to consider another's argument

Remind students how to break down a multisyllabic word that is unfamiliar: look for word parts, such as prefixes and suffixes *(un-, -able)*, and find a meaningful base word *(reason)*.

Think about the earlier example of hearing music at your cousin's wedding, connecting it to a merengue performance you saw, then using that experience to describe the merengue to your cousin. That's what you're going to practice here; not dancing, of course, but using the connections you make to the text.

If a character experiences something that reminds you of something you've experienced, ask yourself, "How does that connection help me better understand what I'm reading?" The answer might be that you can feel what the character feels. If the setting in something you read reminds you of the setting in a movie you saw, you might be able to better understand what you're reading because you can picture it so clearly. If something you read reminds you of something you heard on the news, you might be able to better understand the situation by asking questions about why both of these things happen.

The excerpt you are about to read is from Linda Sue Park's *Project Mulberry*, a novel about family, friendship, and what it means to "be American." In the **Response Notes**, record connections you make as you read. Afterwards, you'll reflect on how those connections help you understand the text better.

Response Notes

from **Project Mulberry** by Linda Sue Park

Patrick and I became friends because of a vegetable.

Not just any vegetable.

A cabbage.

And not just any old cabbage. A Korean pickled cabbage. Which isn't a round cabbage like Peter Rabbit would eat, but a longer, leafier kind. It gets cut up and salted and packed in big jars with lots of garlic, green onions, and hot red pepper, and then it's called *kimchee*. Kimchee is really spicy. Koreans eat it for breakfast, lunch, and dinner.

I don't like kimchee. My mom says that when I was little, I used to eat it. She'd rinse off the spiciness and give me a bite or two. When I got to be six or seven years old, she stopped rinsing it. Most Korean mothers do that, and most Korean kids keep eating it.

Not me. I hated the spiciness, and I still do. My mom keeps telling me I should eat it because it's refreshing. But what's so refreshing about having your mouth on fire?

My family used to tease me about not liking kimchee. My dad said maybe it meant I wasn't really Korean. "We should have your DNA tested," he'd tell

Before

CRITICAL READING SKILL

Using Your Connections for Understanding Most students readily make personal connections when they are reading. Some, however, need help learning how to make such connections to enrich their understanding of the text. This lesson helps students use their connections by asking: *How does this connection help me understand what I*

am reading? As students work at making better use of connections, they become more aware of the reading strategies they use and become better able to use those strategies as they read a variety of texts.

RESPONSE NOTES Remind students to jot down their connections in their Response Notes. Emphasize that the notes can be phrases or words; they do not have to be complete sentences. Tell students they will refer to those notes later in the lesson.

me. The seven-year-old snotbrain named Kenny who lives with us—otherwise known as my little brother—would wave big pieces in front of me and threaten to force me to eat them.

Another thing about kimchee is, it has a really strong smell. Even though it's stored in jars, you can still smell it, right through the jar and the refrigerator door. It sends out these feelers through the whole house.

Three years ago, when I was in fourth grade, we were living in Chicago. I'd made friends with a girl named Sarah. The first time she came over to play, she stopped dead in the entryway and said, *"Eww!* What's that smell?"

I'd never really noticed it. Smells are funny that way—they can sort of disappear if you live with them all the time. But Sarah was so grossed out that I was really embarrassed.

The exact same thing happened again a few weeks later, this time with two friends, a boy named Michael and his sister, Lily. They *both* stopped dead in their tracks and grabbed their noses. They insisted that we play outside because they couldn't stand the smell.

I asked my mom to stop making kimchee, but she told me I was being unreasonable.

When we moved to Plainfield two years ago, our new apartment didn't smell like kimchee—for about half a day. Then my mom unpacked some groceries, including a big jar of kimchee. *Sigh.* ❖

�֍ Review your **Response Notes** to help you determine the strongest connection you made so far. Describe that connection and how it helps you to better understand the story or influences your response to the story.

Describe a connection you made	How does the connection enhance your understanding of the story?

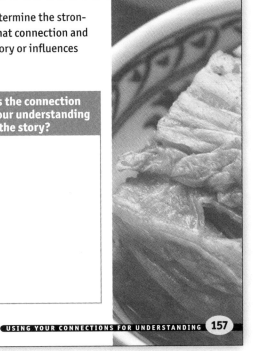

ABOUT THE AUTHOR

Linda Sue Park was born in 1960 in Urbana, Illinois. She is the daughter of Korean immigrants and has drawn on her own experiences to create her stories.

Park is the author of the novels *A Single Shard* (which received the Newbery Medal), *Seesaw Girl*, *The Kite Fighters*, and *When My Name Was Keoko,* as well as two picture books, *The Firekeeper's Son* and *What Does Bunny See?*

Linda Sue Park lives with her family in Rochester, New York. She still has a piece of raw silk made by the silkworms she raised as a research project for this book. For more information, see the author's official website: www.lspark.com.

During

MODELING MAKING CONNECTIONS

If students have difficulty explaining how their connections enhance their understanding, work through one or two together as a class. On a piece of chart paper or the board, draw a graphic like the one on page 157. Say: *I can relate to what the narrator, Julia, is saying. Everyone in my family loves sour-cream-and-onion potato chips. I hate them.*

I like plain chips. They all make fun of me, just they way they make fun of Julia in the story. I can understand how she must feel.

WRITER'S CRAFT

Author-Character Dialogue

Point out that most writers have certain exercises or techniques they use to help make their writing distinctive. Having an imaginary dialogue with your character is an exercise used by many writers. What's different about Linda Sue Park is that she has included her dialogue in her book! Discuss with students why having a dialogue with a character might be a good exercise. Have them give their opinions (supported by reasons) about whether they enjoyed reading the dialogue between Park and her character.

In *Project Mulberry,* the author, Linda Sue Park, inserts an imaginary dialogue between herself and the main character, Julia. It is a technique authors sometimes use to develop the personalities and voices of their characters or to reveal more about themselves. Here's how the story within a story begins:

Every story has another story inside, but you don't usually get to read the inside one. It's deleted or torn up or maybe filed away before the story becomes a book; lots of times it doesn't even get written down in the first place. If you'd rather read my story without interruption, you can skip these sections. Really and truly. I hereby give you official permission.

But if you're interested in learning about how this book was written—background information, mistakes, maybe even a secret or two—you've come to the right place. Some people like that sort of thing. It's mostly conversations between me and the author, Ms. Park. We had a lot of discussions while she was writing. ✢

✳ Read the following excerpts from the dialogue, and take notes about the connections you make between this text and the excerpt you read earlier.

Ms. Park: ...I hated kimchee when I was little. I like it now, but I didn't when I was your age.
Me: Wow. You can remember that far back?
Ms. Park: Very funny. I don't remember everything, of course. But parts of my childhood are quite vivid to me, and I like going there in my mind. You probably will, too, when you're older.
Me: Did your parents grow up in Korea?

Ms. Park: Yes. And my father always did the dishes.

Me: Did you have a bratty younger brother? Is that why you put Kenny in the story?

Ms. Park: I have a younger brother and a younger sister. But neither of them was very bratty. I got along with them pretty well when we were kids.

Me: A sister would be *much* better... ❖

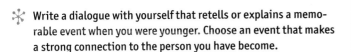

✳ In what way does the excerpt you read earlier influence your understanding of this excerpt?

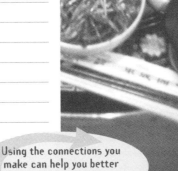

✳ Write a dialogue with yourself that retells or explains a memorable event when you were younger. Choose an event that makes a strong connection to the person you have become.

Using the connections you make can help you better understand and remember the text you are reading.

Planning Your Writing Before students write their response to the question on page 159, have them think about what they are going to say. Remind them to provide reasons for their opinions. Have students ask themselves these questions: *Did the dialogue give me insight into Julia's personality? What did I learn? After reading this, how do I feel about Julia? Why?* After students have made notes about what they want to say, have them write their answer to the question. (see page 31 for information on punctuating dialogue.)

Quick Assess

✳ Can students explain how making connections can enhance their understanding of a story?

After

READING/WRITING CONNECTION

Have students write a descriptive essay about a food their whole family enjoys. As they write their descriptions, they should answer these questions for the reader: *When is the food served? What does the food look like? Is it cooked or eaten raw? Is it served warm or chilled? Does it have a distinctive odor that fills the house? Is it spicy, mild, sweet, or salty? Is it noisy or messy to eat?*

Students will read a story, make personal connections, and describe how the connections influenced their appreciation of a story.

BACKGROUND KNOWLEDGE

Help students relate to the relationship between the characters in the story by connecting it to something in their own experience. Ask them these questions: *Do you and a friend prefer certain foods? What types of food do you both enjoy? Is there a food you dislike but your friend enjoys? How does your taste in food influence your friendship?*

Tell students they are going to read about the relationship between Julia and her friend Patrick.

Often the connections you make influence how you respond to what you read. Think back to the merengue example just once more. Imagine that you absolutely loved the performance you saw. That connection to the music at the wedding might make you respond with pleasure because you are hearing it again. It might inspire you and make you want to dance. When you're reading, the connections you make can help elicit your emotional (how you feel) and intellectual (what your brain thinks) responses.

If, for example, you learned about General Trujillo in Social Studies class, that connection to the plot of *Before We Were Free* (in the first unit in this book) might influence your response to what happens to Anita's family. Or, if you could relate to April in *The Egypt Game,* when she said she rarely had anyone to play with, your response to her odd actions might be very sympathetic.

Read the next excerpt from *Project Mulberry*. In the **Response Notes,** record connections you make as you read. After, you'll reflect on how those connections influence your response to the text.

Response Notes

from Project Mulberry by Linda Sue Park

I met Patrick on our second day in Plainfield, a Saturday morning. Actually, I saw him on the first day; he was hanging around on his front steps three doors down, watching the movers. Him and his three brothers as well. I noticed him right away, not because of the way he looked—brown hair in a normal boy-haircut, a few freckles, a gap between his front teeth that predicted braces in his future—but because he seemed to be the closest to my age. The other three boys were little, younger even than Kenny.

On the second day, I took a break from unpacking and went out to have a good look at our neighborhood. There they were again, the four boys, like they'd never moved off the steps. This time there was a girl with them, too, but she was a lot older.

Patrick came down the steps and said hello and told me his name. I said hi back and told him mine.

"Can I see inside your house?" he asked.

"Sure," I said.

...As we walked in the door of my house, Patrick tilted his head and sniffed. I braced myself for his reaction.

"Whoa," he said. "What's that? It smells great!"

Before

CRITICAL READING SKILL
Using Your Connections for Response

Making connections enhances one's understanding of a story. It can also influence the way a reader responds. In this lesson, students should ask themselves: *How do each of my connections affect, or influence, my responses to what I am reading? How have each of my connections affected what I want to know after reading the*
selection? How has each affected how I feel after reading the selection?

RESPONSE NOTES   Remind students to record their responses, since they'll use their Response Notes later in the lesson.

During

RESPONDING TO TEXT   Provide examples of ways you have responded to something you read. For example, you might talk about a time when you felt sad (happy, mad, surprised) while you were reading because you knew what it felt like to go through what the main character was experiencing.

That was the beginning of Patrick's love affair with kimchee. Whenever he eats dinner with us, my mom puts one bowl of kimchee on the table for the family and gives Patrick a whole private bowl for himself. He eats it in huge mouthfuls, sometimes without even adding any rice. I can hardly stand to watch him.

Maybe he's the one who needs his DNA tested. ❖

✳ With a partner, discuss the connections you made and how they influence your response to the story.

Describe a connection you made	How does the connection influence your response to the story?

Collaboration Have students work with a partner to chart their connections. As they talk about them, they might want to add other connections. Let students know that this is understandable, since often we don't realize we've made a connection until we talk with someone else about a text.

Students should think about the connections they are making as they read the selection. After reading, they should reflect on how those connections shaped their responses to the text.

Reflecting Remind students to focus on their responses to the selections from *Project Mulberry: Could you picture yourself in Julia's place? Did you laugh, or did you feel embarrassed like her? Did you like Patrick? Did he remind you of someone you know?*

Make sure students provide examples from the story to back up their responses.

Quick Assess

✳ Did students note connections they made with the text?

✳ Were they able to express how those connections affected their understanding of the text?

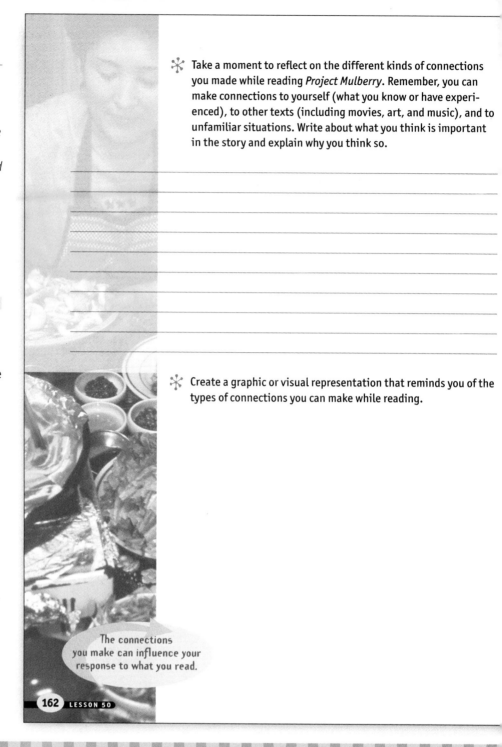

✳ Take a moment to reflect on the different kinds of connections you made while reading *Project Mulberry*. Remember, you can make connections to yourself (what you know or have experienced), to other texts (including movies, art, and music), and to unfamiliar situations. Write about what you think is important in the story and explain why you think so.

✳ Create a graphic or visual representation that reminds you of the types of connections you can make while reading.

The connections you make can influence your response to what you read.

162 LESSON 50

After

BOOK CONNECTIONS Have students set up a display of recommended books. Students can clip notes to the books telling why the book is special, how they responded to it, and why. Invite students to select from the books during independent reading time. Students can then meet in book groups to talk about the books they have read and share the connections they made.

Exploring Multiple Perspectives

Have you seen athletes argue with the officials, fans, or other players? Do you sometimes argue with your friends or your parents? Heated arguments rarely cause anyone to change his or her mind.

However, if you structure and present an argument well, you can convey your opinion effectively. For example, if you want to go somewhere special with your friends, you may wish to have a later curfew. In order to convince your parents, though, you will want to form an **argument** with responses to any objections they raise. A review of a new movie is another type of argument. Reviewers inform you of their opinion and support the argument with details and examples of why they like or do not like the movie.

In this unit, you will learn how to evaluate arguments presented by people with a variety of viewpoints. You will also learn how to structure your own argument.

163

UNIT OVERVIEW
In this unit, students learn that the author's purpose and perspective and the audience influence how an argument is constructed.

KEY IDEA
Well-structured arguments allow writers to present their opinions to specific audiences effectively.

CRITICAL READING SKILLS
by lesson
51 Understanding the author's perspective

52 Identifying support for an argument

53 Structuring an argument

54 Recognizing opposing viewpoints

55 Evaluating an argument

WRITING ACTIVITIES
by lesson
51 Express an opinion on the effectiveness of an argument.

52 Explain which argument is more convincing, based on the evidence.

53 Write an e-mail presenting an argument to a specific audience.

54 Write a paragraph that refutes opposing arguments.

55 Write an evaluation of the structure of an argument.

Literature

■ *All I Really Need to Know I Learned in Kindergarten* by Robert Fulghum (nonfiction excerpt)

Best-selling author Robert Fulghum offers advice about how to live life well and fully, based on what we teach children, such as playing fair, sharing, and cleaning up one's own mess.

■ "Battle of the Belts" by Karen Epper Hoffman (magazine article)

Writer Karen Epper Hoffman presents arguments in the controversy over installing seat belts in school buses.

■ *The Greatest: Muhammad Ali* by Walter Dean Myers (nonfiction excerpt)

Myers presents the complex issue of boxing and a sympathetic view of Ali as a man "who has been knocked down in his life," but who "has had the courage to rise."

■ *Green Planet Rescue* (excerpt) Robert R. Halpern

Halpern stresses the importance of safeguarding the planet's plant life.

ASSESSMENT To assess student learning in this unit, see pages 236 and 257.

Students will read and analyze persuasive text to determine the author's purpose and evaluate the effectiveness of the argument.

BACKGROUND KNOWLEDGE

Ask students about their time in kindergarten. What was it like? What lessons or rules did they learn? After students have read the Fulghum excerpt, compare the class discussion to Fulghum's excerpt.

Preview terms and concepts to ensure understanding of the references: "the little seed in the Styrofoam cup" refers to a common kindergarten activity; Dick-and-Jane books were early readers back in the 1950s; the Golden Rule teaches that you should treat others as you want others to treat you.

VOCABULARY

sanitation cleanliness

extrapolate to predict a future situation by drawing on similar situations in the present or past

Give an example of extrapolating: *Parents and teachers are always telling us to wash our hands before we touch food. I extrapolate from that that clean hands equal good sanitary habits.* Then discuss the meaning of *sanitation* as it's used on page 165.

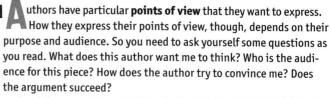

Authors have particular **points of view** that they want to express. How they express their points of view, though, depends on their purpose and audience. So you need to ask yourself some questions as you read. What does this author want me to think? Who is the audience for this piece? How does the author try to convince me? Does the argument succeed?

Read the excerpt from *All I Really Need to Know I Learned in Kindergarten* by Robert Fulghum. As you read, put a check in the **Response Notes** by the sentences that tell you the author's opinion.

Response Notes

from ALL I Really Need to Know I Learned in Kindergarten by Robert Fulghum

All I really need to know about how to live and what to do and how to be I learned in kindergarten. Wisdom was not at the top of the graduate-school mountain, but there in the sandpile at Sunday School. These are the things I learned:

Share everything.

Play fair.

Don't hit people.

Put things back where you found them.

Clean up your own mess.

Don't take things that aren't yours.

Say you're sorry when you hurt somebody.

Wash your hands before you eat.

Flush.

Warm cookies and cold milk are good for you.

Live a balanced life—learn some and think some and draw and paint and sing and dance and play and work every day some.

Take a nap every afternoon.

When you go out into the world, watch out for traffic, hold hands, and stick together.

Be aware of wonder. Remember the little seed in the Styrofoam cup: The roots go down and the plant goes up and nobody really knows how or why, but we are all like that.

Goldfish and hamsters and white mice and even the little seed in the Styrofoam cup—they all die. So do we.

And then remember the Dick-and-Jane books and the first word you learned—the biggest word of all—LOOK.

Before

CRITICAL READING SKILL
Understanding the Author's Perspective Effective arguments usually begin with the author's opinion. Sometimes the author tries to convince the reader through straightforward details and reasons; other times the author might use satire or other subtle ways to convince the reader. If a reader cannot understand what technique the author is using to present an argument, the reader might miss the message. Knowing "where the author is coming from"—the writer's *perspective*—helps readers understand and evaluate the author's opinion.

Ask students to discuss arguments they have had or seen. Help them see the differences between effective and ineffective arguments. Point out that an argument does not need to result from anger. It can just be about presenting different points of view. Let them know they are about to read a selection written from the point of view of an adult man who is presenting the argument, or opinion, that he learned the most important lessons in his life when he was in kindergarten.

RESPONSE NOTES As students read, remind them to put a check mark next to sentences that express the author's opinion. (See *Daybook* page 225 for more about marking text.)

Everything you need to know is in there somewhere. The Golden Rule and love and basic sanitation. Ecology and politics and equality and sane living.

Take any one of those items and extrapolate it into sophisticated adult terms and apply it to your family life or your work or your government or your world and it holds true and clear and firm. Think what a better world it would be if we all—the whole world—had cookies and milk about three o'clock every afternoon and then lay down with our blankies for a nap. Or if all governments had as a basic policy to always put things back where they found them and to clean up their own mess.

And it is still true, no matter how old you are—when you go out into the world, it is best to hold hands and stick together. ❖

�֎ Briefly answer the following questions:

■ What is Fulghum's purpose in writing this?

_____

■ Who is his audience?

_____

■ How good is his advice for this audience?

_____
_____

�֎ Readers also evaluate an author's argument by how convinced they are. Complete the following statement in a few sentences.

I (am or am not) convinced by Robert Fulghum because

_____
_____
_____
_____
_____
_____
_____
_____

Understanding the author's perspective helps you evaluate his or her opinion.

ABOUT THE AUTHOR
Born in 1937, Robert Fulghum grew up in Waco, Texas. He has worked as a ditch-digger, a newspaper carrier, a ranch hand, and a singing cowboy, and for years he was a Unitarian minister in the Pacific Northwest. An accomplished artist and musician, he also taught drawing, painting, and philosophy at the Lakeside School in Seattle. For more about Robert Fulghum, visit his website: www.robertfulghum.com/authorbio.php.

TEACHING TIP
Writing Support A good writer considers the audience before writing. If a writer is presenting an opinion to people who disagree with it, the writer will have to make a strong case that responds to the counterarguments. For help with the questions on page 165, ask students these questions: *Why do you think Fulghum wrote this piece? Did he want to convince people he was right or simply what is right? Who is Fulghum's audience?*

Quick Assess

✷ In their paragraphs, did students present a clear opinion about the author's perspective? Did they back up their opinions with reasons and examples?

During

IDENTIFYING OPINION Remind students that an opinion is a belief or a judgment. An opinion cannot be proved by facts, but it can be supported by facts or experience. Discuss what makes the following statements opinions:

✷ *"Wisdom was not at the top of the graduate-school mountain, but there in the sandpile at Sunday School."*

✷ *"Everything you need to know is in there [in the list] somewhere...Ecology and politics and equality and sane living."*

Help students understand that although they may agree with Fulghum, that does not mean that his statements are factual.

After

READING/WRITING CONNECTION As a class, create a brochure for students entering sixth grade. Ask your students to contribute several statements of advice based on their beliefs and experience. Compile this "collected wisdom" to pass on to new students.

Students will examine an author's point of view on a safety issue and respond to the author's evidence.

BACKGROUND KNOWLEDGE

Explain that seat belts for motor vehicles haven't always been mandatory. Yet, as more statistical information has proved that seat belts save lives, more and more states have passed laws requiring seat belt use. The issue of whether or not people should wear seat belts on buses is still being debated. Have students connect the issue to their own experiences (are there seat belts on the buses they ride?) and consider the issue before reading.

VOCABULARY

mandate to require as if, or actually, by law

unanimous agreed upon by all

compartmentalize to separate into different compartments or small areas

Discuss how the words *mandate* and *unanimous* might be used in a debate about a law. Why would something be mandated? Must a vote be unanimous for something to become law? Invite students to name things that might be *compartmentalized,* such as food on a tray and then predict how the term might relate to a discussion of seat belts on a bus.

Support for an argument can come from the author's background or values, as was the case for Robert Fulghum. It can also come from other sources. Expert testimony, facts, and anecdotes—short personal stories that illustrate your point—can all be effective.

"Battle of the Belts" is about the controversy over installing seat belts in school buses. Read the essay to see what the argument is. Mark the **support** Hoffman uses for each side of the "battle" in the **Response Notes**.

Response Notes

"Battle of the Belts" by Karen Epper Hoffman

When Matthew Mandell took his son to meet the school bus that was to take him on a field trip from the Bronx to Lower Manhattan, he was shocked to find the vehicle had no seat belts. Mandell and the other parents protested and ultimately refused to send their kids on the outing. "No child should be in a moving vehicle without a seat belt," he says.

Mandell's surprise is understandable. New York state passed a law in the '80s mandating seat belts on new school buses (although those that predate the law can still be used). Only New York, New Jersey, and Florida require seat belts be installed in new buses; a similar law is going into effect in California in July [2005]. The latest state to join the debate is Illinois—where the state legislature is considering a measure to mandate seat belts on buses.

We can't imagine cars without seat belts; why aren't buses subject to the same regulation? To start with, there's no unanimous agreement they're even necessary. School buses are constructed with high, thickly padded, closely spaced seats that protect passengers by "compartmentalizing" them in a crash, say Charlie Gauthier, executive director of the National Association of State Directors of Pupil Transportation Services. Studies conducted in the late '80s confirmed that compartmentalization works and concluded that seat belts would provide little or no benefit in these vehicles—and may, in some cases, cause injuries.

Consider the figures. Roughly the same number of kids drive or walk to school as take a bus: about 24 million. Yet each year, approximately 169 children are killed being driven to school by an adult, while about a dozen die in school bus crashes. "With or without seat belts, the safest place for a kid to be is on the school bus," Gauthier says.

Plenty of people disagree with Gauthier—the National PTA and the American Academy of Pediatrics support school seat belt laws—and Alan Ross, president of the National Coalition for School Bus Safety, says getting kids in the habit of buckling up every day can save their lives later on.

Before

CRITICAL READING SKILL

Finding Support Point out that identifying the support a writer uses to convince readers of his or her viewpoint is an important part of comprehending and evaluating an argument. If the support is flawed, the argument will be, too. If the support is inadequate, the argument will not be convincing. Tell

students that in this lesson they will be looking at ways in which an author supports the points of view she is presenting.

RESPONSE NOTES Karen Hoffman supports her argument with expert testimony, anecdotes, facts, figures, and opinions. Have students find examples of this support in the text and mark it in the Response Notes (e.g., the fourth paragraph). Tell students they will use these notes to complete the chart on page 167.

Seat belts can add $3,000-$6,000 to the cost of a new bus and reduce the number of seats up to 25 percent or more because the newly designed seats take up more room. So districts would have to buy more buses, and pay more mechanics and drivers. These expenses are sticking points in passing legislation that mandates seat belts on buses—or even getting the laws introduced into state legislatures. Lawmakers question whether financially strapped school districts can assume these added costs. Until they can, the kids might just need to hang on tight. ◦

❋ People disagree on the value of seat belts in school buses. The author gives evidence from both sides. Use the graphic organizer to sort the details.

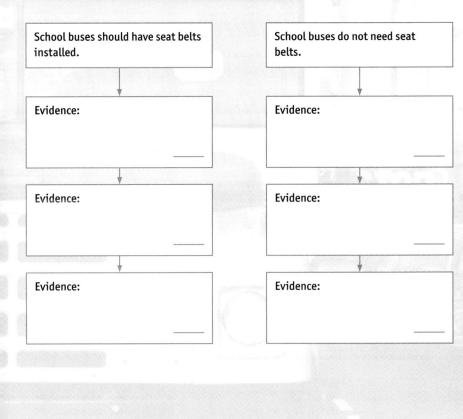

School buses should have seat belts installed.

Evidence:

Evidence:

Evidence:

School buses do not need seat belts.

Evidence:

Evidence:

Evidence:

Differentiation If you think that students will have difficulty following the arguments and supporting details in the selection, preview the graphic organizer on page 167 after you have read the first paragraph aloud. Show students how to use it, putting the opening anecdote in the first evidence box in the left-hand column. Then instruct students to stop after each paragraph to complete the next part of the organizer.

For students who need more of a challenge, ask them to research one more piece of evidence for each side of the argument presented in the article.

TEACHING TIP

Collaboration Ask students to work individually to write the evidence in the boxes. After they are finished, they can get together with a partner to label the types of evidence they have found. You may need to circulate to help them or, if students have little experience with supporting evidence, you may want to make this a whole-class activity so you can be sure everyone has examples that fit each category.

During

Read aloud the first paragraph. Tell students that the ride from the Bronx to Lower Manhattan is a long one through busy city streets. Ask who agrees with Mr. Mandell that the bus should have had seat belts. Discuss students' reasons for agreeing or disagreeing. Then go on to the rest of the article, either reading aloud or asking students to read silently.

After all have finished reading, show students how to use the graphic organizer

on page 167. They should be able to find three pieces of evidence for each side of the argument. Here are examples of types of evidence:

E Charlie Gauthier says that compartmentalizing passengers replaces the need for seat belts.

Fi Approximately 169 children are killed each year while being driven to school in cars.

A Mr. Mandell refused to let his son go on the field trip.

Fa Three states have laws, California's will go into effect soon, and the Illinois legislature is considering such a law.

O We can't imagine cars without seat belts; why aren't buses subject to the same regulation?

WRITING SUPPORT

Using Examples to Support an Opinion To reinforce the importance of evidence in creating a convincing argument, students will write a paragraph explaining which argument is more convincing to them and why. Remind them that they should provide examples to show which evidence provided by the author most influenced their answer. Model using examples with a think-aloud: *The National PTA and the American Academy of Pediatrics support school seat belt laws. The PTA and the pediatricians should know about how to protect children. That's an example of why I think there should be seat belts on school buses.*

Quick Assess

* Were students able to identify the types of evidence in the selection?

* Did students clearly state which argument is more convincing to them?

* Do students offer at least one way in which the evidence helped determine their position?

* In each evidence box on page 167, label the type of evidence the author uses.

  E = expert testimony (An expert gives his or her opinion.)

  Fi = figure (A number or percentage is given.)

  A = anecdote (A short story is used to illustrate a point.)

  Fa = fact (The writer uses a statement that can be proven true by consulting a reference source or using firsthand experience.)

  O = opinion (Hoffman tells what she thinks.)

* Write a paragraph telling which argument is more convincing to you and why. Include an explanation of how the evidence influenced your answer.

> Using different kinds of evidence can make an argument more convincing.

After

APPLYING THE STRATEGY

Ask students to find another article that presents two sides of an argument (newspapers and television-network Internet sites are good places to search). Then have them use a graphic organizer similar to that on page 167 to sort the evidence for the two sides.

An effective argument is structured around a **main idea** supported by **details** and reasons. Look at the two pieces you read in Lessons 51 and 52. Select one to represent in a cluster in order to show how the details support one of the main ideas. In the large oval, write the main idea of the piece you selected. In the smaller ovals, write supporting details.

Title _____

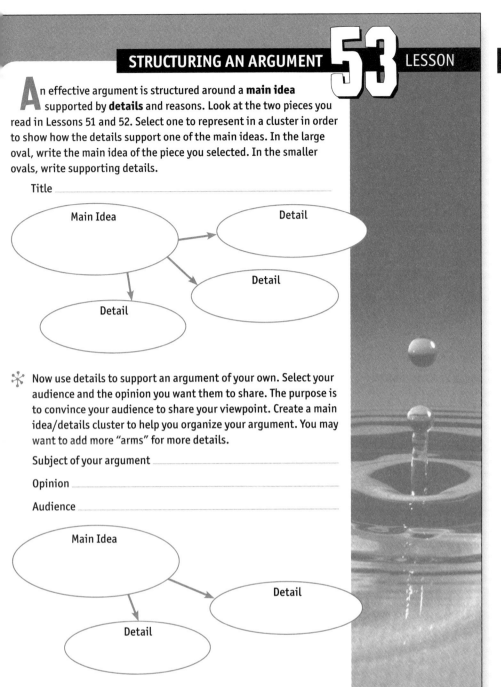

❋ Now use details to support an argument of your own. Select your audience and the opinion you want them to share. The purpose is to convince your audience to share your viewpoint. Create a main idea/details cluster to help you organize your argument. You may want to add more "arms" for more details.

Subject of your argument _____

Opinion _____

Audience _____

Students will use a graphic organizer to record the main idea and supporting details from an argument they have read and use it to organize and write a persuasive e-mail to their audience.

BACKGROUND KNOWLEDGE

Remind students that a main idea is an important point the writer is trying to make and the details are the examples and facts the writer provides to support or explain the main idea. With argument, the main idea is the opinion the writer is expressing, and the details are the examples, facts, and reasons that make the opinion more convincing to the reader.

Before

CRITICAL READING AND WRITING SKILL

Structuring an Argument Make sure that students understand that the structure of an argument will vary depending on the author's purpose and audience, but arguments always consist of a main idea and details that support it. In this lesson, students graph an argument they have read and then use a graphic to organize an argument they will write.

Using a Graphic Organizer Clusters are one of the most common and most effective graphic organizers for helping students map relationships between ideas. By expanding a cluster, students reinforce the idea that all details and examples should connect back to the main idea. Remind students to think about the relationship between the main idea and the details.

EXTRA SUPPORT

Differentiation Help students narrow their writing topics so they have a supportable argument. Have them think about where they can find facts and examples to support their argument (the Internet, books, interviews, personal experience). Encourage them to write down opposing viewpoints they'll need to respond to in their argument.

Quick Assess

✳ Did students map the argument of one of the previous selections?

✳ Were students able to choose a topic and fill out a main idea and details cluster to plan their own argument?

✳ Did students write a persuasive e-mail message presenting their argument in an effective way?

✳ Write an e-mail presenting your argument in the space below. Begin by clearly stating your main idea. Then build your argument using supporting details. Strengthen your argument by including evidence of different types and from different sources.

Send

To:

From:

Subject:

Date: Time:

Writers use details and reasons to support the main idea of an argument.

170 LESSON 53

During

MAPPING AN ARGUMENT

Allow students to select the piece to use for the first cluster on page 169. You may want to model filling in the cluster by writing the main idea (for example, school buses don't need seat belts) and a detail (school buses are compartmentalized for safety).

Once students understand how to map an argument this way, have them fill in the rest of the cluster. Then have them focus on planning their own argument.

Once students have finished planning, have them write their persuasive message on page 170.

After

APPLYING THE STRATEGY

Have students create a main idea and details cluster for other pieces of persuasive writing, such as a letter to the editor of a newspaper or magazine or a review of a book or movie. After students have mapped the main idea and supporting details, have them write a short paragraph about how effective they found the argument to be.

T here are at least two sides to every argument. Writers of convincing arguments know that the best way to counter **opposing viewpoints** is to tackle them head-on by explaining how and why the opposing arguments, or counter arguments, are wrong.

As you read this excerpt from *The Greatest: Muhammad Ali* by Walter Dean Myers, ask yourself: What is Myers's viewpoint on the importance of this famous fighter and on prizefighting as a sport? How does Myers handle opposing viewpoints? Circle words or phrases that help you answer these questions.

Response Notes

from The Greatest: Muhammad Ali by Walter Dean Myers

In examining the life of Muhammad Ali, his personal and professional choices, the fighters he faced in the ring, one wonders if it is morally right to allow young men to risk their health and future for the prizes to be found in a fighting career. So many young people have come to the ring from the farms and from the ghettos—Jews, Italians, blacks, Irish, Latinos—all looking for the elusive dreams of fame and fortune. As the fight game grows, and it is growing, perhaps we don't have the right to deny these young people their chance to succeed. But because we know that in so many cases that quest has ended in the physical ruin of lonely warriors who have dropped off the sports pages and out of the public view, we should at least, as Muhammad Ali has done, try to make sure that when people do sacrifice their goods, it is not their only way to secure human dignity.

Courage does not mean letting go of fear. It means having the will to face one's fears, to face the dangers in one's life, and to venture forward to do that which is morally right. Writers have said that Ali was afraid of Liston, that he was afraid of going into the army, that he was afraid of turning away from the Nation of Islam. There were things of which he was afraid, but he was big enough, courageous enough, to face everything that came his way. He has been knocked down in his life, and he has had the courage to rise. ❖

❖ What is your impression of Muhammad Ali from Myers's description?

_____

_____

OPPOSING VIEWPOINTS **171**

S tudents will learn that an important element of an argument is an opposing viewpoint, or counterargument.

BACKGROUND KNOWLEDGE

Ask students to share what they know about Muhammad Ali. (Ali is an intelligent man and was one of the best boxers ever.) Explain that while boxing has many rules designed to protect boxers, it is still a brutal sport. Even the most highly trained and skilled boxers get injured, sometimes permanently. Ali now has a nervous system disorder that prevents him from speaking clearly or moving easily. Many doctors attribute this condition to brain damage he suffered while boxing.

VOCABULARY

ring platform on which a boxing match takes place

ghetto poor part of a city in which most of the inhabitants are of a single racial or ethnic group

Nation of Islam a social and political organization of African American Muslims

Have students read the selection, circling any unfamiliar words. After reading, they can revisit these words by examining context clues.

Before

CRITICAL READING SKILL
Opposing Viewpoints In this lesson, students will see how effectively persuasive writers acknowledge opposing arguments. By acknowledging other viewpoints, writers or speakers present themselves as reasonable people who have carefully considered the many sides of the argument. As a result, the argument is more convincing.

Remind students that they have found viewpoints in previous lessons. Ask them to discuss what was easy and what was hard about identifying the view points. Use those insights to help students think about how to find Myers's viewpoint.

RESPONSE NOTES Make sure students circle words and phrases that help them identify Myers's viewpoint and how he handles the opposing point of view. (Myers acknowledges other viewpoints in the second paragraph.)

Collaboration Have students work in pairs to share their e-mails from lesson 53 and identify opposing viewpoints. Encourage students to help each other think of another point of view or argument that needs to be addressed. Students can write their paragraphs and then meet again with their partners to see if the argument is addressed effectively or if any changes need to be made.

Quick Assess

✳ Did students identify words and phrases that indicate the author's viewpoint? Did they identify words and phrases that show how the author addresses opposing viewpoints?

✳ Do students' paragraphs effectively acknowledge and then address an opposing viewpoint?

From the title of his book, you probably think that Myers admires Ali. You are correct. In this selection, he looks at the arguments people have raised against boxing and against Ali, and then he supports the position that we should admire Ali. Use a highlighter to mark the details and arguments that represent Myers's viewpoint. Use a different color to mark the details and arguments of the opposing viewpoint.

✳ In the chart that follows, write Myers's viewpoint at the top of the left column. Write the opposing viewpoint at the top of the right column. Under each heading, write the details from the article that support each viewpoint.

Myers's viewpoint	Opposing viewpoint:
Details:	Details:

✳ Review the e-mail you wrote in Lesson 53. What opposing viewpoint might your audience have? Write an additional paragraph that describes and refutes, or argues against, that argument.

> Writers include and argue against opposing viewpoints to strengthen their own arguments.

During

After students have read the excerpt once, have them discuss the questions that appeared before the selection, using the annotations they made in the text.

Help students understand that Myers's viewpoint is that it might not be "morally right to allow young men to risk their health and future for the prizes" of boxing. He then acknowledges the other side, saying "perhaps we don't have the right to deny these young people the right to succeed." Myers's resolution is that we need to make sure that when people do sacrifice their "goods," their health and future, as Ali did for boxing, that they can acheive dignity in more than one way. Once students have finished filling out the chart on page 172, have them use what they've learned about addressing opposing viewpoints to add to the letter they wrote in Lesson 53.

After

READING/WRITING CONNECTION

Ask students to write a review of a movie, book, or television show that involves boxing. In their reviews, have students argue whether or not boxing should be legal. Remind them to address opposing viewpoints in their reviews.

EVALUATING AN ARGUMENT **55** LESSON

When you **evaluate an argument,** you decide whether the argument is convincing. To do that, you need to consider how the author has structured his or her argument.

As you read this excerpt, think about the author's viewpoint and the support for it. Also think about the author's purpose. Circle or underline any strategies he uses, such as using supporting details and facts and arguing againt an opposing point of view. Record your observations in the **Response Notes.**

from Green Planet Rescue by Robert R. Halpern

"Endangered" sounds like something scary, and it is. "Danger" is right there in the middle of it. But when the subject is endangered plants, it's hard to see what all the fuss is about. Plants just grow, don't they? Weeds sprout in every open space, so what's the problem? There are always plenty of green things out there—everywhere we look. Why is any one plant species all that important?

Plants are not great as pets, but they are our companions on this planet. They are important in our lives and in the lives of every other animal. They produce the basic resources for life on Earth. There may be 380,000 or more different species of plants and we know little about many of them. Some species live in such special and small habitats that we haven't even found them yet. Can we afford to find out what life without a particular species would be like?

An endangered species is one with a small population whose survival is threatened. Human populations are growing. New roads, buildings, dams, farms, and grazing areas are spreading over the landscape so that little real wilderness is left anywhere. An endangered species will disappear if these conditions continue. An endangered species needs help. Today 20,000 to 25,000 of the plant species on Earth are endangered, vulnerable, or rare. We may be losing something important without even knowing much about it. ❖

Response Notes

❊ What is the main point of this article? What is the author's viewpoint in his argument?

_____

_____

_____

_____

EVALUATING AN ARGUMENT **173**

Students will analyze a persuasive piece for how well the author states a main idea, uses evidence to support and strengthen the argument, and refutes opposing arguments.

BACKGROUND KNOWLEDGE

Talk with students about the concept of *endangered.* Help them understand that *endangered* refers to a living thing that is in danger of becoming extinct, or dying out. Talk about what people do to keep a species of plant or animal life from becoming extinct. Remind them that people's behavior can help. Invite students to share any knowledge they might have about endangered animals or plants (for example, the bald eagle or rare orchids in the Everglades).

VOCABULARY

species a group of organisms that are similar and that can produce young that are fertile

habitat the type of environment in which an organism generally lives

Review the meanings of the words as part of the discussion in the Background Knowledge section above. Invite students to explain why an argument about protecting endangered plants and animals would use these words.

Before

CRITICAL READING SKILL

Evaluating an Argument Remind students that evaluating an argument does not require that you agree or disagree with it. Evaluating an argument means judging its validity, or how well the details support the main idea. Have students ask these questions when they read a persuasive piece:

❊ What is the author's point of view?

❊ Is the point of view well supported?

❊ What is the author's purpose?

❊ Does the author include a counter-argument?

During

INTERACTING WITH THE TEXT

After students have read the passage and have asked strategic questions about how the author makes the argument, have them evaluate it based on the criteria covered in lessons 51-54. Ask them to assign a grade to it and explain their reasons.

Differentiation Key to evaluating an argument is understanding the author's purpose, or intent, for writing. Help students determine the author's purpose by asking questions such as these:

✳ Why do you think the author wrote *Green Planet Rescue*?

✳ What message does the author want us to understand?

✳ What does the author want us to do?

Help students conclude that Robert Halpern is worried about endangered plants and what their possible extinction means for life on Earth. He probably wants to make readers aware of the issue (inform) and, perhaps, convince us to take action to save endangered species (persuade).

Quick Assess

✳ Did students assign a grade to the selection and give reasons for that grade?

✳ Imagine that you are a teacher, and one of your students turned in this article for an assignment on endangered species. On the following form, give it a letter grade based on how well the student supports his or her argument. Remember, you are deciding how effective the argument is, not whether you agree with the writer's viewpoint.

Does the author

- clearly state his or her main idea?
- use different kinds of evidence to strengthen the argument?
- provide details to support the main idea?
- refute opposing arguments?

Grade assigned for this article: _____

Reasons for this grade: _____

_____

_____

_____

_____

_____

_____

_____

To evaluate an argument, look for how well the details and facts support the author's opinion.

After

ORAL DEBATE Have students work in pairs to present opposing viewpoints to the argument. Students can apply what they've learned about the art of argument as they present their points of view in an oral debate.

Focusing on Language and Craft

Did you ever think about words having a life of their own? Words come from deep inside us, and they are all around us. It's easy to take them for granted.

Read this short poem by a famous American poet, Emily Dickinson. She wrote these words more than one hundred years ago.

A word is dead when it is said
Some say—
I say it just begins to live
That day—

When we write, we can be careful with our words. We can think about the exact meaning we are trying to convey. We can choose our words so that each word counts. The poems you are going to read in this unit will all be small poems, poems made up of very few words. But each word will be important. In the poems that you write, each word will be important, too.

175

UNIT 12
FOCUSING ON LANGUAGE AND CRAFT

Lessons 56–60, pages 176–190

UNIT OVERVIEW

Students will study small poems by William Carlos Williams, Robert Frost, Basho, and other poets to learn how to read and write short forms of poetry.

KEY IDEA

In a small poem, every word counts. Learning to read and write short poetry can help you appreciate the importance of language and word choice in all types of writing.

CRITICAL READING SKILLS
by lesson

56 Reading actively to understand a poem
57 Responding to short forms of poetry
58 Comparing and contrasting images
59 Analyzing word choice
60 Making leaps of imagination

WRITING ACTIVITIES
by lesson

56 Write two small poems.
57 Complete a Know/Think/Wonder chart.
58 Compare two poems.
59 Complete a chart about opposites.
60 Write haiku.

Literature

■ **"This Is Just to Say"** and **"The Red Wheelbarrow"** by William Carlos Williams (poems)

Williams is a master of saying a lot in just a few words, as shown in two of his best-known poems.

■ **"The Sun Coming Up"** by Jim Tipton (haiku)

Tipton selects just the right images to evoke thoughts of morning.

■ **"Fire and Ice"** by Robert Frost (poem)

Frost uses strong imagery to pack a powerful punch in his poem about opposite emotions.

■ *Various untitled haiku* by Basho and *Three tanka* by Fran Claggett

Haiku and tanka are related forms of poetry. Both use a spare amount of text to create images.

ASSESSMENT To assess student learning in this unit, see pages 237 and 260.

Students will closely read small poems that capture a moment and draw a picture to describe the moment.

BACKGROUND KNOWLEDGE

Connect to students' personal experiences by asking if they have ever eaten food that they weren't supposed to, such as food that was being saved for someone else or for a special occasion. Ask: *Did you get in trouble? What happened? Did you have to apologize?*

VOCABULARY

icebox refrigerator

Explain that iceboxes were early types of refrigerators that were insulated chests filled with blocks of ice. Some people continue to use the word *icebox* to refer to a refrigerator.

Have you ever put notes on your refrigerator door with a magnet? Have you found notes that someone in your family has put there for you? There's a story that suggests that William Carlos Williams, a doctor and a poet, put this note on the refrigerator door for his wife.

Response Notes

This Is Just to Say by William Carlos Williams

I have eaten
the plums
that were in
the icebox

and which
you were probably
saving
for breakfast

Forgive me
they were delicious
so sweet
and so cold ❖

❋ Read the poem again. This time, make notes in the **Response Notes** about what you notice. For example, are there any unusual words? Does the apology sound sincere? Does the missing punctuation make the poem hard to read? How many sentences would there be if it were punctuated like prose?

In this small poem, Williams deals with just one brief moment. It depicts an everyday sort of episode, something that just happened. When Williams wrote the poem, he "magnified" the moment; his "note" captures that moment, and it became a poem that has been read thousands of times.

Most people have an urge to write a poem of their own after reading this one. Try your hand at writing a similar poem.

176 LESSON 56

Before

CRITICAL READING SKILL

Reading Closely to Understand a Poem Explain that small poems often focus on brief moments or events and zoom in on, or "magnify," them. A strategic reader knows how to look at a small poem closely—as if through a magnifying glass—to notice word choice, form, punctuation, and other devices that give clues to the poem's meaning. As students read "This Is Just to Say," encourage them to think about why this poem is so often reprinted. Is one reason the simple, straightforward message? Is it the imagery or the language? Do people usually like poems with mundane messages?

During

POETRY MECHANICS After students have read "This Is Just to Say," ask: *What makes this a poem and not just a simple note?* (line breaks and lack of punctuation; divided into three parts; elegant, formal tone). To help students see how the mechanics of the poem affect the message, write it as a regular paragraph: *I have eaten the plums that were in the*

* Make some notes or draw a picture about a small thing you have done that might require an apology. (You can make it up.)
  - What did you do?
  - Who else was there?
  - What are some words that capture that moment?

* Now, write a poem in the style of Williams's poem. Follow this format:

I have _____

that _____

and which
you _____

for _____

Forgive me
they _____
so _____
and so _____

* Share your poems with others in the class. When you read yours aloud, remember to speak clearly, slowly, and with feeling!

Now, read another short poem by William Carlos Williams. Write your comments in the **Response Notes.**

The Red Wheelbarrow
by William Carlos Williams

so much depends
upon

a red wheel
barrow

glazed with rain
water

beside the white
chickens. ❖

ABOUT THE POET
William Carlos Williams (1883–1963) was not only a poet but a novelist, playwright, and doctor. He was famous for writing about the themes of every-day life and common people. A close friend of the poet Ezra Pound, Williams became one of the biggest influences on modern American poetry.

WRITING SUPPORT

Choosing a Topic To help students fill in the blanks and follow the pattern of Williams's poem, encourage them to write specifically about taking or bor-rowing something that they shouldn't have. Students can change the pro-noun *they* to *it* in the third-to-last line if they are writing about only one item.

---

icebox and which you were probably saving for breakfast. Forgive me. They were deli-cious—so sweet and so cold! Then ask: *Do you read the note the same way you read the poem? Would a note have the same effect?*

MAKING INFERENCES AND VISUALIZING After students read "The Red Wheelbarrow" and draw their pictures on page 178, have them share their inferences and visualizations with the class. Then, to help students inter-pret the first line of the poem, ask: *Why is a wheelbarrow important?* (It carries heavy loads and moves things; it helps

to complete the work.) Then reword the beginning of the poem and verbalize it or write it on the board for students: *A lot of important things could not get done without . . .*

Collaboration Pair visual learners with students who have strong verbal skills to write "photographic" poems. The visual students can draw or describe out loud what they see in their minds; their partners can help put it in writing.

Quick Assess

✻ Do the students have entries in each column of the chart?

✻ Do the entries in the first column reflect what students should have learned in this lesson?

✻ Do the notes in the third column reflect a genuine desire to learn more about haiku?

✻ Draw a picture of the moment this poem describes.

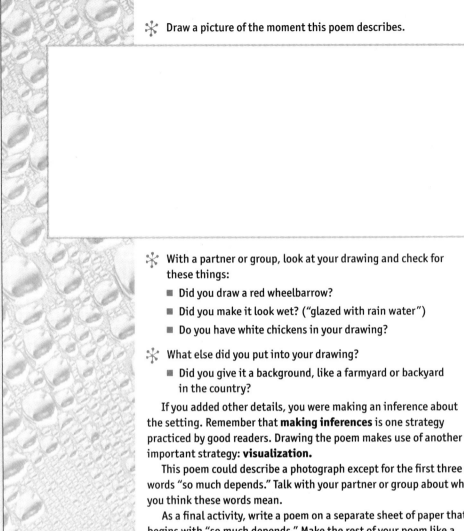

✻ With a partner or group, look at your drawing and check for these things:
- Did you draw a red wheelbarrow?
- Did you make it look wet? ("glazed with rain water")
- Do you have white chickens in your drawing?

✻ What else did you put into your drawing?
- Did you give it a background, like a farmyard or backyard in the country?

If you added other details, you were making an inference about the setting. Remember that **making inferences** is one strategy practiced by good readers. Drawing the poem makes use of another important strategy: **visualization.**

This poem could describe a photograph except for the first three words "so much depends." Talk with your partner or group about what you think these words mean.

As a final activity, write a poem on a separate sheet of paper that begins with "so much depends." Make the rest of your poem like a photograph, using only words that describe the picture you have in your mind. Remember, make every word count in this magnified moment.

Magnifying a moment leads to writing that is as vivid as a photograph.

After

SCIENCE CONNECTION Give students magnifying glasses and have them explore an area inside or outside the classroom, looking for something to study up close (such as a strand of hair, a leaf, or a stone). Have students take detailed scientific notes about their objects—what they look like, what's around them, etc. Then have students write small poems describing their objects without naming them. Students can read their poems aloud and invite classmates to guess the object.

In these next lessons, you are going to read and write a kind of small poem called **haiku.** A haiku is a Japanese poetic form that is very popular worldwide. There are haiku clubs and organizations in the United States in which people write and share haiku. The form is popular because

- it appears to be very simple,
- it features familiar subjects, and
- it invites the reader to give it meaning and significance.

What moment is captured by this haiku, written by the well-known Colorado poet Jim Tipton?

The Sun Coming Up by Jim Tipton

the sun coming up . . .
five eggs
in the iron skillet ❖

Response Notes

✳ With a partner, talk about this poem:
- What colors do you see?
- What kind of skillet is it? What color?
- What can you hear?
- Can you smell the eggs cooking in the skillet?
- Is it cold or warm at dawn?
- Do you feel the warmth of the stove or fire?

✳ Which of these things do you know because the poem actually tells you? Which do you know because you have learned to pay attention to the language and to **make inferences?**
   Put a check beside each question that you could answer because the poem told you. Put a star beside each one that you answered because of an inference you made.

Students will identify and respond to contrasting images in nature poems and begin writing their own haiku.

BACKGROUND KNOWLEDGE
To prepare students for studying haiku, you may want to review with students the concepts of imagery and sensory language (taught in Lessons 23 and 25). These literary devices are key components of haiku and critical to understanding and appreciating the art form.

VOCABULARY
haiku a Japanese poetic form contrasting two images, often of nature, which has 3 lines of 5, 7, and 5 syllables; spelled the same in both singular and plural forms

---

Before

CRITICAL READING SKILL
Understanding Haiku Explain that in haiku, two distinctly different images are connected to create a striking image for the reader. Reading haiku requires paying close attention to the images and making inferences about them in order to see their relationship. Read through the introduction with students and then read the haiku aloud. Ask: *What are the two images in this poem?* (sunrise and frying eggs) *How are they connected?* (Both suggest the color yellow, roundness, heat, early morning.) Then have students work with a partner to complete the rest of the page.

Collaboration Use the Corners technique to have students discuss the haiku for the seasons:

1. Assign a different season to each corner of the room. Divide students evenly among the corners.
2. Have students in each corner read and discuss the haiku for that season.
3. Regroup students and repeat step 2 until all students have been in each corner.

Randy Brooks, a poet, publisher, teacher, and webmaster, has worked with children in schools, introducing them to haiku and leading haiku writing workshops. He writes,

Haiku capture moments of being alive conveyed through sensory images. They do not explain nor describe nor provide philosophical or political commentary. Haiku are gifts of the here and now, deliberately incomplete so that the reader can enter into the haiku moment and experience the feelings of that moment for his or her self.

Haiku are usually made up of two fragments, two images that are placed next to each other. Haiku are not sentences. They are two images unified through an instant in time and a particular place. Sentences are too complete and leave nothing for the imagination of the reader. Haiku are imaginative "jump starts," inviting you to complete the scene that the writer begins. ✻

Many haiku deal with some aspect of nature. Books of haiku are often divided into seasons. Each season is divided into sections such as "birds and beasts," "trees and flowers," "human relationships," and "sky and elements."

With your partner or group, read some of the haiku that sixth graders wrote in Randy's workshop. In the **Response Notes**, jot down images you visualize for each haiku.

Response Notes

Spring

tractor in the field . . .
the doe and her fawn
run from the noise

Summer

good surfing waves . . .
a shark
fin circling

Autumn

hot dogs
sizzling on the grill . . .
smoke up to the moon

Winter

power out . . .
the flickering of the candle
in the kitchen

During

WHAT IS HAIKU? Have students read Randy Brooks's comments. Then, to check comprehension, discuss:

✻ *How are haiku like snapshots?* (They capture a brief moment. They don't explain anything or give an opinion—they just let the reader experience the moment.)

✻ *Why are sentence fragments used in haiku?* (Fragments allow the reader to make his or her own connections between images or ideas. Complete sentences don't leave anything to the reader's imagination.)

VISUALIZING IMAGES Invite volunteers to read each haiku aloud. Then have students identify the two images in each poem. (You might point out that ellipses have been used between fragments to help separate the images.) Help students make inferences and draw connections between the two images. For example, for the summer haiku, ask: *Where can you see surfing waves?* (in the ocean) *Where can*

Working with a partner, reread the explanation of haiku that Randy Brooks wrote. Then look at the students' poems again and notice how well they have learned to write haiku. Talk about which ones you like best and why.

In the next lesson, you will write haiku. Before you leave this lesson, do a Know/Think/Wonder chart about haiku. This chart is different from a K-W-L chart. In this chart, you write what you *know* now, what you *think* but maybe aren't too sure about, and what you still *wonder*—what you'd like to understand better.

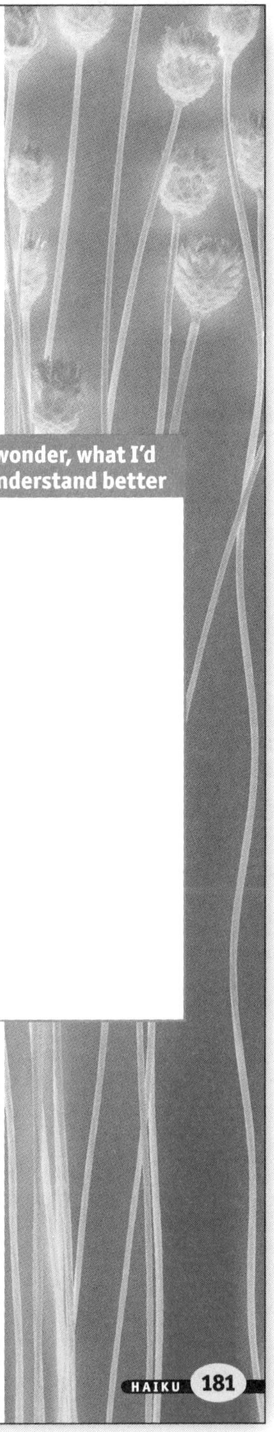

KNOW/THINK/WONDER CHART

What I know about haiku now	What I think but am not too sure about	What I wonder, what I'd like to understand better

Haiku pack a lot of meaning into a few words because of the connections and inferences that the reader makes.

WRITING SUPPORT

Know/Think/Wonder Chart Before students complete the chart, model writing an entry in each column:

Column 1: *I know haiku always connect two images.*

Column 2: *I think haiku are always short, but I'm not positive.*

Column 3: *Is there a limit to the number of words or syllables you can use in a haiku?*

Quick Assess

- Do the students have entries in each column of the chart?
- Do entries in the first column reflect what students should have learned in this lesson?
- Do the notes in the third column reflect a genuine desire to learn more about haiku?

After

you see a shark fin? (in the ocean) *What inference can you make about the subject of the poem?* (It's about looking at the ocean.)

ART CONNECTION Have students make haiku posters. Each student can copy one of the season haiku neatly onto poster board and illustrate the scene or images depicted in the poem. Also have students write an explanation about why they chose the particular haiku and how the haiku inspired the illustrations. The explanation can take the form of a paragraph or a letter to the poet.Display the posters on a wall titled "The Four Seasons."

Students will read and analyze a poem for sensory words that create opposite images to use in an original haiku.

BACKGROUND KNOWLEDGE

Tell students that in this lesson they will read a poem in which the poet contrasts two ways the world might end: by fire and by ice. Explain that visions about the world coming to an end have been around for a long time. For some, the image is based on religious beliefs; for others, it is based on concerns about a natural disaster (such as a flood or a meteor hitting the earth), a nuclear war, or even an extraterrestrial invasion! Invite students to talk about books or movies they are familiar with (such as *War of the Worlds* or *The Day After Tomorrow*) that include images of cataclysm.

VOCABULARY

perish to die or be destroyed

suffice to be sufficient or enough

After discussing the definition of each word, model using each one in a sentence. Then have students write their own sentences for the words and read the sentences aloud.

LESSON 58 OPPOSITE IMAGES, ONE POEM

You have probably heard the statement that "opposites attract." Whether this is true or not, opposites do seem to go together in our language. We contrast *sun and shadow, good and bad, rich and poor, fire and ice.* In preparation for writing your own haiku, it will help to think about opposites.

✳ List some opposites that are common in our language.

_____

_____

Opposites often suggest contrasting images. One pair of opposites is the title of a well-known poem by Robert Frost. Read the poem, making comments in the **Response Notes** about what you notice. What other contrasting ideas and images do you find?

Response Notes

Fire and Ice by Robert Frost

Some say the world will end in fire,
Some say in ice.
From what I've tasted of desire
I hold with those who favor fire.
But if it had to perish twice,
I think I know enough of hate
To say that for destruction ice
Is also great
And would suffice. ✦

✳ What are some ways that "Fire and Ice" is different from the other poems in this unit? How is it the same?

_____

_____

_____

_____

182 LESSON 58

Before

CRITICAL READING SKILL
Comparing and Contrasting Images
Review the definition of an antonym (a word that means the opposite of another word) and list simple examples, such as: *yes/no, true/false, in/out,* etc. Then point out that just as words can have opposites, so can images and ideas. Ask students to visualize a bouquet of flowers and a pile of rocks. Then have students compare the

images. Ask: *How are flowers and rocks opposites?* (Flowers are colorful, alive, delicate; rocks are drab-colored, lifeless, hard.)

PREVIEWING THE POEM Have students read the title and scan for words that are repeated in the poem. How might they be related to each other?

Some things you might have noticed in "Fire and Ice":

- This poem uses a word I don't know: suffice.
- This poem uses rhyme.
- It has punctuation.
- It is about ideas rather than things.
- It is about opposites, how fire or ice might end the world.

✳ You are going to write a haiku using opposite images of animals and plants. Answer the following questions:

What kind of animal are you most like? _____

What kind of plant are you most like? _____

Think about the animal you selected and write the quality that made you select it. It might be a quality like *speedy*, or *graceful*, or *protective*, or *playful*. _____

Do the same thing for the plant. A plant might be *beautiful* like a flower; *strong* like a tree; *prickly* like a rose; *dangerous* like poison ivy or poison oak. _____

Here is a chart filled out by another student. Add your ideas to the chart, using the names of the animal and plant you selected.

Category	Name of animal or plant I am most like	I am most like this animal or plant because of this quality	The opposite of the qualities in Column 2	Name of animal or plant that has the qualities of Column 3
Animal	dolphin	playful	serious	small fish
Plant	oak tree	strong	delicate	blade of grass

EXTRA SUPPORT

Differentiation Students who need extra support completing the writing prompts may benefit from writing a list of qualities about themselves first and then coming up with animals and plants that have those qualities.

During

ANALYZING THE POEM After students have read the poem, ask: *What are the two pairs of opposite images or ideas in the poem?* (fire/ice; desire/hate) *Which emotion does Frost associate with fire, and why?* (desire, because if you act on it without thinking, you can get "burned") *Which does he associate with ice, and why?* (hate, because it's cold and cutting; it freezes people's hearts) One interpretation of

the poem is that the blind compulsions of desire can be so destructive that desire is just as likely to end the world as hate.

COMPARISONS Have students complete the writing prompt on page 182 and share their responses with the class. (Students might mention the following: difference—the season poems are about things, while the Frost poem is about emotions; similarity—all the poems

contain contrasting images of some sort.). Finally, help students complete the rest of page 183. Clarify that the words in the third and fourth columns of the chart should be adjectives, and invite students to use a thesaurus to find antonyms for the fourth column.

Word Choice Remind students to use strong verbs in their sentences to help convey the animals' specific qualities. Point out that in the example shown, the vivid verb *leaps* helps convey the quality of playfulness.

Quick Assess

✳ Did students name both an animal and a plant that they are most like?

✳ Did students list qualities that reflect how the animal and the plant are similar to them?

✳ In columns 3 and 4 of their charts, did students identify animals and plants with opposite qualities?

✳ Did students write sentences about their animals, using strong, active verbs?

Steps in writing your first haiku:

✳ Write a sentence in which the animal in Column 1 does something. Remember the quality you gave it in Column 2.

　■ Example: **The dolphin leaps out of the water beside my boat.**

✳ Now write a sentence having the animal in Column 4 do something that contrasts with the sentence above.

　■ Example: **The small fish hides in schools in the water, not wanting to be caught.**

Save these sentences for the next lesson when you will write haiku of your own.

Opposite ideas can make powerful images in a poem.

184 LESSON 58

After

MORE OPPOSITES For additional practice comparing and contrasting images, have students extend their charts by adding such categories as seasons, colors, types of music, etc.

LISTENING/SPEAKING CONNECTION Students who want an extra challenge can look for additional poems by Robert Frost. Invite students to read the poems aloud and explain the images to the class.

W riting haiku requires close attention to individual words. You must pay attention to **word choice**—finding precisely the right word for what you want to say and making sure each word communicates your thoughts to your readers. Because the traditional haiku uses a set pattern of lines and syllables, you will begin by writing in that form.

Now write your own haiku. Using the sentences you wrote in Lesson 58 as starting points, try to write a poem in the traditional Japanese form of 17 syllables in 3 lines.

✳ Begin by counting the syllables in your sentences.
Example sentences from Lesson 58:

- The dolphin leaps out of the water beside my boat. *(13)*
- The small fish hides in schools in the water. *(10)*

Write your sentences and the number of syllables here:

Sentence 1:

Sentence 2:

✳ Now think of how the two example sentences are related.
- Dolphins appear to be playful, often following boats and interacting with the people.
- Small fish come up for food, but otherwise hide in groups or schools.

✳ The next step is to try to reduce the number of syllables to 17. Begin by cutting any necessary words. For example, you might say, "the dolphin leaps, water splashes." That would be 8 syllables. Then you could say "small fish disappear under waves." That is 8 syllables. Adding up, you have 16 syllables so you can add one more. If you keep playing with the words, you might end up with something like this:

Example: dolphins leap, frolic,   5 syllables
spinning in blue-green waters—   7 syllables
small fish swim below   5 syllables

Students will study the elements of haiku to complete an original poem that uses precise language, creates contrasting images, and follows the traditional pattern.

BACKGROUND KNOWLEDGE

Explain to students that there are different forms of haiku and that some forms have specific patterns, or numbers of lines and syllables. The most common form of haiku has a pattern of three lines—the first and third have five syllables and the middle line has seven syllables. Tell students that this is the kind of haiku they will be writing in this lesson.

Before

CRITICAL READING SKILL
Analyzing Word Choice for Clarity and Precision Write the words *speak, shout,* and *whisper* on the board. Ask: *Which two words are more precise and clear, or tell you exactly how people might talk?* (*shout* and *whisper*) Repeat with other examples, such as *wet/soaked/ damp; smell/odor/fragrance;* and *flower/ daisy.* Then ask: *Why are precision and*

clarity important in haiku? (because you have only a few words to create an overall image or idea)

SYLLABLES Review the concept of syllables and have students practice identifying syllables by:

✳ counting out the syllables in their own names.

✳ looking up multisyllabic words in the dictionary and writing the words with syllable breaks.

✳ playing a game in which partners take turns giving each other a number and composing a sentence with exactly that many syllables.

Form: Line Breaks Remind students that:

✣ Each line of the poem does not have to be a complete sentence.

✣ The break between images can come between the first and second lines, or between the second and third lines.

EXTRA SUPPORT

Differentiation For students who need extra support, guide them through the first step of converting their original sentences to three lines, without worrying about the number of syllables in each line. Then students can adjust the number of syllables and polish the haiku on their own.

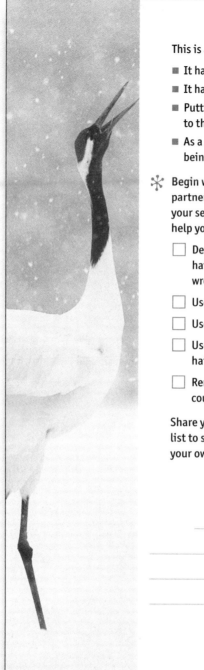

This is a traditional haiku in several ways:

■ It has three lines of 5, 7, and 5 syllables.

■ It has two images or pictures: dolphins and small fish.

■ Putting the two images in the same poem requires the reader to think about how they are related.

■ As a reader, you might be led to think about the small fish being food for the dolphins, but that is not stated in the poem.

✣ Begin working on your poem. You might want to work with a partner on your first poem, exchanging ideas about how to make your sentences into traditional haiku. Use the checklist below to help you with your writing.

☐ Delete and add whatever words you want. Your finished haiku doesn't have to be tied to the original sentences you wrote. They were just jumping-off points.

☐ Use images of things you can see, smell, taste, touch, or feel.

☐ Use strong verbs. Have your animal do something.

☐ Use adjectives and adverbs to help the reader see your haiku images.

☐ Remember that, in a haiku, every word and syllable must count!

Share your finished haiku with another student. Use this check-list to see whether you need to delete or change any words. Use your own paper for your drafts. Write your finished haiku here:

_____ (title)

_____

_____

by _____ (your name)

186 LESSON 59

During

WRITING HAIKU After students have worked through *Daybook* page 185 independently, discuss the haiku at the bottom of that page, how it evolved from the original sentences, and how it demonstrates the characteristics listed at the top of page 186. Then go over the haiku-writing checklist before students begin drafting their own poems. Point out that modifiers (adjectives and adverbs) can help create strong images, but they also add more syllables. Precise nouns and verbs don't need modifiers and probably have fewer syllables.

REVISING Have students hold a peer conference to discuss their drafts with a partner. Partners can make suggestions about word choice and can check each other's poems to make sure they have the correct number of lines and syllables.

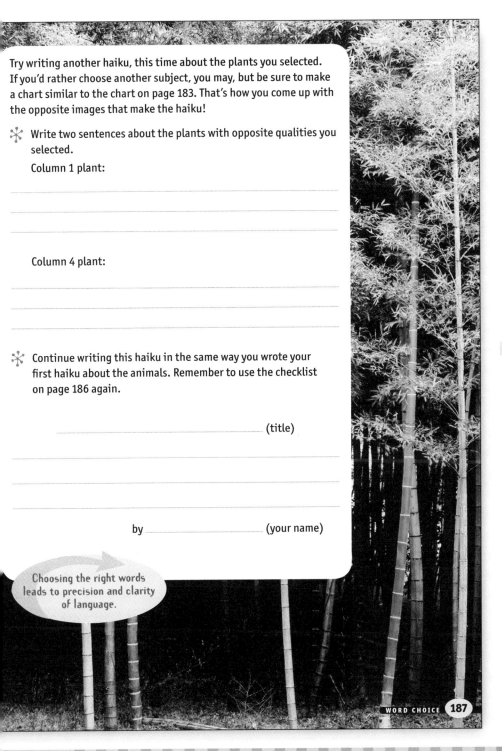

Try writing another haiku, this time about the plants you selected. If you'd rather choose another subject, you may, but be sure to make a chart similar to the chart on page 183. That's how you come up with the opposite images that make the haiku!

✳ Write two sentences about the plants with opposite qualities you selected.

Column 1 plant:

_____

_____

Column 4 plant:

_____

_____

✳ Continue writing this haiku in the same way you wrote your first haiku about the animals. Remember to use the checklist on page 186 again.

_____ (title)

_____

_____

by _____ (your name)

Choosing the right words leads to precision and clarity of language.

Collaboration After students have written their haiku, have them use the Interview technique to share their poems with the rest of the class:

1. Have partners read their haiku to each other and discuss the images—i.e., how they're opposite, how they're related, what overall idea or insight they convey, etc.

2. Have students read their partners' haiku to the class and explain in their own words the images and insights conveyed.

Quick Assess

✳ Do students' poems contain two opposite yet connected images?

✳ Do students' poems have three lines, with five syllables in the first and third lines and seven syllables in the middle?

After

READING/WRITING CONNECTION

Have students reread William Carlos Williams's poem "The Red Wheelbarrow" on *Daybook* page 177. Then have students write a comparison and contrast paragraph to discuss what the poem has in common with haiku and how it is different. Students can discuss their paragraphs in small groups or read them to the class.

LESSON **60** **LEAPS OF IMAGINATION**

Students will read and connect contrasting images in traditional and nontraditional pattern poems to write more pattern poems.

ABOUT THE POET

Matsuo Basho (1644–1694) was born in the Japanese province of Iga, near Kyoto. He began writing poetry while serving as a young samurai, or Japanese warrior. After his master died suddenly, Basho chose to leave home rather than serve a new master. Basho continued to write poetry and eventually became a teacher with a large following, living in huts built for him by his students. In 1684, feelings of discontent led Basho to set out on a series of journeys, which he wrote about in several travel journals and anthologies. Basho died in Osaka of a stomach illness, after writing this last hokku (an early form of haiku):

Traveling sick;
My dreams roam
On a withered moor.

Influenced by Zen Buddhism, Basho's verse was known for having a mystical quality and for expressing universal themes through simple, natural images—from the harvest moon to the fleas in his cottage.

O ne thing to remember about haiku is that they require leaps of imagination. Most haiku use more than one image, as you learned in the last two lessons. The reader must make a leap of imagination to see how the two images can be connected. Different readers will find different ways to make these connections.

One of the greatest writers of the haiku form is Basho. The name Basho (banana tree) is a pseudonym he adopted around 1681 after moving into a hut beside a banana tree. At the time of his death, Basho had 2,000 students, all of whom were eager to learn from the master.

Here are some of Basho's poems. As you read, make notes or sketches around the poems to show what the haiku make you think of and how they make you feel.

Remember: it is the reader who completes the thought of haiku. You need to make the leaps of imagination!

Response Notes

Haiku by Basho

Spring departs
Birds cry
Fishes' eyes are filled with tears ❖

Clouds separate
the two friends—migrating
Wild geese ❖

An old pond!
A frog jumps in—
Splash! in water. ❖

Poverty's child—
starts to grind the rice
and gazes at the moon. ❖

Before

CRITICAL READING SKILL

Making Leaps of Imagination Explain that making a leap of the imagination means using your skill at making inferences along with your imagination to fill in the gaps in a story or to create a mental picture. Point out that we do this all the time in everyday life. Say: *If your parents ask you questions about whether you would take care of a dog if you had one and then*

you see them looking at websites for pet shelters, you might guess that your parents are going to get you a dog. You have just made a leap of the imagination!

BASHO'S POEMS Before students read Basho's haiku, explain that they have been translated into English by Jim Tipton, the poet who wrote the haiku about the eggs in Lesson 57. Point out that the English translations don't strictly follow the traditional haiku form that students have learned about, but that the original Japanese versions probably did.

Share your ideas about Basho's poems with a partner or a group.

- Which did you like best? Why?
- Which made use of two images? (Did you draw both images?)
- What connections could you make between the images when there were two of them?

Basho's poems don't seem to be written in the traditional haiku form. We are reading translations. In fact, his poems have been translated by so many people that there are many different versions.

Another Japanese form related to the haiku is the tanka. The tanka starts like the haiku with three lines of 5-7-5 syllables, then adds two more lines of seven syllables each. This gives you a chance to add more details than you can include in three lines. Here are three original tanka written just for the readers of this book. You will see that you can write haiku and tanka about any subject. Read these tanka alone, in pairs, in groups, or as a class. Which form of poem do you prefer?

Use your **Response Notes** to tell what you think and feel about these three tanka.

Three Tanka by Fran Claggett

The girl twirls into
the room, her purple-fringed skirt
making a circle
around her. When she stops, her
moving purple world stands still. ❖

Walking on the beach,
a crow startles me. I watch
its wings form patterns.
Circles and black lines scratch out
letters written on the sand. ❖

The boy hurls the ball.
Crash! goes the window. Inside,
a grown-up boy ducks
from ball and shattering glass.
He throws it back. Yells "Hey!" Grins. ❖

TEACHING TIP

Collaboration Students can use the Fishbowl technique to discuss the poems on *Daybook* page 188:

1. Half of the class sits in a close circle, with the other half sitting around the outside of the circle.

2. Students in the inner circle discuss the poems, using the prompts on *Daybook* page 189 as the students on the outside listen carefully.

3. Students switch places and repeat step 2. Now the students on the inside can include in their discussion any responses to what the first group said.

During

MAKING LEAPS   Model a leap of the imagination using a think-aloud about one of Basho's poems: Read the poem that begins "Spring departs" and say: *The first line is about spring ending. The second and third lines are about birds and fish crying. So, I imagine that the birds and fish are sad that spring is over.* Then have students take turns reading aloud the poems on *Daybook* page 188 before they make their sketches and notes.

TANKA   Invite volunteers to read aloud each tanka. Then have students reread the poems independently and write their Response Notes. Afterward, have students take turns telling which poem they liked best and why, and why or why not they prefer this form to the shorter, more traditional haiku.

Quick Assess

✳ Did students write a haiku or tanka in the correct form?

✳ Are students' poems about nature? Are the poems based on observations or experiences?

✳ Do students' poems contain contrasting images?

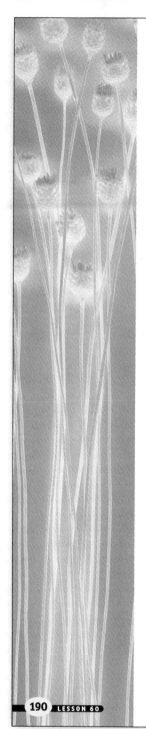

✳ Now you are ready to write more haiku or tanka. They may be traditional or non-traditional. Here are some suggestions for getting started.

■ Go for a walk and closely observe the weather, the trees, the wildlife, and outdoor smells and sounds. Make notes in a notebook you keep for this purpose.

■ Look at little things through a magnifying glass: the movement of an insect or worm, soil, or a piece of wood.

■ Write a haiku structured on two contrasting smells, sounds, or any combination of two sensory impressions.

■ See if you get an idea about the contrasts—rising and falling, delicate and firm—but don't try too hard! If the contrast is not based on an observation or experience, your reader won't be able to imagine it.

✳ Use your own notebook for making notes.

✳ Copy your best poem here. You might want to illustrate your poem and share it with the class.

> Haiku requires that the writer and reader connect the images with a leap of imagination.

After

ART CONNECTION Have students make haiku greeting cards. Students can use a poem they wrote for this unit, or they can write a new poem with a specific person or occasion in mind. They should add an image (drawing, clip art, cutout) somewhere on their card. When the card is finished, students can make envelopes and send them. Ask them to write you a short, informal note explaining the reasons for their decisions:

✳ How does this poem fit the recipient?

✳ How does the image fit the poem?

✳ Why did you decide to place the image where it's placed?

Lessons 61–65, pages 192–206

UNIT OVERVIEW

In this unit, students will examine the writing style of Gary Paulsen and how he incorporates real-life adventures and challenges into his work to explore both internal and external conflicts.

KEY IDEA

Studying an author's work and life can lead to a better understanding of the author's style, ideas, and the craft of writing in general.

CRITICAL READING SKILLS
by lesson

61 Analyzing author's style

62 Recognizing character traits

63 Reading about personal challenges

64 Reading about external challenges

65 Reading autobiographical text

WRITING ACTIVITIES
by lesson

61 Imitating the author's style.

62 Write a short scene about a character.

63 Complete a chart to explore changes in a character.

64 Write about a character's challenges.

65 Write notes for an autobiographical sketch.

Studying an Author

Reading several works by one author helps you see where stories come from. Gary Paulsen has written more than 130 books of fiction and nonfiction. Most of what he writes comes from his own adventures. Paulsen has landed a plane in an emergency, battled an angry moose, and taken dangerous spills during the Iditarod dogsled race—challenges his fans will recognize in his stories.

One of Paulsen's best-known characters is Brian Robeson, who stars in four books. Gary Paulsen says, "When I set out to write the Brian books I was concerned that everything that happened to Brian should be based on reality, or as near reality as fiction could be. I did not want him to do things that wouldn't or couldn't really happen in his situation. Consequently I decided to write only of things that had happened to me or things I purposely did to make certain they would work for Brian." For example, Paulsen spent several days finding the right rock and then four hours trying to use a hatchet against the rock to light a fire, just for one scene in a book.

An author that serious about his writing deserves further study!

191

Literature

- *The River* by Gary Paulsen (novel excerpt)

Brian Robeson (from the *Hatchet* series) returns to the wilderness with a psychologist who wants to learn about Brian's survival techniques. In the excerpt, Brian finds Derek, the psychologist, near death, having been struck by lightning.

- *Dancing Carl* by Gary Paulsen (novel excerpt)

Two boys get to know Carl, a troubled war veteran who lives and works at the town ice rink.

- *Dogsong* by Gary Paulsen (novel excerpt)

A fourteen-year-old boy in Alaska faces hunger and cold and the need to provide for his sled dogs.

- *Woodsong* by Gary Paulsen (autobiography excerpt)

Paulsen describes a real-life encounter with a large, hungry bear.

ASSESSMENT See page 238 for a writing prompt based on this unit.

Students will read an excerpt from an adventure story to analyze the author's style and techniques used to create excitement and build tension.

BACKGROUND KNOWLEDGE

To develop background knowledge about the character of Brian Robeson, invite students who have read *Hatchet* to share their favorite parts of the book and to describe the main character, Brian (13 years old, dealing with parents' divorce, smart, resourceful, determined to survive). Point out that in *The River*, Brian is 15 and returns to the wilderness. Have students think about how Brian might feel about going back. Ask: *Do you think he wants to be in the wilderness again?*

VOCABULARY

blurred out of focus, unclear

Brainstorm with students what might cause someone to have blurred vision (being tired or ill, not wearing one's glasses, having a head injury, etc.)

LESSON 61 AN AUTHOR'S STYLE

Riding on a sled down a snowy mountain behind a pack of dogs . . . surviving on your own in the wilderness . . . facing an angry bear close up. As Gary Paulsen explores these situations in his books, he uses language and a writing **style** that help the reader feel the excitement, the intensity—and sometimes the danger—of a challenge.

In *Hatchet*, Brian Robeson survives alone in the wilderness for fifty-four days with nothing but a hatchet. In *The River*, Paulsen continues Brian's story. Brian goes back into the wilderness with Derek Holtzer, a psychologist who wants to learn about Brian's survival techniques.

As you read the excerpt from *The River*, pay attention to the words Paulsen uses. In the **Response Notes**, jot down your responses as you read. These can be anything you notice about Paulsen's writing or your opinions about his writing.

Response Notes

from **The River** by Gary Paulsen

He rolled on his side. His body felt stiff, mashed into the ground, and the sudden movement made his vision blur.

There.

He saw Derek—or the form of Derek. He was facedown on his bed, his right hand out, his left arm back and down his side. Blurred, he was all blurred and asleep—how could he be all blurred? Brian shook his head, tried to focus.

Derek was still asleep. How strange, Brian thought—how strange that Derek should still be asleep in the bright daylight, and he knew then that Derek was not sleeping, but did not want to think of the other thing.

Let's reason it out, he thought, his mind as blurred as his vision. Reason it all out. Derek was reaching for the radio and briefcase and the lightning hit the tree next to the shelter and came down the tree and across the air and into Derek and he fell . . .

No.

He was still asleep.

He wasn't that other thing. Not that other word.

But Brian's eyes began to clear then and he saw that Derek was lying with his head to the side and that it was facing Brian and the eyes weren't closed.

They were open.

He was on his side not moving and his eyes were open and Brian thought how strange it was that he would sleep that way—mashed on his stomach.

He knew Derek wasn't sleeping.

Before

CRITICAL READING SKILL
Analyzing an Author's Style Explain that an author's style is *how* he or she says something—the type of words, the tone of voice, the sentence structure and length, and the use of literary devices such as figurative language, imagery, and dialogue. Tell students that as they read the excerpt, they should ask themselves:

✻ Are the sentences short and simple or long and complex?

✻ Does the writing sound casual or formal?

✻ What sensory language and details does Paulsen include? What images do they create?

✻ Is there dialogue? Is it realistic?

SETTING A PURPOSE Remind students that successful readers identify a purpose for reading. Review the last paragraph of the introductory text. Have students underline the last part of the first sentence: they will be reading to notice and comment on Paulsen's language and word choice.

He knew.

"No. . . ."

He couldn't be. Couldn't be . . . dead. Not Derek.

Finally, he accepted it.

Brian rose to his hands and knees, stiff and with great slowness, and crawled across the floor of the shelter to where Derek lay.

The large man lay on his stomach as he'd dropped, his head turned to the left. The eyes were not fully open, but partially lidded, and the pupils stared blankly, unfocused toward the back of the shelter.

Brian touched his cheek. He remembered how when the pilot had his heart attack he had felt cool—the dead skin had felt cool.

Derek's skin did not have the coolness, it felt warm; and Brian kneeled next to him and saw that he was breathing.

Tiny little breaths, his chest barely rising and falling, but he was breathing, the air going in and out, and he was not the other word—not dead—and Brian leaned over him.

"Derek?"

There was no answer, no indication that Derek had heard him.

"Derek. Can you hear anything I'm saying?"

Still no sign, no movement. ❖

❋ Look at the notes you took while you read. How do Paulsen's words and writing style make you feel about Brian and the challenges he faces?

AN AUTHOR'S STYLE **193**

During

SENTENCE STRUCTURE After students have read the excerpt, point out that some of the sentences are long and contain a lot of *and*s, while others are short and choppy. Explain that this gives the narrative a train-of-thought feeling; it helps the reader see things through Brian's eyes and experience exactly what Brian is thinking.

WORD CHOICE Draw students' attention to the fact that the author repeats certain key words throughout the passage. For example, have students skim the excerpt and note all of the occurrences of the word *asleep* (or *sleeping*). Ask: *What effect does repeating this word have?* (It shows how hard Brian is trying to convince himself that Derek is not

dead.) Now ask: *What word is suggested, or implied, repeatedly but not actually used until the end?* (dead) *How does Paulsen "talk around" the word, and why?* (By using phrases such as "that other thing," "not that other word," and "not dead," he shows Brian avoiding the idea that Derek could be dead and also builds suspense.)

Differentiation In this excerpt, Paulsen uses the pronoun *he* frequently. In fact, the excerpt begins with *he,* and the pronoun does not have an antecedent. Explain to students that *he* refers to the main character of the story (Brian). In the third paragraph, *he* refers to Derek. Work through the passage with students, making sure they understand to whom *he* refers.

TEACHING TIP

Collaboration Before students complete the writing prompt on page 193, have them share their Response Notes with a partner, comparing what they noted about the author's style and discussing how it affects the way they perceived the character. Then have students complete the prompt independently.

STUDYING AN AUTHOR **193**

WRITING SUPPORT

Style To help students mimic Paulsen's writing style and to spark ideas for their paragraphs, you may want to provide students with examples of short, "staccato" sentences that build excitement and tension:

Time was running out.
What was that noise?
His hands shook.
Maybe...just maybe.
It was worth a try.
Oh, no!

EXTRA SUPPORT

Differentiation Before writing their paragraphs, students who need help getting started may benefit from oral support prior to writing. Have them work with you or a partner to make predictions about what might happen next. Prompt students with questions such as: *Will Derek wake up? What can Brian do to save him? What dangers do they face?*

Quick Assess

✳ Do students' paragraphs continue the story in a believable way?

✳ Did students imitate Paulsen's style?

✳ Do students use their writing to build tension and excitement?

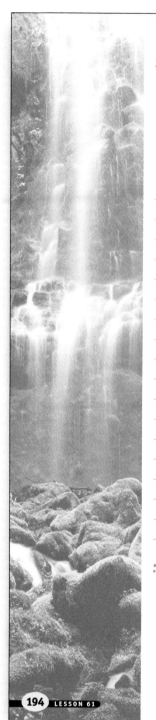

✳ Look at the many short sentences and paragraphs Paulsen writes. Listen as you take turns reading the passage aloud with a partner. Paulsen's writing has been called "staccato"—it reads in short "bursts."

Now try using Paulsen's staccato style. Continue Paulsen's story from this point, using words and sentences that continue to build the tension. Some sentences should be short, only 4 to 6 words long.

_____

_____

_____

_____

_____

_____

_____

_____

_____

_____

_____

_____

✳ Read the passage you wrote aloud to a partner. Ask your partner if he or she noted the staccato sentences. Is your partner feeling the tension in your continuation of the story?

A writer's style can affect the impressions readers get as they read.

After

READING/WRITING
CONNECTION Have students choose another passage from *The River* or one of the other books in the Hatchet series (*Hatchet, Brian's Winter,* and *Brian's Return*) and write a paragraph about how it exemplifies Paulsen's writing style. Students can read their excerpt and paragraph to the class.

The character of Carl in *Dancing Carl* is based on Paulsen's own father. Paulsen's father came home from World War II with both physical and mental scars. In the story, Carl returns many years after the war to the small town where he grew up.

In this excerpt, Marsh (the narrator) and his friend Willy are at the local ice rink. They know that Carl returned from the war with "troubles," and that the town council helped him by giving him a job at the rink and lodging in the warming house. In the warming house, as they get ready to play hockey, Marsh and Willy see Carl act in a surprising way. As you read the excerpt from *Dancing Carl,* write your ideas about what Carl is like in the **Response Notes.**

from **Dancing Carl** by Gary Paulsen

Response Notes

No matter how much you do in the summer, no matter how hard you work or run, your ankles always get weak. The muscles you use for skating don't get used in the summer and it's like everybody has to start all over in the fall, or the first part of winter when the ice forms and gets tight.

The next day was a Friday. School was school. But everybody brought skates and after school we hit the rinks and it was cold and dusky and we went into the warming house to put our skates on.

It was packed. It usually is the first few times after the ice is formed. But this time for some reason there were a lot of little kids, three and four, and like always they were having a rough time.

After skating gets going the warming house isn't so crowded. People skate and come in for a little, then back out, and cycle through that way. But when it first opens they just pack in and the little kids get pushed sideways until they're all in one corner, standing holding their skates, pouting and some of them starting to cry and always before they just had to fight it out or wait until the bigger kids were done and out skating.

But now there was Carl.

He was in the back of the shack and he stood up and he moved into the middle and he took a little girl by the hand and shouldered people out of the way and moved to the benches by the door. There were other kids sitting there, high-school kids suiting up for hockey and he looked at them.

That's all he did. Just looked at them, standing up with his flight jacket unzipped and the little girl holding onto his hand and Willy and I were sitting where we could see his eyes.

Students will explore how an author develops a main character in a story, using description, dialogue, and clues from other characters.

BACKGROUND KNOWLEDGE
Students will read an excerpt from *Dancing Carl,* a story is set in 1958 in a small Minnesota town. Ice skating was (and still is) popular in this northern state. Ask students to discuss how people act at a crowded rink, pool, or other recreation spot. How do people treat one another?

VOCABULARY

dusky dim, shadowy; nearing sunset

warming house building where people, especially skaters or skiers, come in to get warm and rest

flight jacket a style of leather jacket worn by airplane pilots; sometimes called a "bomber jacket"

After going over the definitions, have students do word associations for each word—e.g., for *dusky,* students might say "late afternoon, playing outside, almost dark."

Before

CRITICAL READING SKILL
Recognizing Character Traits Point out that a good writer creates characters who are not only memorable but realistic and believable. Gary Paulsen based Carl on a real-life person—his own father—but since we don't know Paulsen's father, we must use reading strategies to understand Carl. Explain: *Sometimes a writer clearly describes a character's appearance, personality, and/or other traits; at other times the reader must pay close attention to what the character says and does to get a clear picture of the character.*

RESPONSE NOTES Encourage students to mark places in the text where Paulsen gives clues to Carl's character, either through actions or physical appearance. (For tips on marking text, see *Daybook* page 225.)

ABOUT THE AUTHOR

Gary Paulsen is the author of more than 175 books for young adults. Born and raised in Minnesota and a two-time competitor in the Iditarod dog sled race, Paulsen has based much of his writing on personal experience and the themes of survival and outdoor adventure. His books *Hatchet*, *Dogsong*, and *The Winter Room* won the Newbery Honor Award. For more information, see http://www.randomhouse.com/features/garypaulsen/about.html.

TEACHING TIP

Collaboration You may want to have students use the Roundtable technique to brainstorm Carl's character traits:

1. Divide students into groups. Have groups sit in circles. Assign one student in each group to be the note-taker.

2. Have students go around the circle, each student naming a trait, while the note-taker keeps a list of the traits.

Response Notes

"They look hot," he said to me, leaning close to my ear. "His eyes look hot."

And they did. They almost glowed when he looked down at the kids who were sitting on the bench.

For a second or two they didn't do anything, and I think maybe they didn't want to do anything either. But the eyes cut through them, and they moved sideways and some of them got up and they left a place for the little girl and still Carl stood, looking down.

They moved more, made a wider place, and then the people in the center of the room parted and Carl raised his hand and the children who had been pushed down and down came through and they started to use the bench by the door and from that time on whenever the little kids came in they used that part of the bench and nobody else would use that place. Not even the grown-ups who came to skate to the music. ❖

✳ What does Marsh learn about Carl in this scene? Brainstorm a list of character traits—words that describe Carl's personality.

196 LESSON 62

During

GRAPHIC ORGANIZER

Character Web After students have read the story and completed their list of character traits, use the Character Map on page 269 to categorize information about Carl. Then invite students to name things that Carl does (e.g., holds the girl's hand; shoulders people out of the way; stares down at kids) and things about his physical appearance ("hot" eyes; unzipped flight jacket). Add these to the chart. Then have students name traits that each action or physical characteristic demonstrates: e.g., kindness, protective of people in need, intimidating, able to motivate others with just a look, forceful, angry. Finally, have students fill in the rest of the Character Map.

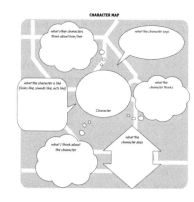

CHARACTER MAP

✳ After reading about Carl and the little girl, think about a time when someone acted in a surprising way. Describe what you observed.

✳ Make a list of words that describe the person in your description.

✳ How might the character have changed after the indicent you described?

Basing a character on a real person helps a writer create characters that seem vivid and real.

Quick Assess

✳ Did students identify at least two character traits?

✳ Do students' scenes clearly demonstrate those traits through the character's actions, words, and/or appearance?

✳ Can students identify how an author develops a character (description, dialogue, actions)?

After

DRAMATIZING THE STORY

To further explore how characters are brought to life, have students work in small groups to turn the scene at the warming house into a skit. Encourage students to think not only about Carl but also Willy and Marsh. What clues does Paulsen give about their characters? What do they say and do? How might students portray them in the skit to make their characters even more realistic and believable? Have students practice and perform their skits for the rest of the class.

COMPARING AUTHORS' STYLES

Have students examine novels by authors other than Paulsen to see how they convey character traits. Students can set up a 3-column chart to show techniques used by Paulsen and two other authors. Does each author use a variety of techniques? How do the techniques differ from each other?

Students will investigate the challenges and conflicts in a story to understand character development.

BACKGROUND KNOWLEDGE

Remind students that Carl fought in World War II. During that war, which took place from 1939 to 1945 (American involvement began with the bombing of Pearl Harbor on December 7, 1941), the U.S. Army Air Corps used planes to drop bombs on the enemy. Help students visualize a B-17 by sharing images from a website such as http://www.centennialofflight.gov/essay/Air_Power/B-17_29/AP28.htm. Then explain that models of these and other planes became popular toys.

VOCABULARY

B-17 a bomber plane used in World War II; also known as the "Flying Fortress"

banking tilting sideways when making a turn

newsreels short films about current events

Have a volunteer demonstrate a plane banking. Then explain that, before TVs were widely available, newsreels kept people informed, especially during wartime. The films were often shown at movie theaters.

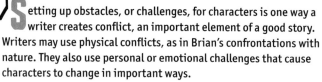

LESSON 63 PERSONAL CHALLENGES

Setting up obstacles, or challenges, for characters is one way a writer creates conflict, an important element of a good story. Writers may use physical conflicts, as in Brian's confrontations with nature. They also use personal or emotional challenges that cause characters to change in important ways.

In this passage from *Dancing Carl,* Marsh brings a model of a World War II B-17 airplane to the rink to show Carl. Through Carl's reaction to the model, Marsh and Willy begin to understand the emotional scars that Carl still carries as the result of the war. As you read the excerpt, write your ideas on why Carl reacts as he does—and why the model affects him so strongly—in the **Response Notes**.

Response Notes

from **Dancing Carl** by Gary Paulsen

Somehow we got to the rink, either with the B-17 flying and carrying me along or with me holding it down, and there wasn't anybody skating.

Not even any kids. So we went in the warming house half figuring it would be closed but Carl was sitting on his bunk. He smiled when we came in, then his face tightened in a quick frown when he saw the plane but I didn't think anything of it.

We knocked snow off and I put the skates and stick in a corner. There was nobody else in the warming house either.

"What's that?" he said, pointing at the stick model.

"It's a model I made. It's a B-17."

"I know that. I know what it is. I mean why do you have it here at the rink?"

"I told him he was crazy . . ." Willy started, laughing.

"Get it out of here."

His voice was quiet, almost like a still pond. Not mad sounding or sad, maybe a little afraid, but so quiet and still that I couldn't quite hear it.

"What?"

"Please take it outside. The model. Please take it out now."

"But it's just a model. If I take it out the wind will tear it apart." Like I said, I had a lot of work in it. I'd probably ruin it later, the way you do with models. Maybe put lighter fluid on the tail and send her off a roof. But that was later, now it was still a fresh model and I hated to just throw it out in the snow and let the wind tear it apart. "I'll put it over in the corner."

"Did you have something to do with B-17's during the war?" Willy asked and it was something he shouldn't have asked, not then, not ever.

Before

CRITICAL READING SKILL

Character Development Explain that in well-written fiction, the main characters usually face challenges. A challenge may be a conflict with people, with nature, or with other *external* factors. Or it may be a personal or emotional challenge that creates *internal* conflict. Point out that Carl's conflict, or challenge, is personal. He is struggling with emotions and memories related to the war. Even though the war was external—something outside of Carl—his current challenge is internal—overcoming his feelings. The reader learns about the character through the way he handles the conflict.

RESPONSE NOTES Tell students that as they read, they should mark text that gives clues to Carl's internal feelings. For example, students might underline *his face tightened in a quick frown* in the second paragraph.

Carl turned from the plane to Willy and there was a hunted look in his eyes. No, more than that, more a torn thing, a broken thing—as if something inside had ripped and torn loose and left him broken and he looked at the model and his face wrinkled down and I knew it wasn't a model anymore, knew he wasn't in the warming house.

"Colors," he said, whispering. "Colors red and down and going around and around in tighter and tighter circles. Hot. Colors hot and alive and going down."

Willy stepped back. "I'm sorry. I didn't mean to say anything ..."

But it was done. His whisper changed to a hiss, hot and alive, and he stood in the warming house and got into the open place by the door. I dumped the model in a corner, dumped it without looking, and moved away.

Carl stood with his arms out, still making that hissing sound, and I wondered if I could get out of the warming house and go for help, get the police, but he was by the door and I was afraid to go past him. Not afraid that he'd do something to me, afraid that I'd hurt him somehow.

So I stood, we stood, and Carl moved his arms even tighter out and the hiss changed to a kind of growl and I realized that he was a plane, a large plane, and I could see it wheeling through the sky, engines rumbling and I knew then that it was a B-17.

Through two, then three loops around the open area in the warming house Carl moved, turning and banking slowly and I swear you could see the plane.

Then something happened. Something hit or hurt the plane, one arm, one wing folded up and over and the plane went down, circling in a great spiral as it went down.

I mean Carl. Carl went down. But it was a plane, too. There in the warming house there was something that Carl did that made him seem a great bomber with a broken wing going down, around and down and I could see it. See the smoke and the explosion as the shell took the wing, the way I'd seen it in newsreels, and then the plane coming down, all the lines coming down, down to the ground in a crash that was like a plane and like a bird, too. ❖

✳ Marsh describes Carl as "torn" and "broken." What does he mean by this?

During

CHARACTER BEHAVIOR After students have read the excerpt, go through the passage together and track the sequence of Carl's reactions—from smiling when the boys first come in, to frowning and his voice growing quiet, to his breaking down and "becoming" the plane. Then guide students in completing the writing prompt by asking: *What might be "broken" inside a person besides body parts?*

CHANGE IN A CHARACTER Point out that an author creates challenges or conflicts that cause a character to change or develop in important ways. Have students complete the chart on *Daybook* page 200 to explore how Carl might have changed. For example, in the left column, students might write "brave, strong, forceful, likes adventure, likes flying"; in the right column, they might write "easily upset, absorbed in his own thoughts, quiet, angry."

Collaboration Have students work in pairs to complete the chart on page 200. The first student can write an entry in the "Before the War" column, and the second student can write the corresponding entry in the "After the War" column.

Quick Assess

✳ Did students list at least three traits in the "Before the War" column?

✳ Did students list traits in the "After the War" column that show how Carl changed?

✳ Use the chart below to explore how Carl's experiences in World War II changed him. The first excerpt from *Dancing Carl* in Lesson 62 gives us a glimpse of what Carl might have been like before the war. Use the character traits you brainstormed on page 196 to help you describe what kind of person Carl might have been. Then use the second excerpt to describe what Carl is like as a result of the war.

Before the War	After the War
Carl may have lacked compassion.	Carl protects those who can't stand up for themselves.

> When you read about a character confronting a challenge, try to figure out how and why the experience changes the character.

After

LISTENING/SPEAKING CONNECTION To explore Carl's personal challenges more deeply, have students work in pairs to write a dialogue between Marsh and Willy in which they discuss Carl's behavior, how the war has affected him, and what they might do to help him. Then have partners perform their dialogues for the class.

In many of Paulsen's books, the main characters deal with the challenges of nature—hunger, cold, the fear of being lost. Paulsen not only depicts the struggles characters face, but he also explores what the characters need to do and think in order to survive the challenges.

Dogsong is not a true story, but it is based on Paulsen's experiences with dog-sledding. The main character, Russel Susskit, is a fourteen-year-old Eskimo boy. Russel becomes friends with Oogruk, an old man who teaches him about dogs, sledding, nature, and the "Old Ways." Russel then goes on a journey of his own, where he meets with many challenges at the hands of nature.

As you read from *Dogsong* (which Paulsen has called his favorite book), put an "X" in the **Response Notes** near any parts that focus on challenges in nature.

from Dogsong by Gary Paulsen

When the first dog started to weave with exhaustion, still pulling, but slipping back and forth as it pulled, he sensed their tiredness in the black night and stopped the team. He had a piece of meat in the sled, deer meat from a leg and he cut it in six pieces. When he'd pulled them under an overhanging ledge out of the wind and tipped the sled on its side, he fed them. But they were too tired to eat and slept with the meat between their legs.

He didn't know that they could become that tired and the knowledge frightened him. He was north, in the open, and the dogs wouldn't eat and they were over a hundred and fifty miles to anything. Without the dogs, he would die.

Without the dogs he was nothing.

He'd never felt so alone and for a time fear roared in him. The darkness became an enemy, the cold a killer, the night a ghost from the underworld that would take him down where demons would tear strips off him.

He tried a bite of the meat but he wasn't hungry. Not from tiredness. At least he didn't think so.

But he knew he wasn't thinking too well, and so he lay down between the two wheel-dogs and pulled them close on either side and took a kind of sleep.

Brain-rest more than sleep. He closed his eyes and something inside him rested. The darkness came harder and the northern lights danced and he rested. He was not sure how long it might have been, but it was still dark when one of the dogs got up and moved in a circle to find a better resting position.

Response Notes

Students will analyze an author's use of conflict (challenges in nature) to develop a story.

BACKGROUND KNOWLEDGE

Ask students what they know about dogsledding. Some students may be familiar with the Iditarod, the annual dogsled race from Anchorage, Alaska, to Nome, Alaska, a race in which Gary Paulsen has competed twice.

VOCABULARY

weave to move in and out or from side to side

wheel-dogs specially trained dogs that steer a sled (chariot) across frozen, snow-covered ground

northern lights streaks of light seen in the night sky in the northern hemisphere; aurora borealis

go down to die: an animal handler's expression

runners blades under a sled that help it move over snow or ice

Point out that *runners* and *weave* are multiple-meaning words. Compare their common definitions (*runner:* a person who runs; *weave:* something you do with a loom) to the definitions used in the story. For *northern lights,* show pictures from a website such as http://www.geo.mtu.edu/weather/aurora/.

Before

CRITICAL READING SKILL
Reading about External Challenges
Review with students what they learned in Lesson 63 about personal challenges and internal conflict. Then explain that Gary Paulsen also frequently writes about another kind of conflict—"person vs. nature." This type of conflict is an example of a character facing an *external* challenge, one that is outside of the character. Point out that in much of Paulsen's writing, the challenge is *literally* outside. Characters face extreme weather, difficult terrain, wild animals, hunger, injury, and even death. They must use not only their own skills but natural resources to survive. Have students look for ways in which Russel does this as they read *Dogsong*.

SETTING A PURPOSE Remind students that good readers read for a purpose. Review the last paragraph of the introductory text, which tells students what to look for when they read: parts of the text that focus on challenges in nature. Students are asked to mark those parts with an X: for example, the second paragraph.

Visual Learners Show images of the Iditarod, sled dogs, and the northern lights to help students visualize the setting of the story. See websites such as the following: www.iditarod.com, www.dogsled.com, and www.geo.mtu.edu.

Differentiation Support students in answering the writing prompt on page 202 by providing oral support prior to writing. Talk about what the dogs provide. Then make a list: transportation, warmth, protection, companionship, and so forth.

Response Notes

The dog awakened the remainder of the team and they all ate their meat with quiet growls of satisfaction that came from their stomachs up through their throats. Small rumbles that could be felt more than heard.

When they'd eaten they lay down again, not even pausing to relieve themselves. And Russel let them stay down for all of that long night. He dozed now with his eyes open, still between the two wheel-dogs, until the light came briefly.

Then he stood and stretched, feeling the stiffness. The dogs didn't get up and he had to go up the line and lift them. They shook hard to loosen their muscles and drop the tightness of sleeping long.

"Up now! Up and out."

Out.

They started north again, into a land that Russel did not know. At first the dogs ran poorly, raggedly, hating it. But inside half a mile they had settled into their stride and were a working team once more.

But they had lost weight.

In the long run they had lost much weight and it was necessary for Russel to make meat. He didn't know how long they could go without meat but he didn't think it could be long.

He had to hunt.

If he did not get meat the dogs would go down—and he was nothing without the dogs. He had to get food for them.

The light ended the dark-fears but did not bring much warmth. Only the top edge of the sun slipped into view above the horizon, so there was no heat from it.

To get his body warm again after the long night of being still he held onto the sled and ran between the runners. He would run until his breath grew short, then jump on and catch his wind, then run again. It took a few miles of that to get him warm and as soon as he was, the great hole of hunger opened in his stomach and he nearly fell off the sled. ❖

202 **LESSON 64**

❊ "Without the dogs he was nothing." What do you think Paulsen means by these words?

_____

_____

_____

_____

_____

During

CONNECTING TO THE TEXT After students have read the passage, ask: *How would you feel if you were in Russel's shoes? What things would scare you the most or be the hardest for you? The dark? The cold? Hunger? Concern for the dogs? How would you cope?* Have students discuss what Russel might have to do to survive. Then have students answer the writing prompt on page 202 and share their responses.

COMPLETING THE CHART As students complete the chart on page 203, suggest that they think about their answers to the questions in the preceding discussion to help them identify and rank Russel's challenges.

✳ Choose four challenges in nature that Russel encounters. Put them in order from 1 (the most crucial, or life-threatening) to 4 (the least crucial). After each challenge, explain why you ranked the challenge as you did. (For example, "It's important to have enough food, but if Russel doesn't stay warm, he won't be able to hunt.") Compare your chart with others in a small group.

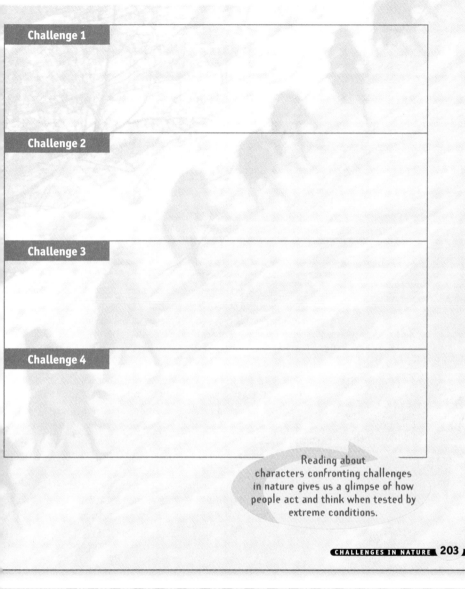

Challenge 1

Challenge 2

Challenge 3

Challenge 4

Reading about characters confronting challenges in nature gives us a glimpse of how people act and think when tested by extreme conditions.

Collaboration After students have compared their charts in small groups and reached consensus, have a member from each group report on the group's chart and how individual rankings within the group were similar and/or different.

Quick Assess

✳ Did students identify four nature-related challenges in their charts?

✳ Did students effectively explain why they ranked the challenges as they did?

After

READING/WRITING CONNECTION Have students imagine they are Russel and write a journal entry about what happens next. What challenges face Russel? How does he deal with these challenges? Remind students to write in first-person, from Russel's perspective. Then invite students to read the rest of *Dogsong* to find out what really happens to him and how it compares to their predictions.

BOOK TALK If students have read any of Paulsen's books, have them prepare a book talk to entice their fellow classmates to read more of Paulsen's work. A good book talk includes a brief summary (without giving away the ending!), a personal evaluation of the book, and a recommendation to the audience.

RESEARCH Invite students to look for print resources and visit www.pbs.org/wnet/nature/sleddogs/index.html to learn more about the Iditarod and dogsledding.

Students will read an excerpt from an author's autobiography to analyze how real-life experiences influence a story.

BACKGROUND KNOWLEDGE

In this excerpt from *Woodsong,* students have an opportunity to read about one of Gary Paulsen's own encounters with the natural world. Point out that, like many of his characters, Paulsen has struggled with challenges in nature and has eventually come to understand that humans must live cooperatively with the natural world, including animals. Have students discuss their own encounters with wild animals (in their backyard, on a family outing, etc.) and/or encounters they have read or heard about in the news.

VOCABULARY

coherent consistent within itself; logical

menace threat of danger

rummaging hastily searching through the contents of a container

After discussing the definition of each word, have students suggest examples of when each word might be used. For example, discuss *coherent* in the context of writing a paper, *menace* as related to a dog, and *rummaging* in terms of a full backpack.

Gary Paulsen has based fictional stories on real people and real experiences, but he has also written about his own experiences. In *Woodsong,* an **autobiography,** he talks about his sled dogs and competing in the Iditarod, a grueling dogsled race across Alaska.

In this selection, Paulsen is describing a time when he burns left-over food to dispose of it—and the smell attracts a big, hungry bear that Paulsen calls "Scarhead." As you read the excerpt, think about what Paulsen is learning from the experience. Write down your ideas in the **Response Notes.**

from **Woodsong** by Gary Paulsen

Response Notes

He was having a grand time. The fire didn't bother him. He was trying to reach a paw in around the edges of flame to get at whatever smelled so good. He had torn things apart quite a bit—ripped one side off the burn enclosure—and I was having a bad day and it made me mad.

I was standing across the burning fire from him and without thinking—because I was so used to him—I picked up a stick, threw it at him, and yelled, "Get out of here."

I have made many mistakes in my life, and will probably make many more, but I hope never to throw a stick at a bear again.

In one rolling motion—the muscles seemed to move within the skin so fast that I couldn't take half a breath—he turned and came for me. Close. I could smell his breath and see the red around the sides of his eyes. Close on me he stopped and raised on his back legs and hung over me, his forelegs and paws hanging down, weaving back and forth gently as he took his time and decided whether or not to tear my head off.

I could not move, would not have time to react. I knew I had nothing to say about it. One blow would break my neck. Whether I lived or died depended on him, on his thinking, on his ideas about me—whether I was worth the bother or not.

I did not think then.

Looking back on it I don't remember having one coherent thought when it was happening. All I knew was terrible menace. His eyes looked very small as he studied me. He looked down on me for what seemed hours. I did not move, did not breathe, did not think or do anything.

And he lowered.

Perhaps I was not worth the trouble. He lowered slowly and turned back to the trash and I walked backward halfway to the house and then ran—anger growing now—and took the rifle from the gun rack by the door and came back out.

Before

CRITICAL READING SKILL
Reading Autobiographical Text

Remind students that an autobiography is the story of someone's life written by that person. It relates experiences, ideas, and events from that person's point of view. Point out that reading an author's own account of something that has happened in his or her own life helps us connect with the author and contributes to our understanding and enjoyment of his or her stories. Tell students that as they read Paulsen's account about the bear, they should look for similarities between Paulsen and some of his characters.

RESPONSE NOTES Remind students that successful readers read for a purpose. In this case, the purpose is to find out what the author learned from the experience with the bear. Have students underline the last two lines of the introduction to help them remember the purpose for which they are reading and what they should record in the Response Notes.

He was still there, rummaging through the trash. I worked the bolt and fed a cartridge in and aimed at the place where you kill bears and began to squeeze. In raw anger, I began to take up the four pounds of pull necessary to send death into him.

And stopped.

Kill him for what?

That thought crept in.

Kill him for what?

For not killing me? For letting me know it is wrong to throw sticks at four-hundred-pound bears? For not hurting me, for not killing me, I should kill him? I lowered the rifle and ejected the shell and put the gun away. I hope Scarhead is still alive. For what he taught me, I hope he lives long and is very happy because I learned then—looking up at him while he made up his mind whether or not to end me—that when it is all boiled down I am nothing more and nothing less than any other animal in the woods. ❖

✳ Compare Paulsen's experience with the bear to a challenge faced by one of the characters in his novels. Think about the characters you've read about in this unit or use your knowledge of other books by Gary Paulsen. Record your ideas in the chart.

Paulsen's challenge	How Paulsen changed

Character's challenge	How character changed

Differentiation Struggling readers may need help understanding who "he" is at the beginning of the excerpt. Model a think-aloud. Say: *I figured this out by noticing that first Paulsen talks about throwing a stick at "him," and then at the end of the third paragraph Paulsen says that he hopes he never throws a stick at "a bear" again. "He" must refer to the bear.*

WRITER'S CRAFT

Author's Style Direct students' attention to the top of page 205 and ask what they notice about the text. (Some sentences are very short, some are really fragments.) What effect do the short sentences and fragments have on the reader? Discuss how authors use techniques to convey a message or feeling to the reader. In this case, the short sentences draw attention to an important part of the excerpt.

During

CONNECTING WITH THE AUTHOR

After students have read the passage, ask them to explain whether or not they agree with Paulsen's decision not to shoot the bear. Then have students discuss what he means when he says he is "nothing more and nothing less than any other animal in the woods."

IDENTIFYING CHALLENGES

Work with students to complete the first row of the chart on page 205. Ask: *What was Paulsen's challenge?* (having a bear rush at him and then having to decide whether to kill it) *How did Paulsen change as a result of this conflict?* (He realized the bear deserved to live; that he was

no better than the bear.) Have students complete the second row of the chart independently or with a partner. Then have students share their responses.

Autobiographical Text Remind students to write in the first person (use pronouns *I, me, my*) and to include specific details in their account of the experience, such as where and when it occurred and who was there.

Quick Assess

✳ Did students describe a challenging experience? Did they include specific details about it?

✳ Did students name at least one thing they learned from the experience?

✳ Did students name at least one way in which the experience changed them?

✳ Think about a challenging experience that you have faced. Write notes for an excerpt from your autobiography. Describe the experience, what you learned from it, and how it changed you.

The experience

What I learned from it

How it changed me

> Writers share events from their lives not only to tell what happened, but also to tell what makes those events important.

After

READING/WRITING CONNECTION
Have students turn their autobiographical notes into a finished piece of writing. Then invite volunteers to read their personal narratives to the class.

COMPARING GENRES For further experience with autobiographical texts, have students read additional excerpts from *Woodsong* or another one of Paulsen's autobiographical texts (such as *Guts: The True Story Behind Hatchet and the Brian Books* or *Winterdance: The Fine Madness of Running the Iditarod*). Then have students compare Paulsen's autobiographical writing to his fiction writing. Ask: *Which did you enjoy reading more? Why?*

UNIT 14
ASSESSING YOUR REPERTOIRE

Lessons 66–70, pages 208–220

UNIT OVERVIEW

Students will use the reading and writing strategies and skills they have studied in the *Daybook* as the basis for drafting and writing an assessment piece.

KEY IDEA

Assessing your use of reading and writing skills and strategies shows you where you have grown in confidence and ability.

CRITICAL READING AND WRITING SKILLS

by lesson

66 Studying an author

67 Exploring multiple perspectives

68 Focusing on language and craft

69 Writing to show what you know

70 Putting it all together

WRITING ACTIVITIES

by lesson

66 Connect text with experience.

67 Write "What if...?" statements.

68 Make notes about your name.

69 Write an assessment piece.

70 Write a reflective letter.

Assessing Your Repertoire

The goal of this Daybook has been to help you become a more confident reader and writer. As you read and write on your own, you won't need to think through every strategy each time you open a book or get ready to write. You have gained confidence, just like an experienced rock climber or skateboarder. And just like an experienced athlete, you will become even more confident over time.

In the Daybook, you have practiced strategies and skills that build reading and writing confidence, and you stopped to measure your progress. In this last unit, you will read two short stories by award-winning author Sandra Cisneros. You will use the skills and strategies you have practiced throughout this book and will check to see how well you have learned them.

207

Literature

- "Eleven" from *Woman Hollering Creek and Other Stories* by Sandra Cisneros (short story),

A young girl muses on the different aspects of being eleven as she experiences a very frustrating birthday.

- "My Name" from *The House on Mango Street* by Sandra Cisneros (short story)

In this story, Esperanza Cordero, a young girl growing up in the Hispanic quarter of Chicago, talks about how she feels about her name.

Students will interact with a text to predict, connect, and visualize as they read.

BACKGROUND KNOWLEDGE

Activate prior knowledge by discussing birthdays and other special days and how they are celebrated. Tell students that many people plan special events to reflect on their accomplishments. Invite volunteers to share any stories about special events that may not have met their expectations and how this made them feel at the time. Tell them that this story is about a girl who has a bad day at school on the day she turns eleven, which causes her to think about what being eleven really means.

Sandra Cisneros, author of the two stories you are going to read, is the daughter of a Mexican father and a Mexican American mother. She was the only girl in a family of seven children. Her family moved between Chicago, where she was born, and Mexico, where her father had many relatives. Her stories often reflect her life in both places.

Cisneros writes, ". . . I currently earn my living by my pen. I live in San Antonio, Texas, in a violet house filled with many creatures, little and large." Pictures of her often show her with four dogs!

Her first book to attract attention and receive many awards was *The House on Mango Street*. This is the story of Esperanza Cordero, a young girl growing up in the Hispanic quarter of Chicago. The story is told in a series of small journal entries, the kind you might write in your own journal or diary. Together, they reflect the ups and downs of the everyday life of Esperanza. They show her in moments of sadness and moments of joy. If you read the whole book, you get a rich picture of all the dimensions of one young girl. The story in the next lesson called "My Name" is from this book.

You will also read one of Sandra Cisneros's best-known stories, "Eleven," which is from her book, *Woman Hollering Creek and Other Stories*. It has also received many awards.

INTERACT WITH THE TEXT

Read the story "Eleven," using the **Response Notes** to predict, question, connect, or visualize as you read.

Response Notes

"**Eleven**" from *Woman Hollering Creek and Other Stories* by Sandra Cisneros

What they don't understand about birthdays and what they never tell you is that when you're eleven, you're also ten, and nine, and eight, and seven, and six, and five, and four, and three, and two, and one. And when you wake up on your eleventh birthday you expect to feel eleven, but you don't. You open your eyes and everything's just like yesterday, only it's today. And you don't feel eleven at all. You feel like you're still ten. And you are—underneath the year that makes you eleven.

Like some days you might say something stupid, and that's the part of you that's still ten. Or maybe some days you might need to sit on your mama's lap because you're scared, and that's the part of you that's five. And maybe one

Before

CRITICAL READING SKILL

Studying an Author Remind students that knowing about an author can add to their understanding and appreciation of the author's writing. Sandra Cisneros is one of the most widely read and taught authors in middle schools. Ask your students if they have read anything else by Cisneros. If they have, ask them to tell about what they read and what they

thought about it. You might summarize the information about Cisneros in About the Author or read it aloud to the class.

RESPONSE NOTES   Review with students what they've learned in previous lessons about interacting with the text. In their Response Notes, ask them to write predictions, questions, connections and images that come to mind as they read.

day when you're all grown up maybe you will need to cry like if you're three, and that's okay. That's what I tell Mama when she's sad and needs to cry. Maybe she's feeling three.

Because the way you grow old is kind of like an onion or like the rings inside a tree trunk or like my little wooden dolls that fit one inside the other, each year inside the next one. That's how being eleven years old is.

You don't feel eleven. Not right away. It takes a few days, weeks even, sometimes even months before you say Eleven when they ask you. And you don't feel smart eleven, not until you're almost twelve. That's the way it is.

Only today I wish I didn't have only eleven years rattling inside me like pennies in a tin Band-Aid box. Today I wish I was one hundred and two instead of eleven because if I was one hundred and two I'd have known what to say when Mrs. Price put the red sweater on my desk. I would've known how to tell her it wasn't mine instead of just sitting there with that look on my face and nothing coming out of my mouth.

"Whose is this?" Mrs. Price says, and she holds the red sweater up in the air for all the class to see. "Whose? It's been sitting in the coatroom for a month."

"Not mine," says everybody. "Not me."

"It has to belong to somebody," Mrs. Price keeps saying, but nobody can remember. It's an ugly sweater with red plastic buttons and a collar and sleeves all stretched out like you could use it for a jump rope. It's maybe a thousand years old and even if it belonged to me I wouldn't say so.

Maybe because I'm skinny, maybe because she doesn't like me, that stupid Sylvia Saldivar says, "I think it belongs to Rachel." An ugly sweater like that, all raggedy and old, but Mrs. Price believes her. Mrs. Price takes the sweater and puts it right on my desk, but when I open my mouth nothing comes out.

"That's not, I don't, you're not...Not mine," I finally say in a little voice that was maybe me when I was four.

"Of course it's yours," Mrs. Price says. "I remember you wearing it once." Because she's older and the teacher, she's right and I'm not.

Not mine, not mine, not mine, but Mrs. Price is already turning to page thirty-two, and math problem number four. I don't know why but all of a sudden I'm feeling sick inside, like the part of me that's three wants to come out of my eyes, only I squeeze them shut tight and bite down on my teeth real hard and try to remember today I am eleven, eleven. Mama is making a cake for me tonight and when Papa comes home everybody will sing Happy birthday, happy birthday to you.

But when the sick feeling goes away and I open my eyes, the red sweater's still sitting there like a big red mountain. I move the red sweater to the corner of my desk with my ruler. I move my pencil and books and eraser as far from it as possible. I even move my chair a little to the right. Not mine, not mine, not mine.

ABOUT THE AUTHOR

Sandra Cisneros was born in 1954 in Chicago, Illinois. As a child, Cisneros moved frequently and spent a lot of time visiting her paternal grandmother in Mexico. The frequent moves were difficult for her, and Cisneros found comfort in writing. Her experiences as an outsider have given her a special empathy for characters who struggle to sort out who they are and where they belong. Additional information about Sandra Cisneros can be found at http://www.sandracisneros.com.

During

MODELING INTERACTING WITH THE TEXT You might want to begin by reading the first part of the story aloud, stopping periodically to talk about your own processing of the text. Model predicting, making inferences, making connections, and reflecting. For example, model making inferences using this think-aloud: *Mrs. Price doesn't seem to realize how she's making Rachel feel. I know this because she says of course it's Rachel's sweater and then she moves on to the math problem.*

After you have modeled some of the strategies, have students read the rest of the story, using the Response Notes to record their own processing of the text.

When students are finished reading, ask them to reflect on the process by completing page 211.

Similes Cisneros uses figurative language superbly. Her analogies help make the text immediately accessible to her readers by comparing what's happening to something familiar. Remind students that a simile is a comparison of two objects that are not alike that uses *like* or *as,* for example, "The sun rose like a sleepy child awakening to a new day." Have students go through the text and find at least three examples of similes. *(Examples of similes in the story:*

❉ *page 209, paragraph 2: "the way you grow old is kind of like an onion or like the rings inside a tree trunk or like my little wooden dolls that fit one inside the other"*

❉ *page 209, last paragraph: "the red sweater's still sitting there like a big red mountain."*

❉ *page 210, paragraph 1: "and it's hanging all over the edge like a waterfall"*

❉ *page 210, last paragraph: "I want today to be far away already, far away like a runaway balloon, like a tiny o in the sky")*

Invite students to suggest alternatives for some of the similes they find.

In my head I'm thinking how long till lunchtime, how long till I can take the red sweater and throw it over the schoolyard fence, or leave it hanging on a parking meter, or bunch it up into a little ball and toss it in the alley. Except when math period ends Mrs. Price says loud and in front of everybody, "Now, Rachel, that's enough," because she sees I've shoved the red sweater to the tippy-tip corner of my desk and it's hanging all over the edge like a waterfall, but I don't care.

"Rachel," Mrs. Price says. She says it like she's getting mad. "You put that sweater on right now and no more nonsense."

"But it's not—"

"Now!" Mrs. Price says.

This is when I wish I wasn't eleven, because all the years inside of me—ten, nine, eight, seven, six, five, four, three, two, and one—are pushing at the back of my eyes when I put one arm through one sleeve of the sweater that smells like cottage cheese, and then the other arm through the other and stand there with my arms apart like if the sweater hurts me and it does, all itchy and full of germs that aren't even mine.

That's when everything I've been holding in since this morning, since when Mrs. Price put the sweater on my desk, finally lets go, and all of a sudden I'm crying in front of everybody. I wish I was invisible but I'm not. I'm eleven and it's my birthday today and I'm crying like I'm three in front of everybody. I put my head down on the desk and bury my face in my stupid clown-sweater arms. My face all hot and spit coming out of my mouth because I can't stop the little animal noises from coming out of me, until there aren't any more tears left in my eyes, and it's just my body shaking like when you have the hiccups, and my whole head hurts like when you drink milk too fast.

But the worst part is right before the bell rings for lunch. That stupid Phyllis Lopez, who is even dumber than Sylvia Saldivar, says she remembers the red sweater is hers! I take it off right away and give it to her, only Mrs.Price pretends like everything's okay.

Today I'm eleven. There's a cake Mama's making for tonight, and when Papa comes home from work we'll eat it. There'll be candles and presents and everybody will sing Happy birthday, happy birthday to you, Rachel, only it's too late.

I'm eleven today. I'm eleven, ten, nine, eight, seven, six, five, four, three, two, and one, but I wish I was one hundred and two. I wish I was anything but eleven, because I want today to be far away already, far away like a runaway balloon, like a tiny *o* in the sky, so tiny-tiny you have to close your eyes to see it. ❖

VISUALIZE

✳ Draw a picture of how you think Rachel feels when she is sitting in her classroom with the ugly red sweater. In the space below, write how you feel about Rachel's reaction to the sweater.

MAKE CONNECTIONS

Think of times when you didn't feel as old as you were.

✳ Make notes about one memory you have when you felt younger than you were.

- What made you feel younger?
- How old were you?
- How old did you feel?

✳ Jot down as many details as you can remember about that memory. You will use these notes in a later lesson.

✳ Write a sentence about whether you think boys and girls both have experiences like Rachel's, when they don't feel as old as they are.

Responding to the emotions of the characters in a story helps the reader get more meaning from it.

Collaboration Students should respond to the Visualize activity independently, making sure they write a sentence about what they have drawn. Then have students work in small groups to discuss the questions in the Make Connections section. Rather than having a Recorder in the group, ask students to write their own notes on page 211 as they make connections to their individual experiences. After students have written a sentence in response to the last prompt, discuss the issue as a class, inviting students to talk about their experiences.

Quick Assess

✳ Did students interact with the text as they read by writing in their Response Notes?

✳ Were students able to find at least three similes in the story?

✳ Did students draw a picture of Rachel and write a sentence explaining what they drew?

✳ Did they participate in the discussions and make notes to use later as they write about their own experience?

After

RESEARCH CONNECTION Have students research other stories, essays, poems, and interviews in which Sandra Cisneros explores the issue of age. Have them take notes and then report to the class in writing or in an oral presentation. Encourage them to make comparisons between what they've learned about Cisneros's view of age in "Eleven" with what they learn from their research.

ORAL HISTORY CONNECTION

Have students interview their parents or other adults to see whether they ever have feelings about being younger than they are. Have students ask the adults if they remember how they felt when they turned eleven. Students can bring their notes from their interviews to share in class.

Students will examine an author's perspective to speculate "what if" the story were told from a different point of view.

One of the ways to read a piece of literature is to think "what if?" the story were different in some way. For example, how would your **perspective,** or point of view, change if the title or a character changed?

✳ Talk with a partner about how you might read this story differently if the title were different.

  ▪ What other title would fit this piece? Would another title be more or less effective than "Eleven"? Write your thoughts.

_____

_____

_____

_____

✳ Talk with a partner about how the story would change if it were told from a different perspective.

  ▪ What if "Eleven" were a story of a boy at that age instead of a girl? How do you think the story would be different?

  ▪ What if you were a student in Rachel's class who remembered this moment of insensitivity toward Rachel? How do you think you would feel about this story now?

_____

_____

_____

_____

_____

✳ Make up three or four additional "what if" speculations and share them with your partner or writing group.

_____

_____

_____

_____

_____

Before

During

CRITICAL READING SKILL
Exploring Multiple Perspectives
Remind students of what they have learned about exploring multiple perspectives— that it is a valuable way of interpreting things from different viewpoints. One way to get at these different ways of seeing text is to ask the question, "What if...?"

GROUNDED SPECULATION
Have students answer the questions on page 212, working alone, in pairs, or in a small group. After they have finished, ask them to try to find lines in the story that support their ideas. This will not be possible for all of their answers, but it will help them see whether their answers would substantially change the meaning of the story.

✳ Choose one of the "what if" speculations. Make some planning notes about details you could include when you write about this speculation. Save these notes.

_____
_____
_____
_____
_____
_____
_____
_____
_____
_____
_____
_____
_____
_____
_____
_____
_____
_____

Speculating leads to new ways of making meaning from a story or poem.

After

DRAMA CONNECTION   Invite students to work in small groups to act out one of their "What if...?" scenarios, such as the incident from the teacher's point of view or the story with a boy as the central character. Give groups time to plan and rehearse their skits. Then allow each group to present its skit to the rest of the class.

Students will explore how a writer uses language in poetic ways.

BACKGROUND KNOWLEDGE

Activate prior knowledge by having students talk about their names: their whole names, their family nicknames, what their names mean, whom they're named after, and so on. Ask them to write their whole names and then just the name they use most often. Have them write just one sentence that begins, "My name...."

Read the story "My Name" from *The House on Mango Street* by Sandra Cisneros, using the **Response Notes** to mark any places where you are aware of the influence of the Spanish language. You may want to make other comments about your reactions as you read, too.

"My Name" from *The House on Mango Street*
by Sandra Cisneros

Response Notes

In English my name means hope. In Spanish it means too many letters. It means sadness, it means waiting. It is like the number nine. A muddy color. It is the Mexican records my father plays on Sunday mornings when he is shaving, songs like sobbing.

It was my great-grandmother's name and now it is mine. She was a horse-woman too, born like me in the Chinese year of the horse—which is supposed to be bad luck if you're born female—but I think this is a Chinese lie because Chinese, like Mexicans, don't like their women strong.

My great-grandmother. I would've liked to have known her, a wild horse of a woman, so wild she wouldn't marry. Until my great-grandfather threw a sack over her head and carried her off. Just like that, as if she were a fancy chandelier. That's the way he did it.

And the story goes she never forgave him. She looked out the window her whole life, the way so many women sit their sadness on an elbow. I wonder if she made the best with what she got or was she sorry because she couldn't be all the things she wanted to be. Esperanza. I have inherited her name, but I don't want to inherit her place by the window.

At school they say my name funny as if the syllables were made out of tin and hurt the roof of your mouth. But in Spanish my name is made out of softer something like silver, not quite as thick as sister's name—Magdalena—which is uglier than mine. Magdalena who at least can come home and become Nenny. But I am always Esperanza.

I would like to baptize myself under a new name, a name more like the real me, the one nobody sees. Esperanza as Lisandra or Maritza or Zeze the X. Yes. Something like Zeze the X will do. ⟡

Before

CRITICAL READING SKILL
Focusing on Language and Craft
Remind students about the discussion they had in Lesson 66 about Cisneros's use of similes in her writing. Point out that one of the other things that Cisneros does well in her writing is to use sensory and descriptive language. Cisneros evokes color, sound, feeling by using well-chosen adjectives, alliteration ("softer something than silver"), similes, and images.

RESPONSE NOTES   Tell students to mark places in the text where they are aware of the influence of the Spanish language. Model finding this influence by using a think-aloud: *In the first paragraph, the author says that in Spanish her name means too many letters. But then she goes on and explains what her name means by presenting images of sadness and waiting and a muddy color and sad songs. These images give me a better idea of what Esperanza really means in Spanish.* Encourage students to mark other places in the text where Cisneros uses poetic imagery and language.

Cisneros uses language in poetic ways.

✳ What do you think Esperanza means when she says " . . . in Spanish my name is made out of softer something like silver"?

_____

_____

✳ Write your name. Then write what you think your name could be "made out of."

_____

_____

✳ What do you visualize when you read the phrase "the way so many women sit their sadness on an elbow"?

_____

_____

✳ Find another example of a poetic use of language in "My Name."

_____

What if you had a different name? Would it affect who you are?

✳ Jot down names that you may have tried at different times in your life.

_____

_____

✳ Think about whether you would act differently if you had another name.

_____

_____

✳ Do different people call you by different names? Make notes about any of these names and how you feel about them.

_____

_____

WRITER'S CRAFT

Imagery Cisneros weaves vivid images into her writing. Her sentences flow in a conversational way, and her words paint clear pictures for the reader. Students may need help understanding some of the imagery in "My Name," but with a little guidance they should be able to appreciate how effective it is. Talk about the image of Esperanza's great-grandmother sitting at the window "the way so many women sit their sadness on an elbow." Ask students to talk about what the author means by that. What do they visualize when they read that phrase? Help them picture a woman looking out a window with her head leaning against her palm as her elbow rests on the window sill. Ask them how that image helps them understand more about Esperanza's great-grandmother.

During   After

FOCUS ON AUTHOR'S USE OF LANGUAGE   Read this piece aloud, emphasizing the rich imagery that Cisneros uses. Then have students write their responses to the first four items on page 215. Have students share some of their responses, using them as a basis for discussion.

Then ask students to write their responses to the questions regarding their names.

LANGUAGE/ART CONNECTION

Ask students to create their own poetic images. A student's image can be about his or her name or about a sport (for example, "Soccer is like a prairie fire as the players race across the field, scorching the ground beneath them.") Encourage students to illustrate their images with drawings or photos. Display the final products on a bulletin board.

Differentiation   Help any students who are having difficulty selecting a topic for their cluster. Ask them: *Which of the questions was the most interesting to you? Which answer would you like to say more about?* Tell students they don't have to write a finished piece; they can just jot down some ideas in the cluster at the bottom of the page or expand on their answer on another sheet of paper.

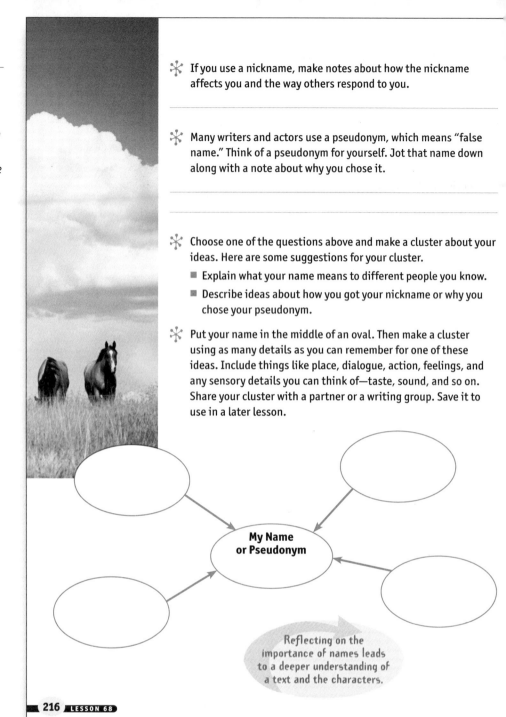

✳ If you use a nickname, make notes about how the nickname affects you and the way others respond to you.

✳ Many writers and actors use a pseudonym, which means "false name." Think of a pseudonym for yourself. Jot that name down along with a note about why you chose it.

✳ Choose one of the questions above and make a cluster about your ideas. Here are some suggestions for your cluster.
  ■ Explain what your name means to different people you know.
  ■ Describe ideas about how you got your nickname or why you chose your pseudonym.

✳ Put your name in the middle of an oval. Then make a cluster using as many details as you can remember for one of these ideas. Include things like place, dialogue, action, feelings, and any sensory details you can think of—taste, sound, and so on. Share your cluster with a partner or a writing group. Save it to use in a later lesson.

My Name or Pseudonym

Reflecting on the importance of names leads to a deeper understanding of a text and the characters.

WRITING TO SHOW WHAT YOU KNOW — 69 LESSON

In this lesson you will review the work you did in Lessons 66-68. This will prepare you to write a piece that shows what you have learned about how authors get messages across to their readers.

Here are the notes you should have from your work:

1 **A memory:** notes about one memory of a time when you didn't feel as old as you were (from Lesson 66)

2 **Other ways you might read "Eleven":** speculations on ways you might read the story "Eleven" differently (from Lesson 67)

3 **Poetic language** from "My Name" (from Lesson 68)

4 **How your name has been important to you:** notes about your name—other names people call you, nicknames, names you wish you had, how your name has been important (from Lesson 68)

✳ Review your notes. Choose one topic to develop into a personal essay. Write the topic you have selected here.

_____

_____

Using the notes you have as a starting point, make additional notes.

✳ If you have chosen to write about an incident, an event that happened, be sure to include such details as

- time and place
- what actually happened
- who was there
- what people there said
- how it ended

Tell how you felt about the incident at the time and how you feel about it now.

_____

_____

_____

Students will review the strategies they have learned and build on the work they have done in this book to write a personal narrative.

BACKGROUND KNOWLEDGE

The background students bring to this lesson is what they've learned about critical reading and writing skills over the year. Students will also draw on the specific work they have done in this unit. Have students review what they did in Lessons 66–68 in order to make a good topic choice for their written assessment.

Before

CRITICAL WRITING SKILL
Writing to Show What You Know

Help students understand that this is their chance to draw on what they've learned about being good readers and writers. Review what they've learned about interacting with the text, studying an author, exploring multiple perspectives, and focusing on language and craft.

Talk about how they've learned to use these strategies when they read but also how to apply these techniques to their own writing.

* If you have chosen to write about another way to read the story, be sure to include the following.
  - what you think should be changed
  - why you think your ideas would improve the story
  - how your changes would affect the characters

Use these writing lines to plan your writing.

_____
_____
_____
_____
_____
_____
_____
_____
_____
_____
_____
_____
_____
_____
_____
_____
_____

You are now ready to write a draft of your paper. Use your notes, and write at least a page on regular notebook paper. Use details so that your audience has a clear picture of your story or your ideas.

Using notes, drawings, and other prewriting material helps in writing organized and detailed papers.

During

WRITING A DRAFT Have students review the writing choices listed at the top of page 217. Have students write down some ideas as to what they want to include in their narrative. Check each student's topic, and then have students use the checklists at the bottom of page 217 and the top of page 218 to plan their writing. Once they've finished planning, have them begin writing the first draft on their own paper. In the next lesson, they will have a chance to revise and make a final copy.

As with any craft, one very important part of writing is looking to see how it can be improved. This is called *revision* because you *see (vision)* it *again (re-)*. Work with a partner to decide how you can improve your writing. Ask each other questions such as the ones below. Then, use the list to help you evaluate your own writing.

- Does the beginning get your attention so you want to read more? If not, how could it be improved?
- Do I stay on topic? If not, where do I get off topic?
- Do I use "vivid verbs" to show action? Where are some places where I could use stronger verbs?
- Do I use specific, concrete details and sensory language to make my piece come alive? Where could I use more details?
- Is the ending satisfying? Does it sound "finished"? If not, what could I do to make a better ending?
- Are my sentences complete? Do I use a variety of sentences? If not, where do I need to make changes?
- Have I checked for any spelling or punctuation errors? If not, do it now!

Characteristics of my paper	Really good!	So-so (about average)	Needs improvement!
Does it have a catchy beginning?			
Does it stay on topic?			
Does it use vivid verbs?			
Does it use details and sensory language effectively?			
Does it have a good ending?			
Does it use complete sentences?			
Are the words spelled correctly?			

After you have made the changes that you think will strengthen your writing, make a final copy.

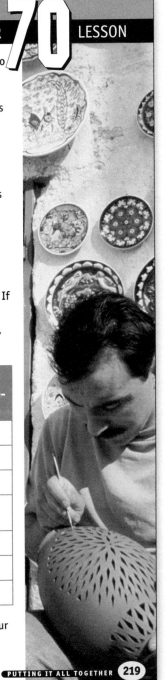

Students will revise their personal narrative to write a final copy and reflect on their progress toward meeting their goals of reading and writing effectively.

TEACHING TIP

Collaboration Have students conduct a writing conference with their partners to review their narratives. Encourage reviewers to give helpful and specific feedback on what works and what might need revision. Tell them to use the questions on page 219 to evaluate the writing. Make sure that the writers know that they are the final decision makers on what they want to say and how to say it. Once students have marked their revisions, tell them to prepare their final copies. If possible, have them put the essay aside for a day or two before proofreading. You may want to build in time for students to trade essays again for final checks of spelling and punctuation.

Before

During

CRITICAL WRITING SKILL

Putting It All Together Let students know that their final writing for this unit will be their opportunity to show what they have learned about being a good writer. Have them think about what they have learned about the ways other writers draw the reader in and keep the reader's interest. Encourage them to take the time and thought to make this piece an example of their best work.

TURNING A DRAFT INTO A FINAL PAPER
Provide support for students who need help deciding what needs to be revised in their work. Talk about the characteristics of a good narrative. You may want to point out the writing rubric on page 219 to let students know how you're going to evaluate their final essay. Once students have finished their final copies, have them share their work with the class.

A FINAL REFLECTION

As you worked through this book, you had many opportunities to learn and practice skills and strategies to become a better reader and writer. You have read stories, poems, and essays, using these skills and strategies.

In this final reflection, identify one strategy you have perfected during your work with the *Daybook*. Think about whether you have met another of the goals: that you now really *like* to read and write. Then write a note to a friend that explains how your work with the *Daybook* has helped you become a better reader and writer.

Using a list of traits of good writing makes self-assessment easier.

After

REFLECTING Ask students to write a letter in which they evaluate what they have learned about reading and writing from the lessons in the *Daybook*. Have them write about how they've improved as readers and writers. Encourage them to give specific examples of what they found helpful and to set new goals for applying what they've learned.

Becoming An Active Reader

Reading can entertain, inform, and reward. Reading also requires some hard work on the part of the reader. The sections that follow will help you get the most out of your reading.

The **reading process** section will guide you through reading a text. It will help you think about how to prepare to read (before reading), what to think about as you read (during reading), and how to get the most out of your reading by reflecting on it (after reading).

The **reading actively** section will show you how to interact with a text in order to get the most meaning out of it. It will show you how to engage with a text by using your brain and your pen—both at the same time!

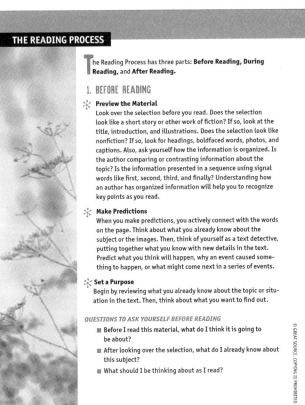

THE READING PROCESS

The Reading Process has three parts: **Before Reading, During Reading,** and **After Reading.**

1. BEFORE READING

❋ **Preview the Material**

Look over the selection before you read. Does the selection look like a short story or other work of fiction? If so, look at the title, introduction, and illustrations. Does the selection look like nonfiction? If so, look for headings, boldfaced words, photos, and captions. Also, ask yourself how the information is organized. Is the author comparing or contrasting information about the topic? Is the information presented in a sequence using signal words like first, second, third, and finally? Understanding how an author has organized information will help you to recognize key points as you read.

❋ **Make Predictions**

When you make predictions, you actively connect with the words on the page. Think about what you already know about the subject or the images. Then, think of yourself as a text detective, putting together what you know with new details in the text. Predict what you think will happen, why an event caused something to happen, or what might come next in a series of events.

❋ **Set a Purpose**

Begin by reviewing what you already know about the topic or situation in the text. Then, think about what you want to find out.

QUESTIONS TO ASK YOURSELF BEFORE READING

■ Before I read this material, what do I think it is going to be about?

■ After looking over the selection, what do I already know about this subject?

■ What should I be thinking about as I read?

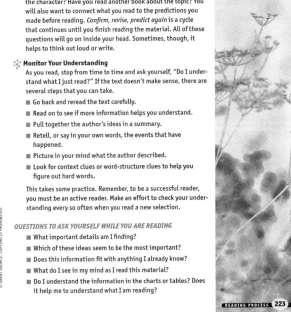

2. DURING READING

❋ **Engage with the Text**

As your eyes look at the words, your brain should be working to make connections between the words and what you already know. Have you had an experience similar to that of one of the characters in a story you are reading? Do you know someone like the character? Have you read another book about the topic? You will also want to connect what you read to the predictions you made before reading. *Confirm, revise, predict again* is a cycle that continues until you finish reading the material. All of these questions will go on inside your head. Sometimes, though, it helps to think out loud or write.

❋ **Monitor Your Understanding**

As you read, stop from time to time and ask yourself, "Do I understand what I just read?" If the text doesn't make sense, there are several steps that you can take.

■ Go back and reread the text carefully.

■ Read on to see if more information helps you understand.

■ Pull together the author's ideas in a summary.

■ Retell, or say in your own words, the events that have happened.

■ Picture in your mind what the author described.

■ Look for context clues or word-structure clues to help you figure out hard words.

This takes some practice. Remember, to be a successful reader, you must be an active reader. Make an effort to check your understanding every so often when you read a new selection.

QUESTIONS TO ASK YOURSELF WHILE YOU ARE READING

■ What important details am I finding?

■ Which of these ideas seem to be the most important?

■ Does this information fit with anything I already know?

■ What do I see in my mind as I read this material?

■ Do I understand the information in the charts or tables? Does it help me to understand what I am reading?

---

3. AFTER READING

❋ Summarize
Reread to locate the most important ideas in the story or essay.

❋ Respond and Reflect
Talk with a partner about what you have read. What did you learn from the text? Were your predictions confirmed? What questions do you still have? Talking about reading helps you to better understand what you have read.

❋ Ask Questions
Try asking yourself questions that begin like this:

Can I compare or contrast . . . evaluate . . . connect . . .
examine . . . analyze . . . relate . . .

❋ Engage with the Text
Good readers engage with a text all the time, even when they have finished reading. When you tie events in your life or something else you have read to what you are currently reading or have read, you become more involved with your reading. In the process, you are learning more about your values, relationships in your family, and issues in the world around you.

QUESTIONS TO ASK YOURSELF AFTER READING

■ What was this article about?
■ What was the author trying to tell me?
■ Have I learned something that made me change the way I think about this topic?
■ Are there parts of this material that I really want to remember?

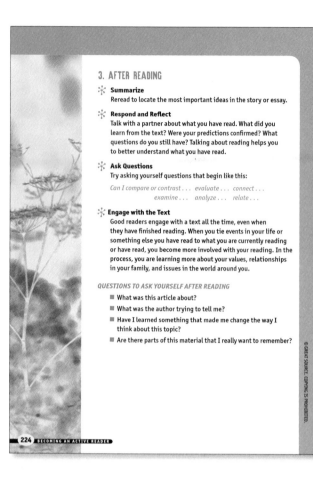

Make the effort to stay involved with your reading by reading actively. Your mind should be busy reading the text, making connections, making predictions, and asking questions. Your hand should be busy, too. Keep track of what you are thinking by "reading with your pen." **Write** your reactions to the text or connections that you can make. **Circle** words you don't understand. **Draw** a sketch of a scene. **Underline** or **highlight** an important idea. You may have your own way of reading actively. You may develop a style that works better for you, but here are six common ways of reading actively.

MARK OR HIGHLIGHT The most common way of noting important parts of a text is to write on a sticky note and put it on the page. Or, if you can, mark important parts of a text by highlighting them with a marker, pen, or pencil. You can also use highlighting tape. The highlighted parts should provide a good review of the text.

ASK QUESTIONS Asking questions is a way of engaging the author in conversation. Readers who ask a lot of questions think about the text more and understand it better. "Why is the writer talking about this?" "Is this really true?" "What does that mean?"

REACT AND CONNECT When you read, listen to the author and to yourself. Think about what you are reading and relate it to your own life. Compare and contrast what the text says to what you know.

PREDICT Readers who are involved with the text constantly wonder how things will turn out. They think about what might happen. They check their thoughts against the text and make adjustments. Sometimes the author surprises them! Making predictions helps you stay interested in what you are reading.

VISUALIZE Making pictures in your mind can help you "see" what you are thinking and help you remember. A chart, a sketch, a diagram— any of these can help you "see." Sometimes your picture doesn't match what you think the author is telling you. This is a signal to reread to check your understanding of the text.

CLARIFY As you read, you need to be sure that you understand what is going on in the text. Take time to pull together what you have learned. Try writing notes to clarify your understanding. Another way of checking to see that you understand is to tell someone about what you have read.

---

aggressor a person or country that attacks another

apparatus equipment for a specific purpose

architect a person who designs buildings or other large structures

arcing [AR king] moving in a curved path

argument persuasive language consisting of a main idea supported by details and reasons

associate be with; play with

author's purpose the reason an author writes a specific piece

autobiography an author's story of his or her own life

B-17 a bomber plane used in World War II; also known as the "Flying Fortress"

banking tilting sideways when making a turn

bar graph a graph in which bars represent data values

barrio [BAR ee oh] a Spanish-speaking area of a city

benevolent showing kindness or generosity

bickering spiteful arguing and quarreling

binoculars a device made up of two small telescopes that are attached in the middle. You can look through this device with both eyes to make distant things look bigger.

Black student movement a group of African American college students who fought for equal rights during the 1960s

bloomers loose-fitting women's underwear

blurred out of focus, unclear

bonds something, like rope, that is used to restrain

bow the front part of a ship

bulkhead a separate section of a ship or plane

burial chamber a room that serves as a tomb

cadence rhythmic sound of speech

caravan a trailer; a large truck with furniture in it that can be used as a home

causes and effects the ways in which events (causes) bring on other events (effects)

characterization the way an author develops the people, animals, and imaginary creatures in a story

climax the highest point, or turning point, in the action of a story

coherent consistent within itself; logical

communal shared by many people

compartment a separate space or room

compartmentalize to separate into different areas

compounded increased by combining

concussion damage due to a hard blow

con permiso [cohn pair MEE soh] excuse me

conveyor belt a continuously moving belt used to transport materials from one place to another

crane a long-legged, long-necked bird that wades in marshes and wetlands and soars over open areas

---

creaky raspy; having a grating or squeaky sound

credible believable

critical reading a reading strategy that involves understanding and evaluating information outside a text

crow's nest a small lookout platform that is near the top of a ship's mast

deafening so loud as to cause hearing loss

dehydrating causing a lack of moisture

denounce to publicly speak out against

description a basic technique an author uses to create pictures in the mind of a reader

devoured eaten up

diagram an illustration that shows the parts of something or how it works

disabled impaired; not able to function properly

disposition usual mood or temperament

distress confused anxiety

drenched soaking wet

dungeon an ancient prison often found in a castle basement

dusky dim; shadowy; nearing sunset

eccentric strange; odd

ecstatic extremely happy; joyful

Egyptologist person who studies artifacts of ancient Egypt

elicit to bring forth

el Polo Norte [el POH loh NOR tay] the North Pole

engineer someone who designs or plans things

evaluate an argument to decide whether an argument is convincing

excruciating intensely painful; agonizing

existence life

exposition the part of the story, usually the beginning, that explains the background and setting and introduces the characters

extrapolate to predict a future situation by drawing on similar situations in the present or past

falling action the part of a story that follows the climax; it contains the action or dialogue necessary to lead the story to a resolution or ending

figurative language a way that poets convey more images with fewer words; techniques include metaphor and simile

filling station gas station

flight jacket a style of leather jacket worn by airplane pilots; sometimes called a "bomber jacket"

flirting behaving in a tempting way

foibles small weaknesses or mistakes

forage to search for food

forensic referring to the use of science or technology to find facts or evidence

fowls domesticated birds that are used for food, such as chickens, ducks, and turkeys

frantically in a hurried and disorganized manner

fretted worried

full steam without any hesitation

---

game wild animals, fish, and birds hunted for food

gangsters criminals; outlaws

glint a sparkle; a flash of light

go down to die: an animal handler's expression

gratitude thankfulness, appreciation

grindstone a large stone that is used to sharpen or polish knives and tools

gruesome horrifying, disgusting; repulsive

guileless not deceitful

guillotine (GHEE oh teen) a device in which a large blade drops down and chops off someone's head; here, a metaphor—the nod "chops off" any more questions

habitat the type of environment in which an organism generally lives

haiku a Japanese poetic form contrasting two images, often of nature, which has 3 lines of 5, 7, and 5 syllables; spelled the same in both singular and plural forms

haughtiness snobbishness; pride

heedful carefully paying attention

hieroglyphic an ancient system of writing that includes pictures and symbols

icebox refrigerator

illumination understanding; awareness

imagery language used by a poet that encourages a reader to make mental pictures as he or she reads

images mental pictures created by a reader as he or she reads

immeasurably impossible to measure; exceedingly

industrial relating to the commercial production and sale of goods

ineffable impossible to describe

inferences reasonable guesses

inquisitorial trying to get information in a hostile, cruel, or harsh way

interact to engage with by reacting to, remembering, wondering about, asking questions of, or getting ideas from something or someone

interacting with the text "carrying on a conversation" with a text; a strategy for effective reading that involves circling, underlining, and writing notes

internment being confined, especially in wartime

intervals spaces between each point

jolt a sudden bump or jerking movement

karate a martial art, or style of self-defense, from the island of Okinawa

khaki (KAK ee) sturdy, yellowish brown cloth

la abuela [lah ah BWAY lah] the grandmother

la familia [lah fah MEE lee ah] family

la isla [lah EES lah] island

languishing losing strength; withering away

lofty high; soaring

lounge [noun] a place for people to sit and relax

lounge [verb] relax

lynch to murder by hanging

main idea [subject] + [what the author says about the subject] = main idea; the central focus of a piece of nonfiction

make inferences a reading strategy that involves making reasonable guesses by putting together something you have read in a story with something you know from real life

making connections a reading strategy that involves comparing what you are reading to something you already know

mandate to require as if, or actually, by law

mason a stoneworker; a craftsman who works with stones or bricks

mechanical relating to machines or tools; automatic

menace threat of danger

merciless showing no mercy or pity

metaphor a technique of figurative language in which one thing is described in terms of something else

meticulously carefully; with attention to detail

monolith a large block of stone

nada [NAH dah] nothing

Negro a person of African descent. NOTE: *African American* is now strongly preferred.

newsreels short films about current events

Nile The longest river in the world, flowing about 6,677 km (4,150 mi) through eastern Africa

northern lights streaks of light seen in the night sky in the northernmost parts of the northern hemisphere; aurora borealis

onslaught overwhelming amount

opposing viewpoints sides of an argument different from that of an author or speaker

Oriental Asian; from the region that includes Asia south of the Himalaya Mountains. NOTE: *Asian* is now strongly preferred.

papier-mâché (PAY per muh SHAY) a material made from paper mixed with glue or paste that can be shaped when wet and becomes hard when dry

pathos something that makes people feel sympathy or sorrow

peat partially decomposed vegetation found in bogs

peril danger

perish to die or be destroyed

periscope an instrument with lenses and mirrors that helps one see things that are not in the direct line of sight

perspective the point of view or angle from which you see a subject

persuade to try to convince others to feel the same way you do

pew a long bench of seats in a church

pharaoh a king of ancient Egypt

pillar architectural column

plight a bad or difficult situation

plot how the characters and events in a story are connected

Plymouth a car made by a company called Chrysler

poetic license bending of writing rules by a poet

point of view how one sees an event; perspective

poised balanced in readiness, waiting

political prisoner a person who has been put in jail for his or her political views prediction an educated guess about upcoming events that is based on background knowledge and clues from the present

prediction an educated guess about upcoming events that is based on background knowledge and clues from the text

protracted extended; taking place over a long time

pulverize to pound, grind, or crush into small pieces

quarry a large area from which stone is dug, blasted, or cut out

radiocarbon dating a way to determine the approximate age of an ancient object by measuring the amount of carbon-14 it contains

reeds tall grasses that grow in wet areas

reflecting taking time to think about what you have read

refuse [REF-yoos] garbage

reluctantly not eagerly

repercussions bouncing-back of sounds

repertoire a performer's collection of abilities

repertoire of skills and strategies a collection of learned abilities needed by an effective writer or reader

resolution the end of a story, in which the problems are resolved or the story gets "wrapped up"

revenge punishment of somebody in return for harm done

ridiculous silly

rising action the central part of a story during which various problems arise, leading up to the climax

rule the afternoon to have complete control over

rummaging searching hastily through the contents of a container

runners blades under a sled that help it move over snow or ice

sanitation cleanliness

Sanitation Laborer someone who cleans up garbage

scamper to run quickly and playfully

scolding yelling at; criticizing

scrupulously thoroughly; in keeping with the law or rules

sensory language language that appeals to the reader's senses

sequence the order of events

serials stories presented in installments or in a series

setting the time and place of a story

simile a technique of figurative language in which the characteristics of one thing are described in terms of something else using the word *like* or *as*

sinkhole a sunken area where waste collects

slackening easing up

solitary done alone

somber sadly serious

sorrow sadness

species a group of organisms that are similar and that can produce young that are fertile

speech a talk given to an audience

squatting crouching; sitting on one's heels

stern [adjective] strict; severe

stern [noun] the back part of a ship

steward assistant to passengers on a ship

stole a long scarf worn around the shoulders

story line the sequence of events in the order they are told in a story

strategic reader one who uses a repertoire of skills and strategies to help in understanding texts

style one's unique way of expressing oneself

subject the person, place, or thing a writer has written about in a piece of nonfiction

suffice to be sufficient or enough

support information a writer or speaker uses in trying to persuade an audience

taking notes a way to organize ideas by making short written comments about what one is reading

taunts teases; insults

taunting mocking; teasing

tic a small, repeated movement

transcendent extraordinary; going beyond the usual limits

tremor a trembling, shaking movement; a small earthquake

troubled worried; bothered

tumultuously in a way that is full of commotion; disorderly

unanimous agreed upon by all

un cero [oon SAIR oh] a zero

unconscious not aware

unfettered not restrained

unreasonable unwilling to consider another's argument

vestibule a waiting area or room

visualizing a reading strategy in which a reader makes mental pictures of what he or she is reading about

vulnerable at risk of being harmed

warming house building where people, especially skaters or skiers, come in to get warm and rest

wary cautious; worried

weave to move in and out or from side to side

weighty serious and important

wheel-dogs specially trained dogs that steer a sled (chariot) across frozen, snow-covered ground

woldwellers fictional creatures that live alone in forest trees

word choice the conscious decision of a writer to use specific words to convey an image

ACKNOWLEDGMENTS

10, 13, 20, 22 From *Before We Were Free*. Copyright © 2002 by Julia Alvarez. Published by Dell Laurel-Leaf in paperback in 2003 and originally in hardcover by Alfred A. Knopf Children's Books, a division of Random House, New York. Reprinted by permission of Susan Bergholz Literary Services, New York. All rights reserved.

18 From *Latin American Politics and Development, Fifth Edition,* by Howard J. Wiarda, Copyright © 2000 by Westview Press. Reprinted by permission of Westview Press, a member of Perseus Books, LLC.

26, 29 "All Summer in a Day" by Ray Bradbury. Reprinted by permission of Don Congdon Associates, Inc. Copyright © 1954, renewed 1982.

33, 36 "Hearing the Sweetest Songs" by Nicolette Toussaint from Newsweek 5/23/1994. All rights reserved. Reprinted by permission.

42 From *The Search for Delicious* by Natalie Babbitt. Used by permissions of Farrar, Straus and Giroux, LLC.

42 From *A Wrinkle in Time* by Madeline L'Engle. Used by permissions of Farrar, Straus and Giroux, LLC .

44, 47 From *Danny: The Champion of the World* by Roald Dahl, illustrated by Jill Bennett, text and illustrations copyright © 1975 by Roald Dahl Nominee Limited. Used by permission of Alfred A. Knopf, an imprint of Random House Children's Books, a division of Random House, Inc.

53 From *An Island Like You, Stories of the Barrio* by Judith Ortiz Cofer. Published by Orchard Books/ Scholastic Inc. Copyright © 1995 by Judith Ortiz Cofer. Used by permission of Scholastic Inc.

58, 60 From *The Titanic* by Richard Wormser. Used by permission of Parachute Press.

67, 69 From "John Thayer: Becoming a Man aboard the *Titanic*" by Phillip Hoose. Used by permission of Farrar, Straus and Giroux, LLC.

70 Jennifer Kirkpatrick/National Geographic.

72 "Karate Kid" copyright © 1996 by Jane Yolen. First appeared in *Opening Days, Short Poems,* published by Harcourt Brace. Reprinted by permission of Curtis Brown, Ltd.

75 "Skiing" copyright © 1971 by Bobbi Katz. Used with permission of the author.

77 "Swimming" from *A Tree Place And Other Poems* by Constance Levy. Copyright © 1994 Constance Levy. Used by permission of Marian Reiner for the author.

79 "The Base Stealer" by Robert Francis, from *The Orb Weaver* © 1960 and reprinted by permission of Wesleyan University Press.

81 Special permission granted by *Weekly Reader.* All rights reserved.

86 Excerpt from *A Summer to Die* by Lois Lowry. Copyright © 1977 by Lois Lowry. Reprinted by permission of Houghton Mifflin Company. All rights reserved.

89 Excerpt from *The Silent Boy* by Lois Lowry. Copyright © 2003 by Lois Lowry. Reprinted by permission of Houghton Mifflin Company. All rights reserved.

93 Excerpt from *The Giver* by Lois Lowry. Copyright © 1993 by Lois Lowry. Reprinted by permission of Houghton Mifflin Company. All rights reserved.

96 Excerpt from *Gathering Blue* by Lois Lowry. Copyright © 2000 by Lois Lowry. Reprinted by permission of Houghton Mifflin Company. All rights reserved.

99 Used by permission of Lois Lowry.

102 "Eagle Boy" from *Native American Animal Stories* told by Joseph Bruchac. Used by permission of Fulcrum Publishing.

108 "Salmon Boy" from *Native American Animal Stories* told by Joseph Bruchac. Used by permission of Fulcrum Publishing.

118 Elie Wiesel Foundation for Humanity.

119 "To You" from *The Collected Poems of Langston Hughes* by Langston Hughes, copyright © 1994 by The Estate of Langston Hughes. Used by permission of Alfred A. Knopf, a division of Random House, Inc.

121 Excerpt from *Farewell to Manzanar* by James D. Houston and Jeanne Wakatsuki Houston. Copyright © 1973 by James D. Houston. Reprinted by permission of Houghton Mifflin Company. All rights reserved.

123, 124 From *The Gold Cadillac* by Mildred D. Taylor, copyright © 1987 by Mildred D. Taylor, text. Used by permission of Dial Books for Young Readers, A Division of Penguin Young Readers Group. A Member of Penguin Group (USA) Inc., 345 Hudson Street, New York, NY 10014. All rights reserved.

132, 135 From *Egyptian Pyramids* by Anne Steel. Used by permission of Hodder & Stoughton.

138 Reprinted from *The Ancient Egyptians* by Elsa Marston with permission of Marshall Cavendish

139 From WGBH Educational Foundation, copyright © 2000 WGBH/Boston

142 From *Cat Mummies* by Kelly Trumble, illustrated by Laszlo Kubinyi. Text copyright © 1996 by Kelly Trumble. Illustrations copyright © 1996 by Laszlo Kubinyi. Reprinted by permission of Clarion Books, an imprint of Houghton Mifflin Company. All rights reserved.

144 Excerpt from *How to Make a Mummy Talk* by James M. Deem. Text copyright © 1995 by James M. Deem. Reprinted by permission of Houghton Mifflin Company. All rights reserved.

148, 151, 153 Reprinted with the permission of Atheneum Books for Young Readers, an imprint of Simon & Schuster Children's Publishing Division, from *The Egypt Game* by Zilpha Keatley Snyder. Copyright © 1967 Zilpha Keatley

156, 160 Excerpt from *Project Mulberry* by Linda Sue Park. Copyright © 2005 by Linda Sue Park. Reprinted by permission of Clarion Books, an imprint of Houghton Mifflin Company. All rights reserved.

164 From *All I Really Need to Know I Learned in Kindergarten* by Robert L. Fulghum, copyright © 1986, 1988 by Robert L. Fulghum. Used by permission of Random House, Inc.

166 George Lucas Educational Foundation

171 From *The Greatest: Muhammad Ali* by Walter Dean Myers. Published by Scholastic Inc./ Scholastic Press. Copyright © 2001 by Walter Dean Myers. Reprinted by permission.

173 From *Green Planet Rescue* by Robert R. Halpern. Used by permission of The Zoological Society of Cincinnati.

175 "A Word is Dead" by Emily Dickinson. Reprinted by permission of the publishers and the Trustees of Amherst College from *The Poems of Emily Dickinson,* Thomas H. Johnson, ed., Cambridge, Mass.: The Belknap Press of Harvard University Press, Copyright © 1951, 1955, 1979,1983 by the President and Fellows of Harvard College.

176 "This Is Just to Say" by William Carlos Williams, from *Collected Poems: 1909-1939, Volume I,* copyright © 1938 by New Directions Publishing Corp. Reprinted by permission of New Directions Publishing Corp.

177 "The Red Wheelbarrow" by William Carlos Williams, from *Collected Poems: 1909-1939, Volume I,* copyright © 1938 by New Directions Publishing Corp. Reprinted by permission of New Directions Publishing Corp.

182 "Fire and Ice" from *The Poetry of Robert Frost* edited by Edward Connery Lathem. Copyright 1923, 1969 by Henry Holt and Company. Copyright 1951 by Robert Frost. Reprinted by permission of Henry Holt and Company, LLC

191 From *Guts* by Gary Paulsen, copyright © 2001 by Gary Paulsen. Used by permission of Random House Children's Books, a division of Random House, Inc.

192 From *The River* by Gary Paulsen, copyright © 1991 by Gary Paulsen. Used by permission of Dell Publishing, a division of Random House, Inc.

195, 198 From *Dancing Carl* by Gary Paulsen. Reprinted with the permission of Atheneum Books for Young Readers, an imprint of Simon & Schuster Children's Publishing Division. Copyright © 1983 Gary Paulsen.

201 From *Dogsong* by Gary Paulsen. Reprinted with the permission of Atheneum Books for Young Readers, an imprint of Simon & Schuster Children's Publishing Division. Copyright © 1985 Gary Paulsen.

204 From *Woodsong* by Gary Paulsen. Reprinted with the permission of Simon & Schuster Books for Young Readers, an imprint of Simon & Schuster Children's Publishing Division. Text copyright © 1990 Gary Paulsen

208 "Eleven" from *Woman Hollering Creek and Other Stories* by Sandra Cisneros. Used by permission of Random House.

214 "My Name" from *The House on Mango Street* by Sandra Cisneros. Used by permission of Random House.

ILLUSTRATIONS

137: © Great Source; **142 *m:*** © Laszlo Kubinyi. Reprinted by permission of Houghton Mifflin Company. All rights reserved.
All additional art created by AARTPACK, Inc.

PHOTOGRAPHY

Photo Research AARTPACK, Inc.

Unit 1 **9:** © Kris Timken/Getty Image; **10:** © Ryan McVay/Getty Images; **11:** © Ryan McVay/Getty Images; **12:** © Martin Hospach/Getty Images; **13:** © Royalty-Free/Corbis; **14:** © Royalty-Free/Corbis; **15:** © Royalty-Free/Corbis; **16:** © Royalty-Free/Corbis; **17:** © Ryan McVay/Getty Images; **18:** © Ryan McVay/Getty Images; **20 *t:*** © PhotoDisc/Getty Images; **20 *b:*** © PhotoDisc/Getty Images; **22:** © Royalty-Free/Corbis; **23:** © PhotoDisc/Getty Images; **24:** Royalty-Free/Corbis.

Unit 2 **25:** © Lawrence Lawry/Getty Images; **26:** © Royalty-Free/Corbis; **27:** © PhotoDisc/Getty Images; **28:** © Royalty-Free/Corbis; **29:** © Shaen Adey/Gallo Images/Getty Images; **31:** © Shaen Adey/Gallo Images/Getty Images; **32:** © Royalty-Free/Corbis; **33:** © DynamicGraphics Inc./Inmagine; 34: © MedioImages/Getty Images; **35:** © DynamicGraphics Inc./Inmagine; **36:** © Pixtal/Inmagine; **37:** © Royalty-Free/Corbis; **38 *t:*** © MedioImages/Getty Images; **38:** © Pixtal/Inmagine; **39:** © Royalty-Free/Corbis; **40:** © Royalty-Free/Corbis.

Unit 3 **41:** © Teri Dixon/Getty Images; **42:** © Adalberto Rios Szalay/Sexto Sol/Getty Images; **44:** © Wilfried Krecichwost/Getty Images; **45:** © Wilfried Krecichwost/Getty Images; **47:** © Royality-Free/Corbis; **48:** © Royality-Free/Corbis; **49 *b:*** © DesignPics/Inmagine; **50:** © Brand X Pictures/Inmagine; **51:** © Image Source/Getty Images; **53:** © Image Source/Getty Images; **55:** © Image Source/Getty Images.

Unit 4 **57:** © Diane Macdonald/getty Images; **58 *m:*** © Sun Source/The Baltimore Sun; **58 *l:*** © Royalty-Free/Corbis; **60:** ©PhotoDisc/Getty Images; **61:** ©PhotoDisc/Getty Images; **64:** © Royalty-Free/Corbis; **65:** © Royalty-Free/Corbis; **66:** © Royalty-Free/Corbis; **67:** © Royalty-Free/Corbis; **69:** © Royalty-Free/Corbis; **70 *t:*** © Royalty-Free/Corbis; **70 *b:*** © Stockdisc/Getty Images.

Unit 5 **71:** © Angelo Cavalli/Getty Images; **72 *t:*** © IndexStock/Inmagine; **72 *m:*** © TongRo/Inmagine; **72 *b:*** © Natphotos/Getty Images; **73:** © IndexStock/Inmagine; **74:** © Natphotos/Getty Images; **75:** © Royalty-Free/Corbis; **76:** © Royalty-Free/Corbis; **77:** © DAJ/Getty Images; **78:** © DAJ/getty Images; **79:** © Royalty-Free/Corbis; **80:** © Royalty-Free/Corbis; **81:** © Nancy R Cohen/Getty Images; **82:** © Royalty-Free/Corbis; **83:** © PhotoDisc/Getty Images; **84:** © PhotoDisc/Getty Images.

Unit 6 **85:** © Colin Hawkins/Getty Images; **86:** © Erin Hogan/Getty Images; **87:** © PhotoDisc/Getty Images; **88:** © PhotoDisc/Getty Images; **89:** © Royalty-Free/Corbis; **90:** © Royalty-Free/Corbis; **91:** © Digital Zoo/Getty Images; **92 *t:*** © PhotoDisc/Getty Images; **92 *m:*** © Image Source/Getty Images; **93:** © Tim Hibo/Getty Images; **96:** © Royalty-Free/Corbis; **97:** © Royalty-Free/Corbis; **99:** © Royalty-Free/Corbis; **100:** © Royalty-Free/Corbis.

Unit 7 **101:** © Hisham F Ibrahim/Getty Images; **102:** © Medioimages/Getty Images; **103:** © Tom Brakefield/Getty Images; **104:** © Tom Brakefield/Getty Images; **106:** © Tom Brakefield/Getty Images; **107:** © Tom Brakefield/Getty Images; **108:** © Diana Miller/Getty Images; **109:** © Diana Miller/Getty Images; **110:** © Diana Miller/Getty Images; **111:** © Royalty-Free/Corbis; **112:** © Charles C Place/Getty Images; **113:** © Bettmann/Corbis; **114:** © Univ of Washington Libraries, Special Collections, NA 2463; **115:** © PhotoDisc/Inmagine; **116:** © Univ of Washington Libraries, Special Collections, NA 2210.

Unit 8 **117:** © Royalty-Free/Corbis; **118 *l:*** © John Wang/Getty Images; **118 *b:*** © John Wang/Getty Images; **119:** © John Wang/Getty Images; **120:** © PhotoDisc/Getty Images; **121:** © Itaru Hirama/Getty Images; **123:** © Comstock/Inmagine; **124:** © Royalty-Free/Corbis; **125:** © Royalty-Free/Corbis; **126:** © Royalty-Free/Corbis; **127:** © Royalty-Free/Corbis; **128:** © Mike Spring/Getty Images; **129:** © Comstock/Inmagine; **130:** © Brand X Pictures.

Unit 9 **131:** © GDT/Getty Images; **132 *t:*** © Petr Svarc/Getty Images; **132 *b:*** © Petr Svarc/Getty Images;**133 *t:*** © Adam Crowley/Getty Images; **133 *ml:*** © Royalty-Free/Corbis; **133 *mlc:*** © Royalty-Free/Corbis; **133 *mrc:*** © Royalty-Free/Corbis; **133 *mr:*** © Royalty-Free/Corbis; **134:** © Petr Svarc/Getty Images; **135 *t:*** © Derek P Redfearn/Getty Images; **135 *b:*** © Derek P Redfearn/Getty Images; **136:** © Brand X Pictures/Inmagine; **137:** © Adam

Crowley/Getty Images; **138:** © Gerard Rollando/Getty Images; **139:** © Pankaj & Insy Shah/Getty Images; **141:** © Gerard Rollando/Getty Images; **142 *t:*** © Alistair Duncan/Getty Images; **143 *t:*** © Derek P Redfearn/Getty Images; **143 *b:*** © Pankaj & Insy Shah/Getty Images; **144 *m:*** © www.mummytombs.com; **144 *l:*** © PhotoDisc/Getty Images; **146:** © Adam Crowley/Getty Images.

Unit 10 **147:** © Royalty-Free/Corbis; **148:** © Royalty-Free/Corbis; **149:** © Royalty-Free/Corbis; **150:** © Stockbyte/Getty Images; **151:** © Izzy Schwartz/Getty Images; **152:** © PhotoDisc/Getty Images; **153:** © Gordon Osmundson/Corbis; **154:** © Royalty-Free/Corbis; **155:** © Gordon Osmundson/Corbis; **156:** © Brand X Pictures/Inmagine; **157:** © DAJ/Getty Images; **158:** © Izzy Schwartz/Getty Images; **159:** © Jeff Greenberg/Photo Edit; **160:** © David Young-Wolff/Photo Edit; **161:** © DAJ/Getty Images; **162 *t:*** © Jeff Greenberg/Photo Edit; **162 *b:*** © Jeff Greenberg/Photo Edit.

Unit 11 **163:** © Alain Pons/Getty Images; **164:** © Sheila Terry/Photo Researchers, Inc.; **165:** © Royalty-Free/Corbis; **166:** © PhotoDisc/Inmagine; **167:** © PhotoDisc/Inmagine; **168:** © Royalty-Free/Corbis; **169:** © Comstock/Jupiter Images; **171 *t:*** © Bettmann/Corbis; **171 *b:*** © PhotoDisc/Getty Images; **172:** © Rim Light/PhotoLink/Getty Images; **173 *t:*** © Spike Mafford/Getty Images; **173 *b:*** © Royalty-Free/Corbis; **174:** © PhotoDisc/Getty Images.

Unit 12 **175:** © Royalty-Free/Corbis; **176:** © Royalty-Free/Corbis; **177:** © Royalty-Free/Corbis; **178:** © PhotoDisc/Getty Images; **179:** © Comstock Images; **180:** © Don Farrall/Getty Images; **181:** © PhotoDisc/Getty Images; **182 *t:*** © Royalty-Free/Corbis; **182 *b:*** © Karl Weatherly/Getty Images; **183:** © Karl Weatherly/Getty Images; **184 *t:*** © Tom Brakefield/Getty Images; **184 *m:*** © Tom Brakefield/Getty Images; **185:** © Royalty-Free/Corbis; **186:** © Royalty-Free/Corbis; **187:** © Royalty-Free/Corbis; **188:** © Royalty-Free/Corbis; **189:** © Don Farrall/Getty Images; **190:** © PhotoDisc/Getty Images.

Unit 13 **191:** © Robert Cable/Getty Images; **192:** © PhotoDisc/Getty Images; **193:** © Maurice Joseph/Getty Images; **194:** © PhotoDisc/Getty Images; **195:** © Steve Mason/Getty Images; **196:** © Royalty-Free/Corbis; **197:** © Steve Mason/Getty Images; **198:** © Royalty-Free/Corbis; **199:** © Royalty-Free/Corbis; **200:** © DesignPics/Inmagine; **201:** © Royalty-Free/Corbis; **202:** © Royalty-Free/Corbis; **203:** © John A Rizzo/Getty Images; **204:** © Royalty-Free/Corbis; **206:** © Royalty-Free/Corbis.

Unit 14 **207:** © Royalty-Free/Corbis; **208:** © Royalty-Free/Corbis; **209:** © Royalty-Free/Corbis; **210 *t:*** © Kent Knudson/PhotoLink/Getty Images; **210 *m:*** © Brand X Pictures; **210 *b:*** © Kent Knudson/PhotoLink/Getty Images; **211:** © Royalty-Free/Corbis; **212:** © Royalty-Free/Corbis; **214 *t:*** © Royalty-Free/Corbis; **214 *b:*** © Royalty-Free/Corbis; **215 *t:*** © Laurent Hamels/Getty Images; **215 *m:*** © Laurent Hamels/Getty Images; **215 *b:*** © Laurent Hamels/Getty Images; **216:** © Royalty-Free/Corbis; **217:** © Ken Usami/Getty Images; **218 *l:*** © Ken Usami/Getty Images; **218 *r:*** © Nigel Hillier/Getty Images; **218 *m:*** © PhotoDisc/Getty Images.

Becoming an Active Reader **221:** © Image Source/Getty Images; **222–224:** © Kaz Chiba/PhotoDisc/Getty Images; **225:** © Jamie Kripke/Getty Images.

WRITING PROMPTS — 226

ASSESSMENTS — 239

REPRODUCIBLE GRAPHIC ORGANIZERS — 268

WRITING PROMPTS

The following Writing Prompts are designed for use at the end of each unit of the *Daybook*. You can assign the prompt in a single class period, or you may prefer to have students write over a period of two or three days with time for peer conferences, revising, editing, and reflecting.

Since each prompt is based on the literature and strategies from the corresponding unit, assign the prompt when students have finished the unit. Allow students to refer to their *Daybooks* so they can use the selections as they write.

Please note: The Writing Prompts for Unit 7 and Unit 14 are contained within those units.

✳ **Evaluation criteria accompany each prompt.**
Go over the criteria with students before they begin each assessment so they can use the criteria to inform their writing. Tell students to use resources such as dictionaries or computer programs to check spelling and grammar.

LITERATURE CONNECTION

- *Before We Were Free*

Interpretive Writing, Option 1

In the "Author's Note," Julia Alvarez wrote, "I won't ever forget the day in 1960 when my parents announced that we were leaving our native country of the Dominican Republic for the United States of America. I kept asking my mother why we had to go. All she would say, in a quiet, tense voice, was 'Because we're lucky.'"

Responding Think about why Alvarez's mother said, "Because we're lucky." Make a list or a cluster of possible reasons. Then explain why you think her mother made this statement. Use examples from the Author's Note and the excerpts from *Before We Were Free* to support your view.

Persuasive Writing, Option 2

Anita's parents insisted on staying in their country to fight for change. Julia Alvarez's parents came to the United States. Both families had strong opinions.

Responding Write a page stating your opinion on which set of parents made the best decision. Remember that an opinion is a belief. Give reasons for your opinion and make a strong case for others to be persuaded to agree with you. Use quotations and examples from the selections in Unit 1 to support your view.

Evaluation Criteria

The writer responds directly to the prompt and

* develops and supports the ideas with details and examples
* organizes the writing logically (ideas followed by support)
* uses a personal writer's voice that appeals to the reader
* makes effective word choices
* varies sentence structure and writes fluent sentences
* edits and proofreads for accurate copy

LITERATURE CONNECTION
- **"All Summer in a Day"**

Narrative Writing

William and the other students acted as a group when they kept Margot from experiencing "all summer in a day." Most people have had the experience of doing something or going along with something that was not true to their character because they felt pressure from a group.

Responding Write about a time when you were part of a group and did something that you didn't think you should do. Maybe you just "went along with the crowd." Include details such as who was involved, what happened, how you felt at the time, and what you think of what you did. (You don't need to use real names.)

Evaluation Criteria

The writer responds directly to the prompt and

* develops and supports the ideas with details

* organizes the narrative logically (beginning, middle, ending)

* uses a personal writer's voice that connects with the reader

* makes effective word choices

* varies sentence structure and writes fluent sentences

* edits and proofreads for accurate copy

LITERATURE CONNECTION

- *Danny the Champion of the World*
- "Abuela Invents the Zero"

Expository Writing, Option 1

Look back at Unit 3, on pages 41-56 of the *Daybook*. Assume that a good friend of yours was sick and missed most of the week in which you learned about the elements of a story. Your friend has read the excerpts from *Danny the Champion of the World* and the story "Abuela Invents the Zero," but your friend hasn't learned about the elements of a story and asks you to write an explanation of what makes up a story.

Responding Write an informative letter to your friend explaining the elements of a story. Use examples from *Danny the Champion of the World* and "Abuela Invents the Zero" to illustrate your points. Make your explanation clear and direct. Make sure you cover all the elements of a story that you have learned about.

Expressive-Descriptive Writing, Option 2

Look back at the story "Abuela Invents the Zero" on pages 51-56. At the end of the story, Connie is sent to her room to "consider a number (zero) I hadn't thought much about—until today." What do you think Connie will think about?

Responding Write a diary entry that Connie might have written as she sits in her room after her experience. Think about what happened with Abuela at church and Connie's confrontation with her mother when she got home. Use events in the story to make your entry as specific as possible. Think about Connie's "voice" in the story and see if you can capture what she sounds like.

Evaluation Criteria

The writer responds directly to the prompt and

- ✳ develops and supports the ideas, using examples from the stories
- ✳ organizes the writing logically
- ✳ sounds knowledgeable (1) or conveys the voice of the character (2)
- ✳ uses terms correctly (1) or uses words the character might use (2)
- ✳ varies sentence length and structure
- ✳ edits and proofreads for accurate copy

LITERATURE CONNECTION

■ "John Thayer: Becoming a Man Aboard the *Titanic*"

Persuasive Writing

You know from your readings about the *Titanic* that the code of ethics on the ship was that women and children should be saved first. You read that John watched his mother and his sister be given a place in a lifeboat while he and his father were not.

What is your opinion of the ethics of this code? Do you think women and children should be saved first in case of a disaster, such as the sinking of a boat, a fire in a crowded theater, or rapidly rising floodwaters?

Responding Write a persuasive essay that presents your opinion on whether officials should save women and children first in case of a disaster. State your opinion. Then give reasons for your opinion. You may use examples from the selections in Unit 4, as well as from other reading or your own experience. Remember to think about other perspectives and address them in your argument.

Evaluation Criteria

The writer responds directly to the prompt and

* develops and supports the position with evidence from the selection and addresses at least one other perspective

* organizes the writing logically (introduction, body, conclusion)

* uses a voice that conveys knowledge of and interest in the topic

* avoids weak verbs such as *do, go,* and *get*

* varies sentence structure and writes fluent sentences

* edits and proofreads for accurate copy

LITERATURE CONNECTION

■ Poems about Sports

Persuasive Writing

In Unit 5 of the *Daybook*, you focused on figurative language used in poems about sports. You saw how strong verbs, similes, and metaphors make writing about a sport vivid and exciting.

Responding Imagine that you are the sports columnist for your school newspaper. Persuade people at your school that a certain sport should be supported better by the students. Explain in detail what benefits it would bring to the students if it were valued more. Use language that is specific to the sport. Try to include some comparisons in the form of similes or metaphors. Before you write, make a chart of words you associate with that sport. Use words and phrases from your chart when you write your paper.

Name of the Sport: _____

Nouns	Verbs	Adjectives and Adverbs	Similes and Metaphors
Names of things associated with the sport (equipment, playing field, uniforms, and so on)	Actions associated with the sport (running, jumping, hitting the ball, and so on)	Descriptive language used in talking about the sport (such as *swift*, *graceful*, *powerful*, and so on)	Images that create a vivid picture of the sport being played

Evaluation Criteria

The writer responds directly to the prompt and

✳ supports the position with specific information about the sport

✳ organizes the writing logically (states a position, supports the position, wraps up)

✳ uses an objective, polite voice to convince the reader

✳ makes effective word choices

✳ varies sentence structure and writes fluent sentences

✳ edits and proofreads for accurate copy

WRITING PROMPT

LITERATURE CONNECTION

■ **Lois Lowry's Speeches**

Expressive-Descriptive Writing

From the excerpts that you read from Lois Lowry's speeches, you learned that she is most interested in how people relate to each other and she gathers her ideas from events in her own life. One of the reasons people like reading Lois Lowry's books is that they can relate to the feelings she expresses through her characters.

Imagine that you are having a conversation with Lois Lowry, talking about things that matter in your own life. You realize from her books that she is very easy to talk to. Think about two things: 1. What would you want to *ask* her? and 2. What would you want to *tell* her? Make some notes about these two questions.

What would I want to ask her?	What would I want to tell her?

Responding Write your conversation with Lois Lowry. You can write it as a conversation, making up Lowry's answers to your questions, or you can write it as a letter to send to her for her to answer the questions. Be sure to include some references to what you have read in Unit 6 that show you are familiar with some of her thoughts and feelings.

Evaluation Criteria

The writer responds directly to the prompt and

❖ shows knowledge of the topic by referencing Lowry's work

❖ organizes the writing logically

❖ uses a natural-sounding and respectful voice

❖ makes effective word choices

❖ varies sentence lengths and beginnings

❖ edits and proofreads for accurate copy

LITERATURE CONNECTION

- **"The Perils of Indifference"**
- *Farewell to Manzanar*
- *The Gold Cadillac*

Interpretive Writing

In Unit 8 of the *Daybook,* you read a number of selections about having the courage to stand up against indifference and oppression. Choose the excerpt from that unit that you found most interesting and persuasive.

Imagine that the writer of the selection you chose is going to visit your school. Your teacher has asked you to introduce the writer to your class. To make the introduction effective, the teacher has asked you to

✳ tell what you inferred about the author as a person from reading this excerpt

✳ tell what you found persuasive about the selection

✳ ask one or two questions of the author

Responding Write the introduction. In your introduction, be sure to include

✳ how you used inference to learn about the author as a person

✳ what you found persuasive about the author's writing

✳ the questions you want to ask the writer

You may want to look at the chart on page 126 to review how authors use persuasive language.

Evaluation Criteria

The writer responds directly to the prompt and

✳ develops and supports the ideas, including references to the author's work

✳ uses transition words such as *therefore, because,* and *in conclusion* to connect ideas

✳ uses a personal writer's voice that connects with the reader

✳ uses synonyms and pronouns to avoid repeating words

✳ varies sentence structure and writes fluent sentences

✳ edits and proofreads for accurate copy

LITERATURE CONNECTION

■ **Excerpts About Ancient Egypt**

Expository Essay

In Unit 9 of the *Daybook*, you learned about the importance of graphs and other visual texts. Review the unit to see how the visuals sometimes *take the place of* written text and how in other places they *support* the written text. Now think about how often you get your information from visuals in your everyday life.

To plan your writing, use a two-column chart. In the left column, write the name of the visual source, such as the name of a news show. In the right column, list what information you get from that source, such as what's happening around the world.

Responding Write an essay about the different visual sources you use for information, such as movies, television ads, illustrations in science and social studies books, diagrams in math books, billboards, and other places where information is presented visually. Write a strong beginning that describes how you use visual sources of information. The middle section will explain the details of the visual sources: where they are found, how you have used them, how they are different from print or audio sources. Conclude with a summary of the benefits of visual information. Be sure to give your essay a title. Include your own visuals, such as maps, diagrams, or photos.

Evaluation Criteria

The writer responds directly to the prompt and

✷ develops and supports the ideas with details from the selections and real life

✷ uses transition words such as *first, finally, therefore,* and *as a result* to connect ideas

✷ uses a knowledgeable voice to convey information

✷ makes effective word choices

✷ varies sentence structure and writes fluent sentences

✷ edits and proofreads for accurate copy

✷ includes visuals and a title

LITERATURE CONNECTION

- *The Egypt Game*
- *Project Mulberry*

Expository Writing

In Unit 10, you made connections from what you read in the excerpts from *The Egypt Game* and *Project Mulberry* to your own life experiences. In making these connections you focused on comparing and contrasting, asking the questions "What are the similarities?" and "What are the differences?"

Responding Write an essay that explores the connections between two things. You can choose two books, two television shows, two movies, two songs, two schools, or any other two things you want to compare. In your comparison, give specific examples to show the similarities and the differences. Before you create your draft, fill out the chart to help you plan your writing. In your essay, you can list the similarities and then the differences. Or, you can go point by point, listing what is the same and different about each point. The beginning should state what you are going to talk about in your essay. The ending should sum up what you said. Be sure to give your essay a title.

	Similarities	*Differences*
First thing		
Second thing		

Evaluation Criteria

The writer responds directly to the prompt and

⁂ develops and supports the ideas with specific details

⁂ uses transition words such as *similarly, likewise, however, otherwise,* and *although* to organize ideas

⁂ uses a knowledgeable voice to convey information

⁂ makes effective word choices

⁂ varies sentence structure and writes fluent sentences

⁂ edits and proofreads for accurate copy

WRITING PROMPT

LITERATURE CONNECTION

■ **Nonfiction Selections in Unit 11**

Persuasive Writing

The authors in Unit 11 use different kinds of evidence to make their arguments convincing. Some of them present an opposing viewpoint to balance an argument. Set up a situation in which you want to convince a parent or other authority figure to give you permission to do something you want to do. Think of three different reasons (arguments) you should be able to do it.

What I want permission to do:

____

____

Three reasons that I should be able to do it:

1. ______________________________________
2. ______________________________________
3. ______________________________________

Responding Write a letter to an adult that explains why you think you should be able to do something. Decide how to present your reasons. You can start with the strongest one or end with it. Support your argument with evidence. Address an opposing viewpoint, also known as a counterargument. Consider your audience and use language that is appropriate. Be sure to use conventional business letter format: heading, inside address, salutation, body, closing, and signature.

Evaluation Criteria

The writer responds directly to the prompt and

- supports the argument with evidence and counters an opposing argument with a counterargument
- organizes the reasons from most to least important or the other way around
- uses a positive voice
- avoids wordiness and repetition of words
- varies the sentence beginnings and lengths
- edits and proofreads for accurate copy

LITERATURE CONNECTION

■ **Poetry**

Expressive-Descriptive Writing

In Unit 12, you read many different types of poems and focused on how poets use imagery and description to create vivid pictures in the reader's mind.

Imagine yourself in a particular place and look at the scene in front of you. Make a quick sketch of the scene.

Responding Write a poem about the scene you just drew. It can be any form of poem, such as a haiku, a rhyming poem, or free verse that doesn't follow a set form.

Before you begin writing, look at your drawing and brainstorm descriptive words and images you want to use in your poem Then write your first draft. Read it aloud to see how it sounds. Remember, no matter how short your poem is, you may want to revise it more than once until you get it just the way you want it. Also, remember to include a title for your poem.

Evaluation Criteria

The writer responds directly to the prompt and

　　✿ develops ideas with sensory details

　　✿ organizes the description logically

　　✿ uses a knowledgeable voice to describe a real place

　　✿ uses sensory language

　　✿ writes text that is easy to read aloud

　　✿ edits and proofreads for accurate copy

WRITING PROMPT

LITERATURE CONNECTION

- *The River*
- *Dancing Carl*
- *Dogsong*
- *Woodsong*

Narrative Writing

Gary Paulsen is a masterful storyteller. As you learned in Unit 13, many of his books have characters who cope with the challenges of nature—hunger, cold, the fear of being lost.

Responding Write about a time when you experienced a challenge in dealing with nature or a challenge that involved another person. Be sure to set the scene and tell what happened. Describe the animals or people who were part of the experience. Tell what you learned from the experience and how it changed you.

Before you write, plan your writing by making a few notes about what you want to say.

The challenge I faced: _____

What I learned from the experience: _____

How I changed as a result: _____

Evaluation Criteria

The writer responds directly to the prompt and

* develops and supports the ideas

* organizes the narrative logically (beginning, middle, ending)

* uses a personal writer's voice that connects with the reader

* uses specific nouns and precise verbs

* varies sentence structure and writes fluent sentences

* edits and proofreads for accurate copy

The *Daybook* assessments are designed to help you evaluate students' progress toward understanding what they read. The assessments include a Pretest, four Reading Strategy Assessments, and a Posttest, as described below. Each assessment includes one or two passages that were created for the assessment and are based on the types of selections found in the *Daybook*.

PRETEST

The Pretest has one long and two short, paired literature selections. This test is designed to be administered at the beginning of the school year. Because each of the sixteen questions covers a particular reading strategy, the test can help you determine students' beginning levels and indicate what you might need to emphasize in your teaching. The test also provides a baseline for measuring students' progress through the *Daybook*.

READING STRATEGY ASSESSMENTS

These assessments can help you monitor students' progress and inform your teaching plans for using the *Daybook*. Each assessment requires students to apply a particular reading strategy to a selection of literature. Units not listed below are assessed only through the more appropriate method of the writing prompts (see page 225). The following list shows the strategy focus of each assessment and suggests when to administer the assessment.

Assessment	To be administered after . . .
1. Interacting with the Text	Unit 2 or Unit 9
2. Making Connections	Unit 3 or Unit 10
3. Exploring Multiple Perspectives	Unit 4 or Unit 11
4. Focusing on Language and Craft	Unit 5 or Unit 12

Note: If you administer the assessment after completing the first unit and students do not score well, you may want to administer the assessment again after the second unit of instruction for the same strategy.

POSTTEST

The Posttest contains the same types of selections and the same number of questions as the Pretest and measures the same strategies. It should be administered at the completion of the *Daybook* to help determine how much progress students have made.

DIRECTIONS FOR ADMINISTERING ASSESSMENTS

To administer, distribute copies of the test pages to each student. Have students write their name at the top of each page. Then have students read the selections and answer the questions. For multiple-choice questions, students should choose the best answer to each question and circle the letter of the answer. For written-response questions, students should write their answers in complete sentences on the writing lines provided on the test page.

DIRECTIONS FOR SCORING ASSESSMENTS

All multiple-choice items are worth 1 point each; written-response questions are worth 2 points each. (A partially correct written response may be awarded 1 point.) Use a copy of the Scoring Chart on page 244 to record students' scores.

Pretest & Posttest—Add the total number of points earned and write the result under "Points" on the Scoring Chart for each test. To find the "Percent," multiply the total points × 5. (For example, 15 points × 5 = 75%).

Reading Strategy Assessments—Add the total number of points earned and write the result under "Points" on the Scoring Chart for each assessment. To find the "Percent," multiply the total points × 10. (For example, 7 points × 10 = 70%).

Students should score at least 70% correct on each test. For students who score 70% or lower, you may want to analyze the test responses more closely and focus instruction on particular strategies.

Multiple Choice   (1 point each)

Item	Answer	Reading Strategy
1	**D**	Making Connections: Setting
2	**C**	Making Connections: Point of View
3	**B**	Making Connections: Character
4	**D**	Making Connections: Story Line and Plot
5	**C**	Exploring Multiple Perspectives: Cause and Effect
6	**A**	Making Connections: Theme

Written Responses   (2 points each)

7	**Answers vary.**	Acceptable responses will state that Nicole feels close to her grandmother and will support this statement with evidence from the story. (Interacting with the Text: Making Inferences)
8	**Answers vary.**	Acceptable responses will consist of two complete sentences that logically extend the story and reflect an understanding of the story's characters and plot. (Interacting with the Text: Predicting)

Multiple Choice   (1 point each)

Item	Answer	Reading Strategy
9	**B**	Interacting with the Text: Main Idea
10	**D**	Interacting with the Text: Author's Purpose
11	**A**	Exploring Multiple Perspectives: Sequence of Events
12	**A**	Focusing on Language and Craft: Word Choice
13	**B**	Focusing on Language and Craft: Simile
14	**C**	Exploring Multiple Perspectives: Author's Perspective

Written Responses   (2 points each)

15	**Answers vary.**	Acceptable responses will identify the National Weather Service as the source of information and will suggest a plausible way in which the author might obtain the information. (Exploring Multiple Perspectives: Author's Credibility)
16	**Answers vary.**	Acceptable responses will identify "Tyrel's Journal" as the eyewitness account and will mention at least one way in which the passage reflects an author's experience. (Exploring Multiple Perspectives: Eyewitness Accounts)

READING STRATEGY ASSESSMENTS ANSWER KEY

ASSESSMENT 1   Interacting with the Text

Answers: 1–A   2–A   3–B   4–D   5–C   6–B   (1 point each)

Written responses   (2 points each)

7 **Answers vary.** Acceptable responses will make a prediction about Mallory's attempt to climb Mount Everest and will state whether it was accurate. It also would include supporting evidence from the passage.

8 **Answers vary.** Acceptable responses will indicate that successful climbers do not receive as much recognition as Hillary and Norgay because they were the first to reach its summit and the feat has become more commonplace.

ASSESSMENT 2   Making Connections

Answers: 1–C   2–A   3–D   4–C   5–B   6–D   (1 point each)

Written responses   (2 points each)

7 **Answers vary.** Acceptable responses will indicate that the first part of the story occurs at (or outside of) an antiques shop in the present time.

8 **Answers vary.** Acceptable responses will explain that Matt didn't want to learn what happened to Erik, and he believed he could keep from learning Erik's fate if he put the photograph away.

ASSESSMENT 3   Exploring Multiple Perspectives

Answers: 1–A   2–A   3–B   4–D   5–D   6–C   (1 point each)

Written responses   (2 points each)

7 **Answers vary.** Acceptable responses will mention at least two factual details that can be verified with reference sources.

8 **Answers vary.** Acceptable responses will identify "Moon Memories" as an eyewitness account and mention at least one way in which the passage reflects an eyewitness experience.

ASSESSMENT 4   Focusing on Language and Craft

Answers: 1–C   2–B   3–D   4–A   5–B   6–D   (1 point each)

Written responses   (2 points each)

7 **Answers vary.** Acceptable responses will explain that the poem describes a batter hitting a home run and the crowd cheering.

8 **Answers vary.** Acceptable responses will indicate that the imagery describes clouds and will relate in some way the clouds' shape and/or texture, which helps the read visualize an image.

Multiple Choice
(1 point each)

Item	Answer	Reading Strategy
1	B	Making Connections: Point of View
2	D	Making Connections: Setting
3	C	Making Connections: Character
4	A	Exploring Multiple Perspectives: Cause and Effect
5	C	Making Connections: Story Line and Plot
6	D	Making Connections: Theme

Written Responses
(2 points each)

7 **Answers vary.** Acceptable responses will indicate that Angie feels satisfied or happy, pleased that she has made friends, or something similar, and will give supporting evidence from the story. (Interacting with the Text: Making Inferences)

8 **Answers vary.** Acceptable responses will consist of two complete sentences that logically extend the story and reflect an understanding of the story's characters and plot. (Interacting with the Text: Predicting)

Multiple Choice
(1 point each)

Item	Answer	Reading Strategy
9	B	Interacting with the Text: Main Idea
10	A	Interacting with the Text: Author's Purpose
11	C	Focusing on Language and Craft: Simile
12	C	Exploring Multiple Perspectives: Sequence of Events
13	A	Focusing on Language and Craft: Word Choice
14	B	Exploring Multiple Perspectives: Author's Perspective

Written Responses
(2 points each)

15 **Answers vary.** Acceptable responses will indicate that by identifying herself as a school principal, the author enhances her credibility and helps to persuade readers to accept her point of view. (Exploring Multiple Perspectives: Author's Credibility)

16 **Answers vary.** Acceptable responses will relate Kyle's emotional and health problems to having too many scheduled activities. (Exploring Multiple Perspectives: Eyewitness Accounts)

READING ASSESSMENTS

SCORING CHART

Daybook 6

CLASS _____

TEACHER _____

Student Name	Pretest		Assess 1		Assess 2		Assess 3		Assess 4		Posttest	
	Date / Points	%		%		%		%		%		%

Name _____

Date _____

DIRECTIONS: Read this passage about what happens when Grandma moves in with a 12-year-old girl and her parents. Then answer questions 1–8.

Helping Hands

Nicole handed the phone to Dad but stayed close by to listen. She had not recognized the voice on the other end and wondered who it might be. Dad said hello with a casual tone, but obvious concern tightened his features as he listened to the caller. "Oh, that's terrible," Dad declared immediately. Then, after listening some more, he seemed to relax, adding, "Well, that's reassuring news, I suppose. Thank you for calling, Lucia."

Mom was coming in from the garden as Dad hung up and announced, "That was my mother's friend, Lucia Alonso. My mother has taken a fall and broken her right arm. She's going to recover fully, thank goodness, but she's in a cast from her hand to her upper arm. She can't drive, of course, so she's going to need a lot of assistance until her cast comes off."

"Your mother will come here, of course," Mom said without hesitation. "She can take Nicole's room, and Nicole can sleep in the family room."

But Dad seemed uncertain. "You know how much my mother values her independence," he pointed out. "Perhaps we should make some other kind of arrangements so she can stay in her own apartment. Maybe between you and me and Mrs. Alonso, we could do all her shopping and errands for her."

"Nonsense," Mom replied. "Your mother lives an hour away, so that arrangement would be completely impractical." Then Mom smiled at Nicole and added, "Besides, Nicole would like nothing better than to have Grandma recuperate right here with us. Isn't that right, Nicole?

Nicole nodded enthusiastically. "We'll have a fantastic time together!"

For about a week, Nicole and Grandma did have a fantastic time together. Every afternoon when Nicole got home from school, Grandma was all ears, eager to hear how the day had gone. She listened as Nicole practiced the piano and exclaimed that it was amazing how much Nicole had improved her technique. And she spent a rainy Saturday afternoon perched on a stool in the kitchen, teaching Nicole how to make scrumptious cornbread. Until that day, Grandma had kept the recipe to herself. By passing it along, she made Nicole feel special.

But then one day, Nicole noticed a change in Grandma. Instead of greeting Nicole after school, Grandma stayed in her room. When Nicole knocked on her door, Grandma sounded irritated. "I'm resting, Nicole," was all she said.

A few hours later, Nicole called Grandma to the dinner table. Grandma took her seat silently beside Nicole as Mom and Dad brought the plates to the table. They had prepared Grandma's favorite meal of grilled steak, corn on the cob, and tossed salad. When Grandma didn't even acknowledge the special effort, an awkward silence settled over the table. Grandma picked at her salad for a while before putting down her fork.

Trying to smile, Dad asked, "Is there something wrong with your dinner, Mom?"

"I'm sure it's delicious," Grandma answered tartly, "but with only one useful hand, I can't eat the rest of it."

Dad gasped and reached for Grandma's plate. "I'm sorry, Mom, I wasn't thinking!" he exclaimed. "Here, I'll cut up your steak and butter your corn for you."

But Grandma shook her head, pushed her chair away from the table, and stood up. "No thank you, son," she said quietly, "I just don't have much of an appetite tonight."

A half hour later, Nicole went to the family room to practice the piano. There she found Grandma sitting in the easy chair, reading a book. Without a word, Nicole sat on the piano bench and started playing her newest piece. It was a difficult one, and the fingering for the left hand was especially tricky. Again and again, Nicole played the wrong keys, making harsh, unpleasant chords. Finally, she heaved a loud, exasperated sigh.

That's when Grandma got up from her chair and came to sit beside Nicole on the left side of the piano bench. "You know, Nicole," she began, "I've spent the day feeling sorry for myself. This clunky old cast has made me feel helpless, and extremely dependent on you and your parents."

When Grandma paused for a moment, Nicole gently touched her cast and said, "I think I can understand that, Grandma."

Grandma chuckled and said, "But now my sulk is over and I'm ready to brighten up, so let's tackle this piece together. You play the right hand, and I'll play the left."

She lifted her left hand to the piano keys. Nicole smiled and lifted her right hand. As they peered together at the music book, Grandma murmured, "Ready, set, begin." ❖

❊ QUESTIONS 1–6: Circle the letter of the best answer to each question.

1. Where do most of the events in this story take place?

   A in Grandma's apartment

   B at Nicole's school

   C in Mrs. Alonso's home

   D at Nicole's house

2. Who is telling this story?

   A Mom and Dad

   B Nicole

   C someone outside the story

   D Grandma

3. Which words best describe Grandma's behavior at the beginning of her visit?

   A rude and hurtful

   B generous and kind

   C quiet and withdrawn

   D silly and playful

4. What happens at the *climax*, or high point, of this story?

    A Grandma falls and breaks her arm.

    B Grandma arrives at Nicole's house.

    C Grandma shares her cornbread recipe with Nicole.

    D Grandma listens to Nicole struggle to play the piano.

5. What upsets Grandma most in this story?

    A being seriously injured

    B the way Mom and Dad cook

    C losing her independence

    D the way Nicole plays the piano

6. By the end of this story, Grandma comes to accept the idea that —

    A everyone needs help sometimes.

    B it's better to depend on friends than family.

    C a child can't understand a grownup's problems.

    D you should never admit to feeling helpless.

❋ QUESTIONS 7 and 8: Write your answers on the lines.

7. How does Nicole feel about her grandmother? Support your answer with a detail from the story.

_____

_____

_____

_____

_____

8. Write two sentences that continue the story as if you were the author.

_____

_____

_____

_____

_____

DIRECTIONS: Read these two passages about a tornado that struck several towns in New York state. Then answer questions 9–16.

Otsego County Shaken by Tornadoes

The people of Otsego County in New York are used to severe weather. They've seen their share of blizzards and ice storms. Heavy rains and flash flooding also happen from time to time. But when tornadoes whirled through the county in 1998, everyone agreed that they'd never seen anything like that before.

The tornadoes struck on Sunday, May 31. For most residents, there was no warning. On that day, the weather seemed fair enough for gardening and spring cleaning. Even when the afternoon sky quickly darkened in the west, no one imagined a tornado was approaching. A thunderstorm, maybe, but not a tornado. Tornadoes just didn't happen in these steeply rising hills of upstate New York.

In all, five tornadoes struck in and around Otsego County that day. According to the National Weather Service, two had wind speeds of up to 157 miles an hour. A third tornado was even more powerful, with winds up to 206 miles per hour. The tornadoes downed trees and power lines. They ripped off roof shingles, shutters, and doors. They lifted and tossed parked cars, and they sent residents scurrying for cover. For a community unaccustomed to dealing with tornadoes, the human toll was remarkably small—only one person died, killed by a fallen tree. Afterward, residents had to cope with damage to their homes and days without power. Many could not travel by car until crews removed trees or downed power lines from roads.

The people of Otsego County rolled up their sleeves and got to work. There was storm debris to be cleared. There were properties to repair. In places hardest hit by tornadoes, the process took months. Gradually, life returned to the way it used to be.

Except for this one difference: now, in Otsego County, when the skies suddenly darken and the wind whips up, people stop to wonder if a tornado is on its way. ❖

Tyrel's Journal

I was stretched out comfortably on Mama's bed, watching a Sunday afternoon movie on television. Although I was dimly aware that the sky had grown dark and a strong wind was kicking up, I continued watching. Then I heard Mama's anxious, urgent voice coming from the backyard. "Tyrel!" she yelled. "Get downstairs! Go to the basement—*NOW!*"

I looked out the window and saw Mama at the clothesline, struggling to take down the sheets she had just hung up to dry. As she yanked the clothespins off one damp sheet, the wind lifted it off the line and flung it into the air. For a moment, it looked like a dancing, twisting ghost. Then it smacked against the window where I stood. Mama saw me and screamed, "*Go to the basement!*"

Mama raced inside in time to meet me at the top of the basement steps, and as we scrambled down, I asked Mama what was happening. "I have no idea!" she exclaimed. "It's almost like a tornado—but it couldn't be!" Bewildered, we peered out a small, high window into the backyard. We could see our neighbors' lawn furniture tumbling crazily across our yard. We could see our lilac bushes leaning over in the wind until they were nearly parallel to the ground. And then we heard a loud, ominous *CRACK!* followed by a swooshing sound as our big old fir tree gave way and fell toward the house. "Look out!" exclaimed Mama, but we were both too petrified to say anything more.

Ten minutes later, when the winds had subsided, Mama and I ventured outside to see where the fir tree had fallen. It lay across a caved-in section of roof directly above my mother's room—where I had been watching television.

Mama and I wandered into the street, where all of our neighbors were doing the same thing—looking with dazed disbelief at the destruction caused by the sudden, terrifying winds. Sometime later, when we learned that the storm was, in fact, a tornado, it was almost impossible to believe. None of the neighbors, not even the elderly ones, had ever heard of a tornado in Otsego County. Now it was an experience we'd never forget. ❖

✳ QUESTIONS 9–14: Circle the letter of the best answer to each question.

9. **What is the main idea of Passage 1?**
   A Severe weather is common all year round in Otsego County.
   B People were astonished when powerful tornadoes struck in Otsego County.
   C The damage caused by tornadoes in Otsego County has been repaired.
   D Tornadoes were once rare in Otsego County, but now they are common.

10. **In Passage 1, the author's main purpose is to —**
   A warn people about the dangers of tornadoes.
   B compare tornadoes with other kinds of severe weather.
   C give information about Otsego County's weather.
   D describe an unusual tornado event in upstate New York.

11. **In Passage 2, what happened just before Mama yelled to Tyrel?**
   A A strong wind started to blow.
   B Tyrel turned on the television.
   C Lawn furniture tumbled across the yard.
   D Mama ran inside the house.

12. **In Passage 2, words such as *yanked*, *raced*, and *scrambled* suggest actions that are —**
   A hurried.
   B useless.
   C graceful.
   D careful.

13. **Which sentence from Passage 2 is a simile?**

    A The sky had grown dark.

    B The sheet looked like a dancing, twisting ghost.

    C The lilac bushes leaned over in the wind.

    D The tree lay across a caved-in section of the roof.

14. **When Tyrel saw where the tree had fallen, what was probably his strongest feeling?**

    A worry that the television was destroyed

    B regret that the old tree was lost

    C relief that he had escaped unharmed

    D fear that more trees were about to fall

✳ QUESTIONS 15 and 16: Write your answers on the lines.

15. **From what source did the author of Passage 1 get information about the wind speeds of the tornado? Tell how you think the author found this information.**

_____

_____

_____

_____

_____

16. **Which passage is an eyewitness account of the day the tornadoes struck Otsego County? Tell how you know.**

_____

_____

_____

_____

_____

_____

INTERACTING WITH THE TEXT

DIRECTIONS: Read this passage about climbing the world's highest mountain. Then answer questions 1–8.

Because It's There

In 1924, a climber named George Mallory was preparing to climb Mount Everest, the world's highest peak. At the time, no one had ever reached the top of Everest. Few could imagine even trying such a dangerous feat. But Mallory found it easy to explain why he would risk his life to climb Everest. "Because it's there," he said simply.

Sadly, Mallory and his climbing partner, Andrew Irvine, died trying to reach the summit. But their deaths seemed to inspire other climbers. For 29 years, team after team tried and failed to climb Everest. Finally, in 1953, partners Edmund Hillary and Tensing Norgay reached the peak. The whole world cheered their bold, brave feat.

Not surprisingly, Hillary and Norgay's success inspired even more climbers. With each passing decade, the number of climbers to reach the top of Everest has grown. Successful attempts are common now. This is due in large part to huge improvements in climbing gear. Modern gear helps climbers endure weather and wind conditions that would have turned back earlier climbers—or killed them. The climbing routes are also a bit easier to scale now because ladders and ropes have been fixed in place on the way to the summit. Finally, today's climbers can keep in radio contact with the base camp and call for help if trouble strikes.

To be sure, climbing Mount Everest is still an extremely risky challenge. Just since 1990, more than 70 people have lost their lives on the mountain. As time goes on, though, more and more people have decided that the risk is worth taking. Like George Mallory, they want to climb Mount Everest simply because it's there. ❖

CLIMBERS TO REACH MOUNT EVEREST'S SUMMIT

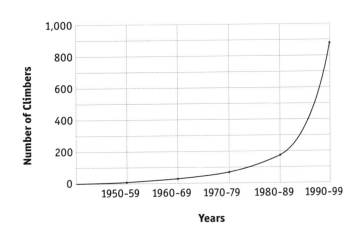

Name _____ Date _____

✴ *QUESTIONS 1–6:* Circle the letter of the best answer to each question.

1. **What is this passage mostly about?**

   A the appeal of climbing Mount Everest
   B the lives of great climbers
   C the weather on Mount Everest
   D the importance of climbing gear

2. **Which aspect of climbing Mount Everest has remained the same over the years?**

   A the weather and wind conditions
   B the clothing worn by climbers
   C the difficulty of climbing up the mountain
   D the ability to call for help

3. **The graph best illustrates which of these statements from the passage?**

   A For 29 years after Mallory's death, no one succeeded in climbing Mount Everest.
   B The number of climbers to reach the top of Mount Everest has grown each decade.
   C Climbing Mount Everest is still extremely risky.
   D Since 1990, over 70 climbers have died on Mount Everest.

4. **According to the graph, about how many climbers reached the summit of Mount Everest in the 1990s?**

   A 100
   B 200
   C 500
   D 900

5. **The author's main purpose in this passage is to —**

   A tell some entertaining stories about the lives of mountain climbers.
   B explain the story behind George Mallory's famous words.
   C tell how the challenge of climbing Mount Everest has changed over the years.
   D persuade more people to climb Mount Everest.

6. **The information in this passage suggests that, in the next decade, the number of people who will reach the summit of Mount Everest is likely to —**

   A be the same as the last decade.
   B keep increasing.
   C drop off sharply to almost zero.
   D decline slightly.

✳ *QUESTIONS 7 and 8:* Write your answers on the lines.

7. As you read the first paragraph, what prediction did you make about George Mallory? Write your prediction and tell whether it matched the text. Include a detail from the passage to explain how close your prediction was.

_____

_____

_____

_____

_____

_____

_____

_____

8. Do you think people who climb Mount Everest today get the same kind of recognition that Hillary and Norgay did? Explain your answer.

_____

_____

_____

_____

_____

_____

MAKING CONNECTIONS

Name _____

Date _____

DIRECTIONS: **Read this passage about a young man named Matt, who finds a special photograph. Then answer questions 1–8.**

The Photograph

Matt spotted the framed photograph in the window of a neighborhood antiques shop. It was a family portrait of a couple and two young children, which Matt guessed was more than 100 years old. He was curious to know who the people were and what had become of them, so he stepped into the shop to find out.

"I haven't got a clue," said the shop owner. "Some folks just like collecting old pictures. That's why it's here. If you want it, you can have it for five bucks."

Digging into his pocket, Matt produced three dollars, two quarters, a dime, and a penny. "Close enough," said the shop owner as he handed the photograph to Matt.

That night, Matt studied the photograph. He noticed the man's hand resting gently on his wife's, the affectionate tilt of her head toward his cheek, the ease of their smiles, and the contentedness of the children nestled on their parents' laps. Obviously, they were a happy family.

With the picture on his bed table, Matt fell asleep. Before long, he saw the family gathered at a ship's boarding ramp. The man embraced and kissed his children and then his wife. She pulled the photograph from her dress pocket and pressed it into her husband's hands. "I will send for you as soon as I can," the man promised as he walked up the ramp.

Matt woke in the morning knowing one thing with certainty: the images and words of his sleep were not a dream. They were the family's true story, which the photograph somehow had the power to transmit to him. Hoping the photograph had still more to reveal, Matt waited impatiently for the day to end so he could try to learn more.

When Matt finally drifted off to sleep that night, he saw the man again, dressed in the clothes of a factory worker. The man was sitting at a table, reading over a letter he had just written. The letter was dated May 12, 1889. *Dearest Claudia*, it began. *Johnstown, Pennsylvania, is so filled with immigrants from Germany that it feels almost like home to me. I have taken a job at the Cambria Iron Factory. By working hard and living frugally, I will soon save enough money to pay for the voyage for you and the children. I can hardly wait until we are all together again. Your loving husband, Erik.*

When he woke, Matt felt an unbearable dread. He'd once read about a terrible flood that had devastated the factory town of Johnstown on June 1, 1889, killing more than 2,000 people. He knew that Erik could have been one of the many

DAYBOOK (6) © GREAT SOURCE. COPYING IS PERMITTED; SEE PAGE ii.

residents who escaped with their lives that day. But if he wasn't—if Erik had perished without ever seeing his family again—Matt did not want to know. So he put the photograph away on a shelf in the back of his closet.

That night, Matt slept deeply, undisturbed by any images of the family in the photo. It was as if he had drawn a dark, heavy curtain on their story. ❖

✳ QUESTIONS 1–6: Circle the letter of the best answer to each question.

1. Who is the narrator of this story?

    A the owner of the antiques shop

    B Claudia

    C someone outside the story

    D Matt

2. The details of this story suggest that Erik was —

    A loving and hardworking.

    B selfish and impatient.

    C fearful and anxious.

    D carefree and loving.

3. Which of these events happened last?

    A Erik got ready to board a ship.

    B The family posed together for a photograph.

    C Erik wrote a letter to Claudia.

    D A terrible flood struck Johnstown, Pennsylvania.

4. Which event takes place at the climax of the story?

    A Matt finds the photograph in the antiques shop.

    B Matt studies the photograph closely.

    C Matt realizes Erik might have died tragically.

    D Matt puts the photograph away in a closet.

5. Which sentence states a theme of this story?

    A Long ago, life was simpler than it is today.

    B Tragedy can strike unexpectedly.

    C Knowledge of history is seldom useful.

    D Some people will never find happiness.

6. Matt's actions in this story suggest that he is —

    A witty and charming.

    B wasteful and foolish.

    C bold and daring.

    D curious and sensitive.

✳ *QUESTIONS 7 and 8:* Write your answers on the lines.

7. What is the setting at the beginning of this story? Tell *where* and *when* the first part of the story takes place.

_____

_____

_____

_____

_____

8. Why did Matt put the photograph on a shelf in the back of his closet?

_____

_____

_____

_____

_____

_____

EXPLORING MULTIPLE PERSPECTIVES

DIRECTIONS: Read these two passages about an historic event that took place in 1969. Then answer questions 1–8.

All the World Was Watching

Over the years, TV has allowed us to witness important events, as they unfold, in the comfort of our homes. Since most of these events occur right here on Earth, the fact that we can watch them on TV fails to impress most of us. But in the summer of 1969, TV achieved a great feat: the live broadcast of the first moon landing. As people around the world watched the images of the *Apollo 11* astronauts walking on the moon, they could hardly believe their eyes.

   Apollo 11 blasted off from the Kennedy Space Center on the morning of July 16. At that moment, nearly nonstop TV coverage of the space flight began. On their third day in space, astronauts Neil Armstrong and Buzz Aldrin moved from the main ship, the *Columbia*, to the *Eagle*, the small craft that would carry them to the moon. They stayed just long enough to do an equipment check. As the astronauts worked, millions of viewers watched them from Earth.

   But the real excitement began on July 20. That afternoon, Armstrong and Aldrin returned to the *Eagle*. They switched on the power, and the small craft separated from *Columbia*. When it touched down on the moon, Armstrong announced, "The *Eagle* has landed." Then he and Aldrin began preparing to explore the moon's surface, and about six hours later, Armstrong finally emerged. By this time, nearly 600 million people were glued to their TV sets. As Armstrong made his way down the ladder, he stopped to activate a camera. The image of Armstrong on TV held viewers spellbound as he continued down. At last, Armstrong stepped on the moon, saying, "That's one small step for man, one giant leap for mankind." For those watching from Earth, that step certainly seemed giant. ❖

Moon Memories

When I was a child, my family always took a week's vacation on Cape Cod in Massachusetts. We always stayed in a rented beach cottage. The cottage was a tight fit for our family of eight and completely lacking in frills. But my father always dismissed our complaint that there was no TV. "We're here to swim and watch the sun set over the ocean," he'd say. "We don't need the idiot box for that."

   But in the summer of 1969, my father made an exception to this policy. We had rented the cottage in July during the week that the *Apollo 11* astronauts were to

Name _____ Date _____

make their historic moon landing. As we loaded our station wagon with suitcases, beach gear, and a week's worth of dry goods, my father emerged from the house, straining under the weight of our TV. "The first men on the moon—I wouldn't miss that for the world," he huffed.

As soon as we got to the cottage, my father plugged in the TV and turned the dial to the local CBS station. Then he adjusted the antenna until the black-and-white picture came in clearly. "Listen up," he commanded as we looked on. "No one is to change the channel or move the antenna." None of us had to ask why. My father considered Walter Cronkite, the CBS news anchor, the only broadcaster worth listening to during the moon mission.

I'm sure we swam and watched some sunsets that week, but I don't recall any of that. What I do recall are the hours spent in front of the TV as we followed *Apollo 11*'s progress. Most of all I remember the day the astronauts landed on the moon. It was a hot afternoon, and the eight of us were squeezed together on the sofa and floor, holding our breath as the *Eagle* dropped toward the moon's surface. Its descent, narrated by Walter Cronkite and faceless voices from the Kennedy Space Center, seemed to take forever. But finally, we heard Neil Armstrong's announcement: "The *Eagle* has landed." Amazingly, the usually calm and steady Cronkite was almost speechless. As he pulled off his glasses and shook his head, all Cronkite could manage was, "Oh, boy . . . Whoo!" I remember how my brothers and sisters and I jumped up and down, yelling and whooping. And I remember how my father, his arm around my mother, threw back his head and let out a loud cheer. ✚

✳ QUESTIONS 1–6: Circle the letter of the best answer to each question.

1. **According to Passage 1, what happened on the morning of July 16, 1969?**

   A The *Apollo 11* astronauts blasted into space.

   B The *Columbia* separated from the *Eagle*.

   C The *Eagle* dropped toward the moon's surface.

   D Armstrong and Aldrin checked the *Eagle's* equipment.

2. **According to Passage 1, as Armstrong climbed down from the *Eagle*, he paused on the ladder so that he could —**

   A switch on a camera.

   B help Aldrin climb out of the *Columbia*.

   C say, "That's one small step for man . . ."

   D put on his spacesuit.

3. **The author of Passage 1 was mainly interested in —**

   A encouraging young people to become astronauts.

   B showing how the first moon landing captivated TV viewers.

   C explaining how difficult it was to send humans to the moon.

   D describing what astronauts do in space.

4. In Passage 2, the author's father brought a television to the beach cottage because —

   A his children persuaded him.

   B he didn't want to miss any of his favorite programs.

   C he expected a lot of bad weather during the vacation.

   D he wanted to see the historic moon landing.

5. Which detail from Passage 2 can be checked in a reference source?

   A The family usually spent their vacation without a TV.

   B The family went swimming and watched sunsets in the summer of 1969.

   C Walter Cronkite was the only broadcaster worth listening to during the moon mission.

   D Neil Armstrong spoke the words, "The *Eagle* has landed."

6. Which event is described in detail in both passages?

   A *Apollo 11* blasts off.

   B Armstrong and Aldrin leave the *Columbia*.

   C The *Eagle* lands on the moon.

   D Armstrong steps on the moon.

✳ QUESTIONS 7 and 8: Write your answers on the lines.

7. Write two details from Passage 1 showing that the author relied on research to write the passage.

   _____

   _____

   _____

   _____

   _____

8. Which passage is an eyewitness account of how the first moon landing was covered on TV? Tell how you know.

   _____

   _____

   _____

   _____

   _____

   _____

FOCUSING ON LANGUAGE AND CRAFT

DIRECTIONS: Read these two poems. Then answer questions 1–8.

Home Run

Any lumberjack would envy my swing —
a swift, strong, effortless slice.
But timber is my tool, not my target.
And the crack you hear when I connect
is not a splintering trunk,
but a soaring missile,
perfectly round, covered in white leather and bound with red stitches.
And the sound that follows is not the thud of a falling tree.
It is the roar of the crowd. ❖

— *Janet Callahan*

Skyscapes

Like a butterscotch candy,
gleaming and golden,
the sun sinks —
threading its way
through orange-pink tufts
of cotton candy
that stick to the sky
at sunset.

Like paint on a canvas,
fluid and blue-black,
the darkness spreads—
overtaking all light
except for the glitter
of distant diamonds
that adorn the sky
at night. ❖

— *Janet Callahan*

DAYBOOK (6) © GREAT SOURCE. COPYING IS PERMITTED; SEE PAGE ii.

Name _____

Date _____

✳ *QUESTIONS 1–6:* **Circle the letter of the best answer to each question.**

1. **In "Home Run," what is the speaker doing?**
   - **A** chopping down a tree
   - **B** standing in a crowd
   - **C** swinging a baseball bat
   - **D** walking through the woods

2. **In "Home Run," the phrase** *soaring missile* **is a metaphor for which of these?**
   - **A** an ax
   - **B** a baseball
   - **C** a tree limb
   - **D** a loud roar

3. **The speaker's tone in "Home Run" is best described as —**
   - **A** silly and playful.
   - **B** mysterious and solemn.
   - **C** cautious and timid.
   - **D** confident and proud.

4. **In "Skyscapes," the poet compares the sun to a —**
   - **A** butterscotch candy.
   - **B** thread.
   - **C** piece of gold.
   - **D** painting.

5. **In "Skyscapes," the phrase the** *glitter of distant diamonds* **is a metaphor for —**
   - **A** sunlight.
   - **B** stars.
   - **C** the moon.
   - **D** clouds.

6. **"Skyscapes" uses the image of paint on a canvas to describe —**
   - **A** a stormy sky.
   - **B** the sky at sunrise.
   - **C** a clear sky.
   - **D** the sky at night.

Name _____

✳ *QUESTIONS 7 and 8:* **Write your answers on the lines.**

7. **What happens in "Home Run"? Describe the brief moment this poem depicts.**

_____

_____

_____

_____

_____

_____

8. **In "Skyscapes," what are the "orange-pink tufts of cotton candy"? Explain why the poet would use such a phrase.**

_____

_____

_____

_____

_____

_____

_____

DIRECTIONS: Read this passage about a sixth grader and what she discovers. Then answer questions 1–8.

The Yearbook

Angie thought back to the day Mr. Ng handed out the yearbook order forms in homeroom. That day was in late September, and she was still getting used to being in middle school. "You really should order the yearbook," Mr. Ng had urged the students. "Take my word for it. By the time the yearbook comes out in June, you'll be eager to have all your new friends sign it. Then, for years to come, the yearbook will be a souvenir of your fantastic year in sixth grade."

New friends . . . fantastic year . . . . The words would have irritated Angie if she weren't so fond of Mr. Ng. Since she liked and trusted him, though, she heard the words differently. They were, she decided, a prediction—a promise, even—that things would improve. So Angie had gone home that afternoon, filled out the order form, and folded it into an envelope with a twenty-dollar bill. Then, soon after she turned in the envelope to Mr. Ng, she forgot all about the yearbook.

In some ways, Angie had adjusted quickly to Centerville Middle School. Because she was a serious student with good study habits, the schoolwork didn't throw her. Once she'd figured out the layout of the school building, she actually liked switching classrooms and teachers all day long. And having her own locker, rather than a classroom cubby, made Angie feel rather grown up.

However, moving on to middle school was also difficult for Angie in a way. Lee and Bonita, her two friends from Hale Elementary, weren't in any of her classes. They didn't even have the same lunch period. This realization snuffed out Angie's excitement about middle school like dirt thrown on a fire. Then, because he was concerned, Angie's dad encouraged her to meet with the guidance counselor to see if her schedule could be changed so she could share some classes with her old friends.

"I'm sorry, Angie," Ms. Franklin had explained crisply. "It's against school policy to change a student's schedule for strictly social reasons. If we allowed that, students would be changing schedules all the time." Then, with a smile softening her face, Ms. Franklin added, "Academic skills are just part of what you'll learn in middle school, Angie. You'll also learn to spread your wings a bit and make new friends. Trust me, it'll happen."

Now Angie was sitting in homeroom, leafing through her brand-new copy of the yearbook. The first picture she came across was Trish, from science class. They had become friends on a field trip to the science museum. They'd spent the whole bus ride singing theme songs from old TV shows. The next picture Angie spotted was of Seth, who sat in front of her in social studies and was always turning around to joke and gossip with her. Angie turned several more pages until she found Nadifa's picture. Angie would always remember the day she had left her lunch at home and sat by herself in the cafeteria, her stomach empty and growling. Then Nadifa, a girl

Name _____

Date _____

she didn't know, noticed and offered to share her lunch. Angie had accepted gratefully, and from that moment, she knew Nadifa would be a friend.

Closing the yearbook, Angie remembered what Mr. Ng had said—his prediction about new friends and a great year. She realized how fast the year had gone since that day, and now she couldn't wait to ask her friends to sign her yearbook. ❖

✳ QUESTIONS 1–6: Circle the letter of the best answer to each question.

1. This story is told by —

    A Ms. Franklin.
    B someone outside the story.
    C Mr. Ng.
    D one of Angie's friends.

2. Where is Angie as this story takes place?

    A in the cafeteria
    B in Ms. Franklin's office
    C in her elementary school
    D in her homeroom

3. Which words best describe how Angie felt when she decided to order the yearbook?

    A happy but nervous
    B angry and afraid
    C lonesome but hopeful
    D excited and confident

4. Why was moving on to middle school difficult for Angie?

    A She was separated from her elementary school friends.
    B It was confusing to have so many teachers.
    C The school work was too hard for her to manage.
    D She had trouble finding her way around the building.

5. What does Angie do at the *resolution* of this story?

    A She fills out the order form for the yearbook.
    B She talks to Ms. Franklin.
    C She looks through her new yearbook.
    D She finds out that her old friends are not in her classes.

6. By the end of this story, Angie comes to understand that —

    A most adults remember what it's like to be a kid.
    B one good friend is all anyone really needs.
    C school gets harder as you get older.
    D making new friends is part of growing up.

✳ *QUESTIONS 7 and 8:* **Write your answers on the lines.**

7. **At the end of the story, how does Angie feel about her year in sixth grade? Tell how you know.**

_____

_____

_____

_____

8. **Write two sentences that continue the story as if you were the author.**

_____

_____

_____

_____

DIRECTIONS: **Read these two passages about how busy some children are—and how busy they should be. Then answer questions 9–16.**

PASSAGE 1

Keep Children Active and Learning

"I'm bored. There's nothing to do."

My daughter was coming to me with this complaint several times a week. For a while, I did my best to come up with projects and activities to amuse her. Finally, my well of ideas dried up. When I huffed, "I'm not an entertainment center; you'll have to solve this problem yourself," my daughter spent the rest of the day watching TV reruns, while I scolded myself for being a bad parent.

Why? I'm not just a mother. I'm also a school principal. From my years of experience, I know that children are like sponges, ready to soak up knowledge, ideas, and skills. The interests they develop in their early years often stay with them their entire lives, helping them to develop enjoyable hobbies and sometimes even leading to rewarding careers.

So I decided to take action, using the resources that were readily available in my community, starting with my daughter's own middle school. Rather than coming straight home each day, she decided to join the theater club and the school chorus. These activities keep her busy every afternoon, Monday through Thursday. On Fridays, she volunteers at the public library, helping the children's librarian sort and stack books.

These days, my daughter is too busy—and having far too much fun—to spend the afternoon watching reruns. Maybe she'll become an actress, a singer, or a librarian someday. Or maybe not. What's important is that what she's learning now will stay with her for life. ✛

PASSAGE 2

Children Need Free Time

My young patient sat silently as his mother described his symptoms. "Kyle is tired all the time, and he has moods. He's always snapping and grumbling. Lately he's been getting stomachaches and doesn't have much of an appetite. I don't know what could be wrong with him."

I wasn't too surprised when my physical examination didn't detect a problem. Then I asked Kyle to describe his daily routine.

"Which day?" he replied sarcastically. "On Mondays it's soccer practice and drum lessons. On Tuesdays it's Spanish Club and swim team. On Wednesdays . . ."

Kyle continued to list each day's activities, and by the time he'd finished, all of us—Kyle, his mother, and I—knew exactly what the problem was. Like many kids his age, Kyle was simply too busy for his own good.

Parents who encourage their children to get involved in numerous activities have good intentions. They want to give their children opportunities to learn and develop interests and skills that will improve their lives. Yet having too many of these activities can be unhealthful for kids. Being overly busy causes stress, irritability, and burn-out. Rather than enjoying all the activities to which they commit, children end up resenting the fact that they don't have enough downtime to hang out with friends or be alone with their thoughts.

Kyle and his mother didn't leave my office that day with a prescription for a medicine that would make him feel like his old self again. But they did leave with the knowledge that Kyle, like all kids, needs a healthy balance between scheduled activities and free time. Having enough time each week for doing absolutely nothing—that's the sure cure for what was ailing Kyle. ✛

❋ **QUESTIONS 9–14:** Circle the letter of the best answer to each question.

9. **Which sentence best states the main idea of Passage 1?**
   - **A** Children need to amuse themselves.
   - **B** It's good for children to have a variety of activities.
   - **C** Watching TV keeps children from doing other activities.
   - **D** Communities have great resources for children.

10. **The author's main purpose in Passage 1 is to —**
   - **A** discuss the benefits of involving children in activities.
   - **B** identify several good activities for children.
   - **C** describe the challenges of being a parent.
   - **D** help children choose activities that will lead to careers.

11. **Which sentence from Passage 1 is a simile?**

   A There's nothing to do.
   B I did my best to come up with projects and activities.
   C Children are like sponges, ready to soak up knowledge.
   D I decided to take action, using the resources that were readily available.

12. **Which event described in Passage 2 happened last?**

   A Kyle started getting stomachaches and lost his appetite.
   B Kyle's mother took him to a doctor.
   C Kyle's mother realized that he needed more free time.
   D Kyle listed all his activities for each day of the week.

13. **In Passage 2, the words *snapping* and *grumbling* suggest —**

   A annoyance.
   B excitement.
   C calmness.
   D fear.

14. **The author of Passage 2 probably thinks that Kyle's mother —**

   A does not really care about Kyle.
   B did not realize how Kyle's busy schedule was affecting his health.
   C should ask another doctor to examine Kyle.
   D will ignore the advice to let Kyle have more free time.

✳ *QUESTIONS 15 and 16:* Write your answers on the lines.

15. **Why do you think the author of Passage 1 mentions in her writing that she is a school principal? Explain.**

16. **The author of Passage 2 states, "But having too many activities can be unhealthful for kids." What information about Kyle does the author present that supports this statement?**

Graphic organizers are great for helping students organize their thinking, whether they are analyzing something they've read; planning their own writing; or exploring relationships among words, phrases, and ideas.

CHARACTER MAP, Page 269

Using a Character Map allows readers to notice, record, and organize details from various perspectives. It can also be used for planning the writing of a story or a character sketch.

PLOT DIAGRAM, Page 270

Keeping track of the events of the plot helps readers comprehend and remember the action of the story. While many stories have the five-part structure presented in unit 3, some stories may have fewer or more parts. This diagram can also be used for planning the writing of a story.

THEME ORGANIZER, Page 271

This graphic offers students a step-by-step way to organize their thinking about the important messages and ideas in a story. Because *theme* can be a fairly abstract concept, students benefit from collecting concrete details as they try to understand and articulate a theme.

WORD SPLASH, Page 272

Use this graphic to preview the vocabulary in something students are about to read. First give students the list of key vocabulary that they may not know but will need to understand in order to get the key concepts in the story. Then provide them with definitions or have them find their own definitions to write next to the words. Ask them to suggest the subject of the article and tell why they think so, accounting for all of the words and phrases. Once you have discussed the possibilities, read the selection independently or as a group. Discuss students' guesses and how close they are to the actual text. Make sure students understand that the point of the activity is to get them thinking about the words; it is not about guessing correctly. Surprises should be welcome. They will inspire interesting discussions about word meanings and language.

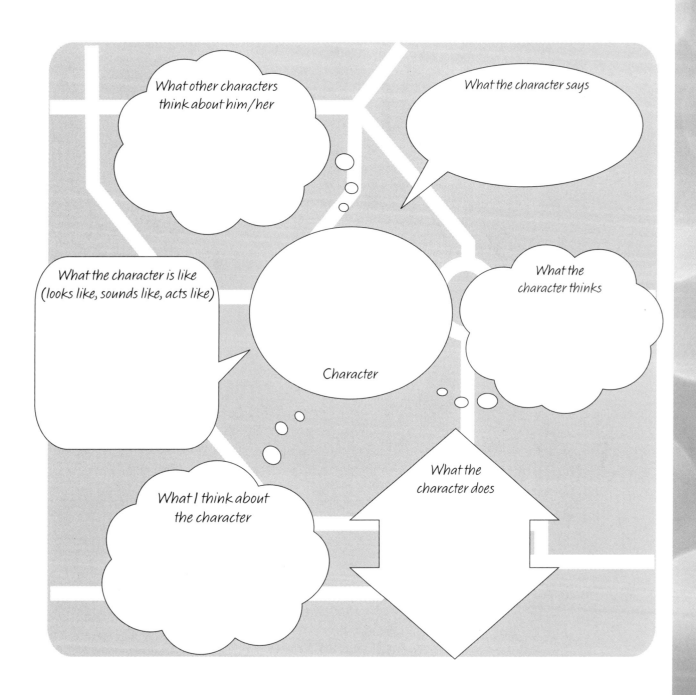

What other characters think about him/her

What the character says

What the character is like (looks like, sounds like, acts like)

What the character thinks

Character

What I think about the character

What the character does

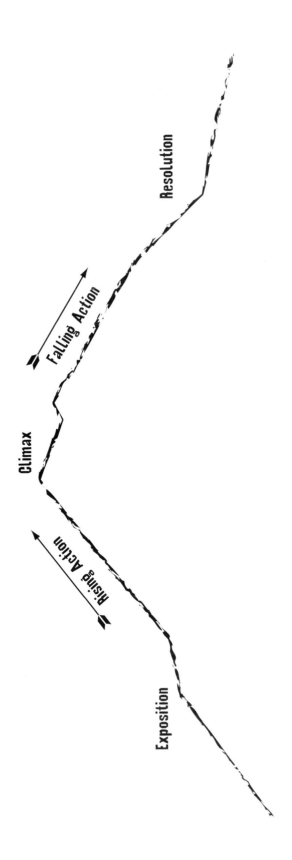

1. Important Quotes   What I Think About This

2. What Characters Do and Say

Meaning to the Story

3. Big Ideas

4. Lessons Learned

SELECTION VOCABULARY

Write the selection vocabulary on the lines below. Write a definition for each word. Read the words and their definitions and then guess what the selection will be about. Remember, all the words will be used in the selection. Compare your guess with your classmates and talk about the reasons for each person's guess. Then read the selection to see if anyone's guess was close to the topic.

Word   **Definition**

What the selection will be about _____

INDEX